THE POLISH
CHALLENGE

THE POLISH CHALLENGE

KEVIN RUANE

BRITISH BROADCASTING CORPORATION

To the memory of
my Polish friend
Martin Sullivan

Plates i–viii are between pages 112–13 and plates ix–xvi between pages 208–9.
They are reproduced by permission of the following:
The John Hillelson Agency Ltd plate iv top (Alain Dejean/Sygma), v (Alain Keler/Sygma), xi top (Jean-Pierre Laffont/Sygma), xiii bottom left (Michel Philippot/Sygma), xv bottom Sygma; Keystone Press Agency Ltd front and back covers, i top left & right, iii top, iv bottom, vi top, vii top, viii, ix centre, xii top, xiii centre; Polish Agency Interpress Photoservice vii bottom, xi centre & bottom, xiii bottom right; Popperfoto x top left, xii bottom, xiii top, xvi inset; Puls Publications/Stanislaw Skladanowski iii bottom; Rex Features Ltd ix top & bottom left, x centre, xiv bottom, xv top; John Topham Picture Library i bottom, ii, vi bottom, ix bottom right, x top right & bottom, xiv top & centre, xvi main picture. The map and Appendix C are by Line and Line.

Published by the British Broadcasting Corporation
35 Marylebone High Street, W1M 4AA

ISBN 0 563 20054 5 (hardback)
      0 563 20041 3 (paperback)

First published 1982
© British Broadcasting Corporation 1982

Filmset by August Filmsetting, Warrington, Cheshire
Printed in England by Mackay of Chatham Ltd

CONTENTS

The illustrations are between pages 112–13
and pages 208–9.

PREFACE

One day writers will be able to attempt a considered history and analysis of the upheavals which began in Poland in July 1980. This book does not pretend to do that because not all the facts are known. But an attempt at a coherent narrative has been made possible by the voluminous and continuous flow of information from the radios, television, press and news agencies not only of Poland but of its Warsaw Pact allies as well.

All this material, recorded and documented by the BBC's Monitoring Service, is of exceptional value because the spirit of the Polish 'renewal' expressed itself vividly in the way the media throughout Poland threw off the old constraints of strict Communist censorship and spoke out frankly and honestly for the first time in many years. Martial law brought that and many other things to an end, but this book may, at least, ensure that what was said in Poland before it will not be forgotten.

Most, though not all, of the book is based on the work of the BBC's Monitors. My thanks go to them, to the engineers and technical staff who helped them, and to the Report Writers whose selection and editing made possible a task that would otherwise have been almost physically beyond me. I am grateful too for helpful advice from Chris Pszenicki and Jan Repa of the BBC's Central European Service and for the sympathy and encouragement of my researcher and Monitoring mentor, Ramon Silva.

As is customary, I have simplified the spelling of Polish names by omitting the barred L (Ł) and other diacritical marks in words like zloty and Lodz. I have also used the English names for places like Warsaw and Cracow.

K.R.
January 1982

FOREWORD

The strikes in Gdansk in August 1980 did not at first appear to differ much from previous flurries in Eastern Europe. The Hungarians in 1956 and the Czechs in 1968 recorded their resentment of Communist constraints, but Soviet tanks quickly forced them to step sharply back into the ranks. Sullen superficial calm was restored and the subservient Communist news media assured the world that little local difficulties had been overcome and that the Soviet bloc was as solid as ever.

In Poland there were also periodic signals of discontent. In 1956 in Poznan, in 1970 in Gdansk and in 1976 near Warsaw Poles took to the streets to signal that Big Brother was going too far, usually because of his periodic (very reasonable) attempts to reduce meat subsidies. Polish intellectuals, peasants, students and Roman Catholics had groused persistently, but it was the cheap meat issue which occasionally brought the workers to their side. The Government, constantly misled up to the eleventh hour by complacent reports from the Party and the media, always knew that it had to act when the workers lined up with the habitual malcontents. In 1956, 1970 and 1976 a formula of concessions and leadership changes restored order and the demonstrators stopped protesting. Ringleaders thereafter found life difficult and vanished from the public eye.

But in August 1980 the Government's formula did not work. Concessions and leadership changes were tried by Gierek, an experienced and reasonable man, but this time the appetite for reform merely fed upon the concessions and changes and grew stronger. The crisis has settled in and is still with us. The imposition of military rule in December 1981 dramatically marked the end of over a year of negotiations with Solidarity. The Polish Government decided that it could not continue to govern unless it imposed its will by force. The Soviet Government rejoiced that the Poles were at last taking the tough line recommended by Moscow since August 1980. The Americans took the contrary view. The west Europeans and the Vatican deplored the bloodshed but stuck to the middle ground. Poland has come to a turning point in post-war history, and events in Poland are bound to affect the whole Soviet bloc and the rest of our interdependent world. The moment is clearly right for an authoritative book. Fortunately, authoritative information is abundantly available.

Thanks to the BBC's Monitoring Service and correspondents, day-by-day records of happenings and debate in Poland have been produced for many months. Until 1980 such access to information and the political process would have been unthinkable. But supporters of Lech Walesa realised from the start that news of their activities could reach the whole world simultaneously via the media if only they made the facts available. Accordingly, they ensured that the international news machine would receive the right fuel: factual reports, access to leaders, fly-on-the-wall facilities at meetings. For the first time since 1939 the world was able adequately to follow day-by-day events in Poland. Only since the military takeover has there been renewed uncertainty about the facts of Polish life.

Not surprisingly, Soviet jammers were switched on in August 1980. Soviet bloc authorities have long resented the ability of Western broadcasts to leap over the Iron Curtain into millions of homes. Since 1980 Polish homes have been regularly supplied with the facts of the Polish situation through trusted services such as the BBC, and it is wholly appropriate that Kevin Ruane, steeped in Soviet-bloc experience, should set in print the many gems picked up by the BBC Monitoring Service. Richly endowed with material and skills, Ruane has splendid subjects for his book: drama at a flashpoint of East–West relations, another chapter in the tortured history of Poland, a game for the highest stakes, and probably the end of the era which started at Yalta.

Indeed, Walesa's influence spreads far beyond Poland and puts all Stalin's heirs in a quandary. Stalin carried his allies with him in imposing by force a post-war settlement in Eastern Europe disliked by most of its inhabitants, and installed Communist regimes wherever the Red Army had been. His East European defensive bastion was to be permanent and inviolable. Foster Dulles challenged Stalin's concept and spoke of the possibility of rolling back the bastion's frontiers. But until 1980 the Russians moved promptly to counter any threat to the bastion's solidity. Only in 1980 did they hesitate to follow their own tough precedents and move into Poland. Despite the Soviet-approved military takeover, whoever rules Poland still has to deal and negotiate with the Roman Catholic Church and the forces which threw up Solidarity and Walesa.

Ruane's book provides a fascinating day-by-day commentary. The reasons underlying the prolonged reluctance of the Russians to do more than threaten deserve attention, as do the prospects for the future. Briefly, Poland has always been a strange bedfellow in the Soviet bloc, strangely un-Communist in that eighty per cent of the land is privately owned and the majority of Poles practising Roman Catholics, now proud of their Polish Pope. Throughout their terrible history, in their frontierless country flanked by aggressive Germans and Russians, the Poles have retained a Polishness and a reputation for courage and non-conformism. Christian and Western-looking for a thousand years, and Communist within the Eastern bloc for only thirty-five, Poles in the late 1970s became increasingly critical of their authoritarian State for its failure to fulfil their rising expectations. Bad harvests, Western recession, lack of incentives, rash borrowing, lengthening queues and arthritic austerity added to their discontents and confirmed their feeling that they would fare better if their straitjacket were loosened. Increasingly, they found it hard to believe that their interests were adequately upheld by the Party and aspired to choose their own representatives.

Unsatisfactory representation was the issue which dominated the events of August 1980. Workers' resentment of their economic plight and of the constraints on self-help was widely publicised, and in private, for reasons of prudence, criticism grew of the arrangements imposed on them in 1945. Indeed, one might well wonder why the Gdansk explosion did not come sooner. It might well have done if post-war Poland had not in many ways been a satisfactory country, far more homogeneous than pre-war Poland. Thirty-five million patriotic Poles now live in a compact and relatively rich country without the minority problems which complicated Polish life before the second world war. They have performed prodigies of reconstruction and industrialisation, and Polish Communists and Catholics have cooperated for the good of Poland, each recognising the other's contribution – two oxen harnessed to the same Polish plough.

Many predicted, when the explosion came in 1980, that the Russians would invade Poland to restore the solidity of their bastion. But it soon became clear that there was no easy course of Soviet action. Walesa's success in establishing Solidarity, independent of the Communist hierarchy, to represent Polish workers was anathema to the Polish Party and even more so to the Soviet and other East European Parties. Solidarity challenged the Communist creed itself and threatened the foundations of Stalin's post-war security system, for Poland is the largest East European country, and through it run the lines of communication between the Soviet Union, where the Warsaw Pact weapons are made, and East Germany where so many of them are deployed.

Until December 1981 no satisfactory course was open to Moscow. Walesa had not mounted the barricades, but adopted a Ghandiesque formula of passive resistance which proved highly successful. He insisted that Solidarity challenged neither the Communist regime nor Poland's position within the Soviet bloc. The Russians knew they would find almost total non-cooperation and be unlikely to succeed where the Polish authorities failed. They would find that Polish workers, peasants and priests were in favour of Walesa and totally antagonistic to Russian invaders. Non-cooperation by day and bullets in the back by night provide an unattractive prospect. Hence Soviet efforts to get the Polish Government to discipline the trouble-makers. Hence repeated Soviet demonstrations of armed force. Hence the chorus of criticism from every Communist country. But, for month after month, no invasion.

At last, in December 1981, the Polish Government did what Moscow had been urging it to do since August 1980. It argued that it could not go on governing if Solidarity persisted in calling strikes. It acted to avert economic collapse by asserting itself and calling on Polish workers and believers to save Poland by working. But suspended Solidarity, and detained Walesa, could not be disregarded. They must participate in Poland's future. The debate on how continues. Still, neither the Polish authorities nor Solidarity have easy options. Production is disastrously low, shortages are rife and foreign exchange reserves non-existent. The question still before Poland is whether the industrial muscle of the workers can be harnessed to essential work and not used negatively to achieve illusory gains.

The Polish Government, Walesa and the Church are unanimous in their view that all Poles must unite to get the economy going again. Military rule is essentially temporary. The centrally-directed system has collapsed and nothing has taken its place. Somehow they must provide incentives, perhaps on the Yugoslav or Hungarian pattern, so that coal will be dug, goods produced, food grown and distribution achieved. Soldiers can enforce curfews and censorship, but bayonets cannot cut coal.

Despite American and Soviet snarling over Poland, its stability is an interest common to NATO and the Warsaw Pact. East and West must hope that Jaruzelski, Glemp and Walesa will harness themselves, as Gierek and Wyszynski did, to the Polish plough. With abundant resources, skills and patriotism, Poland's situation is still by no means hopeless. When I first went to Poland before the war, with my father busy on the *Cambridge History of Poland*, Poland seemed a far more complicated country than it now is. In my four years at the Embassy in the mid-seventies, Poland seemed set on a course of modest progress. The exhilaration of August 1980 has now turned sour, the soldiery are in power and the situation is precarious and unpredictable, but a combination of Polish virtues and the support of her friends in East and West should see her through to better days. Already her creditors are showing forbearance, and the need for generosity towards her is better recognised. Whatever the dangers and difficulties, Poland must be preserved from both external and internal anarchy. This book will greatly help its readers to understand what has happened since August 1980, and what the possibilities are for the future.

Norman Reddaway
February 1982

PROLOGUE

Poland has a history of more than one thousand years. It has been a Communist state for less than forty. It is wedged between three other Communist states, the Soviet Union, Czechoslovakia and East Germany.

The apparatus of power is roughly the same as in any 'socialist' state in the Soviet orbit. The country is run by the Communist Party which, for historical reasons, is known as the Polish United Workers Party, the PZPR for short. In theory the Party's ruling body between congresses is its Central Committee, now with 200 members, backed up by a lesser number of non-voting 'candidate' or 'alternate' members. In practice, real power has rested with the Central Committee's executive inner cabinet, the Political Bureau or Politburo, which varies in size but usually has about a dozen members. Running the Party's apparatus is a team of Central Committee Secretaries, some of whom also belong to the Politburo. One of these is traditionally the most powerful man in the land, the First Secretary of the Central Committee.

The Communist Party's authority, as in the Soviet Union, is based on the hallowed principle that it exercises 'the leading role in society'. This means that in all aspects of life – politics, economics, education, the arts, the mass media, trade union affairs, and so on – it is the Party that decides. For the record, independence was promised to trade unions back in 1956, but the resultant 'workers self-government council' also included Party officials.

In Poland – unlike the Soviet Union – other parties do exist. But the representatives of the United Peasant Party and Democratic Party who sit in Parliament – the Sejm – along with communist and 'non-party' deputies have had to play a token role, supporting the Communist Party and unable to challenge its power.

In the summer of 1980, the Polish Communist Party had more than 3,000,000 members out of a population of some 35,000,000. But in terms not just of membership but also of loyalty, by far the most 'representative' organisation in Poland was the Roman Catholic Church. The overwhelming majority of Poles are practising Catholics. For them the Church stands not only for the faith but also for national history and national identity. And that feeling of national pride through the Church was strengthened immeasurably in 1978, when Karol Wojtyla, Cardinal Archbishop of Cracow, was elected Pope and became John Paul II. The astonishing news of the election of the first Polish Pope confirmed for many that Poland was not simply a member of the 'socialist commonwealth' of Soviet-bloc states. It meant that Poland had been recognised for what it was in the much wider and much older context of the universal church.

The upheavals that shook Poland in 1980 were occasioned by something far more mundane, an affair of the shopping basket. But one of the main characters in the events that followed happened to be a worker who went to Mass every morning.

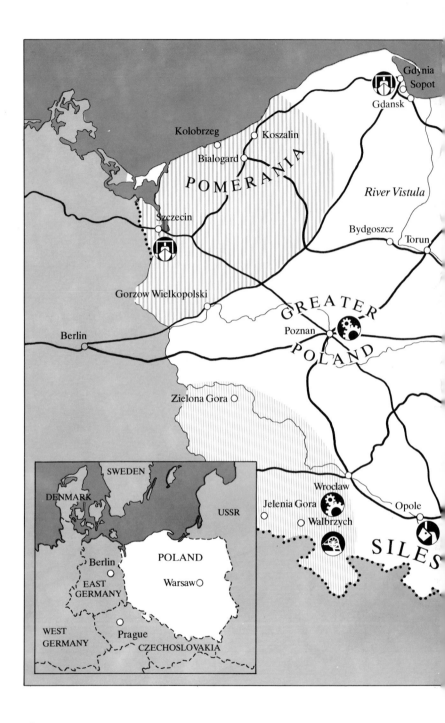

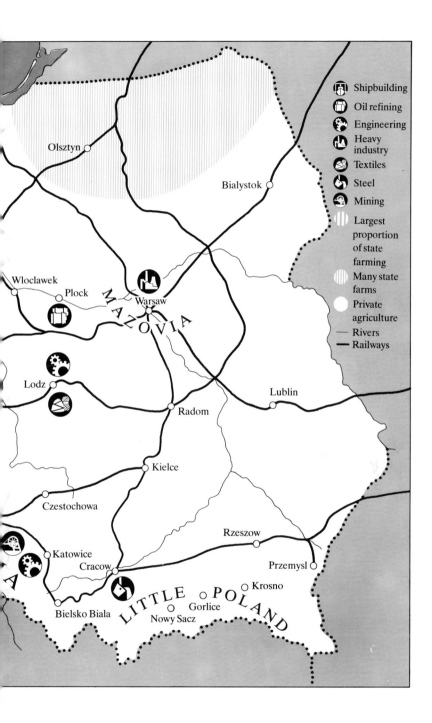

Shipbuilding

Oil refining

Engineering

Heavy industry

Textiles

Steel

Mining

Largest proportion of state farming

Many state farms

Private agriculture

Rivers

Railways

Olsztyn

Bialystok

Wloclawek

Plock

MAZOVIA

Warsaw

Lodz

Lublin

Radom

Kielce

Czestochowa

Katowice

Cracow

Rzeszow

Przemysl

LITTLE POLAND

Krosno

Bielsko Biala

Gorlice

Nowy Sacz

The following abbreviations are used in this book:

CRZZ   Centralna Rada Zwiazkow Zawodowych – Central Trade Union Council
CUKPPW   Centralny Urzad Kontroli Prasy, Publikacji i Widowisk – Central Office for the Control of the Press, Publications and Performances
DPA   Deutsche Presse Agentur – West German News Agency
KOR   Komitet Obrony Robotnikow – Workers' Defence Committee
KPN   Konfederacja Niepodleglej Polski – Confederation of Independent Poland
KSS   Komitet Samoobrony Spolecznej – Committee for Social Self-defence
MO   Milicja Obywatelska – Civic Militia
NIK   Najwyzsza Izba Kontroli – Supreme Chamber of Control
NSZZ   Niezalezny Samorzadny Zwiazek Zawodowy – Independent Self-governing Trade Union
ORMO   Ochotnicza Rezerwa Milicji Obywatelskiej – Voluntary Civil Militia Reserve
PAP   Polska Agencja Prasowa – Polish News Agency
PZPR   Polska Zjednoczona Partia Robotnicza – Polish United Workers Party
ROPCiO   Ruch Obrony Praw Czlowieka i Obywatela – Movement for the Defence of Human and Civil Rights
SB   Sluzba Bezpieczenstwa – Security Service
TASS   Telegrafnoye Agentstvo Sovetskogo Soyuza – Soviet News Agency
ZOMO   Zmotoryzowane Oddzialy Milicji Obywatelskiej – Motorised Units of Civil Militia

1. THE FIRST STRIKES

'Some Changes in the Meat Trade'
It all began rather quietly, while the world was thinking more about the coming Olympics in Moscow. On 1 July the Polish Government introduced measures which raised the price of meat. It did not happen everywhere. The measures were meant to take effect gradually. The Government's caution was not surprising. On two occasions in the previous ten years it had announced rises in the price of meat, only to be forced to rescind them after immediate and violent protest. In 1976, for instance, angry workers actually tore up railway track near the giant Ursus tractor works in Warsaw.

This time, prices were raised before any announcement was made. But strikes followed immediately all the same. One was reported at the Ursus plant, another at a factory making vehicle parts at Tczew, near the Baltic port of Gdansk. None of this was reported by Polish radio or television, but the latter did broadcast an interview with a senior official of Poland's Consumer Cooperatives' Union on the evening of 2 July. In fact it was broadcast twice in a couple of hours, in response to telephone enquiries. The official confirmed that the prices of the best cuts of meat would be going up. But the whole complicated issue was explained more precisely the next day, when the papers published an announcement from the official Polish News Agency, PAP, euphemistically headlined 'Some Changes in the Meat Trade':

Since 1 July several more varieties of meat and poultry have been sold through the network of shops selling higher grades of meat at higher prices. The move affects legs of pork, boneless beef, bacon and rashers, as well as ducks, turkeys and geese. The change will affect restaurants but not factory or school canteens, hospitals or holiday homes.
   In the two-tier structure of meat prices that has existed in Poland

for some years, the share of the higher-class shops has been insignificant up to now. Now they will account for 420,000 out of 2,045,000 tonnes of meat to be distributed through the retail network. The bulk of meat and meat products will still be sold at previous prices.

The communiqué on the change said that the additional revenue will result in lower subsidies for meat production. The money thus saved will be earmarked for improving the lot of the lowest-paid, large families and pensioners.

Changes probably were necessary by any reckoning. Meat prices had remained officially frozen since 1970. But they had done so at the cost of increasingly high subsidies, made worse as a result of poor harvests and the rise in the price of imported fodder. In 1980, for example, meat valued at 90,000,000,000 zlotys was subsidised to the tune of 76,000,000,000 zlotys, or so said the Polish media. In an effort to get round that, the government, in 1977, had introduced a two-tier system of retail outlets. Alongside ordinary shops, selling meat at the frozen prices, there appeared so-called 'commercial' shops selling higher grades of meat at higher prices, sometimes as much as 100 per cent higher. The proportion of the overall meat supply sold in such shops was small but it had grown gradually. What the announcement published on 3 July made clear was that the commercial shops were to get a larger share of the meat supply to sell at higher prices. The other consequence, of course, was that the ordinary shops already suffering from serious shortages would be getting less good-quality meat to sell at the lower prices.

Dissidents Report Strikes
So workers began to strike at individual factories and enterprises throughout the country. In the next three weeks more than thirty different factories were reported to have been affected. The reports of the strikes came not from the official media, which remained silent as usual for weeks to come, but from an organisation that was to figure very largely in the astonishing developments in Poland in the coming months, an unofficial body commonly known by the initials KSS KOR. A dissident organisation, originally known simply as KOR (Komitet Obrony Robotnikow) or the Workers' Defence Committee, it was founded in 1976 after the Government had responded to violent worker protests against a previous rise in meat prices by arresting and sentencing the alleged 'ring-

leaders' of the strike wave – and withdrawing the price rises. Later KOR's intellectual leaders broadened the organisation's scope by renaming it the Committee for Social Self-Defence (Komitet Samoobrony Spolecznej). Its purpose was to provide legal and financial assistance and advice to people seen as victims of government repression, such as that which followed the violent protests of 1976. It is fair to say that KOR, in effect, filled a void in the Polish political and social system. It became an organisation to which people with grievances could have recourse. This may explain why the strikes of July 1980 were different from all previous examples of worker-protest in Poland's Communist history. There was no violence this time. The workers did not take to the streets in a defiant challenge to the Government. Instead they stayed in their factories and went to their managements to demand higher wages to compensate for what they saw as an obvious rise in their cost of living. The workers, moreover, appear to have ignored the established, Soviet-style trade unions, soon to be criticised for not serving the interests of the workers they were supposed to represent.

On Wednesday 9 July Warsaw Radio and television reported that a meeting of what was described as 'the central party and economic leadership' had been chaired that day by Edward Gierek, Poland's Communist Party leader for nearly ten years. It was under his leadership that Poland, in the early seventies, had launched an economic programme of modernisation, expansion and investment backed by huge foreign loans. That programme had gone wrong, so much so that in February 1980 Mr Gierek had dispensed with the services of his close ally and Prime Minister throughout the seventies, Piotr Jaroszewicz, and instituted a policy of greater efficiency, economy and tighter control on investment. It was to review the results of this policy over the first six months of the year that the Wednesday meeting was held. It was not, as far as one can tell, a full meeting of the Party's Central Committee, called especially to discuss the growing industrial unrest. On the contrary, a recording of the proceedings broadcast that night by Warsaw Radio suggests very strongly that it was an occasion for ministers to report publicly on how successfully things were working out. The question of meat sales was mentioned only twice, but not as a problem. There was no mention of strikes. If there was any suggestion of crisis, then it was the general economic crisis, recognised and discussed at the Party's Congress earlier in the year.

Gierek's 'good programme'

And Mr Gierek's own speech was that of a man sticking to his policy and not planning any emergency measures to meet any immediate crisis.

Dear comrades, I agree that we are facing considerable difficulties. But we also have considerable opportunities for overcoming them . . . We have a good programme as set out in the resolutions of the Eighth Congress . . . We shall continue our present line in the current and the coming year . . . In the first half of next year we should like to solve four basic problems. First, we want to increase family allowances . . . Second, we believe greater help must be given to mothers bringing up children on their own. Third, we see an urgent need to increase old age and other pensions. Finally, in spite of the fact that the present economic situation renders wage increases impossible, we feel that we must increase the minimum wage . . . I think this kind of approach and also the provisions of our programme in this field for next year will meet with public approval.

Unfortunately for Gierek, neither his programme nor his apparent disregard for the crisis developing around him, had any effect. Reports of industrial unrest were multiplying and, in a remarkable break with tradition in Communist Eastern Europe, wage-bargaining was taking place at factory level. Many strikes had ended with factory managements granting wage rises to their protesting workers. In some cases the wage settlements offered were being rejected as too small. Some work forces were asking for as much as ten per cent, and some were getting it.

On 11 July the strike-wave spread to Lublin, an important town in the history of Communist power in Poland, for it was there that the Soviet-backed Committee of National Liberation was established toward the end of the Second World War. Now came the news that more than twenty factories and enterprises had gone on strike there. At the same time new strikes were reported from half a dozen other towns, including Poznan and Warsaw. KOR, the dissident organisation now operating as an information centre, was reporting that a total of thirty-three separate strikes had ended successfully with wage settlements averaging ten per cent.

On 15 July the situation in Lublin got worse. As it did so, the Communist Party paper in Warsaw, *Trybuna Ludu*, issued a plea for increased productivity as the best way to balance incomes and the rising cost of living. It maintained that, statistically speaking, earnings were still ahead of the increase in the cost of living. But it made an important admission: 'It must be remembered that a large proportion of employees earn less than the average wage and that the increase in the cost of living is not distributed evenly between social groups.'

On 16 July came reports that striking railway workers had blocked traffic from Lublin to the Soviet border about fifty miles away by abandoning their engines on the main-line track. At the same time, the city's bus and tram system had been brought to a halt. All this was obviously more serious than wage bargaining in factories. The workers' action was affecting the public.

The next day, Gierek was not far from Lublin, addressing a rally of students in the nearby town of Chelm. Western journalists reported him as saying that lack of discipline was exposing the country to great danger. But there was no hint of that from Warsaw Radio, which quoted the Party leader as repeating his familiar line that a way out of the present difficulties lay in decisions that were 'not always simple or popular' and through better and more productive work. A Government spokesman even claimed that the Council of Ministers had noted 'positive signs in socio-economic activity in a number of fields'.

Politburo admits 'Work Stoppages'

But the authorities' apparently complacent disregard for the growing crisis could not last much longer. The next day, Friday 18 July, a Lublin strike committee was said to have been formed. The Communist Party's inner cabinet, the 14-man Politburo, met to discuss the situation there. The fact was announced by the Polish News Agency, PAP, that evening:

The Politburo expressed deep concern over work stoppages in factories, municipal enterprises and the railway junction, as well as over the general situation in Lublin which is causing great discomfort to the city's population. The Politburo stated that, in the present economic situation . . . each workless day deepens existing difficulties and causes extra losses. That is why the Politburo calls on the work forces and citizens of Lublin to restore order and the normal rhythm of work.

The Party leaders made a conditional offer of Government talks:

The Politburo approved Government decisions connected with the implementation of the demand submitted by the industrial work forces as well as the setting up of a commission, headed by Mieczy-slaw Jagielski, a member of the Politburo, Deputy Chairman of the Council of Ministers, and a Parliamentary Deputy for the Lublin Region. After industrial plants undertake normal work, the commission will fully examine the demands submitted and present them to the Polish Government.

So the Party leadership had admitted the strikes, though it preferred to call them by the presumably less offensive term of 'work stoppages'. The Government had also offered to talk on condition that the Lublin strikers went back to work. However the authorities seemed to be hoping for a settlement without too much publicity. On 19 July *Trybuna Ludu* also admitted the strikes without actually mentioning Lublin.

Matter-of-fact, calm and concrete talks about the state of the economy and its problems are always needed . . . The important thing however is that such discussions must not be carried out at the expense of work . . . There are no reasons why any disputes should lead to work stoppages. We are writing about this because periodic interruptions of work have taken place . . . This is a road that leads nowhere.

Later that day, a Polish television commentator in the evening news bulletin was bold enough to mention Lublin by name and also to speak about truth:

In the last few weeks work stoppages have occurred in a dozen or so industrial enterprises. The city of Lublin was particularly affected . . . In every situation one always likes to know the truth and be able to use it . . . It becomes harder and harder to obtain the truth of compli-cated and difficult matters. You have to work out the truth just as you work to produce bread or any other product . . . It has always been the aspiration of the Party leadership under Edward Gierek to make views about reality accord with reality. We all have a com-mon duty. Whatever we do or think we have a duty to bear in mind the opinion of our friends and the opinion of those who are hostile to today's socialist Poland.

For the first time, Poles had been told ever so gently that whatever they did at home had an important international dimension. As they were to be reminded repeatedly in the months to come, strikes could upset Poland's socialist allies and encourage its alleged imperialist enemies. But the television commentator's estimate of the number of strikes was soon to be challenged by what the dissidents in KOR saw as a more truthful picture of the country's industrial unrest.

In the meantime, though, the strikers in Lublin soon decided to go back to work and clear the railway line to the Soviet Union. They did so in exchange for substantial wage concessions. If the authorities were tempted to see the settlement as a response to the Politburo appeal they could not have been complacent for long. Almost immediately new strikes were reported in other areas – in Chelm near Lublin, at the Stalowa Wola steel plant to the south-east, in Warsaw where newspaper delivery drivers struck briefly but successfully on the eve of Poland's national day, in Wroclaw, in Ostrow Wielkopolski, and in Walbrzych in the south-west.

On 28 July there was a brief warning strike by tram drivers in the three-city conurbation of Gdansk, Gdynia and Sopot on the Baltic coast, a place with momentous historical connotations. It was after the armed suppression of worker protests in Gdansk and Gdynia that Edward Gierek replaced Wladyslaw Gomulka as First Secretary of the Central Committee of the Polish United Workers' Party in December 1970. Gierek, however, was no longer in Poland to hear the news from the Baltic coast. On 27 July he had left for his annual holiday in the Soviet Union and the regular visit that the East European Communist leaders were in the habit of making each summer to President Leonid Brezhnev at his holiday home in the Crimea. The two men met on 31 July, and to judge from the official communiqué on their talks they found little or nothing to disturb them, though they did 'brief each other on the situation in their respective countries and about problems which the CPSU [the Soviet Communist Party] and the PZPR are currently trying to solve'. The talks, as usual, were said to have been held 'in an atmosphere of cordiality and complete mutual understanding'. Neither of the two men could have suspected, perhaps, that this would be their last such meeting.

At home in Poland, some hundred factories were said to be on strike.

2. AUGUST CLIMAX

Edward Gierek did not return from his holiday until 15 August. By then the situation was getting out of hand. In his absence, intermittent strikes had continued to break out. They were not mentioned by Poland's official media. In the early days of the month, however, unofficial, dissident sources reported a steadily mounting list of striking factories at places all over the country: Wlochy near Warsaw, Bierun Stary near Katowice in Silesia, Kielce and Tarnow to the south-east, Swidnik near Lublin in the east, and Kalisz and Lodz in central Poland. On the Baltic Coast crane drivers went on strike in the Gdansk shipyards. In Warsaw dustmen also stopped work.

One of the problems apparently facing the authorities was that, as one group of workers managed to win wage rises from their local managements, the word got round and other groups tried to do the same. The Government, having tacitly accepted the wage settlements for more than a month, had no obvious way of stopping them without causing far greater trouble.

'No one will pay our debts'
On 4 August *Trybuna Ludu* countered with the economic argument:

Life is difficult today and it will be difficult for some time to come. Our tumultuous expansion – often getting out of control, dependent too on the world situation and not, of course, devoid of errors – is causing tension and anomalies. Our first requirement if we are to overcome them is a calm assessment of the situation . . . We find many things irritating and painful – poor supplies, queues and price rises, the rise in the cost of living, troubles with bureaucracy, evidence of speculation, the greasing of palms . . . But is stopping work a cure for all that? Is it not something which makes the soil even more fertile for such things? No one will solve our problems for us. No one will pay off the debts we have incurred in speeding up the country's economic expansion. Only we and we alone can overcome our difficulties.

Meanwhile, the West German news agency, DPA, was quoting Jacek Kuron, a founder-member of the dissident organisation, KOR, as saying that Poland's Communist leadership had utterly failed and that the strikes could not be stopped. He did however suggest that the crisis could be overcome if the workers were given the opportunity to 'organise themselves freely'.

There was little sign of anything like that yet, at least on the official surface. But the BBC's East Europe correspondent, Tim Sebastian, reported from Warsaw two days later:

There's every indication that the current series of strikes in Poland has brought about a minor industrial revolution. Even Polish sources admit that the new unofficial wage-bargaining, the open discussion of stoppages in the censored press, the tacit admission that strikes are acceptable – all this is bound to cause irreversible changes in Polish life. As one official here put it: 'After the last few weeks, there is just no way things could ever be the same again.' For a country firmly anchored in the Soviet bloc, that is a remarkable admission, but it reflects both the extent of the changes that have taken place and the realisation that a new economic structure must be created. There is a growing feeling that Poland's economy can no longer be ordered by ideological requirements, but by the genuine requirements of the people themselves.

On 8 August KOR announced that there had been strikes at 150 factories or work-places since the beginning of July. But KOR announced something else. As well as providing information on the strike wave, it was ready, it said, to act as a centre through which various strike committees could contact each other. KOR also offered financial help for the strikers and opportunities to meet expert advisers.

That was a Friday. On the following Monday, the leader of the dustmen's strike in Warsaw was arrested. It looked, for a moment, as though the patience of the authorities was running out. So far the police had not interfered with strikers in any way. But after several hours the man was released. The dustmen's strike was settled, and almost immediately the capital's bus drivers went on strike, followed by the tram-drivers. These were disputes that could not be hidden from the public.

The following day there was a full session of the Warsaw Party organisation, clearly prompted by the growing unrest.

According to an official news agency report, the meeting found that the overwhelming majority of Warsaw's work forces had stayed on the job, but 'work stoppages had taken place' and 'apart from justified demands, claims were made that were unrealistic in the existing economic situation'.

On the same day, the authorities took the unusual step of inviting foreign correspondents to a press conference given by the Communist Party's propaganda chief, Mr Jerzy Lukaszewicz, a member of the ruling Politburo and Head of the Central Committee Department for the Press, Radio and Television. In the event, he became the first Polish leader to use the word 'strike', a fact not reported by the official media. Indeed, the official Polish News Agency report on the press conference is an object lesson in how to say something that amounts to nothing.

Answering questions, Jerzy Lukaszewicz discussed the attainments and problems of Poland's socio-economic developments in the past few years, including the current difficulties stemming first of all from the need to import additional amounts of grains and fodder and the rise in prices of imported raw materials and semi-finished products.

It was the radio in Hungary, of all places, that broadcast, several days later, a recording of some of Mr Lukaszewicz's remarks:

There have been strikes. Yes, we can call them that . . . It is no secret that in our opinion, under socialist conditions, labour stoppages are harmful to the entire working class. It is not a good method of making progress. However once stoppages occur, we must learn how to stop them, always and exclusively by way of negotiations.

Lukaszewicz, in fact, painted a rather rosy picture of the situation, claiming that the worst was over, that everything was being settled amicably, and that there had been no sign that the strikes were aimed against the Communist Party or the country's socialist system.

Looking back, though, perhaps the most important thing Lukaszewicz said was that the strikes must be stopped 'exclusively by negotiation' and not, presumably, by administrative action or the use of force. This was an understandable attitude, perhaps, on the part of any administration headed by Edward Gierek. He knew that on the two major occasions when force had been used against protesting workers, the

Communist Party leader had been brought down. This happened in 1956 when Wladyslaw Gomulka came to power after the Poznan riots in which over sixty people were killed; and it happened again in 1970 when Gierek himself replaced Gomulka after troops had been used against strikers in Gdansk and Gdynia and some fifty people died.

Gdansk Shipyard Strike

On Thursday 14 August the strikes spread to the Gdansk shipyard, and the fact was admitted that evening by Warsaw Radio and television:

Work stoppages have been taking place in some factories and enterprises. Demands concerning wages, work norms and the organisation of work and supplies have been put forward. In the past few days there has been a partial disruption of municipal transport in Warsaw. Work stoppages impeding the normal course of production occurred yesterday and today at light industry enterprises in Aleksandrow Lodzki and Teofilow and in some departments of the Gdansk shipyard.

Work stoppages fill us with concern because they aggravate the already difficult economic situation . . . Many of the issues being raised in the discussions can be and are being dealt with inside the enterprises themselves. Some justified demands are being met. Others require careful consideration and others still, in spite of their importance, cannot be settled either today or tomorrow because we simply cannot afford to do so.

A television commentator, Jerzy Ambroziewicz, took up the issue immediately afterwards:

Demands are being made for higher wages and improved living conditions. Concern over the rising cost of living is understandable, but everyone in Poland knows that the standard of living does not depend on the issuing capacity of the Bank of Poland. You won't solve the problems and stresses of the market by printing money.

A second thought is this: Work stoppages, wherever they have occurred, have also been alarm signals indicating that something is wrong either in the way individuals or institutions work, including institutions of socialist democracy. Individual units and institutions can and should be the object of criticism. They should also be the object of control . . . Poland is a socialist state, and in any image of socialism, even if completely deformed by incompetence and human dishonesty, one should be aware of what we want to do and how to go about doing it.

A readiness to talk more openly about popular grievances was hinted at the next day in the party paper, *Trybuna Ludu*.

No discussion, however bitter, is being ruled out. Many issues need it . . . Nothing is more worrying than the silence of a shut-down factory, than the lifelessness of machines and installations standing idle and silent, producing nothing.

The paper repeated the argument that there was no point in printing extra money if the goods were not being produced to spend it on. 'Wallets may bulge but the queues for staple goods will get longer.'

As for the queues, a Finnish correspondent, Jarmo Jaeaeskelaeinen, put them in their context in a report from Warsaw for Helsinki Radio:

Nobody is starving in Poland, but the price an ordinary citizen has to pay in terms of time, in hours spent to get food for the family, has increased to an excessive level. An hour in a shop is not like queueing at all. Two or three hours is about the average. The housewife who finishes work at four can start getting the dinner ready for the family at eight. If food deliveries to the shops had been regular and if there had been no shortages, the increases in food prices would not have caused strikes but at most some grumbling.

As Gierek returned from his annual pilgrimage to the Soviet Union, tens of thousands of Roman Catholic pilgrims had assembled at the shrine of Our Lady at Jasna Gora in Czestochowa to celebrate the Feast of the Assumption of the Virgin Mary. But Gierek was more concerned with the tens of thousands of workers reported to be on strike, especially on the Baltic coast where the dispute was reported to have spread to Gdynia.

It may be that the Communist Party leader knew more than most people about what had happened in Gdansk the day before his return. What was eventually learned from unofficial sources was that workers in the shipyard had gone on strike following the dismissal of a crane driver and free trade union activist, Mrs Anna Walentynowicz. At 9 am on Thursday 14 August a strike committee was formed and drew up a list of demands. The first was for the reinstatement of Anna Walentynowicz and another free trade union activist who had been dismissed and arrested several times in the previous ten years, a veteran of the 1970 strike committee. His name was Lech Walesa.

During the day, the local Communist Party secretary, Tadeusz Fiszbach, was reported to have attended talks between strikers and management. The first of the strikers' demands was conceded. Mrs Walentynowicz was brought to the Lenin shipyard to address the strikers. Lech Walesa, the unemployed electrician and father of six, had already climbed over the wall to join the strike leaders. Ironically, he had sat in on talks with Gierek back in the early days of 1971.

'Stopping work will settle nothing'

The first major development after Gierek's return on the Friday was a television broadcast to the nation that evening by his right-hand man for many years who had become Prime Minister only a few months earlier, Edward Babiuch. His message revealed greater frankness but it amounted to little more than an appeal.

I fully realise that the public expects a clear answer about what the Government is doing and intends to do to get the country out of its economic difficulties . . . It has to be admitted that in the past we have not always managed to deal with them efficiently. The public has not been given sufficient information about our troubles, about the state of the economy and the growing problems as and when they occurred. We have not prepared ourselves sufficiently for the difficult times which we should have seen as inevitable. Even today, not everyone realises what our country's economic situation is like. To put it bluntly, our country's indebtedness has reached a point which must not on any account be overstepped . . . We have been living and developing on credit.

As for the immediate crisis, Mr Babiuch said there were no miracles in economics and strikes would only make matters worse.

Stopping work not only harms the national economy, it also turns against the working class and working people in general, damaging their vital interests . . . The opponents of People's Poland are trying to use the atmosphere of tension and emotion for their own political ends, putting forward slogans and suggestions which have nothing in common with the aspirations of the working class . . . The world is watching us, wondering how we can manage in these difficult moments. We have reliable allies who also worry about our troubles and believe that we will be able to overcome them ourselves. They wish us success from the bottom of their hearts.

Babiuch's appeal for unity and for work contained nothing essentially new to persuade the strikers to go back to work. The next day, however, one of Poland's official news agencies, Interpress, reported that the strike in the Lenin shipyard had been settled. Foreign journalists were baffled by this because their information was that strikers and management were still very far apart. Some workers were even said to be demanding free trade unions. Something odd did happen that day if we are to believe the local radio in Gdansk which reported the activity of what sounded like flying pickets.

In some enterprises, among others the tram depots, where negotiations ended last night, it had been decided to start work this morning. But when drivers arrived at their depots this morning they found groups there, each several dozen strong and not employees of the municipal transport enterprises. These groups threatened violence and thus made it impossible for the vehicles to leave the depots . . . At the Gdansk shipyard the talks led to almost total agreement and as a result the strike committee decided to end the stoppage.

The following morning, Gdansk Radio reported regretfully that strikes were continuing in many places on the coast.

The strike in the Lenin Shipyard has not ended. As a result of the agreement signed yesterday by the strike committee and the management, members of the work force left the shipyard yesterday with the intention of resuming normal work on Monday. It turned out, however, that a group of several hundred of the work force plus outsiders remained on the premises. This is in contravention of the agreement reached yesterday.

Meanwhile Jacek Kuron, speaking for KOR, had told the West German news agency, DPA, that it was a 'false' strike committee that had declared the strike over. Only a few dozen men, he said, had left the shipyard. Whatever the exact truth is, subsequent evidence suggests that sympathy with workers striking elsewhere had some influence on the continuation of the shipyard strike. It was a kind of solidarity, which also led to the formation (reported by western correspondents) of an inter-factory strike committee, or MKS, set up to cater for the demands of all striking work-forces in the area. This was a key development.

Sunday 17 August was a crucial day. A spate of reports came from the radio in Gdansk. There was an announcement that the Party Politburo in Warsaw had set up a commission under a Deputy Prime Minister, Tadeusz Pyka, who was also a candidate member of the Politburo, to examine the grievances of the striking workers on the Gdansk coast.

Remember 1970
Then came an appeal to the citizens of the three towns of

Gdansk, Gdynia and Sopot from the Provincial Governor of Gdansk, Jerzy Kolodziejski, and the Chairman of the Provincial People's Council, Tadeusz Fiszbach, who was also the local Party secretary. This contained a clear warning:

The atmosphere of the discussion in certain plants has assumed an alarming nature. This applies, among others, to the Gdansk shipyard, where part of the work force has remained on the premises, in spite of the decision taken earlier by the strike committee to go home and end the strike. The workers' discussion has turned into a permanent rally. And it is accompanied by the activities of people who have no connection with the shipyard, who have come from outside and are known for their opposition activities which run counter to the interests of the people's state.

We are doing all we can to solve burning social problems and eliminate everything that causes dissatisfaction. However, the opportunities for rapid improvement are limited. That is why we appeal to everyone to go back to work . . . We appeal to your minds and hearts, to your patriotism, to your prudence and sense of responsibility . . . Citizens, the inhabitants of Gdansk and Gdynia still remember the painful events of December 1970. Mindful of these events, let us preserve calm and a sense of responsibility in everything we do.

That was a warning but not, perhaps, a threat. For according to Gdansk Radio a few hours later, the Executive of the Provincial Party Committee, headed by Mr Fiszbach, had met that morning and decided to compile a full list of all demands and proposals being made by the striking workers. It had then conveyed several proposals to the Party Central Committee in Warsaw. The first was that a Government commission be set up, a suggestion immediately accepted with the appointment of the Pyka commission. But eight other proposals suggested very strongly that the Gdansk Party leaders, far from being opposed to workers' demands, had themselves decided that they must support changes and reform if any settlement was to be reached. They proposed, for instance, that the country's entire housing policy be re-examined, that action be taken without delay to counteract what they called 'the phenomenon of people acquiring excessive wealth'. The executive also suggested a form of meat rationing, better and more hygienic working conditions, greater power for the trade unions, and more rapid changes in the way the economy was managed.

In a television broadcast later that evening, Tadeusz Fiszbach repeated the main points of his earlier joint appeal but also said this:

Differences of opinion are not only natural but indispensable if we are to define remedies . . . In the Poland of 1980 there are no problems on the Gdansk coast, not even the most difficult ones, that cannot be discussed openly and sincerely.

But some of the proposals put up for discussion by the workers far outstripped anything heard so far. From the Lenin Shipyard in Gdansk, now the effective headquarters of the Inter-Factory Strike Committee representing more than twenty enterprises, came a long list of demands. They included a guarantee of the right to strike, freedom of publication and the lifting of censorship, the release of all political prisoners, access to the media for representatives of all churches, and observance of the International Labour Organisation's convention on the freedom of trade unions. The strikers also said they would not resume negotiations until Gdansk's telephone links with the outside world, cut off for some reason, were restored.

Anyone wanting to negotiate, it seemed, would have to enter a shipyard under occupation, guarded day and night by workers, through gates hung with red and white Polish flags and a picture of the first Polish Pope, John Paul II. An open-air mass was celebrated there on the Sunday morning. Foreign journalists were at the shipyard in considerable numbers.

'There are limits'

The next evening, Edward Gierek went on television to talk to the nation about the crisis.

I would like to say as frankly as I can that we are aware that, quite apart from many objective factors, mistakes in economic policy have played an important part . . . We understand the working people's tiredness and impatience with the troubles of everyday life, the shortages, the queues, the rise in the cost of living . . . But strikes do not change anything for the better . . . Together we must find another way.

Gierek made several promises. He said the Politburo had decided to carry out an honest assessment of changes in the cost of living, to freeze the price of meat until autumn 1981, to tighten price controls and to increase child benefits. But while the Government wanted to seek agreement through compromise and understanding, he insisted that this could only work if talks were orderly and serious and agreements were observed.

Attempts by irresponsible individuals and anarchic, anti-socialist groups to use stoppages for political ends and to incite tension are a dangerous aspect of recent events at plants on the Gdansk coast . . . Any actions which strike at the foundations of the political and social order in Poland cannot and will not be tolerated. On this fundamental issue nobody can expect compromise, concession or even hesitation . . . Only a socialist Poland can be a free and independent country with inviolable borders. Our country's socialist system has a significant international importance and is one of the most essential features of the European order created after the second world war . . . There are limits that no one is allowed to cross.

After mildly criticising the official trade unions for symptoms of bureaucracy and being 'detached' from the workers, Gierek appealed to Party members, to patriots, to members of the token United Peasant and Democratic Parties, to Catholics and to the workers of Gdansk: 'We are giving your demands our full attention but we cannot promise to meet them all for that would be a promise we could not keep.'

Gierek's speech was not the only event of that Monday. That was the day the strikes were reported to have spread westwards along the coast to the port of Szczecin. In Gdansk municipal transport was at a standstill and, according to the local radio, railwaymen were trying to repair damage done to the braking mechanisms of fast commuter trains by 'unidentified persons'. In the evening – a sure sign of the desperate concern of the authorities – a plenary session of the Gdansk provincial committee of the Party was attended not just by Mr Pyka, heading the special government commission in the area, but by two members of the Politburo from Warsaw, President Henryk Jablonski and a secretary of the Central Committee, Stanislaw Kania.

On the following day there was no appreciable change. Warsaw Television reported that the sea ports of Gdansk, Gdynia, Kolobrzeg and Szczecin had been standing idle for two days. A total of sixty-eight ships were said to be waiting in the roads at Gdansk and Gdynia, which meant a loss of some one and a half million dollars in fines for that day. In Szczecin, meanwhile, a session of the local Communist Party committee had been joined by three other visitors from Warsaw – two full members of the Politburo, Prime Minister Babiuch and Jerzy Lukaszewicz, and a Deputy Prime Minister and alternate member of the Politburo, Kazimierz Barcikowski. The meeting stressed that outsiders were trying to exploit the strikes. Within twenty-four hours, Barcikowski had been appointed to head a commission to look at the strikers' demands in Szczecin. But the commission already set up in Gdansk under Tadeusz Pyka was not doing too well. A spokesman in Warsaw had already disclosed that Pyka was refusing to deal with the Inter-Factory Strike Committee, which now represented some 170 enterprises. He preferred to deal with individual groups of strikers. This probably explains why, while reporting that the commission was pressing on with its work, the local radio in Gdansk also broadcast the commission's address and repeatedly told listeners how to get in touch with it by telephone. Meanwhile the three towns of Gdansk, Gdynia and Sopot were officially reported to be paralysed. The reopening of schools in Gdansk had been postponed. The mayors of the three towns broadcast an appeal for an end to disruption – 'Let's not permit a situation in which our children will be pleading for food'.

Political 'manipulators' blamed
At the same time the local paper, *Glos Wybrzeza* (the Voice of the Coast), was making great play with reports of outsiders exploiting the situation.

Workers who want to carry out their normal obligations to the city are having their equipment and tools destroyed. Threats are being made about putting vital installations out of commission. Vehicles are not being allowed to transport the most essential commodities ... Where do the expectations and suggestions of the working people end and where does this political game, played by manipulators behind the backs of the workers, begin? ... The presence of these manipulators is no secret to anybody ... They take advantage of the calm and the composure of the authorities, abusing the fact that they have shown restraint rarely seen elsewhere, even in those cases where a firmer stand would be justified. How long can this go on?

Perhaps this indicated continuing argument within the Polish Communist leadership about using stronger measures to put a stop to the industrial disruption. At any rate changes were in the offing. On Thursday morning, 21 August, Gdansk

Radio reported first that Mr Pyka was continuing his work, and then only hours later that he had been replaced as head of the Government commission by another Deputy Prime Minister and member of the Politburo, Mieczyslaw Jagielski, who had already arrived in Gdansk. Pyka had never gone to meet the strikers in the Lenin shipyard. But Kazimierz Barcikowski was beginning his work in Szczecin by going straight to the Adolf Warski shipyard there. In the town of Elblag, just east of Gdansk, yet another alternate member of the Politburo, Jozef Pinkowski, was attending a plenary session of the local Party committee. In Warsaw, Bishop Kaczmarek of Gdansk briefed Cardinal Wyszynski, the Roman Catholic Primate of Poland, on the situation inside the Lenin shipyard.

As that week came to an end, the official media kept up their campaign against the exploitations of the strikes for political aims. *Trybuna Ludu* accused anti-socialist forces of trying to prolong the strikes and denied that there were any political prisoners in Poland. Warsaw television said that each day the strikes in the Gdansk area were costing the country the price of one new hospital. On Saturday, Stockholm Radio broadcast an interview with the Gdansk strike leader, Lech Walesa, whose name was yet to be mentioned by the Polish broadcasting organisations. He said the situation was such that the Government had to negotiate. 'If violence is used, as it was in 1970, we should, of course, go back to work. But what kind of work would that be? Nobody would want to help the authorities.' Walesa suggested that military intervention by the Soviet Union was impossible.

Deputy Premier Jagielski began talks with Walesa and his colleagues inside the Lenin Shipyard the same day. So both in Szczecin and in Gdansk the authorities had been forced to go to the strikers.

Party Leaders sacked
That fact, though highly significant, was less surprising than the changes that took place in Warsaw on Sunday 24 August. Warsaw television announced in the evening that the Central Committee of the Communist Party had met in plenary session and heard a report by Stanislaw Kania. There had also been a speech by Mr Gierek. The Committee had sacked four men from the ruling Politburo – Edward Babiuch, the Prime

19

Minister; Jerzy Lukaszewicz, the Party's propaganda chief; Jan Szydlak, the head of the Trade Union Council; and Tadeusz Wrzaszczyk, a Deputy Prime Minister and State Planning chief. Two men were dropped as candidate members of the Politburo – one of them Mr Pyka, who had failed in Gdansk. Two men joined the Politburo – Stefan Olszowski, whom Gierek had dropped from the Politburo in February, and Jozef Pinkowski, who also became Prime Minister. Another notable point was the election to the Central Committee of Tadeusz Grabski, a man also dropped previously by Gierek after Grabski had objected to official economic policy. At the same time, a meeting of the Council of State carried out a similar reshuffle in the Government. Several new appointments were made, including that of a new State Planning chief, new ministers of finance and foreign affairs, new heads of the state prices and statistical boards, and a new head of radio and television.

The overall effect of the changes, both in Party and Government, and especially the sacking of Babiuch as Prime Minister, was that Gierek had discarded some of the pillars of his ten-year regime, men who had been in charge of economic policy and the mass media. As the Party leader said in his closing speech to the Central Committee, the debate had been 'sharp and painful'. Many speakers came from the scenes of the worst labour unrest: Tadeusz Fiszbach, the Party chief in Gdansk; Jan Labecki, the Party secretary inside the Lenin shipyard; and Stanislaw Miskiewicz, the Party boss in the Szczecin shipyard. The speakers also included two committed journalists, Ryszard Wojna of *Trybuna Ludu*, and the more liberal Mieczyslaw Rakowski, editor-in-chief of the weekly *Polityka*.

'Fundamental change in policy'
Gierek's own speech, broadcast by television, promised further changes.

We are making a fundamental change in the policy of the Party and the State. We are adapting it to present-day realities . . . This will require significant changes in economic plans for the near future . . . We think that the Central Trade Union Council should consider the immediate holding of elections for new trade union authorities wherever work forces want it. These elections should be fully democratic, secret and with an unlimited number of candidates. If the authority of those representative bodies that have recently been formed should turn out to be lasting and established, then their members will find themselves on the newly-elected trade union authorities.

Gierek in fact was offering the strike leaders a chance to be elected and absorbed into an improved version of the existing trade union system. This was a chastened Gierek, a man admitting 'our own mistakes, inconsistencies and delays, vacillation and weakness', but also pleading for trust:

We have appointed to responsible posts those comrades who had earlier observed the irregularities that had been accumulating and who had tried to counteract them, comrades whose voices we failed to heed when we should have done so ... Citizens, our Party honestly wants to correct its policy, but we cannot make empty promises. Nor can we agree to demands which strike at the foundations of the existence of the nation and State.

The Party leader placed less emphasis on the alleged subversion of so-called anti-socialist forces. Maybe he had been impressed by the speech by Tadeusz Fiszbach from Gdansk who virtually contradicted what had been said more than once in the Party paper, *Trybuna Ludu*.

It would be a mistake [Fiszbach told the Central Committee plenum] to imagine that the strike in the Gdansk Shipyard and other enterprises resulted from the activities of a small group of anti-socialist forces or that its roots, course and objectives grew out of a basis that was detached from the working class or was hostile to People's Poland.

In Gdansk, as that plenum was meeting, more than five thousand people attending mass in the Lenin Shipyard heard an appeal read out from Bishop Kaczmarek.

The delegation you have chosen is about to begin meetings with the competent authorities. Proceed calmly and with dignity, demanding the realisation of your just claims but with understanding and without hate. Make your claims. But if it is up to you alone, then be ready to put an end to the standstill and to the sad moments which our beloved coastal region is now experiencing.

'We want new unions'
On Monday, in spite of all the appeals, the strike situation did not improve. But Tuesday brought astonishing developments. It was not simply that the Central Trade Union Council

21

(CRZZ), the controlling body of the official trade unions, dismissed its leader and declared that, if all else failed, unions should have the right to strike. That was amazing in itself in a Communist country. The really memorable event belonged to the world of the media. Gdansk Radio broadcast recordings lasting several hours of Deputy Premier Jagielski's negotiations with the strike leaders inside the Lenin shipyard. The talks were already being relayed live through loudspeakers to the thousands of strikers occupying the shipyard, and foreign journalists were there in force. But it must have taken a very high-level decision to broadcast the proceedings to the populace at large even on local radio. Had any Communist minister ever before been so publicly questioned, challenged and contradicted?

At one point, Jagielski said there were no political prisoners in Poland, to which came the retort: 'We know what the trials looked like. If we're to be honest, I suggest they should be reviewed. The trials were faked.' Jagielski, who had been confronted with twenty-one demands, was having a rough time, as one speaker after another told him plainly what was wrong and what should be done.

Poles are sick of listening to talk about errors and mistakes which go on being repeated . . . The workers must have the freedom to speak out, whether they are right or not . . . The people of the coastal region want to establish new unions, independent and free . . . I think the new unions must have a say in the division of the national income . . . We have been developing and investing for thirty-five years but the people have little to show for it.

And so on and on.

Mr Premier, we don't really understand why the government is trying hard to reorganise the trade unions but doesn't want to agree to the creation of new ones. The old trade unions are so discredited now that we can have no part in them . . .

The opinions published in the media do not mirror the truth . . . The fundamental reason for the economic crisis is the lack of representation of working people when economic decisions are taken . . . Control at all levels can only be ensured by independent, free trade unions . . . The authorities and the present Government have no authority among the workers . . . Only with free trade unions can reform be carried out . . .

Quite simply, we are quitting the present trade unions . . . We are not disbanding them because we do not have the right to do so. We are just leaving.

Mr Jagielski, who had to listen to a torrent of criticism, was once prompted to complain: 'I was hurt by what you have said. I'm only human too.' What the workers were saying was the plainest possible rejection of Gierek's offer to reform the old trade unions. The manner of the rejection, broadcast over the air, though only by the local radio, was startling indication of how far the authorities had given way.

Appeals and warnings

In Warsaw, meanwhile, a campaign was being mounted to appeal to what was claimed to be 'the political maturity' of Poles. On television that night Ryszard Wojna, the journalist who had addressed the Central Committee on the Sunday, read out his latest article for *Trybuna Ludu*. It began straightaway with a warning that if things went wrong Poland could suffer the sort of fate that befell it at the end of the eighteenth century when it was partitioned between Prussia, Russia and Austria. His words immediately prompted the joking comment throughout Warsaw that Austria, at least, wasn't interested. But Wojna was deadly serious:

Despite all efforts, no one can say that we are capable of halting the course of events which could bring the country to a national catastrophe of such dimensions that some people are recalling the drama of the end of the eighteenth century. This is no exaggeration, nor is it an attempt to scare you. Such are the realities of the contemporary world, which is deeply divided by conflict. And for that world, regardless of whether it sympathises with us or not, the interests of Poland are not an overriding consideration. Poland's interests can be safeguarded only by Poles themselves. History has taught us that bitter lesson.

Wojna conceded that the working class had the right to define for itself the aims and tasks of the trade unions, but then he drew a very clear line.

Demands aimed at breaking up the trade union movement and bringing it and the party into confrontation are not justified. Furthermore, such demands are unrealistic . . . There are issues on which there can be no discussion. They are defined by Poland's *raison d'état* and all its considerations and first of all by the political system and the system of alliances to which we belong . . . Our country lies in the centre of the continent in the direct security zone of the world socialist power, the Soviet Union.

In all Soviet-bloc states, the unions work in effect with the

Government and the Communist Party, not against them. Hence the fear that independent unions would become adversaries challenging what is known as the Party's 'leading role in society'. But Wojna also said the Party wanted everyone to become involved in running the country, including 'those who are guided by the Catholic ideology'.

By coincidence, that very evening Cardinal Stefan Wyszynski became involved, apparently against his will. Shortly after the broadcast by Wojna, Polish television carried extensive excerpts of a sermon which he had delivered that day in Czestochowa at celebrations of the feast of Our Lady of Jasna Gora. The Polish Episcopate was to complain later that the sermon, as broadcast, was incomplete and unauthorised, and still later Vatican Radio was to broadcast the whole sermon. But perhaps the chief omission from the Warsaw version was a reference by the Primate to 'atheism that undermined the bonds and cultural potential of this thousand-year-old nation' and a plea 'to leave the Church alone and give it a free hand in its work'. But the version carried by Warsaw television did contain a strong suggestion, which matched the official line, that it would be safer in the present crisis not to press too hard.

Even though man has the right to make his views known – even if this is by refusing to work – we nevertheless know [the Cardinal said] that this is a very expensive argument, so expensive that it burdens the whole national economy and affects the life of the nation, the family and every person in some negative way or other . . . It is never possible to satisfy demands immediately, today. That must be spread over a period of time. So talks must be held . . . We must always have what in Latin is called prudentia gubernativa, the prudence of government.

The Polish Episcopate, chaired by Cardinal Wyszynski, made up for any misunderstanding by issuing a communique calling for a speedy end to the crisis on the basis of solutions acceptable to both sides. According to Vatican Radio it said:

The Second Vatican Council teaches that human rights include the right of employees freely to set up unions which truly represent them and which could help shape economic life, as well as the right of every employee to take part in such union activities.

The next night, 27 August, it was the turn of the editor of *Polityka*, Mieczyslaw Rakowski, to go on television with his appeal. Developments, he said, had given him cause for hope but also for fear. The strikers, he thought, had decided it was

24

now or never but the authorities felt that their chances of satisfying all demands were limited. 'If this situation continues, we will be plunged into economic crisis and chaos.' But that was not all.

Developments reveal the strivings of forces unfriendly to socialism, and I do not mean the strikers . . . Our country is approaching a critical point. The Party to which I belong has committed serious mistakes. But if catastrophe were to occur it would bring no satisfaction to anyone . . . That includes us, members of the Party. After all, we have not been moulded from a clay that is any different from that of the striking workers. We were born in the same land and our bones will rest in the same land . . . The workers have achieved gains of considerable importance. But all that may be wiped out if we allow events to snowball . . . Polish affairs have reached a point where we have to choose our path. There are only two – chaos and self-destruction, or a deep, solemn and sincere improvement in all those spheres of life where many ailments have come to light.

Right to strike
Rakowski's broadcast gave a distinct impression that there were elements in the Communist Party anxious to secure a genuine social contract and make sure that past mistakes, 'crass mistakes' he called them, would not be repeated. He actually said that a system of guarantees against this was being created. The new trade union bill, he said, would guarantee the right to strike.

This, as we have said, was an astonishing achievement for, in theory at least, strikes in Soviet-bloc countries are unnecessary and therefore do not happen. Deputy Premier Jagielski went on television to announce the same thing in a progress report on the Gdansk negotiations. He thought agreement was near on most of the strikers' twenty-one demands. The hold-up was over the status of trade unions.

We share the feeling of the mass of the workers that the activity of the trade union movement up to now has been highly unsatisfactory . . . However, we think that the crisis of confidence can and must be overcome within the framework of the existing union body. This sick body can and must be cured, however painful that may be.

Next day's *Trybuna Ludu* condemned the call for free trade unions. Such a new structure, it said, would be a *de facto* political movement. 'We cannot permit it.' Nothing could be clearer than that. When Mr Barcikowski, the Government negotiator in Szczecin, went on television to deliver a progress report on his talks, there was less emphasis on deadlock. But the question that had aroused the most passion, he conceded, was that of trade unions. Meanwhile strikes seemed to be spreading, as reported by local radios in Bydgoszcz, Lodz and Wroclaw. On Friday they spread to the coalfields of Silesia, perhaps the most important industrial area, an ominous fact that may have persuaded the Government to be even more conciliatory. At any rate, on Saturday morning the radio in Szczecin began a live relay from the Adolf Warski shipyard with surprising words: 'This is 30 August, the thirteenth and last day of the strike.'

What followed was a long outside broadcast of a final meeting between the negotiating parties at which an agreement was announced and its main points read out. The very first point went as follows: 'It has been agreed that, on the basis of expert opinion, self-governing trade unions will be allowed to be set up. These will have a socialist character in compliance with the Constitution of the Polish People's Republic.'

That clearly represented quite an achievement, but 'socialist' self-governing trade unions left room for doubt. The main argument over 'free and independent trade unions' had been in Gdansk. No verdict could be reached until word came from there.

'Independent self-governing trade unions'

In mid-morning Gdansk Radio began broadcasting a relay of a meeting between the Jagielski and Walesa delegations. Agreement was clearly at hand for the proceedings began with one of the strike leaders, Andrzej Gwiazda, reading out a protocol on the strikers' first demand.

It is recognised as advisable to set up new, self-governing trade unions, which would be the authentic representative of the working class . . . By creating new, independent, self-governing trade unions, the Inter-Factory Strike Committee (MKS) declare that they will observe the principles outlined in the Constitution of the Polish People's Republic. The new trade unions will serve the social and material interests of the workers and do not intend to fulfil the role of a political party. They are based on the principle of social owner-ship of the means of production, which constitutes the foundation of the socialist system existing in Poland. They recognise that the Polish United Workers' Party (PZPR) fulfils the leading role in the State. They aim at ensuring that the working people have appropriate means of exercising control, expressing their opinion and defending their interests.

That was the main point of a long list of agreements initialled that day by Lech Walesa, leader of the MKS, and Deputy Premier Jagielski. It represented a compromise between workers determined to have genuinely free trade unions and a Communist Government equally determined to preserve for the Party the monopoly of political control so vital to its survival. Many people in the West as well as the East doubted whether it could work. Jagielski said he was off to Warsaw to report to the Central Committee and promised to be back as soon as possible. Maybe he was dazed by this achievement. At any rate he said some strange things. 'It is Saturday. I am a farmer and I consider Saturday a lucky day. Yes, Our Lady, Our Lady. My parents used to start harvesting on Saturday.'

The Central Committee met on Saturday night and heard a report, once more, from Stanislaw Kania. It also heard reports from Barcikowski and Jagielski. On Sunday Jagielski was back in Gdansk and Poland's national radio in an outside broadcast from Lenin Shipyard relayed the ceremony at which Lech Walesa and Mieczyslaw Jagielski put their signatures to the final agreement in a huge room adorned not only by the national emblem of the Polish eagle but by a crucifix. Both men made speeches. Walesa, in fact, was addressing the nation for the first time. It was also the eve of the anniversary of the German invasion of Poland in 1939.

We are going back to work on 1 September. We all know what that date reminds us of and what we think of on that day. We think about our country and about our national cause, about the common interests of our family which is called Poland . . . Have we achieved everything we wanted to achieve? . . . Not everything, but we all know that we have achieved a great deal . . . We have achieved all that we could achieve in the present situation. We shall achieve the rest, because we now have the most important thing, our independent, self-governing trade unions. This is our guarantee for the future . . . The life of our new trade unions begins tomorrow. Let us ensure that they always remain independent and self-governing . . . I declare the strike over.

Just before the signing Walesa spoke again:

I would like once more to thank Mr Premier and all those elements that prevented any solution by force. We have indeed reached an

27

agreement by negotiation, Poles talking with Poles, without any use of force . . . and that is how it should always be . . . Both sides realised that the elements which were plann . . . [and here Walesa hesitated over his choice of words before he went on] proposing to use force in some way or other have not won. The victors are common sense and prudence, which are represented, as I think we all know, by Premier Jagielski and a certain rather sensible group.

Jagielski, for his part, said that there were no winners or losers and that the main thing now was that the country should put in some solid, hard work. It was never to prove as simple as that for, whatever Walesa had said about not achieving everything, the Gdansk Agreements, as they came to be called, contained a long list of promises and commitments (see Appendix A, page 296) which the Government would find very difficult to implement for some time. And that sowed the seeds of further industrial and political unrest. For the moment, though, the stunning achievement of the Polish workers could only bring hope and promise for the future. On that afternoon of 31 August 1980 one middle-aged worker in overalls found himself facing a film camera inside the Lenin Shipyard. He seemed slightly embarrassed, almost as if he were about to burst into tears. In fact he was very happy at what had happened there that day. 'Now', he said, 'there'll be a chance for justice.'

3. A START TO RENEWAL

On the night of Sunday 31 August, within hours of the signing of the agreements in Gdansk, the local Party activists met there to hear a speech from their leader, Tadeusz Fiszbach. It was an attempt to assess what had happened and Mr Fiszbach was not in two minds. From the outset, he said, the local Party authorities had recognised 'an authentic protest of the working class' and had sent appropriate proposals to the central authorities in Warsaw. The final outcome of the crisis had proved to be 'an historic event in the life of our Party', creating fundamentally new conditions in which the Party had to renew its line. The new self-governing trade unions, which all could join, including Party members, should make a constructive contribution to the protection of workers' interests and socialist democracy. As for the workers, Fiszbach had only admiration.

We think today with appreciation of the working class of the coast, of all the working people who were guided by the good of the homeland during the difficult days of the crisis. Those values were also present among the striking work forces and in the Inter-Factory Strike Committee. In the course of the past few days, invaluable men have emerged there, men fired by the passion to work for the universal good, men with gifts of organisation. Let this whole valuable trend determine the course of future action.

In a sense, Fiszbach had himself emerged as a Party boss who was not afraid of workers or their demands and, like Mieczyslaw Rakowski perhaps, saw hope as well as dangers in the events of August. That very weekend, in fact, people all over Poland were able to read an article by Fiszbach in the weekly edited by Rakowski, the highly respected *Polityka*. It was far more outspoken than his speech.

The strikes, he wrote, were mainly caused by a worsening standard of living and a mood of dissatisfaction prompted by a long list of failings: the progressive centralisation of decision-making, 'voluntarism' in the setting of production targets, a failure of communication in which the views of the public were ignored, a division of the national income that was not always appropriate or just, the excessive growth of individual wealth. He went on to catalogue the inefficiency of the trade unions, bureaucracy, the offhand treatment of citizens, ostentation and sham, the treatment of people, including Party members, as mere instruments, a disregard for grassroots opinion, the failure of the country's mass media, with a reluctance to criticise and the growth of taboo subjects which divided the nation's opinions into two, private and official.

With that unprecedented public indictment of the Gierek regime, Tadeusz Fiszbach, bald and bespectacled, could well have earned from the Western press the title of the first liberal of the August crisis. But his words were overshadowed by the main events. And besides, the world was anxiously watching Moscow for signs of any move or inclination on the Soviet Union's part to do in Poland what it had done in Czechoslovakia in 1968 – intervene in force to halt alleged 'counter-revolution'.

Moscow reports 'counter-revolutionary aims'

On Monday 1 September, as the workers of the Polish coast went back to their jobs, the most authoritative expression of Soviet concern appeared in the Communist Party paper, *Pravda*. The article, which bore the signature Aleksei Petrov, seemed in many ways to be an anachronism, outdated by events. It quoted extensively from *Trybuna Ludu*, its Polish counterpart, which had claimed a few days earlier that 'anti-socialist elements' were trying to prolong the strikes.

It is obvious from press reports [*Pravda* wrote] that anti-socialist elements have succeeded in penetrating several enterprises on the Polish coast, primarily in Gdansk, in abusing the trust of part of the working class and in using economic difficulties for their counter-revolutionary aims.

Many *Pravda* articles are written and even set in type a day or more before publication. But this article was at least slightly different. It actually reported the Saturday evening session of the Polish Central Committee which heard the reports of the Government teams which had been negotiating in Gdansk and Szczecin. It went on:

> However, anti-socialist elements are continuing to put forward political demands, which reveal their true intentions which are far from the economic and social interests of the Polish working class . . . They are doing direct damage to real socialism on Polish soil. They want to destroy the link between the Party and the working class.

Maybe all that was inserted at the last minute on the day before publication. But the fact that Moscow went ahead with the publication of an article that was largely and obviously outdated suggests that it was more concerned to convey its message about 'counter-revolutionary aims' and the threat to the Party. To underline its importance the article received advance publicity, being published by TASS, the official news agency, and broadcast by Moscow Radio's home service on the Sunday evening before publication, at a time when the Gdansk agreements had been signed and their details were known throughout the world. It did not mention anything about the right to strike or the formation of free trade unions; nor did the first Soviet announcement of the agreements the next day.

Moscow was clearly unhappy, as it had been from the start. True to its old tradition of not reporting facts that it did not find politically palatable or even understand, it had not revealed the existence of the strikes until it felt obliged to quote Mr Gierek's broadcast of 18 August referring to 'work stoppages'. After that the Soviet media consistently emphasised the dangers of the unrest being exploited for political ends. It accused the West, in particular American trade unionists and West German 'revenge-seekers', of actively assisting anti-socialist elements in Poland. It claimed that the West was over-dramatising the situation and distorting it 'in the crazy mirror of bourgeois propaganda'. At the same time, Moscow failed to report simple facts, such as Gierek's offer of free elections to trade union bodies. But one thing it did report was maybe more immediately pertinent, an article in the newspaper *Daily World* by the United States Communist Party leader, Gus Hall. According to *Pravda*, he said this:

> The strikes in Poland are not taking place because of any inherent defects in the socialist system. In reality, they are taking place because of weaknesses of leadership and because of distortions of socialist methods.

Soon the Polish Communist Party would itself be passing judgement on its leaders, but in the meantime a celebrated Yugoslav journalist of Zagreb Radio, Milika Sundic, was presenting a more generous view:

The agreement between the Government and the workers was achieved at the last moment, and if the messages and lessons of past upheavals have not been forgotten, all Poles have good reason to mark 1 September as a big victory. The same applies to anyone who has lasting peace in Europe and the world at heart, because any other outcome could have led to bloodshed with unforeseeable consequences both for socialism in Poland and for peace in the world . . . a long time will probably be needed to clarify everything that has happened. However it would not be wise for anyone except the Poles themselves to impose their interpretation. The Poles are quite capable of doing that themselves. Nor would it be wise or right to identify those who won and those who lost. The victors are the Poles, the workers who rebelled and the Government which mustered the strength to understand the workers' dissatisfaction and accept it as justified . . . The agreement has opened the eyes of both of them. Today they can see what they could not see before . . . It has been shown again that there is no such thing as socialism without conflict and that situations of conflict in a socialist country can be resolved only by those who have the mandate of the working class.

During the strikes there were attempts both in Poland and outside it to paint the unrest on the Baltic in various colours and to ascribe to the strikers something they did not want. Perhaps there will be further attempts to do that and it is something to be feared.

As September began, the Polish leaders had their hands full. A broadcast summary of the commitments undertaken in Gdansk and Szczecin comprised a daunting list for any government, let alone one that had suffered a historic political reverse to add to its economic problems. Quite apart from granting the right to strike and form independent trade unions, the Government was committed, among other things, to revising the law on censorship, allowing Sunday mass to be broadcast, speeding up economic reform, preparing a programme of wage rises, considering the release of political prisoners, improving medicine supplies through additional imports, drawing up a programme to improve the housing situation, and a whole series of welfare and labour projects, including higher pensions and work-free Saturdays with pay – most of them with deadlines at the end of the year.

That would have been enough to keep the Government busy. But strikes were continuing, not on the coast but elsewhere, especially in the coal fields of Silesia, perhaps the most important region in the country economically and politically, the former power base of the Party leader, Edward Gierek. What the Government did was quickly appoint a commission to negotiate, as in Gdansk and Szczecin. On Wednesday 3 September an agreement was signed at Jastrzebie committing the Government to even firmer commitments, at least for miners: no Saturday or Sunday working from 1 January 1981, the abolition of the 24-hour working pattern in some mines from 15 September and in others from 1 October, a pledge to submit to Parliament a lowering of the retiring age for underground workers to fifty, and the granting of a full pension to anyone, regardless of age, who had worked underground for twenty-five years.

Whatever that did to ease industrial unrest, it could hardly be expected to increase the production of coal. But the Government apparently had little choice. Indeed, throughout that first week of September the only option open to the authorities was to battle on and try to pick up the pieces. Mr Gierek chaired a meeting of Provincial and Central Committee party leaders, at which the main speeches were made by the new Prime Minister, Jozef Pinkowski, and Stanislaw Kania, a Central Committee secretary. The Government announced measures to curb excessive price increases. A newly appointed Chairman of the Central Statistical Bureau, which provides the facts and figures on the country's economy, said in a radio interview that from now on he would try to increase the honesty and truthfulness of its reports. *Glos Pracy*, the official trade union paper, commented rather ruefully that listening to the voice of the people was a basic law of socialism, and that modernising Poland did not just mean importing technology, it also meant the proper exercise of socialist democracy.

'Anti-socialist incitement'
Poland's allies were not so disposed to see the crisis as an occasion for examining the Communist conscience. They saw it as the work of enemies. In East Germany, the Communist Party daily, *Neues Deutschland*, was upset by the fact that some people in the West saw the possibility of liberalisation in Poland.

The mass media and certain politicians in the imperialist countries are engaged in an unconcealed attempt to interfere in the affairs of our Polish sister country. A whole flood of anti-socialist incitement, ranging from lies and distortion to instructions for staging a counter-revolution and hypocritical attempts to ingratiate themselves with the Polish working people, is pouring from the press, radio and television . . . Those who today profess sympathy for the Polish workers are in fact anti-Polish wolves in sheep's clothing . . . The new 'friends of Poland' are now zealously advocating a so-called 'liberalisation' in Poland . . . There can be no doubt that by liberalisation these people mean something we know from past experience, an attempt to organise counter-revolution against socialism.

In Prague, the Czechoslovak Communist Party paper, *Rude Pravo*, remembered past experience in an article dealing not with Poland but with 'proletarian and socialist internationalism', the principle which had taken Warsaw Pact troops into Czechoslovakia twelve years earlier.

One of the chief plans of international reaction in the crisis-ridden years of 1968–9 was to snatch our country from the family of the socialist community and break our links with the Soviet Union . . . Let us remember all those worries about our freedom, our democracy and our successful development that were expressed in the bourgeois camp and its mass media. But there is also a truth tested by life: when you are praised by your enemy, beware .

At that moment, though, the Polish Communist Party leaders were concerned with trying to prove that Communist rule in their country need not be chronically inefficient or corrupt. On the evening of Thursday 5 September it was announced in Warsaw that the Politburo had appointed a commission to investigate charges against Maciej Szczepanski, the man who had been sacked the previous week from the post of Chairman of the State Committee for Radio and Television. The charges, as it was soon made clear and as everyone knew anyway, were of corruption.

The next morning, the Polish Sejm (Parliament) began what was to be a brief but remarkable session. It opened with a long speech by Prime Minister Pinkowski outlining Government plans for an economic about-turn. He promised to increase wages, family allowances, pensions and welfare benefits, to restrict prices and to put more meat on the market by the chastening expedient for a former meat exporting country of buying from abroad. He also promised limits on investment and comprehensive economic reform.

'Propaganda of success'

But Pinkowski had a more political point to make.

I declare with all my strength that the Government wants to fulfil its obligations. The fundamental guarantee of the lasting nature of the changes that are now taking place lies in the development of socialist democracy . . . We must change a great deal in the style and methods of directing the State and the national economy . . . Observance of the principles of socialist democracy demands openness in public life and consequently systematic and open information about the condition of the State and the national economy. We shall see that information is available because we share the view that co-government and co-responsibility of citizens for the destiny of the country are possible only when the nation is well informed . . . There is a place here for every Pole to take an active part. Party members and non-Party members, believers and non-believers, for all the elements united in the National Unity Front.

And he looked forward to continued understanding and support from the Roman Catholic Church:

I wish to declare with due esteem that recent days have brought evidence of common sense and patriotic solicitude for the country on the part of the leadership of the Church and the vast majority of the clergy.

Pinkowski's words were not insignificant but, in the event, his speech was possibly among the least exciting. His Communist Party colleague, Andrzej Zabinski, a signatory of the agreements in Szczecin and Jastrzebie, recently promoted to candidate membership of the Politburo, added bitter criticism to his call for change.

A mistaken policy on information, the excessively punctilious operation of censorship and local and sectional ambitions determined to achieve favourable comment at all costs, led eventually to a hazardous complacency. We are now paying a high price for this departure from reality.

More biting comments still came from less exalted speakers. Piotr Stefanski, a member of the Democratic Party, which with the United Peasant Party forms the essentially powerless ingredient of the National Unity Front coalition with the Communists, asked why the Sejm should be 'reduced to playing the part of a rubber stamp to endorse decisions taken earlier'. Jan Szczepanski, a respected non-Party deputy, told the House that although the nation had known it was heading for a crisis, neither the authorities nor the mass media had been willing to talk about it. Szczepanski saw grounds for optimism in what he described as the charisma, skills and imagination of the men who had led the August strikes. They could serve as an example to the State administration. Szczepanski also said that the press, radio and television should provide what he called accurate reports of all that was said in the Sejm. There could be no democracy in the State, he suggested, without democracy in the Party. Subsequent speakers said that the Sejm must be given back its full constitutional function as the highest body of State authority.

One of the most telling criticisms of the Government-controlled media came from Karol Malcuzynski, a journalist and broadcaster and President of the Polish Authors' Association. He claimed that control of the mass media had proved to be a mistake in concept and in practice. For years, he said, press, radio and television had been engaged in what he called 'the propaganda of success', a pattern of reporting which always looked on the brighter side of things. The result had been that any discussion of the economic and social costs of Poland's stormy development had been suppressed, and news reporting and news commentaries had been reduced to complete uniformity. Malcuzynski suggested that while no sane person would call for the complete abolition of censorship, there was a need to determine its scope by law.

On the 6 pm news on that Friday, 5 September, Warsaw Radio broadcast a report from one of its correspondents who had gone straight to the studio from the Sejm. He was almost beside himself with excitement.

I have been a parliamentary reporter for more than twenty-five years, but I must say that what I have experienced in the Sejm today is without parallel in the past quarter of a century . . . The Prime Minister's speech launched the debate towards economic reform and the issues of economic policy, but the most important and essential feature of the debate was the question of the renewal of the Sejm itself . . . It was pointed out that in the past, and in recent years in particular, there have been some extremely unpleasant and unwelcome distortions of the work of the Sejm, that it had lost its constitutional function. Nobody deprived the Sejm of its functions in the legislative sense, but in day-to-day experience a method of rubber-stamping, of response by applause in unison, became established . . . The performance of the deputies today fills one with confidence and optimism.

Kania replaces Gierek

As it happened, though, another event, reported in the same news bulletin as that enthusiastic commentary, overshadowed the session of the Sejm. It was announced that Edward Gierek had that morning suffered 'a serious malfunctioning of the heart' and was in hospital under specialist care. Five hours later, past midnight, the radio announced that he was no longer leader of the Polish Communist Party.

The Central Committee of the Polish United Workers' Party held its sixth plenary session on the night of 5/6 September under the chairmanship of Henryk Jablonski, a member of the Politburo and President of the Council of State.

In connection with Edward Gierek's serious illness, the Central Committee released him from the post of First Secretary of the Central Committee and member of the Politburo of the PZPR Central Committee. The Central Committee unanimously appointed Stanislaw Kania to the post of First Secretary. Stanislaw Kania made a speech. The text will be published later.

The Central Committee appointed Kazimierz Barcikowski and Andrzej Zabinski members of the Politburo. Tadeusz Grabski, Zdzislaw Kurowski and Jerzy Wojtecki were appointed Secretaries of the Central Committee.

The plenary meeting will be continued this month.

Edward Gierek's ten-year reign as Party leader was over. The news was not unexpected but few could have predicted that his going would be quite so similar to that of his predecessor. Wladyslaw Gomulka, who had risen to power and left it, like Gierek, after workers had demonstrated their dissatisfaction, had also suffered a minor stroke in the final days of his rule.

The appointment of Kania to succeed Gierek was more of a surprise. Most Western observers had expected Stefan Olszowski, the man sacked by Gierek from the Politburo in February, to take over. Some described him as a 'liberal'. But few had words to describe Kania except to say that he was an 'unknown'. In fact, signs of his probable succession were already there. Stanislaw Kania, who was fifty-three and had reportedly started his working life as an apprentice blacksmith, may have been the quiet man of Polish politics but throughout the recent crisis he had performed a notable function. At each of the crucial meetings of the Central Committee, meetings that could have gone one way or the other, it was he who delivered the opening report. One suspected then

37

that he was in a sense the organiser and director. Moreover, he was responsible in the Party for security and the police, who were not used against the strikers, and for relations with the Church, which played a key role in preaching moderation. Some Western reporters even jumped to the conclusion that Kania must be 'Moscow's man'. Perhaps they were influenced by the tone of the message of congratulations sent to the new leader by Mr Brezhnev. It was broadcast by Moscow even before Warsaw broadcast Kania's speech.

Dear Comrade Kania, Soviet Communists and the working people of the Soviet Union know you as a staunch champion of the people's true interests and well-being, the ideals of Communism, the strengthening of the leading role of the PZPR and the consolidation of socialism in the Polish People's Republic. They know you as a man who stands firmly on the positions of proletarian internationalism and the inviolable friendship of the Polish People's Republic with the Soviet Union and other fraternal socialist states.

Mr Brezhnev expressed 'the firm conviction' that the Polish people, guided by the Party, would soon solve the country's difficulties. To judge from Kania's speech, though, he knew it would not be as easy as that.

'Democracy is not a gesture'
In this, his first public statement as Party leader, Kania made it clear that he was in no doubt about the causes of the crisis or of the duty of the Party and himself.

Words have been used here in one speech or another about my going to be the leader of the Party. No, comrades, the function does not make a leader of a man. And I am not so sure that our Party needs what is signified by this notion of leader.

I am deeply convinced that it is my duty first and foremost to ensure that the collective wisdom of the people should function here in this hall and throughout the Party . . . Our most important task is to restore public confidence in the people's authority, the confidence of the working class and all Party workers . . . Serious mistakes in economic policy and deformations in social life were the fundamental source of the great wave of strikes that has rolled across Poland since July and is continuing today. We are treating the strikes as a sign of workers' dissatisfaction, of workers' protest which, in its main current, was of a purely working-class nature. This was a protest directed not against the principles of socialism nor against our alliances. This was not a protest aimed at the leading role of our Party . . . It was directed against the distortions, against the mistakes in our policy. And that is why the fundamental method of solving such social conflicts as strikes was dialogue, talks patiently and consistently conducted by our comrades. As a result we obtained agreements . . . We shall see to it that all of them are implemented. The fact that we did achieve a political solution to such a sharp social conflict is valuable political and moral capital.

Mr Kania repeated the usual statements of loyalty to the alliance with the Soviet Union and gave a warning against the danger of anti-socialists taking advantage of the situation. But the whole tenor of his speech made it clear that in his view the blame for everything lay at home and that it was up to the Party to change its ways.

We shall go to the sources of the tensions and remove them, so that such a dramatic situation never happens again. But it must be realised that the struggle is not only to regain the trust of the working class. A sharp struggle is also being waged against our adversary. We want to solve the country's difficulties, but our anti-socialist adversary wants to exploit the conflicts that have arisen for goals that run counter to what the workers are striving for . . . We shall act decisively against cases of disruption of order, arbitrary action and disorder, against acts of discrimination against honest and selfless people in their work for Poland. We shall firmly defend the cause of socialism, the vital interests of our state.
  We can, indeed we must, discuss and dispute many issues. We must change no small number of things . . . We proceed from the assumption that democracy is not a gesture by the authorities towards society, but a great and growing need of socialism. For this reason, we are strongly in favour of the full observance of the constitutional rights of the Sejm, of the extension of the powers of the People's Councils, of the genuine renewal of the trade unions . . . We shall ensure too that the new trade unions develop in the way their organisers have said they will . . . We want every patriotically-minded citizen to have a sense and opportunity of taking an active part in national affairs. We want to continue our policy on religion, enriched by new experiences which have served our country well.
  We should ensure that models of socialist society are created throughout the Party – in other words, democracy in the work of the Central Committee and all Party echelons; high standards and a stern attitude to irregularities and to violations of moral principles such as were mentioned in today's discussions . . . We must make sure that our style of work becomes more simple and natural . . . Less standing on ceremony and more objectivity and honesty will help make our work more effective and strengthen the links between the Party and the public . . . We should build the authority of the Party on modesty, simplicity and passion in the struggle against what is bad, what annoys them and offends their sense of justice.

Stanislaw Kania may indeed have appeared to be a simple

man but the ideas he put forward in that speech – virtually unprepared because of the haste with which the plenary meeting was called into session – proved to be a pretty shrewd assessment of the real situation, the mood of the country and the way attitudes were changing. Strikes were continuing intermittently in more than a dozen places and were to continue until well into the second half of the month. One of the aims of the strikers was to make sure that the momentous agreements secured in Gdansk also applied elsewhere. Until the strikes ended, the Government could hardly begin to plan any economic recovery. But it could not end them without first restoring some trust between the Party and the workers. One obstacle to that was a reluctance on the part of some local authorities to change their ways and deal with the workers in the new spirit of conciliation insisted on by Mr Kania. Another obstacle was a deep-seated distrust of the authorities in a nation that had seen similar promising situations go badly wrong in the past. Gomulka in 1956 and Gierek in 1970 had both heralded false dawns. The Editor-in-Chief of the weekly *Kultura*, Dominik Horodynski, had very definite ideas on that.

The present crisis is not the first in People's Poland. Every time Poland has come out of a crisis, it has turned out that the truth and public talk of the truth about us and our affairs was more important than wage rises or the presence of goods in the shops. Alas, each time the situation went back to normal here, people appeared who began to manipulate the truth, usually under a Marxist guise.
All of us have to pay for their manipulations, and the price is higher each time. The highest price is paid by the Party, because such manipulations always break its links with the masses and weaken its leading role . . . To lead is to express the aspirations of the working class, to be able to reconcile sometimes conflicting interests of social groups, regions and sectors of the economy. To lead means restoring the bond with the masses, creating mechanisms to prevent it ever being broken. The key to that is authentic democracy inside the Party.

Party methods must change
Mr Kania, it seems, was already well aware of this. He knew the Party could not be changed overnight. But he also knew that it was largely discredited and had to change. In speeches first in Gdansk and then in the industrial centre of Katowice he said that the Party's position would not be the same, nor

would the position of its members and activists. He acknowledged that there was 'great bitterness' in the Party ranks but insisted that, though things were tough, 'we need a great deal of will-power and a faith that nobody will replace us or the Party in finding a way out of these troubles'. He said he was in favour of calling an extraordinary Party congress. He believed that guarantees should be built into the system, that 'where the authorities have sinned, humility is needed'. For Kania, in words at least, the whole problem was moral as well as political.

There is much that is bad in our society, bad qualities, vices . . . However, it cannot be overemphasised that what is a thousand times more important is what has to be changed within ourselves, how the authorities must change, how the methods of ruling and governing must change, how the methods with which the Party exercises its leading role must change. This is a fundamental topic for discussion. Attitudes to people are the big problem. We have repeatedly spoken about shaping socialist relations among people. But it transpires that this has been one of the causes of the miners' protest. Good pay is not enough, nor will orders suffice. Nothing will replace the feeling of being a human being, a fully honoured citizen of our country, with one's dignity respected as a citizen of our socialist state.

That was the philosophy of Kania's rule, put across at local Party meetings throughout the country in the weeks to come. It is impossible to say from Polish reports whether it provoked any opposition. But the practical implications of the policy may have been a different matter. After one Party meeting in the town of Koszalin, at least, a local radio reporter confessed that never in his life had he witnessed 'such a heated debate'. Speakers, he said, lashed out at the errors that had led to the crisis, claiming that local authorities had in effect been paralysed, forced into 'indiscriminate obedience in carrying out unrealistic decisions', and treated to 'reports which always sounded optimistic irrespective of the actual truth'.

The guest speaker was Kazimierz Barcikowski, now a full member of the Politburo. In a speech covering all aspects of the crisis he dwelt in detail on the economy, admitting that the problems were enormous.

What frightens us most is the progressive escalation of demands. Sometimes you find yourself close to despair. If everyone makes demands and you go round explaining and persuading but your words fall on deaf ears, it sometimes occurs to you that Poland has decided to treat itself to inflation with all the consequences and to live according to the motto 'let's have it come what may'.

But Barcikowski also saw the need for a clean-up inside the Party.

We must assess people more efficiently and see to it that good experts and fine men, leaders and administrators are respected and protected. At the same time we must get rid of worthless people, paltry people both in the moral sense and as regards professional ability. But this too must be done only when their guilt has been established . . . Comrades, let's not repeat the old mistake and simply go from the propaganda of success to the propaganda of self-flagellation.

It is interesting to note how quickly the words of a non-Communist parliamentary deputy were picked up and adopted by the Party.

Party post-mortems continued in the provinces. In Jelenia Gora the local Party secretary wondered angrily why all his hard work to make up shortages of butter, meat and coal had not done any good. His conclusion: 'When a person is cold, it's hard for him to bother his head about socialism.'

Call for purge

A meeting of the Warsaw Party organisation heard one of its secretaries, Henryk Szablak, sum up the 'general feeling of regret and resentment' over the mistakes and the violations of the Party programme. The conclusion, according to Warsaw Radio, was this: 'The process of renewal should start today. It must be accompanied by a purge in which the Party will rid itself of accretions alien to socialism, bad methods of work and dishonest people who often represent only their own interests.'

That was Sunday 14 September. The next day *Trybuna Ludu* put it on record more firmly:

It is a painful matter, but the Party must clear its ranks of individuals who have lost their honesty and given way to the temptations of corruption and an easier life. Contrary to the opinions spread by the Party's enemies, these individuals constitute only a marginal section of the membership, but they cast a shadow on a substantial number of other members who are honest and completely dedicated.

President Jablonski went on television that night to take the message further. He too condemned 'the false and one-sided propaganda of success' and claimed that there was nothing to stop every citizen being provided with 'full and honest information'. The people, he said, must take an active part in the exercise of power.

Having been the object of power, the people must become the subject of power . . . We must all feel responsible for our common destiny if democracy is to become a complete reality. In the immediate future this means, above all, the implementation of the obligations which we have jointly undertaken . . . Establishing the most favourable conditions for the creative efforts of the nation is not possible without combating all social evils . . . Lack of respect for public property, abuse of position for personal gain, bribery, corruption and all other forms of law-breaking do occur in many sectors. In the struggle against these infectious diseases we must be merciless. The only way we can safeguard the sound part of the community is by surgery regardless of where the disease is located.

Only two weeks had passed since the signing of the agreements in Gdansk but already the Party leader, Mr Gierek, had been replaced and a penitent and shaken Party was talking of a purge, an attack on corruption, honest reporting in the media and a place for everyone in running the country. But there was no great excitement over these glittering prospects. Indeed, one rather cynical joke summed up the prevalent attitude in two words: *Wraca nowe* – 'the new is coming back'. Briefly but tellingly, the slogan said that they had heard it all before.

But the Party, under Mr Kania, pressed on with what it had promised. On 19 September Stefan Olszowski made a long speech in Bydgoszcz in which he accused the former leadership of having been 'arrogant, self-willed and neglectful of social consequences'. The same day he also visited Poznan for a Party meeting at which the Provincial Party secretary, Jerzy Zasada, was replaced by a Mr Kusiak. At the same time Kania attended a meeting in Katowice at which the local Party boss, Zdzislaw Grudzien, an old ally of Mr Gierek, was replaced by Andrzej Zabinski. According to one Warsaw Radio report, Grudzien also asked to be released from his seat on the Politburo. Gossip had it that Grudzien and Gierek used to have a fine time at expensive villas down south near Zakopane. But there was far more circumstantial gossip about the scandals concerning Maciej Szczepanski, the former broadcasting chief. Unpublished allegations suggested that he used his post to finance a life-style that featured several private cars, executive aircraft, a yacht, a farm and a couple of villas each providing every luxury including the company of beautiful girls. The Public Prosecutor soon confirmed that investigations had revealed grounds for prosecution and the lifting of Szczepanski's parliamentary immunity. This went some way, no doubt, to satisfying the mood of moral indignation.

Another move which was bound to be welcomed by a predominantly Roman Catholic nation was the news that agreement had been reached in the newly reconstituted Church–State Commission on the regular nationwide broadcasting by radio of 9 am Sunday mass from the Church of the Holy Cross in Warsaw. This was something the Church had been after since the Communists came to power. It was also one of the commitments undertaken by the Government in the Gdansk Agreements. The first mass was broadcast on 21 September. The celebrant was Bishop Jerzy Modzelewski, Suffragan of the Warsaw Archdiocese. There was a sermon. Several notices were also read out, including brief details of a pastoral letter from the Polish bishops warning against the moral dangers to children from some television programmes and reminding television producers that they were 'responsible to their own consciences and to the nation for the upbringing of the new generation of Poles on the basis of healthy and durable moral principles'. It was Mass Media Day, so one of the special prayers was for workers in press, radio and television. The whole service overran by a few minutes to accommodate the singing after mass of the patriotic hymn about fatherland and freedom that is sung in the same way by Polish exiles throughout the world: 'Boze cos Polske przez tak liczne wieki' – 'O God who has protected Poland . . .'

All this helped improve the atmosphere considerably, but it did not lessen in any way the seemingly intractable problem of the economy and the pressing challenge of the new unions.

'Chaos and galloping inflation'
The economy was in a bad way before the strike wave had begun. But figures presented to the Government in the early days of September indicated how damaging it had been. In August, industrial output was twelve per cent below the monthly target, mainly because of the strikes. The total esti-

mated losses to the national economy during the month were put at 30,000 million zlotys. And that did not include losses in foreign trade.

On top of that, prolonged heavy rains had ruined hopes for agriculture. Grain and potato crops would be well down on the previous year; a very difficult fodder situation probably meant that there would be a drop in meat supplies in 1981. Deputy Premier Kisiel, the new State planning chief, revealed in an interview on Warsaw television that the grain harvest would fall short by about 1,500,000 tonnes. So that amount would have to be imported.

Perhaps the best picture of the overall economic crisis was given by Mr Barcikowski in Koszalin when his point was that it would be fatal for the Government to keep on giving in to repeated demands:

If the escalation goes on and we are forced to give in and give in, then indeed, we will find ourselves in a situation from which there is no way out. We are simply threatened with chaos and galloping inflation. This is so because the money we have been doling out so far is not matched by goods in the shops . . .

Of course, the voices of demagogues are to be heard demanding that we should stop exporting one commodity or another from among those which we produce at home. But today we not only cannot limit our exports, we must increase them if we want to keep the mechanism of our economy running. It is already common knowledge that as a result of a bad harvest we have already lost at least 600 million zlotys in hard currency exports.

Our attempts to get some help from socialist countries are proving effective to some extent. This help, of course, is based on credits. Between May and this moment, the Soviet Union has lent us 550 million dollars. This money can be used to buy the necessary raw materials from outside markets. As a result of this we have been in a position to maintain our solvency . . . We are also seeking loans in capitalist countries . . . In all likelihood, the state of affairs in this country today does not make our position any easier. Bankers do not get sentimental about our internal situation. We have become a less credible partner for them, a country lacking internal stability, and talks which had been scheduled earlier are now being postponed.

At that moment, Poland was believed to owe Western creditors some $20,000 million.

As Mr Barcikowski was speaking, though, his colleague, Deputy Prime Minister Jagielski, was in Moscow signing a new economic agreement. The Soviet Union, it must be said, regularly supplies Poland with all its natural gas and sawn timber requirements and some eighty per cent of its crude oil, potash, cotton and iron ore. These supplies had been increased in the troubled months of July and August. Now the Soviet Government agreed to supply Poland for the rest of the year with additional quantities of industrial goods and food to the value of 85 million roubles. According to Warsaw television, they would have cost about $150 million on the Western market. Warsaw also reported that the Soviet Union had earlier granted financial credits – presumably the $550 million offered in May – and postponed the repayment of earlier credits.

The reports of the new agreement virtually coincided with the news that the United States had decided to grant Poland credits of $670 million. While reporting that, Warsaw also confused the layman by noting that the Soviet Union had agreed to grant a ten-year credit of $260 million at low interest and extend the deadline. This meant that the total value of Soviet aid now added up to $690 million, more than the American figure.

All this, to quote Mr Barcikowski's phrase, would help keep Poland solvent. But what was the Polish Government doing about the economy? On 15 September it met and was told that coal production was expected to decline in 1980 by about five million tonnes as compared with the plan. It decided on cuts in expenditure amounting to something approaching 34,000 million zlotys.

On 22 September the Government announced its draft economic plan for 1981. Its declared fundamental aim was to carry out the programme of increases in wages and welfare payments, increase production for the consumer market, protect the standard of living, and press on with housing construction. These points determined its priorities. Huge investment projects, which kept money tied up for a long time, were to be shelved and the cash diverted to producing goods for the shops, housing and hospital construction, and the expansion of exports. To stimulate economic growth, the Government said, it would need additional foreign funds.

Altogether the plan was simple and could have been dictated by the workers who struck in August. But it was from them, towards the end of the month, that the Government faced its greatest challenge since the signing of the Gdansk Agreements.

Solidarity comes to town

The Government had started the month clearly hoping that although it had been forced to bow to the demand for new, independent trade unions, the old ones, gathered under the controlling umbrella of the Central Trades Union Council or CRZZ, would continue to operate. On the very first day of the month, the Presidium of the CRZZ met in Warsaw and insisted among other things that the views of the trade unions must not be ignored. It looked forward to the new bill on the unions which it saw as something that would secure conditions for their 'effective work'. But the CRZZ was fighting a losing battle. Within days, another independent, self-governing union had been formed in Wroclaw, a fact reported by Warsaw Radio, but supplemented later by an interview with a representative of the old unions in the city who denied a suggestion in the Catholic paper, *Slowo Powszechne*, that the CRZZ was heading for a quick demise. The paper had predicted that 'the best people' would be moving over to the new unions.

On Sunday 7 September Lech Walesa, the leader of the new union in Gdansk, went to Warsaw with a group of colleagues to meet Cardinal Wyszynski, attend mass in his private chapel and tell reporters later: 'We've won the first round'. A second, more difficult round was now beginning. One of the main problems was that, whereas the CRZZ continued to receive traditional publicity in the official media, the new unions did not. And the emphasis was still on restoring and revitalising the CRZZ.

On Thursday 11 September foreign correspondents in Warsaw including myself were treated to two press conferences. The first was given beneath a bust of Lenin in the headquarters of the CRZZ by its new leader, Romuald Jankowski. Mr Jankowski, a genial man, made plenty of promises about reform but was unable to give any clear idea of how he visualised the relationship between the old unions and the new. He hoped for cooperation with the new unions which he saw, he said, as allies rather than rivals. He also felt there would have to be some sort of joint representation to deal with the Government on such important matters as wages and housing.

A few hours later, just across the street from CRZZ headquarters, the second press conference took place in the Catholic Intellectuals Club. In a much smaller and congested

47

room, hung with crucifixes and pictures of several Popes, a group of workers announced that between fifty and eighty per cent of the work forces of factories in Mazovia, the Warsaw area, had already signed on to join the new, independent unions. The factories included the giant Ursus tractor works, the Municipal Transport enterprise, the Warsaw steel plant, Huta Warszawa, and the huge factory that produces Fiat cars under licence. In one factory, half the founding members of the new union were said to be Communist Party members. The union was non-political and Party members could belong, but no one holding office either in the Party or in management would be allowed to hold office in the union. The workers' main, or at least most impressive, spokesman was Zbigniew Bujak, an electrical assembly worker in his mid-twenties from Ursus, who looked for all the world like a model for one of those famous Soviet socialist realist sculptures of the ideal worker.

Officially the new unions were to have the same rights as the old ones, but the Warsaw workers reported some difficulties in establishing themselves in proper premises. Official obstruction was to be the subject of complaint elsewhere, but in the meantime the idea of independence was spreading to other areas. In the Academy of Sciences there was talk of autonomy in research centres. The Minister of Education said the law on higher education must be changed to make for greater independence and democracy; university senates would be able to elect rectors by secret ballot instead of having them appointed. Journalists in Cracow wrote to Warsaw suggesting that editors be chosen by their colleagues instead of being appointed by the Party. Students at Warsaw University issued a call for independent bodies to represent them. At the same time, the controlling bodies of some of the old unions – the Seamen and Dockers, Metal Workers, Municipal Workers, and others – announced that they were going independent and leaving the CRZZ. Their move received considerable publicity in the official media but it was clear that these were not in any real sense 'new' unions but old ones proclaiming independence while abandoning the sinking ship of the CRZZ.

That was the view, scornfully expressed, at one of the most important events of the month, the first assembly of free trade unionists on Wednesday 17 September in the port of Gdansk.

It was another unprecedented occasion. Some 250 representatives of new unions from all over the country crowded into the hall of what used to be a seamen's hostel to hear Lech Walesa, the hero of the Lenin Shipyard, open the proceedings against a backdrop decorated with the Polish emblem, an eagle and a crucifix. Journalists from all over the world, armed with cameras and recording machines, crowded the aisles as the proceedings were relayed through loud-speakers to crowds of people outside on either side of the building, many of them with their noses pressed against the glass of the windows.

Speaker after speaker got up to report progress in setting up their unions. Some said the authorities were being cooperative; many more complained of official obstruction. There were arguments about the new union statutes which would have to be submitted soon to the Warsaw District Court if the unions were to be legally registered. Walesa himself was originally against a centralised, controlling body. If independence meant anything, he argued, one should not run the risk of falling into the well-known failings of previous centralised authorities. The answer to that was that in some parts of the country, less famous and less populated than Gdansk or Warsaw, the authorities could find it easier to pick off the newly-born unions unless they had the support, clearly and constitutionally expressed, of the big guns of the new union movement.

Overall, though, the meeting gave the impression of a growing movement that could not be ignored. One delegate proudly said that his founding committee would follow the lead of Gdansk and take 130 factories with it. The meeting, which adjourned for a few days, was ignored by the official press. The papers reported instead that more of the old unions, including the Mineworkers, had decided to leave the CRZZ.

One outcome of the meeting was that the Gdansk committee, under Walesa, did take the lead in issuing a strong statement accusing the authorities in many places – but not Gdansk apparently – of trying to sabotage the new unions. It claimed that people wanting to join them were being intimidated, that 'old, discredited union leaders' were trying to halt the new movement by 'lies and provocation'. It complained too of lack of access to the media. Another outcome, reported by the Polish News Agency on the same day, was that the new union movement, as expected, would bear the name of Solidarnosc, meaning Solidarity.

On Wednesday 24 September Solidarity was in Warsaw in force. Walesa and his colleagues drove in a bus covered with the Solidarity banner and Polish flags to the Warsaw District Court to submit a copy of Solidarity's constitutional statutes and apply for its legal registration as a nationwide union with a National Commission based in Gdansk. It was an almost triumphal arrival. As Lech Walesa stepped from the bus with his colleagues he was greeted with cries of 'Leszek, Leszek' from the large crowd that had been waiting for hours, filling the steps to the court, the pavement and part of the road. By the time the union leaders got to the top of the steps and disappeared through the door, making victory signs as they went, the crowd was singing the national anthem.

A decision by Judge Koscielniak on whether Solidarity could be registered was expected in a matter of weeks. But the day was far from over for Walesa and the men of Solidarity. They went on to a meeting with Deputy Prime Minister Jagielski, the man who signed the Gdansk Agreements. Later still Walesa and a few of his colleagues broke even more new ground by giving a press conference in, of all places, the offices of Interpress, one of the official news agencies where, not many weeks earlier, in July, the Party propaganda chief, now sacked, had told foreign journalists that the strikes were virtually over. The official media could not avoid reporting this occasion, another one in which noses were pressed against the windows by curious onlookers outside. But *Trybuna Ludu* reported that Walesa gave 'evasive answers, betraying as it were an underestimation of the country's economic situation'. It did praise him for condemning wildcat strikes, though what he in fact said was that such strikes would continue. Warsaw Radio noted Walesa's statement that he never expressed opinions on political matters, that he was 'only a trade unionist'. In fact, it said, all his answers were brief and to the point. From my own notes I recall that Walesa faced several testing questions from Eastern bloc journalists, including one about his financial position. 'No, I haven't got a Mercedes', he said. 'I have two suits, four pairs of socks, and a father in America who does not send me any money. I have accepted a new flat. My colleagues insisted on that. But we are afraid to put any curtains up in case our neighbours start talking.' It was at that press conference that I first heard Walesa express a desire to emulate the efficiency of workers in Japan.

Another strike call

In spite of Walesa's good humour, Solidarity's relationship with the Government was not proving any easier than was expected. The new union movement was not yet registered as a legal body, but it still had to insist that the Government fulfilled the commitments undertaken in Gdansk. One of these concerned wage rises and according to Solidarity the Government was dragging its feet and seemed unlikely to meet its promised deadline.

On 29 September Solidarity called a one-hour warning strike for Friday 3 October, in protest against what it called violation of the agreements by the Government. A statement from Gdansk said that agreements had been reached in only a few enterprises. Talks had only just started in some, and in others the authorities were trying to deal with the old unions rather than the new. The statement claimed that agreements were being held up because Solidarity had no access to the media.

The strike call came originally from the Gdansk committee alone, but soon it was joined by union committees in other cities, making the strike national. Then it was confirmed that Solidarity leaders were seriously contemplating a general strike later if the warning strike failed to produce any change.

The media avoided mentioning the strike call, but on the last evening of the month Kazimierz Barcikowski addressed the nation on television. His speech was rather like the one he had made in Koszalin earlier in the month. He argued that the Government could do only as much as it could afford; strikes, he insisted, should be treated only as a last resort.

In the name of our common good, we cannot, we must not abuse strikes and regard them as a form of constant pressure or threat on minor matters . . . The public needs a well-functioning economy and internal order. I must say with regret that this truth is not being treated seriously by all the organisers of the new trade unions . . . While talks are being held throughout the country with work forces and representatives of the new trade unions, and while hundreds and thousands of new pay and benefit agreements have been reached with representatives of work forces, a warning strike has been announced in Gdansk for 3 October, with the possibility of its extension nationwide.

51

What is more, in calling the strike and telling the foreign propaganda media about it, those responsible did not even take the trouble to inform Government representatives engaged in continuing talks about their decision . . . I said earlier that we are determined to implement our agreements fully . . . But this makes us wonder whether the authors of the Gdansk decision are really concerned about normal economic effort . . . Perhaps what they are trying to do is maintain social tension and push us into chaos . . . Many questions come to mind here. They must be answered by each and every one of us . . . They are questions for all of us and of great importance for Poland.

September had begun in an atmosphere of some bewilderment but also hope. It ended in bitter anticipation.

4. ALLIANCE FOR REFORM

A large number of people in Warsaw, myself included, failed to see that television appeal against the strike by Kazimierz Barcikowski on the last evening of September 1980. They had gone to the pictures at the Relaks cinema in a side street off the capital's main shopping street, Marszalkowska, for a show that was to draw the crowds for weeks to come. The big picture was *Manhattan*, with Woody Allen, but the main attraction, lasting barely half an hour, was a newsreel report devoted entirely to the strikes of August on the Baltic Coast.

The film had appeared within a month of the strikes ending, a remarkable enough confirmation of the authorities' acceptance of what had happened. No less remarkable was the way in which the strike leaders, the popular heroes such as Lech Walesa, were shown at the height of the crisis inside the Lenin Shipyard being hailed by fellow strikers, holding talks with a slightly quirky but rather sympathetic Mr Jagielski, or simply sleeping as best they could on benches or tables or on the floor. The cinema audience loved it, mainly because of its honest portrayal of the personalities involved, people who until this film had remained almost shadowy figures. They also liked the touches of undoubted humour, such as when the Deputy Prime Minister arrived to begin talks and insisted on introducing himself with deadpan face to each and every one of the strikers' negotiating team as Jagielski, Jagielski, Jagielski . . .

But the most striking and slightly chilling feature of the newsreel was the showing of film never before seen in public, shots of what happened in Gdansk and Gdynia in December 1970 when troops were sent in. Interlaced with the warm colour of the August newsreel, the contrasting black and white pictures of silent streets occupied by tanks and armoured cars and of official buildings charred by fire presented a political contrast between the use of force and the use of negotiation.

After applauding the newsreel and in places even cheering it, the people who left the cinema that night were maybe in a state of some euphoria. After incidents of labour unrest in the past they had been treated at best to official enquiries which allotted the blame. Now they had been shown the pictures and the evidence. And no side had been blamed. Whatever the Government's intentions were in passing the film for public showing, its effect may have been more than they bargained for, coming as it did on the eve of the first token strike since the troubles by those same heroes of Gdansk and their followers elsewhere.

The Government did everything it could to stop the strike. Again Deputy Premier Jagielski went to Gdansk for talks with the Solidarity leaders there. The Government spokesman, at a news conference, denied the Solidarity claim that the authorities were introducing promised pay rises too slowly. As to the new union's second complaint – lack of access to the media – he pointed out that Solidarity already had a column of its own in *Dziennik Baltycki* and other papers on the coast. And on the final complaint, that the authorities in some parts of the country were deliberately obstructing the establishment of the new unions, the spokesman promised that any instance of that would be thoroughly investigated.

Facts of official obstruction were, however, acknowledged by a Warsaw Radio commentator, Jacek Dabrowski:

The atmosphere is poisoned by a lack of trust in statements by the authorities. Trust is prevented from growing by the news, which spreads like lightning, of difficulties encountered by the new trade unions, of difficulties deliberately exacerbated by people who do not sympathise with these unions . . . Such people are not in favour of the new unions because they feel personally threatened. They believe that the authorities and the community are about to rid Poland of all filth. They believe this and they are defending their positions. One should not be surprised that they are obstructing others; everyone everywhere defends his own interests.

The authorities and Solidarity stuck to their guns, both believing they had strong cases. Deputy Premier Jagielski apparently came close to agreement in Gdansk but on the morning of 3 October, the appointed day, Warsaw Radio, through the voice of another commentator, put the last argument against the strike:

Neither the sixty minutes that it will last, nor the losses it will occasion are the most important aspect, although in the present situation they will not be without their significance for our economy. It is the confrontation, putting the issue on the basis of 'an eye for an eye, a tooth for a tooth', that could turn out to be important and dangerous in its effects. The confrontation will have and is bound to have a political character considerably at variance with the demands and desires which were expressed by the port workers and the people of the coast and by so many Poles in the testing days of August.

At noon the strike began and the turnout was impressive. Hundreds of thousands of workers took part in towns all over the country, but in different ways depending on how the local Solidarity leaders decided to make their warning felt. In Warsaw, where only part of the public transport came to a standstill, a small number of factories were affected and there were no walk-outs. Work stopped only in chosen departments. At some factory gates a single Solidarity member stood silently holding the Polish flag. In Gdansk almost everything seemed to come to a standstill except for essential services. In the Katowice area some hundred factories and mines stopped work. In Lodz all public transport came to a halt.

Lech Walesa claimed complete success. 'We showed that we know how to start a strike,' he said, 'and how to end one.' He also said that the threat of a general strike later in the month was being called off. Solidarity had given an impressive performance and the authorities were happy to give the new union more publicity than ever by filling the first ten minutes of its main television news programme with pictures of the strikes in several of the country's main towns. The accompanying commentary condemned the action, of course, but betrayed more sorrow than hostility. What seemed clear was that, in spite of all the warnings, the so-called social contract between the Government and the workers, as represented by the new unions, was far from destroyed. If anything each side had made its point without achieving very much. Of the two, the Government probably came off worse, for although it had argued its case for more sensible behaviour and had stood by it, it knew that among the basic causes of the strike (one that had been admitted virtually by the State radio) was a deep-seated distrust of a Communist Party that had failed to keep its word so many times before.

Party post-mortem

The day after the strike, the Party set about changing that at a meeting of the Central Committee that was to become a landmark in the history of self-criticism and reform. On Saturday 4 October the members of the Central Committee assembled not for a new meeting but for the continuation of the Sixth Plenum (or plenary session), which had been adjourned early in September after electing Stanislaw Kania First Secretary in succession to Edward Gierek. What had become abundantly clear in the intervening weeks was that Gierek had gone not just because of his heart attack, from which he had since been recovering, but because of his political disgrace. It was the disgrace of the Party that was to dominate this latest session.

It began as usual with another report from Stanislaw Kania, ninety minutes long, another post-mortem but much more detailed and outspoken. The strikes of August, in which, he said, many Party members had taken part, were a genuine, mass workers' protest, prompted not by opponents of socialism but by mistaken economic and social policy. It had been unwise to place the country so heavily in debt. It had been wrong to overburden the economy with investments, to ignore the importance of agriculture, to allow such a violent growth of consumption. At the same time, he said, social strains had increased with the accelerated influx of people from the countryside to the towns. The world economic crisis had not helped either.

But Mr Kania made a damning claim:

Reports and evaluations presented to the Politburo used to hide the facts, thus preventing an objective account of the situation that existed at the time . . . The style of government was characterised by arrogance, by hostility to criticism and a disregard of ideas and opinions originating outside the centres of leadership. There is no doubt that in the mid-seventies it was still possible to prevent the economy from entering a blind alley . . .

Sadly, the Party leadership and in particular the Government leadership saw the main chance of balancing the economy through increasing prices. But this was accompanied by hiding or trivialising the true picture of the economic situation and increasing cost of living. Great losses were caused by the so-called propaganda of success, which was conducted with particular insistence by the television service. The biased character of such propaganda did not stand up to common-sense examination. It has to be said honestly at this point that this produced protests among journalists but they were disregarded . . . The convention of spreading news only about successes left no room for criticism.

Mr Kania had himself been in the Politburo, first as a candidate member then as a full member, for most of the seventies, which probably explains another passage in his speech:

It was not an easy matter to oppose the increasing mistakes. The truth about this decade is very complex. The first half did produce many economic and social achievements. The general standard of living in the country went up. The authority of the First Secretary of the Central Committee [Gierek] and of the Chairman of the Council of Ministers [Jaroszewicz] was built on this and we helped to make it so. They were invested with the great confidence of the Party and in their hands was concentrated great power, excessively great power as it turned out. Distortions were gradually building up. All this, however, cannot exonerate the Central Committee and, above all, the Politburo, which should have reacted more resolutely, particularly in the period when the mistakes were clear. After all, reports were getting through about the real state of affairs, although attempts were made to minimise various aspects of the situation, such as the country's indebtedness, in reports to the Politburo.

Some members of the Politburo tried on more than one occasion to have a say in decisions, to correct mistakes . . . But the result of these attempts was slender. There was a fair bit of sycophancy in both central and local government.

No doubt to some people that sounded rather like an apologia, an attempt at self-defence as well as a stern indictment of the style of government under Gierek and the man who had been Prime Minister during most of his reign, Piotr Jaroszewicz. But there were people at the Plenum who had suffered demotion because they had tried to criticise Gierek's economic policy. Stefan Olszowski was one, Tadeusz Grabski another. But Kania was more interested in securing guarantees to prevent the repetition of such 'deformations' in the future. 'A new situation has been created in the country. The old methods cannot be used any more', he warned. 'Patiently, step by step, we must get people to trust the Party's policy.'

Kania believed that the new unions, which members of the Party were helping to set up, would not damage the political unity of the trade union movement – despite the fact that the one-hour warning strike had caused 'particular anxiety and astonishment'. He also looked forward to a greater role for people who belonged to no political party. 'We shall hand over responsible positions in the economy and the administration, at central and local levels, to non-Party experts.' He also promised that the authorities would respect 'the right of the artist to his own viewpoint' and would join journalists in shaping the lines of the mass communications media. But Kania's most telling remarks concerned the Party. While insisting on ideological unity and unity of action, he also demanded that 'the Party must function in such a way that every decision is preceded by free, unfettered discussion'. It was his way of restoring democracy to the old Communist tenet of 'democratic centralism', which in practice usually meant acceptance of the line dictated from the top. Kania wanted top people in the Party to be subject to real control.

Special attention must be paid to ensuring the free election of Party authorities . . . There must be complete freedom to put forward and to discuss candidates. We must define institutionally the duties of the Politburo, the Central Committee Secretariat, the duties of the First Secretary and their relation to the Central Committee. We must create in practice conditions in which the leadership is supervised by the Party, by its statutes and the real will of the majority.

Kania reported that Party organisations had already come forward with numerous proposals on this score. There were demands, he said, for secret balloting in all Party elections, as well as suggestions that there should be a restriction on the length of time people could occupy senior positions. These ideas would be considered, he said, but by themselves they would not ensure democracy. That depended on relations inside the Party and on the quality of its members.

Let there be fewer of us, but let us be resolute and carry conviction . . . There is at present a particularly strong sensitivity, in society and in the Party, to moral and ethical questions. We should deepen and consolidate it . . . The Party Control Commission will now propose that the Plenum should draw Party conclusions from the crass licence and abuses in the management of public assets. Unfortunately, cases of such licence, on a varying scale, were not isolated. This casts a shadow on the good name of our Party and our State. It causes gossip and talk, and that has become a weapon of political struggle. Our position is as follows: every case of dishonesty and abuse is being and will be thoroughly examined by Party control, the Supreme Chamber of Control and the Public Prosecutor's office. Every confirmed fact will be lawfully and severely punished.

Kania was also very conscious of the fact that the errors and the corruption he himself had admitted were good ammunition for people he described as determined opponents of socialism, people who claimed that the socialist system is not capable of being reformed. The best answer to that was to prove that it could.

The policy of accord and cooperation is our country's only chance. It requires patience on the part of the authorities as well as moderation and a sense of discipline on the part of the nation . . . We must lead better and work better. There is no other way . . . Many words of bitter criticism are being uttered today . . . Our Party should glean from this debate everything that is wise and right, everything creative.

Poland needs an alliance of prudent and wise people. Poland needs an alliance of people seeking reforms, people with a sense of responsibility for the destiny of the nation, people who are aware of the fact that changes, if they are to be lasting, must be introduced gradually so as not to demolish but transform the structure of social and economic life.

Careerists, thieves, sycophants
Seventy people spoke in the debate that followed Kania's report to the Central Committee. It was dominated, to judge from the official reports carried by Warsaw Radio and Television and the Polish News Agency, by an outburst of moral indignation. Stanislaw Miskiewicz, Party chief in the Warski Shipyard in Szczecin, regretted that the Politburo report had not named the names of the real people responsible for the present crisis, people, he claimed, who had pursued a policy of absolute personal privilege and should now prostrate themselves before Party and people. The Szczepanski affair, involving charges of high life and misappropriation of funds against the former head of radio and television, was a case of depravity, Miskiewicz said. In future, senior officials should hold office for only two terms at the most.

Zygmunt Wronski, a worker from the Ursus factory in Warsaw, said that all guilty men, without exception, should be brought to account. Wladyslaw Kruk, from Lublin, suggested that people should no longer hold Party and State jobs at the same time. Even Zdzislaw Grudzien, Gierek's old friend who had resigned from his post in Katowice weeks before but was still a member of the Politburo, joined in with a call for the ruthless eradication of evil and the removal of 'careerists' who had abused their authority.

Maybe that speech had something to do with the fiery outburst by Tadeusz Grabski, the man once sacked by Gierek and his colleagues but brought back to the Central Committee during the August crisis. He got to his feet on the Sunday to

59

denounce the 'hypocrisy' of members of the former leadership in offering in speeches now the sort of reforms which they could have offered – but did not – long ago. 'The old truth has been confirmed once again: nothing is more difficult for ham actors than quitting the stage.' Grabski demanded objective and strict judgement on those who had betrayed the Party's trust. He demanded that they should be named.

Today's Plenum can be in no doubt on one issue, that of the personal responsibility of the people who left the leadership at the Fourth Plenum [in August] and the first part of the Sixth Plenum [in September]. Those people have disgraced the Party in the eyes of the nation and the world. There was a time when we put our trust in those people and now we are often ashamed of their names.

Stanislaw Gabrielski, leader of the Socialist Union of Polish Students, was more practical. 'In my opinion, the Party has to get rid of people who are simply thieves and speculators. They should face trial.' Mieczyslaw Moczar indulged in much more vivid language.

Our huge Party has come face to face with the enormous force of justified dissatisfaction and even wrath on the part of the working population . . . We must cleanse our Party of dishonest, immoral and degenerate people . . . We must also free ourselves from slippery and servile people, from sycophants and careerists.

Moczar, at sixty-seven, was a man from the past. In the late sixties he had actually been quite close to becoming Party leader. He is credited with having tried, as Minister of the Interior, to oust Wladyslaw Gomulka and even with planning a coup. He was also held chiefly responsible for the anti-Jewish purge of the administration following the student riots of 1968. After Gomulka's fall in 1970 Moczar became a full member of the Politburo under Gierek, but was dropped after barely a year. Since then he had remained in relative obscurity, still a member of the Central Committee but devoting most of his energies to his job as Chairman of the Supreme Chamber of Control, NIK.

NIK is the watch-dog body designed to expose cases of political abuse and corruption. One would have thought that in the seventies Moczar would have found plenty to expose. In fact during that time NIK was subordinate not to Parliament, as originally planned, but to Prime Minister Jaroszewicz, which meant that it was muzzled. That did not mean that Moczar had not kept records. He had. And it was this that made him such a useful ally for Kania at that moment of unavoidable purge. Some observers half expected Moczar to make a sensational come-back to the ruling Politburo. But it was not yet to be.

When the Sixth Plenum came to an end after an all-night sitting at 6.25 am on Monday 6 October, it was the news of dismissals that caught the eye. Six former leaders had been expelled from the Central Committee: Edward Babiuch, the former premier, and Z. Zandarowski, former Party Secretary, 'for allowing distortions in Party life, for shaping the wrong style of Party work and for inadequate attention to the quality of Party ranks'; Jerzy Lukaszewicz, the former media chief, 'for errors in directing ideological activities and for shaping a propaganda line divorced from reality'; Jan Szydlak, former Trade Union chief, 'for errors in economic policy and for supporting arbitrariness in this field'; Tadeusz Wrzaszczyk, former planning chief, 'for errors in planning and managing the economy'; and Tadeusz Pyka, former Deputy Premier, 'for a wrong style of management and for irresponsible conduct in the first phase of talks with the strike committees in Gdansk'. The resignation from the Politburo of Zdzislaw Grudzien for health reasons was also accepted. As for Edward Gierek, it was decided to take up the matter of his responsibility for the crisis only when he was fit enough to be present at a Central Committee meeting.

There were some promotions and other changes. Kazimierz Barcikowski, already a Politburo member, was appointed a Secretary of the Central Committee. Andrzej Zabinski, another Politburo member, ceased to be a Secretary because of his appointment to replace Grudzien in Katowice. Two new Candidate Members of the Politburo were appointed: Wladyslaw Kruk, the Party chief in Lublin, and Roman Ney, the Rector of the Cracow Mining Academy. Stanislaw Gabrielski, the youth leader, was promoted to membership of the Central Committee Secretariat.

One decision which perhaps satisfied more immediately the prevailing mood of the meeting concerned Maciej Szczepanski, former Chairman of the State Committee for Radio and Television, and his former deputy Eugeniusz Patyk. Both were sacked from the Central Committee after it had found them guilty of 'breaking the law in the way they disposed of budget resources' and of a long list of other offences and misdemeanours. Their local Party committee was asked to apply sanctions. Within a day the two men had been expelled from the Party and a parliamentary committee had lifted their immunity. On the same day, to add to the general atmosphere of righteous retribution, the Warsaw District Court began what Warsaw Radio described as 'one of the most sensational trials in the history of our legal system'. In the dock was another of the star executives of the Gierek era, Kazimierz Tyranski, former director of the Minex Export-Import Bureau, who was accused among other things of receiving more than 700,000 dollars' worth of 'material benefits' from foreign businessmen with whom he was dealing on behalf of the State.

But punishing guilty men was only one aspect of Poland's problem, as one of its leading sociologists maintained in the Party paper, *Trybuna Ludu*, on the day the Central Committee began its meeting. Professor Jerzy Wiatr of Warsaw University said that thirty-five years of Communist rule had made democratic political reforms not only possible but necessary. Warning signals had been ignored in the past, leading to an ossification of political structures which made matters worse. Now it was no longer possible to carry on without reforms not only in the economy but in the country's political mechanisms.

The Central Committee had now gone some way towards doing something about this inside the Party itself. In language which would be astonishing in, for instance, the Soviet Union, there had been open discussion of holding secret ballots in Party elections, of exercising control over the activity of the Politburo and the First Secretary, of introducing a ban on one person holding more than one post, and restricting to two the number of terms individuals could hold high office. It takes only a little stretch of the imagination to visualise what would happen to the largely unchanging Soviet leadership if such ideas were to be applied in Moscow. And if one was to talk of the ossification of Polish institutions after only thirty-five years of Communist rule, surely one could be forgiven for speculating that reform could be desperately needed in the Soviet Union after more than sixty years of it. A look at Soviet broadcasts suggested that the Kremlin was aware of this.

Worried allies

During the Central Committee debate, Stefan Olszowski said that Polish Communists had reason to be sincerely grateful to the Communist Parties of their three nearest neighbours, the Soviet Union, Czechoslovakia and East Germany, for 'the trust shown in us, the economic aid and their support'. But he also conceded that 'fraternal parties are worried about the situation in Poland'.

These worries were demonstrated in different ways. Moscow Radio, for example, had little or nothing to tell its home service listeners about what was really happening in Poland throughout the month of October. The best impression of the situation they received probably came from a five-minute summary of Mr Kania's 90-minute report to the Polish Central Committee on the day it was delivered. Poland was discussed in round-table discussions broadcast by the home service of the radio and by television but neither provided much idea of the scope of the crisis or the frankness with which Polish Communists had condemned the mismanagement and corruption of their former leaders and representatives. The implications of the new mood in the Polish Party and the existence of new, free trade unions were ignored. Emphasis was placed on the determination of the Party to correct previous 'distortions' which had prompted dissatisfaction among 'part of the work force'. Foreign-language broadcasts from Moscow were a different matter, but even they avoided the fundamental issues and concentrated on allegations of Western interference, the allegedly unhappy lot of Western workers and in particular of British trade unions, as well as the 'biased' reporting on Poland by the Western media. Moscow's English-language World Service broadcast a recorded interview with a trade unionist from London, who was asked what lay behind 'vicious' propaganda by papers such as the *Daily Telegraph*. He said he thought 'fear of the success of socialism' was the major reason.

It is strange that the British media would call an English trade unionist who is on strike a traitor . . . It is strange that when a Polish worker goes on strike he becomes a patriot . . . You are fortunate, you have had your revolution, you have made progress, you are determined that the working people shall control the destiny of their own future.

East Germany did not report events in Poland any better

than the Soviet Union but at least the Party leader, Erich Honecker, made some very straightforward references to the crisis. On 6 October, in a public speech, he spoke of 'the subversive activity of anti-socialist forces financed from abroad' and said that the German Democratic Republic could not remain indifferent.

We shall counter any attempts at interference with which foreign reactionaries try to exploit the present difficult situation in People's Poland for their own dark objectives. The counter-revolution must realise that a limit has been set to its power sphere west of the Elbe and the Werra.

On 13 October, in another speech, Honecker alleged that 'imperialist mass media, particularly in the Federal Republic of Germany, have launched an unequalled campaign of incitement against socialist Poland'. Poland, said Honecker, 'is and remains a socialist country . . . We, together with our friends, will make sure of that.' On 28 October practical expression of East German concern came with the announcement that in future East Germans wishing to visit Poland privately and Poles wishing to make private visits to the GDR would have to have prior permission and that would be granted only after they had supplied evidence of an invitation. Previously people had been able to travel with only their personal identification documents. The new regulations were suggested by the East Germans and it was made clear by ADN, the official East German news agency, that while they were temporary they would remain in force until the situation in Poland was stabilised.

Czechoslovak comment was different again. For whereas, like Moscow and East Berlin, it stressed the dangers of anti-socialist elements and Western incitement, Prague seemed to take a far more 'personal' interest in the events in Poland. As we have seen already, within weeks of the signing of the Gdansk Agreements it was reminding people of what happened in Czechoslovakia in 1968. In October, unlike Moscow, it did not hesitate to talk about Poland's new independent trade unions. But it did not conceal its dislike of them. It never gave them the credit of any decent, patriotic intentions. It referred to them disparagingly as the 'so-called new trade unions' or the 'so-called free trade unions', through which anti-socialist elements pushed 'demagogic' demands in an effort to block the Party's attempts to solve the country's problems. That line of argument had, in essence, been heard many times from Warsaw itself. Indeed it was put across with renewed vigour by some Polish papers during October. But the voice of Prague distinguished itself by speaking with a note of certainty, pessimism and scorn quite unlike that of Warsaw. And it differed even more markedly on a quite separate topic, the award to Czeslaw Milosz, the self-exiled Polish poet, of the 1980 Nobel Prize for Literature.

Writers in Poland hailed the award as well deserved and one that was based on correct, artistic criteria. Jerzy Putrament, undeniably an establishment writer, said it had been decided some years back to publish Milosz's works in Poland but this had been frustrated by the 'publishing hierarchy'. President Jablonski sent Milosz a message of congratulations. *Trybuna Ludu* said Milosz's work was marked by concern for the community. *Slowo Powszechne*, the Roman Catholic paper, described him as a 'persistent champion of the dignity, courage and freedom of man'. In Czechoslovakia the Party paper, *Rude Pravo*, said something quite different but very familiar:

The Nobel Prize is in many cases intentionally given to people who have abandoned their nation and its culture, who have no importance in their field. A few years ago it was Aleksandr Solzhenitsyn. This year it is Czeslaw Milosz. This practice deprives the Nobel Prize for Literature of the right to be considered an objective measure of literary value. It is clearly an instrument of bourgeois ideology and culture which, in pursuing class interests, has again given its political attention to an author who has actually made no contribution to the treasury of art, still less to progressive art. While Milosz has produced nothing to enrich his national literature, or world literature, he has made a name for himself as a real intellectual émigré from socialism.

In Slovakia, the local *Pravda* commented that 'Milosz, who deserted the Polish diplomatic service in 1951 and now lives in the USA as a US citizen, is hardly likely to become better known as a poet'.

Dissidents
Such remarks revealed the gulf between Warsaw and Prague. In fact, official Warsaw waged a vociferous campaign against the so-called anti-socialists throughout October. One target was the dissidents of KOR, and in particular Jacek Kuron, who with several of his colleagues had been briefly detained at

the culmination of the strike crisis at the end of August. Another was Leszek Mochulski, the founder in 1979 of a frankly anti-Communist organisation known as the Confederation of Independent Poland, the KPN. He was arrested towards the end of September and was joined in custody by several of his colleagues in the weeks to follow.

One crucial question for Poland's allies was to what extent the strikers in the first place and then the new Solidarity trade union movement were influenced or exploited or even surreptitiously controlled by these groups which came under the blanket title of 'anti-socialist'. In the case of the KPN there could be no doubt. Solidarity did condemn the arrest of Mochulski, but not because it supported his political philosophy. It did so as a matter of principle because, as it had made clear in the Gdansk Agreements, it was against the arrest and detention of anyone for his or her political views. So there was no real connection between the Confederation of an Independent Poland and Solidarity, some of whose members admitted to believing that Mochulski's views were quite unrealistic and slightly mad. His belief, quite simply, was that Poland would not be a decent place in which to live until it threw off what he apparently described, in an interview with a West German magazine, as 'the Communist dictatorship'. To attempt anything like that was, in the opinion of most realistic people in Poland, quite out of the question. Gierek himself had warned that there were limits. Most people accepted that, as the strikers had accepted it, knowing that their protest would never have succeeded if it had challenged Poland's place in the Soviet orbit which had grown out of the post-war settlement in Europe.

Trybuna Ludu, in an article on 18 October, described the KPN philosophy as 'a fatal kind of Don Quixotery', accusing it of substituting nationalism for patriotism:

The Confederation aims at fighting 'the totalitarian Communist regime' to the end and at liberating Poland from alleged Soviet domination . . . Mochulski states that no version or brand of socialism is of any concern to him. As regards diagnosing and curing the ailments of the country's social and economic organism, the platform of Leszek Mochulski signifies an intention to transform the conflict inside socialism – which is quite capable of finding a constructive solution – into an all-out struggle against the socio-political system and the constitutional order.

For the authorities, then, the KPN was a reassuringly simple enemy which made its objectives plain. But, as *Trybuna Ludu* admitted, KOR was a different matter and more complicated:

KOR's slogans are interwoven with thoughts about the working class, sometimes even with echoes of Marxism. Moreover, a considerable number of our critics in this grouping do not negate the socio-political system frontally but obliquely. KOR's criticisms of real deformations and mistakes always constitute part of a much greater picture. It serves to substantiate and give credibility to generalisations about the system being 'beyond reform', about the 'chronic sickness' of the system and thus about the need to struggle for its gradual dismantlement.

The hard core of this grouping treats criticism as a starting point for launching assumptions that constitute a mixture of right-wing revisionist, extreme leftist and simply utopian concepts. In sum, this makes for a platform which in the short term aims at installing itself in political life, and in the long run at using the positions thus gained for dismantling the social and political system permanently.

For the authorities KOR was a difficult problem. Unlike the KPN, which simply declared that the thirty-five years of Poland's Communist history had been a mistake, KOR was the product of that history and spoke in the language of that era. The Party was now talking of reform inside the system. KOR had been doing that for years, even though Jacek Kuron had been expelled from the Party in 1964 and had subsequently been imprisoned for lengthy terms. Similar fates had befallen his colleagues in KOR, such as Adam Michnik and Karol Modzelewski. KOR's position had been strengthened by the success of the workers' strikes in August. The strike leaders were grateful to them for their assistance in spreading the news of what was happening. When Kuron and others were detained towards the end of August, Lech Walesa and the strike leaders in Gdansk told Deputy Premier Jagielski they must be released. And they were.

Since then some KOR activists had become advisers to the new union movement, Kuron among them. And since the authorities had accepted that Solidarity was the product of genuine worker grievance in protest against 'deformations' by Communist Party leaders, they could hardly use the old weapon of arrest and detention against KOR – the sort of action that Moscow and Prague would have had no hesitation in taking – without risking further protest by Solidarity. So the authorities were left with little choice but to hope. Thus, according to Warsaw Radio, Ludwik Krasucki, the author of that 'important' article in *Trybuna Ludu*, held that

people who turned themselves into political opponents or who have been driven into such positions should not be treated as opponents once and for all . . . The accumulating practice of renewal could convince some that one should move towards progress instead of sticking to opposition. In every situation one should persuade, win people over, win them back.

Church

If Poland's allies were discouraged to hear Warsaw Radio advocating that sort of persuasion, they could have been no happier about the apparently growing influence of the Roman Catholic Church in Poland. Solidarity also had Catholic advisers, and not surprisingly. The overwhelming majority of the Polish people are practising Catholics. The Church is generally credited with being the only national organisation which has stood by the people throughout their history. In the days of monarchy the Roman Catholic Primate of Poland had been so revered and respected that he had fulfilled a national role by acting as interrex, head of state between Polish kings. And the current Primate, Cardinal Stefan Wyszynski, had not only survived virtual imprisonment by the Communist authorities for three years in the early fifties but also the creation – believed to have been at Stalin's suggestion – of Pax, a pro-Communist Catholic Front organisation promoting pro-Communist priests. In the Soviet Union the official 'peace-loving policy' is one of the few topics on which the head of the Russian Orthodox Church, Patriarch Pimen of Moscow and All the Russias, is allowed to pronounce for public consumption. Cardinal Wyszynski, in contrast, had never surrendered the right to speak out and, as we have seen, a large portion of one of his sermons in August had been broadcast by television because of what the authorities saw as a valuable appeal for moderation.

The Church's influence had grown not so much in fact as in the degree of public acknowledgement which it now received from the State. In an interview with Hungarian television, Mieczyslaw Rakowski, the editor-in-chief of *Polityka* and a member of the PZPR Central Committee, expressed what was later to become the accepted official line on the Church's role in the Polish crisis:

The Catholic Church and its leadership, in particular Cardinal Wyszynski, represent a realistic and considered attitude in the present situation. At every turn, they take into consideration Poland's fundamental national interests. I would like to see a lot of Poles following this path, taking as their example Cardinal Wyszynski, who behaves and acts like a great statesman . . . The Catholic Church is on the side of the stabilisation of political and social relations. From this we can see that Communists and Catholics are capable of cooperation. This is a positive phenomenon that opens up interesting and promising prospects for the future and for socialism in Poland.

The realistic attitude Rakowski spoke of was the acceptance of the view that there was more danger to national independence than profit in fostering confrontation with a Communist regime that had apparently given up hope of suppressing the faith and even permitted the largest church-building programme in Eastern Europe. In a statement issued after a two-day meeting in the middle of the month, the Polish bishops indicated cautious optimism and seemed to claim that they had been proved right.

The events of recent months which we have witnessed and in which, to a certain extent, we have taken part have permeated every area of the life of society . . . Conscious of their rights and their duties, the workers have underlined the social isolation of those who took upon themselves the task of directing all sectors of public life. The bishops recalled that for a long time, in public statements and in official conversations, they had drawn the attention of the State authorities to the dangerous consequences of the propaganda policy being pursued. However, their voices were not heeded. Today, in the new situation, the bishops are hopeful that the social and political transformations will proceed in the right direction for the common good of the whole nation. The bishops share the concern of the working people. They support them morally and defend their just rights.
All Poles want to feel themselves co-masters in their own house. We must also consider the circumstances, the place and the time. That is why our actions must be sensible and ensure social calm . . . Our work must proceed in the direction of moral renewal in public, social and political life, so that evil may be called evil and good be called good, in the direction of a self-governing society and in the direction of economic progress, the purpose of which is to serve man. This work must be motivated by the principles formulated at the Second Vatican Council.

Most of that text came from a broadcast by Vatican Radio, but most of what is quoted here was also reported by Warsaw Radio. Clearly some of the ideas of Cardinal Wyszynski and

Comrade Kania for practical purposes overlapped. As for the prospects of the 'transformations' and 'renewal', the Chairman of Pax, Ryszard Reiff, published a statement in that organisation's daily, *Slowo Powszechne*, which might well have disturbed the already anxious allies. He spoke of what he called 'multiple-outlook socialism'.

If multiple-outlook socialism is realised in Poland, it could become an example for the future, a universal model, the attractions of which will reach out beyond Poland and the socialist bloc. I am deeply convinced about the irreversibility of further transformations in socialism, through a multitude of outlooks, to make a system that will be better than any other system in guaranteeing people conditions for spiritual and material development.

Cardinal Wyszynski was quite busy in October. Apart from chairing the two-day meeting of the bishops he had a meeting with Roman Catholic deputies of the Sejm, members of the Catholic and Social Circle known as Znak. On 21 October the Cardinal met Mr Kania to discuss 'matters of great importance as regards internal calm and the development of the country'. Earlier, though, he had had talks with Lech Walesa before the Solidarity leader set off on an impressive speech-making tour of the south. It was this meeting that gave neighbouring Czechoslovakia the opportunity to vent its disapproval.

Before setting out on their tour, Walesa and his companions stopped off in Warsaw, where they saw Cardinal Stefan Wyszynski, who promised them full support in their endeavours. The meaning of that support is obvious [said a commentator on Prague Radio]. With the blessing of the Primate of the Polish Roman Catholic Church, it will be easier for Walesa to spread his ideas about the so-called restoration of Poland. Walesa has made no secret for several weeks now of what sort of restoration he has in mind . . . Walesa is proving more and more with every day that passes that he is little concerned about the real interests of the Polish working people and much more about satisfying the interests of anti-socialist forces which enabled him, during the August strikes, to take the lead in the strike movement in Gdansk.

That comment from Prague Radio far exceeded in its hostility and personal animosity anything said either in Poland itself or by any of its other allies. And it is worth noting that the Romanian leader, Nicolae Ceausescu, had also pronounced on Poland by now. In a speech to the Romanian Central Committee, his remarks were clear-cut and unemotional.

We do not wish to interfere in Poland's internal affairs, but I must say, for the knowledge of our Party, that had the country's development problems been solved together with the working class, had proper action been taken in good time, and had a firm attitude been taken against the anti-socialist elements and forces, the known events could not have happened.

The Romanian leadership, noted for the relative independence which it had managed to preserve from the Soviet Union, evidently did not wish to seem excessively concerned by Polish developments. And to judge from their decidedly informative way of reporting events, the same could be said of the Hungarians, who in recent years had quietly achieved some of the economic reforms now desperately needed in Poland. And yet some anxiety was revealed by the fact that *Nepszabadsag*, the Hungarian Party paper, felt the need to publish an interview with the General Secretary of the Hungarian Trade Union Council, Sandor Gaspar. He suggested that for a trade union in a socialist state to be independent would mean that it was opposed to the interests of the class society. In a state where government and unions work for the same objectives, he said, everything can be settled without a strike. 'A strike is not a means of socialist construction.'

Prague Radio was to betray a little more obviously its apprehension lest the idea of independent trade unions might infect Czechoslovak workers. Towards the end of the month, Bedrich Kacirek, Secretary of the Czechoslovak TUC, told home service listeners:

It is essential that we are not deceived and that we understand well why bourgeois propaganda has recently been employing the notions of freedom and independence for trade unions. By its demagogy it is concealing its true interest, which is to blunt trade union unity, this powerful weapon of the working class, and to divert the trade unions from their revolutionary mission.

Solidarity registration dispute
The authorities in Warsaw had long since given up talking in such dogmatic, black-and-white terms. They had admitted that the traditional Communist trade unions had actually failed the Polish working class. They saw the unions' task as more practical than revolutionary, that of serving the basic interests of the workers and their families. But they were also very anxious about the possible political challenge from the new unions and it was this which held up the legal registration

of Solidarity. The whole issue was widely aired in the Polish media. The president of the Warsaw Provincial Court, in an interview for the press which was broadcast at length by Warsaw Radio, explained that the main problem holding up registration was Solidarity's attitude to the Communist Party. In the Gdansk Agreements, he said, the strike committee had stated that the new union recognised that the PZPR plays the leading role in Poland's socialist system. But Solidarity's statutes, submitted to the court on 24 September, contained no such statement.

As Lech Walesa explained in an interview with the youth paper, *Sztandar Mlodych*, the statutes had been drafted in accordance with the Polish constitution, as required by a decision of the Council of State. However, the new unions were 'completely apolitical', so there was no need, according to his argument, to make any political statement at all. *Trybuna Ludu* found this hard to understand and claimed that Solidarity leaders were actually departing from the Gdansk agreements. This was a major issue, one of principle for both sides and one that could provide ammunition to Poland's anxious allies. But it was hardly likely, either, to threaten the new 'social contract' between workers and Government. It had already been admitted that the CRZZ, the old Trade Union Council, had to all intents and purposes ceased to exist, since all its affiliated branch unions had either left it or said they would leave. At the same time the government paper, *Zycie Warszawy*, now under a new and more liberal editor, Mr Jerzy Wojcik, admitted that Solidarity was having a hard time of it, with old unions, in their new guise of independence, refusing to cooperate and even trying to blackmail some members of the new unions.

Solidarity's reputation with Poland's allies, meanwhile, could not have been improved by a hunger strike of thirty-four of its members in the locomotive shed at Wroclaw Central Station. There was a dispute over a new system of wages and benefits for the Polish State Railways. It dragged on for roughly a week with the Minister of Transport appearing on television and deputy ministers actually going to the locomotive shed for talks, before it was settled by a compromise. The hunger strike had also been declared in protest against the delay in registering Solidarity. The argument over that went on while the Military Council of the Warsaw Pact Armed

Forces met in Prague, and then as the Warsaw Pact foreign ministers, including Andrei Gromyko of the Soviet Union, met in Warsaw.

On 24 October the Warsaw Provincial Court announced that it was registering Solidarity, but only after inserting in its statutes a clause stating that the new union did not aspire to become a political party, that it recognised the leading role of the Polish United Workers' Party, and that it did not intend to undermine Poland's alliances. Warsaw television announced the decision as 'good news, very good news'. The newspaper *Zycie Warszawy* said it was good news 'for all those who are in favour of socialist renewal, who believe that the activity of the new unions will usher new values into our life'. Radio commentaries suggested very strongly that the court's decision was prompted not so much by an attempt to shackle or frustrate Solidarity but to get it registered in the only way that was politically acceptable and which got rid of doubts 'at home and abroad'. Franciszek Lewicki, on Warsaw Radio, explained why:

I think registration by the court was essential because Solidarity is a phenomenon of great social significance . . . Since it was born, Solidarity has been the object of great public hopes. It is time those hopes were fulfilled. The important thing is that the union is already functioning. Out of the hot summer of strikes, Solidarity has emerged as a fact, a reality. It is simply obvious to everybody that Solidarity exists. There can be no question of this. It must function and it is in this spirit that the strengthening of the union should take place today.

There seemed little hostility to Solidarity as such in all that, and yet the union's leaders reacted angrily to the court's decision, denouncing it as unlawful. It decided to appeal to the Supreme Court. Three days later Solidarity's National Consultative Commission invited Prime Minister Pinkowski to Gdansk for talks in the Lenin Shipyard. There was inconclusive talk of strikes. Pinkowski replied by inviting Solidarity for talks in Warsaw, and eventually it was agreed that both sides should meet there on 31 October.

Those talks were to stretch into November. In the meantime the political climate became distinctly embittered because of lack of trust and understanding on either side. The official news agency put the Government line rather succinctly:

It can be maintained that the recognition of the leading role of the Party in the Solidarity statutes was a political act. But it is also true that in spite of claims by the union to be apolitical, the absence of any such recognition of the Party's leading role would be a political act too.

In *Zycie Warszawy* a Solidarity member, Jacek Szymander-ski, put his point of view:

People will listen to an appeal for patience and understanding only from an independent, self-governing social organisation which they themselves have created. Solidarity can be destroyed, its activities can be immobilised. But this will not restore lost confidence; and without confidence government is impossible . . . Is there anyone left in Poland who wants to deprive us of our independence, who wants to do away with our movement which now comprises more than seven million members and represents the only chance we have of getting the country out of the crisis by common effort?

On 29 October the Party's Politburo met and expressed dissatisfaction with the way things were going. According to the official news agency, it 'found that the process of normalisation is still too slow. That is the feeling of society. There are growing signs of weariness and even impatience, a yearning for more order and moves to guarantee conditions for peaceful constructive work.'

Kania visits Moscow
The next day Stanislaw Kania, the Party leader, flew to Moscow with Prime Minister Pinkowski for the first meeting with the Soviet leaders since the crisis began. They had talks with President Brezhnev, Prime Minister Tikhonov, Foreign Minister Gromyko, Konstantin Rusakov, a Party Secretary in charge of relations with 'fraternal' countries, and Deputy Prime Minister Arkhipov, who was probably included in the team for talks on economic cooperation.

The meeting, according to the official communiqué, was held in an atmosphere of 'cordiality and identity of views'. There was no hint that the discussions had covered the recent changes in Poland or the new trade unions. Mr Kania, who left for home on the same day, took back what looked like an assurance of continued support from the Soviet leadership.

Comrade Brezhnev expressed the confidence of Soviet Communists and the working people of the Soviet Union that the Communists and working people of fraternal Poland will be able to resolve the acute problems of political and economic development facing them and, relying on the material and spiritual potential built up in the years of people's power, will ensure the growth of the living standards of the working people and the further all-round progress of People's Poland.

But there was another interesting line in the communiqué:

The participants in the meeting resolutely denounced the attempts by certain imperialist circles to mount subversive activities against socialist Poland and to interfere in its affairs.

This was a routine inclusion, no doubt, but alleged outside interference had been used in the past to justify action against internal developments. There was to be far more talk of that possibility in the weeks to come.

5. LIVING WITH SOLIDARITY

'What happens in Poland is a matter for the Polish people and for no one else.' These words of the British Foreign Secretary, Lord Carrington, at a press conference in Warsaw on the last day of October 1980, at the end of a two-day visit, underlined in studiously diplomatic language a widespread anxiety over the possibility of a Soviet intervention in Poland like that in Czechoslovakia in 1968. It did not matter that the Polish Communist Party leader, Stanislaw Kania, had just returned from Moscow with what the Warsaw media saw as a Soviet vote of confidence in the ability of the Polish leadership to pull the country out of the crisis. When Soviet troops joined Polish soldiers in a training exercise in the north of the country in the first week of November, people could be forgiven for remembering that in Czechoslovakia in 1968 manoeuvres had preceded invasion. And Czechoslovak comment did not help. Noting the Western comparisons with 1968, Prague Radio discerned positively sinister motives in them. 'What failed in this country can be realised step by step and in certain circumstances in present-day Poland – such, at least, is the wishful thinking of the Western mass media.' The Czechoslovak trade union daily, *Prace*, claimed that a 'counter-revolutionary situation' had been stirred up in Poland as in Hungary in 1956 and Czechoslovakia in 1968–9. 'The aim is obvious – to set the trade unions against the Communist Party.'

It was very easy, of course, to see the Polish crisis simply in terms of permanent confrontation between Solidarity and the Government and of an ever-present threat of a Soviet-led intervention. It could be argued, in fact, that both East and West took a similarly pessimistic view of the situation. For different reasons they feared that a Communist system which allowed independent unions could not and would not work.

But the whole point of the crisis was that the Poles were determined to make it work, whatever the risks.

An atmosphere of confrontation prevailed as November began. Crisis talks over Solidarity's constitutional statutes continued between Prime Minister Pinkowski and Lech Walesa from the evening of 31 October into the early hours of the next day and were adjourned without any progress. But already there were signs that the danger of a serious protest strike was not so great. In an interview with Paris Radio, the Deputy Editor of Polish Television had predicted a solution 'à la polonaise', with the Supreme Court, to which Solidarity had appealed, taking the offending clause out of the text of the statute and putting it in a preamble. Lech Walesa himself, in an interview with *Polityka*, repeated that Solidarity was not directed against the socialist system. 'Socialism is a good way, so let it be the Polish way.' Days before the Supreme Court ruling was due, Warsaw Radio was referring to Solidarity as 'a movement with enormous social backing, gradually becoming a natural constituent of everyday reality'. And Mr Kania himself told a meeting at the Nowa Huta steel works near Cracow: 'We recommend Party members to take an active part in the trade unions, including Solidarity.'

As for the dispute over Solidarity's statutes, Mr Kania said that that was a legal matter to be settled by the Supreme Court. But it was important that the political declaration made by the new union at its inception should be restated. Mr Kania referred to the 'socialist character of the organisation', which suggested that he misunderstood the strike committee's promise in Gdansk to respect the leading role of the Communist Party and the socialist system. Solidarity had always claimed to be apolitical in a country where only one brand of politics was allowed.

On 10 November, though, the argument was brought to an end when the Supreme Court ruled that the Warsaw Provincial Court had been wrong to change Solidarity's statutes by adding to them. Instead it accepted Solidarity's own suggestion that the political pledges in the Gdansk Agreements which Mr Kania wanted restated should be attached to the statutes as an appendix.

Solidarity immediately called off a strike alert fixed for 12 November. In a public statement it promised to stick to its commitments made in the Gdansk Agreements and its own statutes, and to show a sense of responsibility for the future of Poland. Words like that tempted *Trybuna Ludu* to hope for a partnership between Solidarity and the authorities, a 'community of interests'. But Warsaw Radio seemed far more realistic.

Let's not deceive ourselves that everything will be easy from now on. There are accounts in our country which have still not been settled. There are matters which in the coming weeks, months and perhaps even years will be the subject of discussion and argument. But this is how democracy works. Democracy is based on calm disagreement, discussion and the gradual achievement of the agreements we so badly need.

Solidarity's own statement confirmed that interpretation.

We stand guard over the interests of the workers . . . The future of our country rests in the hands of the working people. Poland is a land of sensible people, who know how to think well and work well. But everyone must be convinced that their efforts are not being squandered through incompetence, bad policies, abuses or corruption.

Both these statements are remarkable indicators of just how far Poland had progressed in little more than two months. The Solidarity declaration, broadcast by Warsaw Radio and read out by a Communist, Bogdan Lis, recognised as a fact of life the possibility of bad Communist government. In contrast, Soviet propaganda depicts the Communist Party as 'the heart, mind and conscience of the people', and therefore virtually incapable of not reflecting the aspirations of the working people. Warsaw Radio's own comment about democracy was also rather suspiciously liberal, for it seemed to recognise that what we might call an adversary relationship is useful and necessary, that disagreement is not always a mark of hostility.

Journalists speak out
This was all part and parcel of a noticeable opening up of the official mass media. The Party leaders had said that the people deserved better, more truthful information, and gradually they were getting it. On the last day of October the Polish Association of Journalists ended a three-day extraordinary congress by electing a new chairman, a rank-and-file Communist, Stefan Bratkowski. Mr Bratkowski, who was to

make quite a mark in the coming months, kicked off with a few modestly startling remarks in interviews with Warsaw Radio and the Government paper, *Zycie Warszawy*. 'Politicians know about politics,' he said, 'we know about journalism. It will be better for the politicians if the newspapers and radio and television bulletins are put together by journalists.' By this time one could detect quite clearly that *Zycie Warszawy* had become the most liberal and forthright of the leading official dailies. *Trybuna Ludu* was more cautiously true to the current Party line, which was not necessarily an easy thing to be in view of the changes taking place. But it was the first paper, it is worth remembering, that spoke of the need for a Party purge. The army paper, *Zolnierz Wolnosci*, was more recognisably hard-line, for ever warning of the dangers of anti-socialist elements exploiting the new unions and reminding its readers of the unbreakable alliance with the Soviet Union.

It was in *Zycie Warszawy* that the new Director of the Press, Radio and TV Department of the Party's Central Committee, Jozef Klasa, explained why so few people believed what they read in the papers. 'This distrust is based on experience; we ourselves have taught the people that information is either tendentious or untrue.' Mr Klasa also admitted to distrust between the authorities and the journalist community. He wanted genuine partnership but warned journalists against sliding from the discredited 'propaganda of success' into the propaganda of defeat. He shared their criticism, he said, of strict control of the press. He understood their idealistic concept of mass media that were absolutely independent.

Work had already begun, meanwhile, on a new bill on censorship. This was the preserve of the Central Office for the Control of the Press, Publications and Performances (CUKPPW); it operated under a decree dating back to 1946 which declared: 'The aim of control is to prevent public opinion from being misled by reports of events which do not accord with reality.' Journalists and lawyers now wanted the office to be subordinate to Parliament rather than to the Prime Minister as in the past because, as Warsaw Radio admitted, 'it used to happen frequently that the head of a department where things were not going too well would, by means of a few telephone calls, make sure that things were reported favourably'.

Some very unfavourable reports were now finding their way on to the teleprinters of the official news agency, PAP. Early in November it reported that Polish agriculture, still mainly in private hands, was passing through a 'real disaster'. On television the Chairman of the United Peasant Party, Stanislaw Gucwa, was able to announce what he must have known for a long, long time, that Polish farming was short of everything – fertilisers, building materials and machinery. It had been short of spare parts, he said, for thirty-six years, which meant ever since the Communists came to power.

Communism and Catholicism
Culture, and especially literature, had also suffered, according to the Minister of Culture and Art, Jozef Tejchma, who was appointed in August after a brief spell as an ambassador. Tejchma, a former member of the Politburo, told *Zycie Warszawy* that this was the result of the application of 'primitive political and personal assessments rather than artistic or ideological ones'. He maintained that 'there should be no barriers or limits to cultural life'. He also detected something calculated to send shivers down the spines of his colleagues in Moscow and elsewhere:

It can be assumed that a dialogue has begun between two kinds of universal humanism, the socialist and the Christian humanisms. In Poland there are various philosophical currents which can be used to build the nation's political unity and form a new society. It is well known that it is thanks to the influence of Catholic thought that Marxism today pays more attention to the problems of individual life, to the search in it for elements of immortality. Under the influence of Marxism, Catholicism has shown greater understanding for the problems of large social groups.

The day after that interview appeared, and perhaps not entirely by coincidence, *Trybuna Ludu* carried an article on the current 'ideological struggle' which insisted that Marxism remained an integral part of 'the spiritual culture of the Polish people'. A few weeks later Stefan Bratkowski, writing again in *Zycie Warszawy*, took the line that socialism in Poland must be a Polish variety, 'a bloom from our own flower bed' as he put it. And he put forward five principles for discussion, the first of which was this: 'In a country with a Catholic majority, where two-thirds of the Party's members believe in God, the political concept cannot rest only on the coexistence of the Party with the Catholic world, but on their cooperation and inter-penetration in social life.'

The political and philosophical implications of these far-reaching suggestions from the Minister of Culture and the journalists' leader were a little difficult to fathom, but at least they reflected something of the real situation faced by a disgraced Communist Party in a Roman Catholic country. Janusz Zablocki, a Catholic Deputy and member of the Znak group, drew the practical implications in a speech to the Sejm in the middle of November.

The country's stabilisation calls for the consolidation of all the forces of the nation, and this is impossible without a Polish historic compromise, a historic compromise of the three main forces which count in the life of our nation today. They are the PZPR, together with the allied parties; Solidarity; and finally, the Catholic forces based on the Church.

All of this was being said in open debate a mere three months after the events which led to the Gdansk Agreements. After a long diet of controlled news and comment, even Poland's second official news agency, Interpress, was able to look back and deride the 'unanimity' which, not so long ago, had had to feature in all reports on the Communist Party's leading bodies.

We had to cover up the differences of opinion, lacquering the grooves . . . We know that people always used to treat that heavenly unanimity as untrue . . . And how much sarcasm was prompted by the reports on the debates in the Sejm, that forest of raised arms, those clapping hands. The show-off unanimity was used more often than not as a means of stifling criticism and frank discussion.

'We are all guilty'
Inside the Party frank discussion was now allowed, but it was bitter, to judge from a television broadcast of extracts from the debate at the Nowa Huta steelworks near Cracow when it was visited by Mr Kania in the first week of November. One dominant theme was the need to punish those who were responsible for the crisis; ordinary Party workers came in for their share of the blame from fellow workers on the shop floor. One speaker accepted some of the blame.

We are all guilty, not only those above us but we, too, who raise our hands high at various comically stage-managed and tasteless plenary meetings and vote without any opportunity for free expression, without a chance to think.

Another speaker complained that although changes were taking place, the middle reaches of the Party seemed completely unmoved.

The rank-and-file think that there has been movement at the top, that something has been done there. The bottom is seething like a cauldron. However, the middle layer is like a belt of clouds around the earth, preventing the rays of the sun from getting through.

The Party was clearly in a bad way. Mr Kania was told that some members had come under pressure to leave the Party, which was not only being blamed by a large part of the workforce for causing the crisis but also accused of never having done anything right. More shocking still were the words of yet another speaker.

The colossus of 3,500,000 people has ceased to be the vanguard of the working class. The events of recent months, which took place before our very eyes, have convinced us of this. And it is hard – is it not? – to work with a Party like this. It is hard to use this huge colossus as an example. Opinion about the Party is not created at Party meetings; it is created where people work and where they live . . . We must come forward with some kind of programme, Comrade First Secretary Kania. It is extremely urgent and we are waiting.

It is very likely that the Communist Party no longer had as many as three and a half million members. But of even more concern to Mr Kania must have been his discovery that nine out of every ten of the Nowa Huta work force now belonged to Solidarity and that a large percentage of Party members there had also joined. At that time, to quote Lech Walesa's figure, Solidarity had seven million members, at least twice as many as the Party. And according to the journalists' leader, Stefan Bratkowski, in an interview with the Yugoslav radio, two-thirds of the Party membership had joined the union. He mentioned the astonishing figures of between 1.8 and two million. Some weeks later a less liberal member of the Party gave the much smaller figure of 700,000, but Bratkowski's point, even if his figures were contestable, was still worth considering. He said that Solidarity was 'not some kind of alien movement which is hostile to the system'.

Mr Kania, in spite of his declared sympathy and friendly attitude to the new unions and in spite of his advice that

Party members should take an active part in them, could not be quite so positive. As the head of a Communist Party that needed the cooperation of Solidarity to get the country out of its economic crisis, he could not, at the same time, ignore the possibility that 'anti-socialist elements' would exploit both the unions and the situation for political ends. At the Nowa Huta meeting he was particularly tough on strikes. He even spoke of civil war.

There are people who want continuous tension, who want to organise mass strikes. In our situation this is bound to lead not only to political tensions, it is leading our economy to real ruin . . . There are also those whose hopes are built on maintaining and stirring up workers' dissatisfaction. There are those who are openly opposing socialism and our alliances. Even the vision of civil war in Poland is not excluded. Such views, such actions cannot be seen as anything other than playing at counter-revolution. So far, we have been acting with exceptional calm, using political methods . . . But today we must say out loud that there are limits. Anybody who strikes at socialism is attacking the independent existence of our nation. We shall defend socialism as we have to defend Poland's independence.

'Silly strikes'
Industrial disputes of various kinds, involving Solidarity, certainly continued throughout most of November, and they took weeks and the personal attention of ministers before they were settled. Health workers began a nationwide protest by simply wearing armbands while continuing work, but eventually they staged a sit-in in Gdansk, supported by students and teachers, before the Government agreed to consider their demands. These were not just for higher wages but better conditions and moves to improve supplies of basic medicines, bandages and so on. A similar dispute took place in the communications industry. There were even several strikes in defence industry enterprises, or so General Wlodzimierz Oliwa, Commander of the Warsaw Military District, told the Sejm.

Another general, Mieczyslaw Moczar, told the Sejm that some of the strikes were 'astonishingly silly'. One at least did sound odd. According to Gdansk Radio, senior pupils at a technical school in Slupsk province boycotted lessons and 'occupied' their hostel demanding the right to smoke and to come and go as they pleased. They also demanded the removal of the headmaster, a woman history teacher and the canteen manageress, all of whom were accused of treating pupils with scant respect and introducing excessively rigid discipline. The strike, which received considerable press and television coverage, ended after six days with the pupils victorious. 'Certain persons' were removed from the school but, as Gdansk Radio added, the strike also left one person with a nervous breakdown after nearly committing suicide, and another receiving treatment in hospital.

General frustration with the way things were going was voiced by Deputy Premier Aleksander Kopec in a speech to the Sejm on 20 November. How could the Government function, he asked, if the Prime Minister was permanently tied up with trade union matters, if Deputy Prime Ministers had to keep travelling round the country negotiating settlements, and individual ministers were also 'distracted' from their work? He told the Sejm with some sadness that, although the authorities were determined to carry out three recently signed agreements on the railways – the first with a large number of railway enterprises, another with Solidarity, and a third with the 'old' railway union – a warning strike was beginning that day and a full railway strike was planned for 24 November. Solidarity, he said, was claiming that the Government was not implementing the agreement it had signed with it and as a result Solidarity slogans and demands were now being broadcast over railway station loudspeakers.

Raid on Solidarity

If that was not enough, Solidarity suddenly became involved in something more than a defiant tussle with harassed ministers – an open clash with the security services, the untouchable guardians of the socialist system. At 4.30 pm on 20 November, while the Sejm was in session, policemen and security men accompanied by a Deputy Prosecutor searched the premises of the district headquarters of Solidarity in Szpitalna Street in Warsaw. The local Solidarity leader, Zbigniew Bujak, was present during the search, after which the police took away copies of a document found in the union's printing and duplicating room. The document was classified. It had been issued internally by Poland's Chief Prosecutor, Lucjan Czubinski, on 30 October 1980 and contained instructions on how to handle dissidents. It was entitled 'Present Methods of Prosecuting Illegal Anti-Socialist Activity'.

The next day a young mathematician who worked in the

Solidarity duplicating room, Jan Narozniak, was arrested and held on a charge of offending against the provisions of the Penal Code on state secrets. Solidarity, in a statement signed by Bujak, immediately demanded that he should be released and threatened to strike if he was not. But Bujak's statement said much more. He claimed that the document represented a threat to Solidarity itself.

The aim of the document is to show that the emergence of independent trade unions is a direct result of all 'anti-socialist' activity. This means that a large section of the judiciary has not accepted the Gdansk Agreement.

The authorities contested this very carefully. The document, they said, did not mention Solidarity, which was a legal organisation, but dealt only with such illegal organisations as KOR, the KPN and another dissident group not mentioned so far, the Movement for the Defence of Human and Civil Rights (ROPCiO). What may have alarmed Bujak was the only reference in the document to independent trade unions. It concerned a book by the KPN leader, Leszek Moczulski, *Revolution Without Revolution*, which allegedly suggested that the seizure of power would follow an expansion of a free press and independent trade unions.

Bujak's statement contained yet another demand, 'that L. Czubinski's role in the violations of the law in the past decade be revealed, especially his responsibility for the persecution of workers at Ursus and in Radom in June 1976'. This was a unique situation if ever there was one. If the Warsaw Solidarity organisation had not responded so promptly to the arrest of Narozniak, attention might well have concentrated on the claim by the Ministry of Internal Affairs spokesman that the search had revealed that Solidarity's premises were being used 'for the illegal duplication of classified documents belonging to a State institution'. In the Soviet Union, one must say, that would have been it; the case would have been cut and dried. In the Soviet Union, we must remind ourselves, there was no such thing as an independent trade union with its own premises or duplicating machines or a union leader free enough to say, as Bujak did, that he never knew the document was on the premises but that, if he had known, he would have got it duplicated anyway. Bujak went much further. Not only did he challenge the police action, he openly suggested that the country's Chief Prosecutor, the guardian of the law, was guilty of breaking the law himself. The reaction in Moscow can only be imagined. But it is at least possible that Mr Bujak's stand was welcomed there as conclusive evidence that these independent unions were inherently hostile to the socialist State.

The Polish authorities did not behave as if that was the case. A representative of the Prosecutor's Office actually visited the Ursus tractor plant, where Bujak worked and where a strike was threatened, to explain that the document did amount to a State secret since it concerned 'persons conducting criminal activity which endangers the State'. The office of the Chief Prosecutor gave a press conference on 24 November to repeat this argument and reveal that a second man, a worker in the duplicating centre of the Prosecutor's Office by the name of Piotr Sapelo, had been arrested. That same morning a Solidarity delegation visited the Prosecutor's Office to demand the release not only of Narozniak but of four dissidents, including Leszek Moczulski of the KPN and W. Ziebinski, leader of ROPCiO, who had recently been detained for organising an 'anti-Soviet' demonstration on 11 November, the 62nd anniversary of Polish independence. Their request was turned down. At noon on 20 November workers in the main assembly section of the Ursus plant stopped work.

Moscow sees threat to defences
It was not a propitious moment. For one thing, a two-hour strike by Solidarity railwaymen brought passenger traffic to a halt on at least two lines. And this was immediately reported by Moscow Radio in its home service and later in the day by the Government newspaper *Izvestiya*, which comes out in the evening.

It is considered in Warsaw that the threat of a general transport strike, called by Solidarity, could affect the country's national and defence interests and disrupt transit rail links through Poland.

Defence interests meant the interests not only of Poland but of the Warsaw Pact and therefore the Soviet Union. Any disruption of 'transit rail links' would affect communications between the Soviet Union and its forces stationed in East Germany. So Moscow Radio was able, for the first time, to present Solidarity as a direct threat to what everyone had recognised as sacrosanct from the start, the socialist military alliance. More than that, the radio was able to say that the warning strike on the railways was seen in Warsaw as proof of 'activity aimed at maintaining tension' and that Solidarity was rejecting offers of cooperation from the 'old' railwaymen's union in a bid for supremacy.

According to Poland's official media, Solidarity was indeed refusing to cooperate with the old union in a bid to settle the dispute. And as it happened, a meeting of the Consultative Commission of the industrial or branch unions, the rump of the official unions that had broken away from the CRZZ and declared themselves independent, also began in Warsaw on 24 November. Their leader, Albin Szyszka, told the meeting that Solidarity had repeatedly rejected offers of co-operation at national level. He complained of attempts to liquidate the industrial unions, of a 'hysterical climate of witch hunts' in which honest trade unionists were being libelled. He even accused the Government of encouraging people to force wage increases that were not real increases at all but galloping inflation. But Mr Szyszka also said much that the authorities would have liked to hear from Solidarity. Denouncing the use of such methods as hunger strikes and the atmosphere of constant turmoil, he said that trade unions in a socialist state should not constitute an alternative centre of power.

When it came to open debate speakers accused the Government of not giving enough support to the old trade unions and of favouritism towards Solidarity. Prime Minister Pinkowski, who was present, was even heckled and shouted down. One speaker demanded that he should sign there and then a resolution pledging equal representation for the industrial unions. Pinkowski refused to sign. Even if he agreed one hundred per cent, he said, a Prime Minister could not be forced to sign anything like that.

Moscow Radio in its home service reported the industrial unions' meeting promptly. It did not mention Mr Pinkowski's embarrassment but it did report the complaints that the Government was being unfair. Moscow also reported the arrests after the discovery of a secret document at Solidarity headquarters in Warsaw. All at once the Soviet Union was able to tell its own people of developments which could obviously be used against Solidarity and even against the Polish

Government. And it was doing this with unaccustomed speed. Presumably it was keenly interested in seeing how the Polish Government handled the Solidarity challenge in three key areas – the railways, the police and security services, and the treatment of dissidents.

Things did not look promising for the Government. The Solidarity leaders in Warsaw raised their demands. Not only did they want Narozniak and Sapelo released along with arrested dissidents; they also said that the people responsible for the allegedly secret document should be identified and punished, that a parliamentary committee should examine whether the activities of the Prosecutor's Office, the uniformed police and the security police were in keeping with the law, and that an investigation ought to be opened concerning people responsible for 'crimes' against protesting workers in 1970 and 1976. Warsaw Solidarity also stated that unless a Government commission went to the Ursus plant by noon on 27 November, the whole Warsaw area would go on a strike alert.

Reminders of 1968
On 26 November, the strikes in Warsaw spread. For the third day running the main assembly section of the Ursus tractor plant was idle. There were stoppages, generally lasting two hours, in at least nine other factories, and they were joined by newspaper delivery drivers and kiosks. *Trybuna Ludu*, as a matter of interest, was attacking Leszek Moczulski, one of the dissidents whom Solidarity wanted released, as a political bankrupt and provocateur whose ideas gave every decent Pole gooseflesh. *Zycie Warszawy* was saying that, regardless of whether Solidarity was right or wrong about the confiscated document, it should not have called a strike. Across the border in Czechoslovakia, Prague Radio said that Solidarity had turned into 'an opposition force which directly threatens socialism and security in Poland'. And in Yugoslavia, in a broadcast over Zagreb Radio, the highly respected Milika Sundic noted that the media in East Germany and Czechoslovakia were increasingly critical of Poland's new trade unions.

The Czechoslovak Communist Party paper, *Rude Pravo*, compares the present situation in Poland with that in Czechoslovakia in 1968. This, undoubtedly, is a signal. It means that the present ferment in Poland can be dealt with only by the methods that were applied in Czechoslovakia.

The first sign of a possible solution came from Solidarity – not the Warsaw branch but from the National Consultative Commission meeting in Gdansk. In a statement reported by Warsaw television on the evening of 26 November the Commission expressed support for what Solidarity had done in the Warsaw region and called for the release of the two men arrested after the search of the Solidarity offices. But it went on to urge all Solidarity members to refrain 'during the present strained situation' from the escalation of pay and other claims. The National Commission announced a ban on the proclamation of strikes which had not been agreed with the union authorities.

Then at 2 am on 27 November Warsaw Radio announced that the Prosecutor had released Narozniak and Sapelo on the provision of a surety by the Chairman of the Polish Journalists' Association, Stefan Bratkowski. A Government representative would be meeting a Solidarity delegation that morning, the radio said, in accordance with the last statement issued by the union, and the state of strike alert was being called off. The news came not many hours after Warsaw television had announced that the railway strike had also ended. It said that the Ministry of Transport had approved proposals from Solidarity on how wage rises earlier agreed upon would be introduced. Whichever way one looked at it, the Government had had to climb down yet again and Solidarity had won.

6. FEARS OF INTERVENTION

As November came to a close, outside concern over Poland continued unabated, especially in Czechoslovakia. The Party papers, *Rude Pravo* in Prague and *Pravda* in Bratislava, the Slovak capital, published an important article on the 'lessons' of 1968. Ostensibly it marked the tenth anniversary of a Central Committee session which drew up a document on that year's crisis, but anyone could be forgiven for believing that the lessons so precisely drawn were meant to apply to Poland in 1980. It spoke scornfully of the so-called Czechoslovak 'revival' at a time when Polish leaders were talking constantly of renewal. It said that in 1968 some Czechoslovak Party leaders had kept on retreating for the sake of personal popularity and allowed the power centres of the socialist state to be paralysed. The 'counter-revolutionary deluge' had been halted only by means of international aid. But it also made direct reference to Poland.

Imperialism has drawn its own lessons from our Czechoslovak lessons. Anti-Communist centres now stress the need for gradual, discreet and unprovocative methods of destabilisation. They are specially careful to make sure that, until the time is ripe, this process specifically avoids any direct questioning of the leading role of the Party, any immediate attacks on the constitutional bodies of the socialist state or any obvious attacks on its obligations under international alliances . . . The recent events in Poland confirm that, in the middle of a difficult crisis, both internal and external enemies are concentrating on one devious goal, that of setting in motion and accelerating some sort of anti-socialist, aggressive trade unionism.

Moscow Radio broadcast generous details of that article in many of its foreign-language services, including Polish. That was on 29 November. The next day the report was in most of the Soviet papers, noting that 'if today the strategists of imperialism think that a convenient time has come to carry out counter-revolution in one of the socialist states, then again they are in for a disappointment'.

That same day, which was a Saturday, the Commander-in-Chief of the Soviet forces in East Germany informed the military missions in Potsdam of the three other wartime allies, Great Britain, France and the United States, that a 24-mile-wide area along East Germany's border with Poland was closed to them and had been declared a temporary restricted area. In effect, the whole border was being closed. It took some days for the news to reach the Western press but when it did it caused a sensation that lasted for weeks. The West faced up to the possibility of a Warsaw Pact invasion of Poland.

Conservatives and counter-revolutionaries
Poland carried on regardless. Less obsessed than the West with the threat of invasion and more concerned than their allies with making 'renewal' work rather than worrying about its risks, the Poles entered another few days of intense political heart-searching. On 1 December another Plenum or plenary session of the Communist Party's Central Committee began in Warsaw. It was preceded by an interesting article in *Trybuna Ludu* which revealed that the Party was being pulled in two directions at once. Zdzislaw Kurowski, a Central Committee Secretary, wrote that 'some Party members' were still unable or reluctant to understand the essence of the changes taking place and 'counting on a return, at some time, to the former style of work, the old methods and system of values'. On the other hand, he said, other members, influenced by 'dubious concepts', including those formulated by 'anti-socialist elements', were departing from Party principles, launching the idea of transforming the Party into some kind of loose structure, bereft of internal unity and incapable of effective action.

To conclude, on the basis of that, that the Communist Party was split would probably be too clear-cut an expression to use. It is more likely that, deprived of the inflexible certainties of the past, it was bewildered and wondering which way to go. Mr Kania, the Party leader, had to contend with that as well as all the problems of the economy and the unions and the anxieties of the allies, as he stood up to speak that Monday morning. The future of the nation, he told the Central Committee, was being decided, but there was no going back on the policy of socialist renewal.

We well understand the internationalist concern and anxiety awakened in the fraternal Parties by the situation in Poland. After all we are an extremely important part of the socialist community. We are grateful to people, particularly our Soviet comrades, for having confidence in our Party, for understanding the nature of our difficulties and for their conviction that we shall find a way out of the crisis which is good for socialism in Poland and for the entire community.

As regards the Party itself, Kania revealed that in the process of restoring 'Leninist norms' more than 500 people had been replaced in leading jobs. Renewal, he said, was meeting considerable obstacles, among them conservative resistance to change.

The Party has not yet adapted to the new situation. In the attitude of many comrades, and sometimes even entire Party organisations, emotion prevails over reason and bitter assessments of the past prevail over constructive conclusions for the future. The Party must not become a debating society or a loose association of sympathisers.

Kania saw the new unions as impatient and emotional.

Nobody can accuse us of lack of patience or of a readiness to compromise or to make concessions designed to head off extreme situations which would be dangerous for the country's security and internal calm . . . But there can be no excuse whatsoever for strikes of a prestige or simply political character. Attempts to force changes in provincial or state authorities or in the management of certain works by threatening a strike or by occupying works or official buildings cause great concern . . . All this shows that certain Solidarity members and organisations are overstepping the limits of trade union activity . . . The overwhelming majority of Solidarity members and sympathisers have nothing in common with this dangerous trend and we count on them not to follow it. The crux of the problem lies in the fact that some links of this genuine workers' movement have been penetrated or are being negatively inspired by groups and persons connected with centres of imperialist subversion. They want to destabilise, harm and overthrow the socialist state in Poland. Their fundamental plan is anti-worker and counter-revolutionary.

At this point in the argument, it might have been expected that an absolutely orthodox Soviet-bloc leader would have gone on to say that, in such a situation, the Party had the right to use 'all revolutionary means' to defend 'socialist achievements'. But Mr Kania said nothing of the sort. He did warn that nobody should count on any leniency from the Party in the defence of the socialist cause but, more important, he reminded the Central Committee of what it had decided in the last few months.

During the crisis of July and August, the Central Committee chose the line of agreement and renewal. This was a decision of far-reaching consequences for the system. It meant a profound transformation in the range and methods of exercising the leading role of the Party. It meant that social organisations were entrusted with an independent and self-governing mandate for wide sectors of public life, in particular the trade unions and youth movements and cultural and scientific activities. We have set a course towards the development of socialist democracy, towards widening the political base of people's power . . . These are very essential changes. It would be naive to think that they have been forced on the Party. Without deliberate support for these changes in the Politburo, in the Central Committee and among broad circles of Party activists, they would have been impossible.

We have chosen this path not because of any illusions that we would be able, in this way, to avert a mass wave of strikes and then go back to the old ways. We have been guided by the desire to gain a stronger social base for socialism in our country . . . We are aware of the fact that the sharp turn we have executed in conditions of tension and conflicts can also bring attacks on socialism and the Party. But we have counted on the strength of our society's prudence and its maturity in understanding the national interests.

Kania's frank assessment of the situation was designed to remind any waverers in the Party leadership that they had gone along with the policy of renewal and could not change it now. He was saying again that using force to tackle the risks for socialism was out of the question, that the Party could not rule without the support of the public. On the eve of his speech, in fact, Lech Walesa had told an audience in Konin that 'every one of us is a Pole first and only then a member of Solidarity. Hence the need to work always in the interests of the country.'

In the Central Committee debate support for Kania's line and for his call for 'an alliance of the forces of common sense and responsibility' came from General Mieczyslaw Moczar, the former Minister of Internal Affairs and current Chairman of the supreme board of the Union of Fighters for Freedom and Democracy (ZBOWiD), the veterans' association.

Our Party's policy boils down to seeking political solutions. This is the correct and only way out . . . Only commonsense can overcome the crisis . . . I support and appreciate Mr Kania for the fact that we have consistently followed this path since the Sixth Plenum. The demand voiced by all PZPR members and all reasonable people is not to let force be used, as that would be a national tragedy.

The debate seemed to stiffen Mr Kania's attitude, though. Protesting that the authorities had been exceptionally patient, and 'in the opinion of some comrades perhaps too tolerant and compromising', he objected to a statement by a 'leading representative of KOR' – in fact, Jacek Kuron – according to which the independent trade unions operating in the Polish Communist system were like rogue trains suddenly introduced on the railways but not running according to the centrally-planned timetable.

In such a situation the logical outcome will be a collision between trains travelling according to different timetables. And here one must ask a question: Does anyone from Solidarity agree with this picture of the role of his union? Who wants to transform the new unions into trains set on a collision course? All those who do toy with such a danger bear a great responsibility before the people.

When the Central Committee meeting ended, General Moczar had been promoted to full membership of the Politburo along with Tadeusz Grabski, and four men had left, completing a remarkable transformation of the Politburo in the space of less than five months. Out of the fourteen occupying seats on the Politburo at the beginning of August, ten had gone, six in disgrace as we have already seen, and the latest four for reasons of health or because they already held state posts (see p. 316). One of them was Alojzy Karkoszka who was replaced in mid-November as Warsaw Party Secretary. In November and December, incidentally, the list of provincial first secretaries that had been replaced rose to at least seventeen. As regards the Government, the November session of the Sejm had approved the replacement of three more ministers and the appointment of a Roman Catholic Deputy Prime Minister, Jerzy Ozdowski.

As for the men of the old regime, Edward Gierek had been invited to the Central Committee but did not appear, pleading ill health. In a special resolution, the Committee put it on record that the former leader bore serious personal responsibility for arbitrariness in economic and social policy, for ignoring economic laws and disregarding criticism, for creating an atmosphere of intrigue and a façade of democracy, and for deciding important matters outside the Politburo and its Secretariat. The Committee decided to drop Gierek from its ranks and instructed him to resign from the Sejm and the State Council, along with several of his former colleagues and supporters.

The West, meanwhile, was more concerned with a much simpler view of Poland, the danger of an invasion by its Warsaw Pact allies. It was only when the Plenum was over that the two stories seemed to meet. In a midnight appeal to the nation, broadcast by Warsaw Radio on 3 December, the Central Committee used words which almost matched the sensational language of reports then appearing in most newspapers of the Western world. It began ominously:

Compatriots, the future of our nation is at stake. The continuing disturbances are bringing our homeland to the brink of economic and moral destruction . . . The time has come for all realistically-minded people in our country to rally round the line of common sense and responsibility . . . The Party appeals to the collective wisdom of the nation. Let us not waste this great opportunity for us all.

Repeating pledges of cooperation with all sections of the nation, with the United Peasant Party and the Democratic Party and also with the Roman Catholic Church, the appeal warned that the cause of renewal and the new forms of self-governing democracy must not be abused against the socialist state.

There are people in Poland who do not hide their counter-revolutionary goals. We shall upset their plans. We cannot allow them to sow anarchy and chaos . . . The arrogance we condemned in the authorities must not be replaced by a new type of arrogance which ignores the legal order or the agreements signed. The strikes, which have been going on for five months now, the disruptions and the low productivity are leading to a progressive worsening of the already difficult economic situation . . . Citizens, let us oppose any further escalation of anxiety. Let us create a front of common sense and responsibility in defence of the socialist renewal.

By this time, news rooms in the West were agog with excitement over the possibility of a Soviet invasion. The news of the closure of the East German–Polish border had been followed by rumours and reports of a build-up of troops on the Soviet border with Poland. The Soviet Foreign Ministry denied that; in an unusual move it told Western correspondents that it had investigated the reports and found them to be fabrications. By that time, though, the Soviet Ambassador in Washington had been summoned to the State Department and told that any Soviet intervention in Poland would have very serious consequences for Soviet–American relations.

In Luxembourg, leaders of the European Community appealed to all signatories of the 1975 Helsinki Declaration to abide by its principles 'with regard to Poland and the Polish people'. In London, fifteen Labour MPs told the Soviet Ambassador that any intervention by his country would strengthen the hand of Moscow's critics, damage détente and escalate the arms race. In the House of Commons the next day, 3 December, the Labour leader, Mr Michael Foot, supported the Prime Minister, Mrs Margaret Thatcher, by saying that any interference with the right of the Polish people to have independent trade unions and enjoy freedom of expression would be a tragedy and a crime. In Washington President Carter issued a public warning that the United States was watching the build-up of Soviet forces on the Polish border with growing concern. American defence intelligence experts were reported to be convinced that Soviet reservists summoned to reinforce units along the border for manoeuvres in the summer had not stood down and that the Red Army was ready and waiting for the political decision for an invasion to be taken. The Central Intelligence Agency was then reported to have concluded that developments could only be a preparation for an invasion.

On 4 December Warsaw announced that the Military Council of the Defence Ministry had met the day before. The Council had expressed profound anxiety at the situation, which was creating a serious threat to the country's social and economic order and to the functioning of the state organism as a whole. If the situation continued, it said, there could be important negative consequences for the country's defences.

Such pregnant words fitted in very well with the current alarm in the West. But nothing in them or in the speeches, resolutions and appeals of the Central Committee meeting gave any suggestion that the Polish leaders really expected an invasion or were afraid of one in the immediate future. Indeed, the head of the Central Committee's Press, Radio and Television Department, Jozef Klasa, accused the West of deliberately stirring up excitement about the alleged plans of the Soviet Union. 'If there's anything our friends do not want,' he told a news conference, 'it is the need to give military assistance in defence of socialism and people's power in Poland. My recent visit to Moscow fully confirmed this.' He conceded, though, that should there be a threat to socialism in Poland, Polish Communists could turn for help to Communists in other countries. But at the moment they could cope without that, he said.

Warsaw Pact summit

Any argument about the significance of that was cut short the next day when it was announced without any warning that a Warsaw Pact summit meeting had been held in Moscow. A long communiqué issued at the end of one day of deliberations contained just a hint that the whole affair had been hurriedly arranged. The delegations attending from Bulgaria, Hungary, East Germany, Poland, Romania, the Soviet Union and Czechoslovakia differed quite strikingly in size and make-up. All were led by the Party leaders and all but one included the Prime Ministers, but the only two to be roughly equivalent were the Soviet and the Polish. They were very strong.

Assisting President Leonid Brezhnev for the Soviet Union were Prime Minister Nikolay Tikhonov, Party ideologist Mikhail Suslov, KGB chief Yury Andropov, Foreign Minister Andrei Gromyko, Defence Minister Dimitri Ustinov, and Konstantin Rusakov, the Party Secretary dealing with fraternal parties. With Mr Kania were Prime Minister Jozef Pinkowski, two Party Secretaries, Kazimierz Barcikowski and Stefan Olszowski, Defence Minister Wojciech Jaruzelski, Foreign Minister Jozef Czyrek and the Minister of Internal Affairs, Miroslaw Milewski. Only one other delegation, that of East Germany, included Ministers of Defence and of the Interior. That had only five members, while Romania and Bulgaria were represented by four people each, and Hungary and Czechoslovakia by only three.

The communiqué dwelt at length on the general international situation and devoted only the last but one paragraph to Poland.

The participants in the meeting expressed confidence that the Communists, the working class, the working people of fraternal Poland will be able to overcome the present difficulties and will ensure the country's further development along the socialist path. It was repeated that socialist Poland, the Polish United Workers' Party and the Polish people can firmly rely on the fraternal solidarity and support of the members of the Warsaw Pact. Representatives of the Polish United Workers' Party stressed that Poland has been, is and will remain a socialist state, a firm link in the common family of the countries of socialism.

The meeting of Party and State figures of the socialist countries was held in an atmosphere of comradely mutual understanding and unity of views.

On the face of it, that represented a vote of confidence in the Polish leadership, not just from the Soviet Union but from all members of the Soviet bloc, including Czechoslovakia which had been especially critical of developments in Poland. The least one could say about the meeting was that it had given Poland a breathing space in which to settle its affairs without help from its allies. That, in fact, is what many Western papers said. But fears and warnings about a possible Soviet invasion persisted until the end of the month. Within a few days of the Moscow summit gathering, the White House issued another statement saying that preparations for a possible Soviet intervention 'appear to have been completed'. American intelligence sources reported the call-up of Soviet reservists. The Pentagon decided to despatch four AWACS reconnaissance aircraft to West Germany. In Brussels, the Canadian Chairman of the NATO military committee said that Soviet forces were in a position to launch an invasion in a matter of hours, never mind days or weeks.

On 10 December that part of the East German–Polish border which had been temporarily closed at the end of November was opened again to Western military missions. But talk of invasion continued, almost dominating the sessions in Brussels of NATO Defence Ministers and then Foreign Ministers. Mr Brezhnev, meanwhile, had gone to India, and his spokesman, Leonid Zamyatin, felt obliged while there with him to deny reports in Indian and some Western newspapers that Soviet troops had actually crossed the Polish border.

Moscow itself was content in its broadcasts to accuse the West of 'hysteria' and of trying to interfere and subvert Poland. It even stuck to its claim, vigorously denied by Washington, that Zbigniew Brzezinski, President Carter's

National Security Adviser, had met some Polish 'political experts' and suggested that the Polish 'opposition' should use armed force. Defence Minister Ustinov, in a speech to a Party conference of the Moscow Military Region, called for increased vigilance in the face of imperialist and reactionary attempts to harm the socialist countries – 'in particular socialist Poland'.

Eventually, in the middle of December a senior Soviet official, Mr Valentin Falin, a former Ambassador in Bonn and currently Deputy Head of the Soviet Party's International Information Department, gave an interview to the West German magazine, *Der Spiegel*, in which he attacked the Western press for spreading 'rumours' of a Soviet invasion and stated categorically that the Soviet Union 'does not intend to interfere in Polish affairs'. A similar denial came in Paris a few days later from an even more senior official, Boris Ponomarev, a Secretary of the Soviet Central Committee. Nevertheless, as Christmas approached Soviet troops were still reported to be in a state of readiness on Poland's borders.

Western 'hysteria'

It would be a mistake to imagine that Western publicity for the invasion scare was welcomed or appreciated in Poland. On the contrary, some of the country's most recognisably liberal publicists themselves were unhappy about the danger to their own efforts from Western reporting. They regarded it as following preconceived ideas more than facts. Stefan Bratkowski, the leader of the journalists' union, told a news conference in Warsaw that in his view newspapers round the world were wrong to report about anarchy and the disintegration of the Polish State.

They should be based on fact, not pre-cooked ideas. Falsely inflated news frequently brings bad results. The responsibility for words was never greater in this country in the past decade than it is today. We see no cause for the hysteria which the Western press is stirring up around Poland. We will be able to repair our house ourselves. We don't need to be reassured. We are aware of how serious the situation is. My voice is that of an optimist. Optimism is our only way out.

Jacek Kalabinski took issue on Warsaw Radio with a recent issue of the American magazine *Newsweek* which had a cover picture of Lech Walesa next to a burning fuse attached to a hammer and sickle. The caption read 'A Threat to Moscow'. Kalabinski was cross.

I think it is high time we said bluntly that renewal in Poland is no threat to Moscow or Ulan Bator or Paris or Brussels. On the contrary renewal in Poland is a chance for socialism and for stability in Europe . . . So we have a request: Don't disturb us with *Newsweek* covers, with alarmist reports from journalists here, statements by politicians or announcements that worker unrest continues in Poland, which is obviously untrue. Don't disturb us as we try to do what we have to do – restore the Republic. After all, the strength and stability of our Republic is in the interests of both Eastern and Western Europe.

Warsaw Radio handled unwelcome Soviet reports differently. On the morning of 8 December, for instance, three days after the Warsaw Pact summit meeting, the Soviet news agency *Tass*, and Moscow Radio in its home service and World Service in English carried the following:

According to reports coming in from various parts of Poland, counter-revolutionary groups operating under the cover of local branches of Solidarity are turning to an open confrontation with local PZPR organisations and also with the administration of some enterprises and establishments. At the Iskra works in Kielce, so-called defenders of the workers' interests have arbitrarily dismissed the management and disarmed the works guard. There have been cases of the disappearance of activists who, at works meetings, expressed their disagreement with the demands of the instigators.
It is noteworthy that over the last few days some Solidarity committees have initiated a campaign to replace trade union officials with people who are openly acting from anti-Government positions. These and other facts show that counter-revolutionaries are taking the situation towards further destabilisation and the aggravation of political struggle.

That report was rapidly reproduced by Sofia Radio, Prague Radio and Television and the East German Radio and news agency, all on the same day. And the Yugoslav news agency, Tanyug, noted that never before had the Moscow media stressed so explicitly that counter-revolution was active in Poland.

These were serious allegations, but they were quietly deflated by Warsaw Radio in three separate news bulletins on the same day, in which it quoted managers and the Party Secretary at the Iskra works in Kielce – the only place specified in the Soviet report – as saying that the factory was working well. The next day, *Trybuna Ludu* said that calm, honest work was in progress at the plant and that this was due, in no small measure, to the creative activity of Solidarity.

Poland's allies, in spite of that Moscow communiqué, did not let up in their criticism of what was happening there, especially Czechoslovakia. Dr Jan Risko, Director General of Czechoslovak Radio, placed the situation in Poland in the same category as what he called 'the intrigues of imperialism and enemies' in East Germany in 1953, in Hungary in 1956 and in Czechoslovakia in 1968. And in yet another reference to the 'lessons' of that fateful year, he drew a picture that was probably meant to be taken to represent at least some aspects of the current situation in Poland.

In Czechoslovakia, the entire crisis-ridden development was strongly affected by the revival and galvanisation of pettybourgeois strata along with their ideas and thinking, by the suppression and weakening of internationalist sentiment, by growing nationalism hand-in-hand with anti-socialism and cosmopolitanism, and last but not least, by the revival of religion.

In fact, the Roman Catholic Church in Poland was a valued national asset, with which the Communist leaders wanted to cooperate for the good of the nation. The joint Church–Government Commission, at its December meeting, agreed that what the nation wanted was the unity of Poles 'regardless of differences in world outlook or political views'. A communiqué on a plenary session of the Polish Episcopate, presided over by the Primate, Cardinal Wyszynski, said that the efforts of 'all Poles' should aim at strengthening the process of renewal – not 'socialist renewal', just plain renewal.

We are facing difficult years. They will demand acts of renunciation, sacrifice and devotion. We must live in the hope that there is a meaning in consciously undertaking these acts for the sake of a better future in a free homeland. A determined will is needed to oppose all attempts to halt the process of national renewal, to stir up differences within society and to exploit existing difficulties for goals alien to the welfare of people and State. Our country, first and foremost, needs internal peace in order to stabilise social life in an atmosphere of rebuilding mutual trust.

The Polish bishops' statement, as broadcast by Vatican Radio, contained no direct criticism of the Polish dissidents, as was curiously reported by both Moscow and some Western papers, and it did not represent any departure from the established Wyszynski line. If internal peace broke down, hopes for national renewal – national, please note, and not socialist – would also disappear. The Church, it seemed, understood very clearly the dangers of the situation in which Poland was walking a tightrope, watched by both East and West, each suspicious and hostile to the other. The big problem was that the Soviet bloc did not think that Poland should be doing it, and besides it could, if it decided it was too dangerous, interrupt the performance and bring the tightrope walker down into its own safety net. And Poland, as those two journalists pointed out, did not want anyone's concentration to be disturbed by alarmist barracking from the other side. On top of that Poles themselves, after so many years of disappointment and corrupt practice, were finding it extremely difficult to trust one another anyway.

Gdansk monument
December, in spite of all its alarms and the realisation of just how difficult things were going to be, did provide some hope for the future. One occasion in particular brought together the three main forces in the country – the Party, Solidarity and the Church – in an act of national reconciliation.

On the evening of 16 December many thousands of people gathered outside Gate Number Two of the Gdansk Shipyard to commemorate the tenth anniversary of the deaths there of forty-five workers, killed by Government troops sent in to quell their protests. In the front row of the mourners were President Jablonski and the local Party Secretary, Tadeusz Fiszbach. Cardinal Franciszek Macharski and the Secretary of the Episcopate, Bishop Bronislaw Dabrowski, were also there, as well as Lech Walesa with colleagues from Solidarity. After the sounding of ships' sirens and the ringing of church bells, the whole crowd sang a patriotic song and watched the unveiling of an impressive monument to the dead, three slender crosses forty-two metres high, each with an anchor affixed to its arms. Mass was said by Cardinal Macharski and messages read out from Cardinal Wyszynski and Pope John Paul II. But before that there were speeches from Lech Walesa and Tadeusz Fiszbach.

Walesa read out the words contained in the monument's act of foundation:

This monument has been erected to those who died as a mark of eternal memory, to those who rule as a warning that social conflicts in the homeland must not be solved by force, to our fellow citizens as a sign of hope that evil can be overcome.

Fiszbach backed Walesa's appeal for calm, law and order with a reminder that united efforts for stabilisation were required not only by Poland's internal interests but by its 'international position, linked to the world through alliances and contacts'. He also made it clear that the Gdansk monument was a symbol of the Party's decision not to use force.

The memory of the December events, though painful, should not and must not divide us. They should unite the nation . . . to ensure that such tragedies should never occur again. That is why, four months ago, we . . . chose the only correct way of solving the August conflict, the path of agreement.

The man largely associated with that policy, Stanislaw Kania, was not at the Gdansk ceremony or in Gdynia or Szczecin where plaques were unveiled to those who died in December 1970. But on 30 December, during a visit to Gdansk, he went to the monument outside Gate Number Two and placed a bunch of flowers. 'Let us hope,' he said, 'that we never have to build such monuments again.'

If he sounded unsure of the future, he had good cause. As the year came to an end, and Lech Walesa was hailed throughout the Western world as Man of the Year, Stanislaw Kania had little reason to be satisfied. But he had considerable achievement to his credit. He had set up an administration dedicated specifically to the use of negotiation rather than force. He had publicly admitted Communist failure and allowed it to be commemorated in a monument to those who had died as a result of it, something quite unprecedented in the Soviet bloc. This in itself was an act of faith of a sort not only in the Communist Party but in the nation. He believed, unlike his allies in the socialist community, that the Communist Party and independent trade unions could work together. But all his experience so far had taught him that this would be difficult to prove.

On New Year's Eve President Jablonski went on television with a candid message for the nation:

We are entering the new year without illusions and without easy promises. During the new year there will doubtless be confrontations between the conflicting interests of various circles, classes and social groups, so the country's difficult economic situation will be revealed more and more sharply . . . We are aware of all this but we also know that no one can take our place in solving our problems . . . that it depends on us alone and on our work what kind of tomorrow we have.

7. TRIALS OF STRENGTH

The new year, 1981, was ushered in without any illusions whatsoever, as President Jablonski had so righly predicted, but there was no immediate confrontation. On the contrary it was very quiet. Industrial unrest had died away at the beginning of December and had not reappeared. Indeed there was time for people to savour the rather optimistic and possibly illusory words of the newly elected President of the Union of Polish Writers. In an interview with *Zycie Warszawy* on the last day of 1980, Jan Jozef Szczepanski looked forward to a new climate in intellectual life.

In 1976 some writers began to print their works through underground publishers. It was an act of common sense, an act of self-defence. It was the literary community's response to official indoctrination and the official monopoly of information . . . The authorities imagined that literature was dangerous . . . But now I believe we can already feel trends conducive to common sense. True we are still bound by old thinking habits and old fears, habits formed by the self-willed operation of censorship over many years. But this must change, even though this change is not easy . . . I believe that all intellectual life in this country will now slowly come back to normal. Free thinking, recently a suspicious activity, will at last make a come-back.

Even the Army newspaper, the most conservative of all the Polish papers, found time to write about culture. As usual, it saw danger ahead. This is how the Polish News Agency reported the article in its English-language service:

Zolnier Wolnosci has sounded an alarm, charging that the media in Poland are increasingly prone to the influence of quasi-modern trends favouring social and national nihilism, sex and primitivism which permeate a whole range of books of poetry, films, songs, theatre productions and paintings, all of them creating a pressure of snobbish terror. The paper pinpoints as the key sources of this trend, social underdevelopment and imperialist ideological subversion ... Preying on errors and depravity, bourgeois propaganda promotes cheap pleasure, sex and pornography to inspire defeatist moods and undermine faith in socialism, a procedure which is particularly intensive at times of internal tension in socialist countries.

Another odd feature of the first week of the year was a report in the Czechoslovak Party daily, *Rude Pravo*, suggesting that Poland was witnessing a return to normal life and that 'honest' members of Solidarity were dissociating themselves from 'anti-socialist and anarchist' elements. This was not the view taken in Moscow. On 1 January a TASS despatch which was given wide publicity on Moscow Radio's home and foreign language services claimed that anti-socialist forces in Poland were urging Solidarity organisations 'to assume the role of a sort of counterbalance to the official organs of power and become an organisation of a political kind'. The report adduced no evidence to support this assertion, but Moscow did not have to wait long for suitable material to present itself.

Five-day week
The seeds of the first major confrontation of 1981 were sown on New Year's Eve, when Warsaw Radio announced that the Presidium of the Government had decided that three out of January's five Saturdays – the 3rd, 17th and 31st – would be 'work-free days'. In the past, Polish workers had had only one Saturday off per month, and one of the main demands of the strikers in Gdansk had been that they should have all Saturdays off. The Gdansk Agreements had stipulated that the Government should submit its proposals for introducing a programme for work-free Saturdays by 31 December. This Government announcement on that very day suggested that the authorities were acting in some haste, and the publicity given in the next few days to the Government's reasons for the decision made it clear that trouble was expected.

The official news agency, PAP, in a long and detailed article quoting estimates from various ministries, concluded that the introduction of a clear-cut five-day week at a time of economic crisis would only make matters worse. Deputy Premier Jagielski argued the Government's case on television. The effects of a sudden reduction in working hours, he said,

106

would be economically intolerable, entailing a lowering of production, the national income and the country's standard of living. Besides, he said, no socialist country had introduced an 'all Saturdays off' system all at once. And in Western countries working hours had been introduced gradually over many years. Mr Jagielski said the Government would entertain various solutions and mentioned two in particular: two work-free Saturdays a month while retaining the normal working weekday, or all Saturdays off provided each of the working days was extended by thirty minutes to make a $42\frac{1}{2}$-hour week.

We are in favour of gradually making all Saturdays free from work with an appropriate adjustment of the length of the working week . . . The Government hopes that its decision will meet with understanding . . . This will be yet another proof of our patriotic, civic responsibility.

Unfortunately for the Government, such appeals were beginning to wear thin. Solidarity's National Consultative Commission began a meeting in Gdansk on the day Mr Jagielski made his broadcast. The next day it adopted a resolution stating quite baldly, according to Gdansk Radio, that from 1 January all Saturdays would be free, without any increase in standard working time and without any cuts in earnings. Workers who did not go to work on Saturday 10 January – a normal working day according to the Government – therefore had the Commission's support.

Whether that amounted to a strike call is a matter for argument. At any rate the Ministry of Labour announced that night that anyone who failed to turn up for work on 10 or 24 January would not be paid. Earlier, a statement from the Ministry, broadcast in full by Warsaw Radio, argued rather convincingly that neither the Gdansk nor Szczecin Agreements obliged the Government to introduce a system of all Saturdays off in 1981. As for the Jastrzebie Agreement, which did specifically concede all Saturdays off from 1 January 1981, the Ministry announced that that clearly applied only to miners.

This was a straight argument about industrial management as well as the interpretation of agreements that had been on paper for months. And it was possible for an outside observer to look at it dispassionately, regardless of ideological persuasion. For those inside Poland that was hardly possible for reasons of past experience and ingrained suspicion. And if we were to believe official reports Solidarity organisations were hardly encouraging the authorities to treat them as harmless and well-meaning newcomers to Poland's political life. On the day the row over the working week came to a head, 8 January, Warsaw television news carried a startling item:

Our correspondents report that in a number of centres, including Wloclawek, Jelenia Gora, Krosno, Olsztyn, Czestochowa and Torun, pressure is being visibily exerted on the apparatus of local authorities. Attempts are being made to force personnel changes in executive posts . . . It has sometimes happened that public buildings have been occupied and that the property of state institutions and organisations has been interfered with. This is simply a manifestation of noisy anarchy hindering the development of law and order.

The bulletin went on to quote *Trybuna Ludu* as saying that some local leaders of Solidarity were among the organisers of these incidents which amounted to 'a deliberate move against the authorities with a view to weakening them'.

Once again the political climate had turned suddenly colder. Stefan Olszowski, a leading member of the Politburo and a man of considerable political skills and versatility, went on television on the eve of the disputed 'working Saturday' to deplore Solidarity's negative response to the Government's proposals for shortening the working week.

The unwillingness to compromise is a new source of unrest . . . In reality it is a trial of strength, a kind of political pressure on the Government. The last few days have revealed other causes for disquiet. Renewed attempts are being made to undermine law and order. For instance, what is the object of attempts in the provinces of Jelenia Gora, Wloclawek, Torun and Radom to exert conspicuous pressure on the machinery of state authority with a view to forcing changes in management posts in those regions? And why at this time, when the Party is carrying out an honest assessment of its work and when those who violated socialist principles, who were bad managers or who showed the wrong attitude to working people are having to take the consequences?

Olszowski asked another question and answered it.

What are some Solidarity activists in the Warsaw region aiming at by drawing up a list of management cadres in the economy, the machinery of State authority and in political life and passing so-called judgment on them? This campaign serves to kindle passions. It is a deliberate attempt to intimidate management cadres. It aims

108

at disorganising economic, state and political life. What the instigators of this activity want is clear: to undermine the organisational structure of social life, not with a view to improving the socialist republic but weakening it.

Also on television that Friday night was the Minister of Labour, Janusz Obodowski. In a lengthy interview in which he faced many probing questions, he made one very clear point: that the Government could settle the whole issue of a shorter working week tomorrow by simply giving all Saturdays off but that would mean a drop in the standard of living of eight to nine per cent.

On Saturday 10 January millions of Polish workers did not go to work, but according to official figures published later, while twenty-four per cent of the work-force stayed away, sixty-two per cent worked normally and thirteen per cent took the day off in lieu of the official day off promised for 31 January. Neither side could claim victory because winning and losing was not really at issue. What the whole exercise did prove was that great damage could be done if the Government and the new unions could not find some way of working more closely together. A similar damaging act of defiance was in prospect on 24 January when the next working Saturday was due. But that was only one of the Government's problems. A second was the series of protest sit-ins in public buildings, mainly to support demands for the sacking of discredited officials.

No to Farmers' Union
A third problem which had been smouldering beneath the surface for months, was the subject of some very strong and unambiguous comments by the Party leader, Mr Kania, on that troubled Saturday. Speaking at a meeting in Warsaw of provincial leaders of the Communist and the United Peasant Parties, he made it quite clear that he was completely opposed to the creation of a union for private farmers along the lines of Solidarity. Moves to set up such a union had begun as long ago as September but the application for registration of Rural Solidarity had been turned down by the Warsaw Provincial Court. An appeal had gone to the Supreme Court and a final ruling was still awaited. Mr Kania would probably have had little reason to worry about the attempt to form this farmers' union, had it not been for certain incontrovertible

facts of considerable importance to the nation's economy.

Poland needed food and the provision of food depended on its farmers. But the overwhelming majority of Polish agriculture was in the hands of small-scale private farmers who had suffered undeniable neglect under the Communist regime and were determined to make sure that in future they had more control over their affairs. The authorities had already admitted that in recent years the state farms, though much fewer in number, had received the lion's share of state aid in investment and machinery. They had promised that from now on the long-established 'agricultural circles' would be reformed and really look after the interests of the farmers in a revitalised countryside. But the farmers would have none of it. And not only did they have their own bargaining counter – the power to withhold produce – they also had the support of both Solidarity and the Church. Indeed a parish priest in a small village off the beaten track not far from Warsaw was one of the prime movers of Rural Solidarity.

The authorities argued that a trade union as such was not the best sort of organisation to look after the interests of private farmers since they were at the same time both employer and employee. But as Mr Kania made clear in his speech to provincial Party leaders gathered in Warsaw, the Communist leadership also saw a political threat in the very idea of setting up Rural Solidarity.

Generally speaking, it is people from outside who have come in for this purpose. And there is no shortage of people whose life histories show their complete alienation as regards the peasants' interests. Nor is there any shortage of people who make no secret of their anti-socialist intentions and – one has to put it even more bluntly – their counter-revolutionary intentions. We know many of their names. Many have their origins in the landed aristocracy. Many have a history of struggle against rural reform. There is no place for an anti-socialist opposition in the countryside.

Mr Kania's uncompromising rejection of a Rural Solidarity must have impressed Moscow Radio which quickly told its home service listeners about it. But the Polish authorities were suddenly exposed to the possibility of defiance and eventual reverses not only on that score but on the issue of the sit-ins and the shorter working week. And Moscow Radio was also telling its domestic audience that 'unfavourable situations' had developed in certain provinces where Solidarity activists had allegedly mounted pickets and stopped people going to work. At the same time, incidentally, the Warsaw region Solidarity organisation had done its own survey of what happened on Saturday 10 January and reported that as many as ninety per cent of the region's work force had stayed away from work – not twenty-four per cent, as claimed by the Government.

No one, it seemed, was in the mood for compromise. Instead there began a bewildering series of protest actions which went on without relief and little clear definition for several weeks.

On Sunday 11 January Warsaw Radio revealed that a three-day protest sit-in at the town hall in Nowy Sacz in south-eastern Poland had been brought to an end when 'the forces of order brought about the evacuation of the hall' while displaying 'the maximum of tact and restraint'. The protest action was the work of Solidarity, which put forward ten demands which the radio did not reveal.

Two days later, several dozen people claiming to belong to Rural Solidarity were reported to have vacated offices in Ustrzyki Dolne, in Krosno province also in the south-east, after occupying them for two whole weeks. The local radio in Lodz reported that students at the university had suspended a sit-in after reaching provisional agreement with the Rector on a series of demands but were maintaining a state of 'protest readiness' while waiting for the Minister of Higher Education to arrive and discuss matters outside the Rector's competence. In Rzeszow, television viewers were told, local Solidarity members had begun a sit-in strike in the former trade union headquarters on 2 January and were now demanding the registration of Rural Solidarity. In Wroclaw two hundred students at the Agricultural Academy were demanding the abolition of exams in political sciences.

In Radom the Provincial Governor himself was under fire from Solidarity. In a lengthy television programme on his quarrels with the union, he read out an invitation he had received from Solidarity to attend a meeting at a certain hour on a certain day to hear 'charges brought by the Commission for the Rehabilitation of Workers and the people of the Radom area against the Provincial Governor'. As the programme made clear in other interviews, the people holding top posts in Radom in January 1981 had been in the same

111

jobs in June 1976 when workers' protests against food price increases were suppressed.

On 16 January a four-hour transport strike took place in Warsaw. It was called by Solidarity in protest against alleged reprisals in the transport department against men who had not worked on Saturday 10 January. The Deputy Mayor of Warsaw had gone on television to protest that the only sanction applied to such people was the refusal to pay wages for that day. His appeal went unheeded.

The accumulating unrest brought a Deputy Prime Minister, Stanislaw Mach, in front of the television cameras to report that, quite apart from the Warsaw strike, there had been short strikes in twelve other provinces and threats of more to come.

The instigators of these undertakings are accusing the Government in various leaflets, in resolutions and through megaphones of not implementing the agreements. They are even accusing it of victimising the strikers. These are lies . . . Solidarity demands that people who did not work on 10 January should be paid. It is against this background that certain regional branches of Solidarity have been organising warning strikes . . . If we are to talk about victimisation, how else can one describe the statement issued by Solidarity in Wroclaw announcing that it will depose any director who attempts to implement the requirements of the Labour Code? This is unacceptable blackmail.

While all this was being said Lech Walesa, the national leader of Solidarity, was away in Rome, completing a five-day visit during which he met the Pope and repeated that his union had no political aspirations. He returned home on Sunday 18 January to a hero's welcome at Warsaw airport, but things did not get any better. Walesa and a Solidarity delegation had talks with Prime Minister Pinkowski about the implementation of the Gdansk Agreements. An official announcement said no more than that. A meeting in Gdansk of the union's National Commission decided on a four-hour warning strike on 22 January, but at the same time said it was ready for talks with the Government on new proposals involving a $41\frac{1}{2}$-hour week with some Saturday working.

More talks with Prime Minister Pinkowski followed. Solidarity representatives led by Lech Walesa demanded that the coming Saturday, 24 January, be a day off work. Government representatives refused and deplored 'the inadmissible

Top left: *Edward Gierek, First Secretary of the Polish United Workers' Party, December 1970–September 1980.*
Top right: *Cardinal Stefan Wyszynski, Primate of Poland until his death in May 1981.*
Bottom: *Workers united, on strike and at Mass, Lenin Shipyard, Gdansk, August 1980.*

The Lenin Shipyard.

Above: *Strikers on the roof as crowds gather outside.*
Left: *On the megaphone crane driver Anna Walentynowicz, whose dismissal prompted the first strike at the shipyard.*
Opposite top: *The negotiations. Strike leader Lech Walesa confronts Deputy Premier Mieczyslaw Jagielski and, on his right, Tadeusz Fiszbach, the Communist Party Leader in Gdansk.*
Opposite bottom: *Walesa, sitting between Jagielski and Fiszbach signs the Gdansk Agreement, 31 August 1980.*

Lech Walesa

Top: *Facing the crowds outside the shipyard gates after signing the Agreement.*
Bottom: *With Anna Walentynowicz at the first national meeting of the free trade union Solidarity in Gdansk in September 1980.*
Opposite: *Carried in triumph by shipyard workers.*

Top: *Stanislaw Kania became First Secretary of the Polish Communist Party on the night of 5/6 September 1980, after it was announced that Edward Gierek was seriously ill in hospital after a 'malfunctioning of the heart'.*
Bottom: *President Brezhnev faces Deputy Premier Jagielski in Kremlin talks which brought promises of Soviet economic and financial aid, 11 September 1980.*

Top: *A hero's welcome for Walesa in Warsaw, where he applied at the District Court for the legal registration of the Solidarity trade union, 24 September 1980.*
Bottom: *Stefan Bratkowski, elected Chairman of the Polish Journalists' Association, October 1980, and expelled from the Communist Party a year later.*

Politburo members.
Top left: *Tadeusz Grabski*. Top right: *Stefan Olszowski*. Bottom left: *Kazimierz Barcikowski*. Bottom right: *Mieczyslaw Moczar*.

abuse of the right to strike'. But while those talks were in progress, Warsaw television confided that it had received scores of telephone calls from viewers complaining that the reports on the first meeting between Pinkowski and Walesa had been too brief and unrevealing. In the avalanche of industrial disputes and negotiations, the people wanted desperately to know what was happening and were not getting the information they needed. Solidarity itself was divided, as Gdansk Radio had reported, over what should be given priority in its talks with the Government. One of the biggest grievances was lack of access to the news and information media and an opportunity to present the union's case as a counterbalance to what was seen as one-sided reporting by the Government.

Divisions in Solidarity and Party
The existence of more fundamental differences inside Solidarity was reported at this time by a Hungarian correspondent on Budapest Radio. Szabolcs Szilyagi suggested that 'extremist elements' were more influential in the Warsaw region and were largely responsible for the tug-of-war over Saturday working. At the same time there was growing evidence that the Party and the Government were facing divisions over their long-term plans. Oddly enough, that same Hungarian correspondent provided one of the first hints of this on Budapest Radio when he interviewed a Polish journalist who wondered whether Poland's political leadership had the courage to press on with economic reform in the face of resistance from those who would lose by it, the members of the central administrative apparatus.

Ideas for the reform were presented at a gathering of Party chiefs from the country's largest enterprises by Tadeusz Grabski, a Politburo member and Central Committee Secretary.

Under the new system, the enterprise becomes the basic, independent economic unit . . . It must operate on the basis of cost accounting and face the consequences of its activities, while observing worker self-government. It means the right of the work force to decide independently on all essential matters as regards the functioning of the enterprise, starting with the organisation of production and ending with staff policy, pay policy and the distribution of earnings.

At first glance, that brief outline of the suggested reform offered a considerable advance on anything permitted in Poland ever before. And it is interesting to read how Mr Grabski, later to be dubbed a political hardliner, warned against opposition to the reform from those whom it would inevitably affect. 'It is necessary to embark on activities to overcome all sorts of prejudice regarding reform. This may take the form of a natural shying away from anything new. It may also take the form of aversion, since the reform changes functional and personnel structures.' Some people, in fact, would have to work differently, sharing authority. Some would lose their jobs.

Addressing that same meeting, another leading member of the Politburo, Kazimierz Barcikowski, said that 'new men, previously unnoticed', were emerging as the Party rid itself of 'superficiality and bureaucratism, moral and ethical misdemeanours'. But he revealed for the first time that 'this sound trend' in Party work was accompanied by extremism.

On the one hand, there is the conservative current, which stems from fear of the changes taking place, fear of the unknown . . . We must also understand that attacks on the Party encourage these fears and favour those who argue against deeper changes in Party policy . . . On the other hand, there is the negative current, supporters of which disparage everything the Party has achieved so far and capitulate in the face of attacks on the Party and the immutable principles of its activity, mainly the principle of democratic centralism . . . The main method of overcoming divergencies should be ideological and political debate . . . But should trends emerge which threaten the unity of Party activity and its ideological and political cohesion, political and organisational steps must be taken to protect the Party from this danger.

The inescapable implication is that, in spite of its much advertised purge of discredited officials, the Party leadership was aware of the possible need to go on purging.

Mr Kania himself addressed the meeting as well, and in a remark that returned the discussion to more immediate practical problems he repeated that there could never be diarchy, or two separate forms of government, in the Polish State. He was referring to the challenge from Solidarity and the continuing spate of industrial and political unrest. But that unrest was all the more difficult to handle because of the natural fears of change among the authorities, especially at the central levels of administration. Those fears, if we are to follow Barcikowski's line of thinking, were heightened by Solidarity activity and prompted attitudes which in turn only encouraged more defiant action on the part of the new unions. It was significant, surely, that even the old industrial trade unions, at a meeting on 21 January, criticised the Government for mishandling the presentation of its ideas on shortening the working week.

The strikes, meanwhile, went on. On Thursday 22 January there were warning strikes in Gdansk, Gdynia and Sopot as well as in Bydgoszcz. On the Friday printers went on strike in Szczecin and prevented the publication of two newspapers. In Warsaw *Zycie Warszawy* failed to appear when printers downed tools along with workers in several factories. The reasons for the strikes varied. In Jelenia Gora province transport workers struck for four hours because there had been no agreement in talks between Solidarity leaders and a Government commission sent to check accusations against past and present members of the local administration. There were also demands for the handing over to the Health Service of a new rest home of the Party Central Committee and a sanatorium being built for the Ministry of Internal Affairs.

On Saturday 24 January millions again stayed away from work in an act of defiance which the Politburo was to admit was worse in some respects than that of two weeks earlier. Again the authorities claimed that more than sixty per cent of the workers had turned up at their jobs, but the Government had suffered another reverse which it had tried desperately to avoid. On the Friday night Warsaw Radio had broadcast a complete list of Government–union negotiations from the previous September to that very day as 'proof that the Government wants to solve all disputes through negotiation'.

More strikes were reported in the next few days in Lodz, Bialystok and the areas of Katowice and Bielsko Biala in the south. The army paper, *Zolnierz Wolnosci*, accused Solidarity of intimidation, aggression and psychological terror.

'Strategy of permanent terror'
Poland's allies were not too happy either. In Moscow the writers' weekly, *Literaturnaya Gazeta*, said that 'the hissing foam of anti-socialism in Poland' was 'music to the ears of the strategists of rolling back Communism'. It was amazing,

it suggested, that there should still be people so naive as to fail to understand 'where the Poles are being called by the sweet-voiced sirens of non-class freedom, or what is threatened by the strategy of permanent chaos, not only for Poland but also for peace and stability in Europe'. In Prague the newspaper *Rude Pravo* said that Marxism-Leninism required 'the dissolution of organisations which have become a base for counter-revolutionary elements'. And in East Berlin, East German Radio reproduced readers' letters said to have been printed in *Trybuna Ludu*.

Nowadays [one of them said] anyone who wants to strike does so when and how he wants. There are occupation strikes, token strikes and general strikes. Even workers in capitalist countries do not have such a choice. Some people think that strikes are better than Christmas because you do not have to go to church or to work and you get paid as if you were on holiday. Young people even say that a 'disco circus' like this is necessary from time to time.

In fact, the strikes were not as amusing as that bitter comment may have suggested. And not everyone, even on the so-called official radio, believed that it was all the fault of the strikers. Jacek Kalabinski called for independent arbitration.

Most people are convinced that the Government is simply unable to talk effectively on such issues as free Saturdays and many other questions, either with the trade unions or with the community. It cannot shake off its old habits, dating from the time when everything was settled by picking up the official phone and the community obediently listened to marathon speeches and pretended that it had been convinced. Today the situation has altered radically. Even the marathon litany of Government negotiations published last week convinces only a few people, since nothing has been achieved as regards the really important issues. The trouble is that although the Government has its arguments and keeps on repeating them, many people do not want to listen.

So the catalogue of strikes on a variety of issues went on growing. In the province of Bielsko Biala in the south, Solidarity proclaimed a general strike, with sit-ins at more than a hundred enterprises demanding that complaints against provincial officials be examined by the authorities. Some ninety plants came to a standstill for four hours in Bialystok province, where the dispute was over censorship. In the Katowice area there was a four-hour strike at some 120 enterprises. In Lodz almost all major enterprises stopped work for three hours and the continuing university sit-in spread to high schools. In Jelenia Gora province, Solidarity's demands received the backing of local officials of the Democratic Party who were normally just ciphers.

On 28 January Solidarity's National Commission, meeting in Gdansk, decided on a one-hour general strike on 3 February on a collection of issues: work-free Saturdays, access to the mass media, censorship, and the right of private farmers to set up a union of their own. Having done that, the Commission instructed union branches to cease all regional and local strikes immediately. In a way, this was a typical Solidarity move: by calling for the general strike, it was emphasising that it had just cause for industrial action; by appealing – in vain, as it turned out – for an end to local strikes, it was trying to take hold of the situation, which seemed to be getting rapidly out of hand, and at the same time being conciliatory.

The move was not before time. Warsaw Radio reported strikes that day and the next in the provinces of Rzeszow – which Lech Walesa was visiting – Przemysl, Bielsko Biala, Lublin, Wloclawek, Gorzow Wielkopolski, Wroclaw, Walbrzych and Jelenia Gora.

Warsaw television broadcast an 'editorial commentary' asking whether this was 'a creeping political revolt for which any excuse is good enough' and noted that although Solidarity had said it would not become a political party, 'some of the demands put forward by local Solidarity chapters have been typical acts of an opposition political party'.

Government warning

On Thursday 29 January the Government issued a statement which offered to continue talks but promised action if necessary to maintain law and order. It spoke of chaos and anarchy entering the life of the State, and said forces hostile to the socialist system were becoming more active. It went on:

In the face of the persisting wave of strikes and in spite of Government efforts, in spite also of the call by the National Consultative Commission of Solidarity on 28 January, the Council of Ministers of the Polish People's Republic states that, on the basis of its constitutional power, it is obliged to ensure law, order and discipline and to provide normal conditions for the normal life of citizens. Bearing this in mind, the Council of Ministers, should this state of affairs persist, will have to take the necessary decisions to assist the

117

normal functioning of works and enterprises in accordance with the best interests of the community.

It is of some importance here to note that according to the statement strikes were continuing in spite of Government efforts and in spite of the Solidarity appeal of 28 January, which could only mean the appeal for an immediate end to local strikes. This point, in an admittedly complex sentence, was made crystal clear even in the Russian version provided by Poland's official news agency. So it was surprising that Moscow Radio and TASS got it wrong. Either by mistranslation or by design, the Soviet version read as follows: 'In view of the wave of strikes, which is continuing in spite of the Government's efforts, and in view also of Solidarity's calls for strikes, the Council of Ministers states . . .'

It did seem that the Soviet media were unable to bring themselves to report anything to the credit of Solidarity. If that was the case, it was still remarkable that Moscow should feel free to adapt to its own purposes the words of a fraternal government, even if the doctored version fitted in more comfortably with the current line from Moscow Radio.

Urged on by the extreme right-wing group KOR and its leaders, the trade union association Solidarity is veering to the right . . . Resorting to threats of blackmail, provocations and now, not infrequently, to physical violence, while stepping up anarchy in the country, the leaders and extremist elements of Solidarity are making increasingly arrogant political demands, thereby putting the union in the position of a political opposition to the Polish Communist Party and Government.

Catholic fifth column
In Czechoslovakia Prague Radio, as usual, spread the blame more personally and more widely.

For Walesa and others, the agreements reached on the coast are not enough. They look on them not as a basis for solving Poland's enormous problems but as a platform from which to attack the system and the principles of socialist construction . . . It is no accident that one can pinpoint the exact date when these forces became active – the day Lech Walesa returned from Rome, where he had consultations with the Pope and other Vatican officials . . . It is clear that the Vatican gave Walesa its instructions and that the Catholic fifth column in Poland is to help the leader of the so-called new trade unions implement these directives.

118

Walesa, in fact, seemed to be working for a settlement. He had talks with Prime Minister Pinkowski for twelve hours and emerged with a form of agreement on shorter working hours and Solidarity's access to the media.

According to a communiqué broadcast by Warsaw Radio, the two sides agreed that a 40-hour week was a desirable target. Both sides would work out a timetable in 1981 for its eventual introduction. In the meantime, and for the rest of 1981, a general principle of three consecutive work-free Saturdays followed by a fourth working Saturday would be put into operation. This amounted, the communiqué said, to the acceptance of a 42-hour week, a neat compromise between the $42\frac{1}{2}$ suggested by the Government and the $41\frac{1}{2}$ proposed by Solidarity. Employees who had not worked on 10 and 24 January would have two work-free Saturdays fewer.

As for the media, the communiqué said that it had been agreed that radio and television would henceforth broadcast reports on resolutions and statements by Solidarity's National Commission, as approved by the union's press spokesman. Local media would do the same for local Solidarity statements. Moreover space would be made in trade union broadcasts for programmes made by Solidarity.

The agreement on access to the media was important but had yet to be tested in practice. That on the shorter working week was the first in which Solidarity had not clearly won the better deal. In an interview later, Lech Walesa said that many of the problems should have been sorted out much earlier. 'We are beginning to learn and to negotiate. If everything goes in this direction, we shall never need to strike.' In Gdansk the local Solidarity branch – Walesa's own – was not entirely pleased with the compromise. According to Warsaw Radio opinions were divided. It was stressed that the Solidarity delegation had departed from its previous stance on many points 'for the good of the country' and as a result members were only partially satisfied.

Solidarity's National Consultative Commission, meeting in Warsaw, also put on record that the results of the talks with the Government fell far behind expectations but decided to accept them 'as the initial stage of the struggle for the union's demands'. The Commission made a point of emphasising that it gave its full backing to private farmers in their efforts to set up a Rural Solidarity. A seemingly chastened

Lech Walesa told television that the union would go on using the strike weapon when necessary and that the continuing strikes in Bielsko Biala and Jelenia Gora were local issues and would have to be treated as such.

Other stikes were continuing in Lodz, in Rzeszow and in Walbrzych province, where eleven farmers had started a hunger strike in the church of St Joseph in Swidnica in support of Rural Solidarity. So no one was satisfied yet, in spite of the agreement on working hours.

As February began, East German Radio claimed that the situation had deteriorated disastrously. 'The leaders of Solidarity are deliberately provoking chaos and anarchy every day,' it declared. 'In league with the ringleaders of the anti-socialist organisation, KOR, these people are flying the colours of counter-revolution.'

Czechoslovak television reported the agreement between Solidarity and the Government but doubted whether it would do any good.

Who can still believe that Walesa's trade unions will really honour their commitments. After all, occupation strikes are still continuing in many places; many administrative buildings remain occupied; slogans are appearing vilifying honest people, accusing them of conservatism and obstructing renewal, as they say in Poland nowadays. But this renewal is a renewal of terror, moral terror, and this has become the fundamental way of influencing life in that country.

But for Poland's Communist leaders the situation could not be so simple. They knew that many Party members belonged to Solidarity. They had admitted that there were conservative extremists inside the Party. Mr Kania, addressing the Commission preparing for the ninth Party Congress, said that Solidarity was definitely being steered in the direction of an opposition party. But as regards contacts with Solidarity, he said, 'we should never ever lose patience'.

Ending the strikes
Patience was not the only quality needed. A clear head was also required to keep track of developments in what was undoubtedly the worst industrial crisis since August 1980. And it took the combined efforts of a whole series of ministers and their deputies, plus Lech Walesa and even, in one case, the good offices of the Roman Catholic Church, to bring it, rather messily, to an end.

The general strike in Bielsko Biala province ended on 6 February after more than ten days. Agreement was reached in the presence of Bishop Bronislaw Dabrowski, Secretary to the Polish Episcopate, after Lech Walesa had argued Solidarity's case against allegedly corrupt officials, and the Minister for Administration, Mr Jozef Kepa, had brought Warsaw's agreement to the replacement of the Provincial Governor and two of his deputies.

In Jelenia Gora the strike came to an end after some twenty days when the Government agreed to hand the newly-built Central Committee rest home over to the Health Service and promised to examine allegations against local officials. The agreement was reached as the Party's Central Committee was again in plenary session. The hunger strike in Swidnica petered out at the same time after all those taking part had been taken to hospital.

On the issue of Rural Solidarity the Government remained firm and the Supreme Court upheld the decision of the lower court that it could not be registered as a trade union. But the issue was far from settled. The Polish bishops, in a statement broadcast by Vatican Radio a day later, insisted that in the country's present situation nothing could be achieved by 'diktat or persistent propaganda'. Their statement went on:

The provision of food for the nation is the basic problem today. The faulty agrarian policy which was pursued for many decades has led to the danger of hunger in our land. The Church has been warning of this danger for a long time. The process of righting the damage done to the Polish countryside will be a lengthy one . . . In the first place, the farmers must be sure that they own the land they till. This must be guaranteed. And their right to free professional affiliation must be recognised. The right of farmers to be free to set up their own federations, according to their will and needs and irrespective of existing federations, is a natural right.

Cardinal Wyszynski, in a sermon in Gniezno which was read out later in the month during the broadcast Sunday mass, put it even more plainly. 'If industrial workers have the right to form associations, then this right must also be granted to workers on the land. In fact, this right does not have to be granted. It simply exists.'

The student strike in Lodz lasted almost thirty days in all and involved many thousands of students who put forward a

121

bewildering series of demands, according to the Government, including some of a political nature. The students emerged with a new independent union, along the lines of Solidarity. A farmers' strike in Rzeszow was the last to finish, on 19 February, with agreement on ending preferential treatment for state farms and a programme for the supply of machinery and building materials for private farming.

A new Prime Minister

None of these strikes achieved everything demanded. Everyone involved in the gruelling confrontation came out of it bruised and tired, and none more so than the Government itself. So there was no great surprise when the Eighth Plenary Session of the Communist Party Central Committee, meeting on 9 February, was told that Prime Minister Pinkowski had resigned and that Army General Wojciech Jaruzelski, Defence Minister and a Member of the Politburo, was being proposed as his successor. Not surprisingly, the news prompted speculation that the authorities had finally concluded that tough action and possibly the use of force under a strong, military man was the only way to end the continuing crisis. In fact, it was far too early to say, though the speeches from Party leaders at the Plenum did suggest a switch to much stronger words at least.

Tadeusz Grabski, presenting the Politburo report, claimed that every day since the registration of Solidarity had brought proof that its leaders and advisers wanted to impose clearly political aims. The union now had to decide which way it was going. Grabski also said that attempts to set up a Rural Solidarity sought to turn the countryside into 'an area of acute political struggle'.

Kazimierz Barcikowski condemned what he called a 'strike terror' with workers allegedly forced to down tools. But he did admit that unless the purge of the Party, which had already led to the expulsion of more than 2000 members, was speeded up and carried out consistently, there would always be pretexts for stirring up tension, as in Bielsko Biala. Solidarity, he said, had behaved very irresponsibly but 'our comrades in Bielsko' were also to blame for minimising the problems and would face the consequences. A few days later the province's First Secretary resigned.

Mr Kania, in a closing speech, said quite clearly that no

Party members should take part in strikes of a political character.

A struggle for power is in progress [he said]. Attempts are being made to weaken the position of our Party and to diminish its role in the state and in society . . . We must nip in the bud all counter-revolutionary trends or attempts. This is not a quiet time. It is a time of crisis. It is not a time of stabilisation. It is a time of struggle. At such a time, the Party must gather all its forces and work with all its strength to calm down emotions, oppose enemies of socialism and create order in public and economic life.

The authorities, meanwhile, were investigating recognised 'enemies of socialism'. According to the office of the General Prosecutor, it had been established that KPN whose leader, Leszek Moczulski, was under arrest wanted to weaken the Polish State and break its alliances with the Soviet Union. It was allegedly receiving support from abroad and had created conspiratorial para-military structures to do so. A separate investigation was said to have found that the Committee for Social Self-Defence, KSS-KOR, was engaged in anti-State activity against Poland's constitutional system and its allies. KOR was also said to be receiving assistance from 'centres of political subversion' abroad.

General Jaruzelski's appointment as Prime Minister was approved by the Sejm on 11 February. He was introduced to the House by Mr Kania as the best man for the job 'when dark, threatening clouds are gathering over Poland'. But he presented him not so much as a strong man liable to take tough action, but as someone enjoying great authority and capable of combining 'State discipline in opposing anarchy and an open mind towards democratic tendencies'. Mr Kania obviously wanted the new Prime Minister not to supervise a crackdown but to save the policy of renewal.

Jaruzelski did seem to be the man for the job. He did not fit the usually accepted image of a Communist Defence Minister, the position he had held since 1968 and was to retain. He looked quite small and slim; he wore dark glasses and gave the impression of being both modest and ascetic. But at fifty-eight he was the longest-serving member of the Party Politburo and his qualifications were impeccable. Quite apart from the fact that he was said to have been educated at the Catholic Marian College near Warsaw, the official records show that in 1943 he joined the Polish Armed Forces in the

Soviet Union and took part in his country's liberation. By 1960 he was Chief of the Polish Army's main Political Directorate. He joined the Politburo in 1971.

Throughout the crisis in Poland, now six months old, General Jaruzelski had remained in the background. It was his good fortune to make his first major national speech in the courteous surroundings of a revitalised and more democratic Sejm. It was an auspicious moment for another reason. For the first time, the whole proceedings of the session were broadcast live on radio – in itself a political achievement, for the words of every speaker were available uncensored to anyone who wanted to listen.

Call for 'ninety peaceful days'

The General created a good impression from the start. 'I am a soldier,' he said, 'so every job, every duty entrusted to me I regard as a service, a service to the nation and to socialist Poland.' As for the task he faced, the new Prime Minister was very firm but also understanding and spoke of hope as well as danger:

The months that have elapsed since the signing of the well-known agreements have yielded many positive changes which give rise to good hopes. They have also yielded serious anxieties. The expected stabilisation has not materialised . . . Both the Government and the trade unions are learning the difficult art of negotiation . . . Mistakes and oversights are occurring. These are unavoidable in the widening field of socialist democracy that has not yet been fully reconnoitred . . . But the sources of the current tensions and conflicts do not lie here . . . Evil, hostile political forces are pursuing activities aimed against socialism, our alliances, our economic stabilisation . . . Working men, millions of whom have found themselves in the new unions for purely union and social aspirations, should not put up with this . . . They should dissociate themselves from political manipulators . . . For over thirty-seven years socialism has created the structure of our national and state life. Attempts to destabilise it mean a weakening of the nation, exposing it to great dangers.

Today the nation faces the greatest danger. Should this destructive process continue, we will be facing the danger not only of economic ruin but of the break-up of social bonds and finally the most fratricidal conflict . . . I state officially that the Government will act honestly and consistently for socialist renewal . . . The arm of the authorities remains immutably, sincerely and amicably stretched out to all men of patriotic good will. But I state with equal determination that the Government has the constitutional duty to defend the values of our state system, to bar the way to those people and processes striving to turn back the wheel of history and achieve a counter-revolution. The gradual process of undermining the stability of the country's life must be arrested . . . To resist this process is not just the business of the authorities, it is also the patriotic duty of all forces of prudence and responsibility, including the millions of members and activists of Solidarity, who support the constitution and believe in the precepts of the socialist system.

It may well be that fewer Solidarity members than the General imagined actually believed in the socialist system to which he referred. But his speech had the virtue of giving a strong impression of respect for his audience and a calm statement of facts. In January industrial output had fallen by ten per cent, productivity by seven per cent and the wage bill had gone up by nineteen per cent compared with the previous year. The country was on a downward slope and the Government could not do its job effectively with the pistol of strikes at its head.

For this reason [he continued] I appeal from this lofty tribune to the trade unions, to all working people to cease all strike action. I appeal for three months of hard work, for ninety peaceful days. We want to use that time to put the basic issues of our economy in order, to take stock, to tackle the most urgent social problems . . . We want to make this time a period for broad social dialogue in a defused atmosphere.

In a number of ministerial changes, General Jaruzelski appointed Mieczyslaw Rakowski, Chief Editor of *Polityka*, as a Deputy Prime Minister and head of a special commission for contacts with the trade unions. The omens were good. In his own speech to the Sejm, Rakowski said that he, like many Poles, linked his hopes for a return to normal working and a better tomorrow with Solidarity. 'For various reasons, Solidarity is creating many anxieties and fears. Yet without Solidarity one cannot imagine the creation in Poland of a system of partnership. That system has to be created.'

The National Commission of Solidarity was in session in Gdansk during the Prime Minister's speech. It did not respond directly to his call for a moratorium on strikes, but in a decision reported the next day it criticised the authorities' record in implementing the August agreements, and at the same time expressed its disapproval of uncoordinated and hastily arranged strikes which, it said, endangered social peace and the union's unity. A few days later, in an interview

125

with *Zycie Warszawy*, a Solidarity spokesman said that the union did not want to set itself up as a second power centre. It wanted to be a recognised and respected social partner. The Prime Minister's speech, he said, gave grounds for believing that social calm could be maintained – in other words, that Solidarity and the new government could get on. That was a turning point of sorts. On 15 February Stanislaw Kania flew to Prague for one day of talks with the Czechoslovak Party leader, Gustav Husak, in which, according to the communiqué, they confirmed their 'identity of views on all basic questions'. On 17 February Kania met the East German leader, Erich Honecker, near Berlin. Once again there was said to have been agreement on all fundamental issues.

Meetings in Moscow

On 22 February Mr Kania arrived in Moscow for the twenty-sixth Congress of the Soviet Communist Party, along with General Jaruzelski, Andrzej Zabinski, the Katowice Party Secretary who was also a member of the Politburo, and Emil Wojtaszek, a candidate member of the Politburo and former Foreign Minister. There, in the Kremlin Palace of Congresses, they heard President Brezhnev's considered view on the situation in Poland.

Our class adversaries learn from their defeats. They act against us with increasing refinement and insidiousness. And wherever mistakes and miscalculations in internal policy are added to the subversive activity of imperialism, the soil is created for increased activity by elements hostile to socialism.

This is what has happened in fraternal Poland, where the opponents of socialism, with the support of outside forces, are endeavouring, by creating anarchy, to turn events onto a counter-revolutionary course. Important political support was given to Poland last December at the meeting of leaders of the Warsaw Pact countries in Moscow. That meeting showed clearly that Polish Communists, the Polish working class, the working people of that country, can firmly rely on their friends and allies. We will stand up for socialist Poland, fraternal Poland and will not leave her in the lurch.

The history of world socialism knows all kinds of trials . . . But Communists have always boldly confronted the attacks of their adversary and won through. That is how it was and how it will be. And let not one have any doubt as to our common determination to secure our interests and to defend the socialist gains of the people.

Mr Brezhnev's words, though definitely strong on paper,

were slightly anodyne. The congress, of course, was no place for warnings to fellow comrades from fraternal countries, but one felt that such words had been heard before in less critical situations, that there was far more to be said than that.

In the event there was. Mr Kania made a dutiful speech to the congress assuring all comrades that counter-revolution would fail in Poland, and then, surprisingly, he went home before the congress ended. But when the congress was over he returned to Moscow to join his delegation for a meeting with exactly the same team of Soviet leaders that had taken part in the Warsaw Pact summit meeting in December: Brezhnev, Andropov, Gromyko, Suslov, Tikhonov, Ustinov and Rusakov. The communiqué on those talks made it clear that the pressure was on.

The participants in the talks noted that imperialism and internal reaction were counting on the economic and political crisis in Poland bringing a change in the balance of forces in the world and on the weakening of the socialist community, the international Communist movement and the whole liberation movement. This makes it especially pressing to give a firm and resolute rebuff to such dangerous attempts. The socialist community is indissoluble. Its defence is the concern not only of each State but also of the whole socialist coalition.

Here, for the first time, the two sides had invoked the argument used by Moscow to justify the Warsaw Pact invasion of Czechoslovakia in 1968, the so-called Brezhnev Doctrine, which claimed that a direct threat to socialism in one member of the Soviet bloc was a threat to all members and therefore the business of all of them. But that was not all. According to the communiqué the Poles pledged steadfast efforts to overcome anarchy and disarray and to strengthen the socialist system. The Soviet leaders had more to say:

The conviction was expressed that Polish Communists have the possibilities and the forces to turn the course of events and remove the dangers hanging over the socialist gains of the Polish people. Soviet people believe that Poland has been and will continue to be a reliable link in the socialist community, as the Polish leaders confirmed once again at the meeting.

That paragraph caused quite a stir, especially in Poland where it was translated in such a way as to suggest that Moscow was telling the Poles to 'reverse the course of events'.

127

Maybe Mr Brezhnev had that in mind. But to be strictly correct, the communiqué was simply using words that the Soviet leader had used in his speech to the congress when he said that enemies of socialism were trying to 'turn events on to a counter-revolutionary course'. Apart from the semantics, though, this was the strongest direct warning to the Polish leadership so far. In effect the Soviet leaders were telling their Polish colleagues this: You know that we will help you out if necessary. You have agreed that it is our business as well as yours. You say you can handle it yourself. You have the means and the opportunity to put things back on the right track. Now it is up to you to do it, as you have promised.

That at any rate was one way of reading it. There were many reasons for believing that the Soviet leaders did not want to intervene directly in Poland. But they could not let the situation slide. The so-called Brezhnev Doctrine was not just an excuse for invading allied countries. It also imposed responsibilities. And if Poland went irreparably wrong, someone would probably have to answer for it in Moscow.

8. BYDGOSZCZ CRISIS

Poland has a reputation for its jokes, and rightly. Frequently self-critical, cynical and highly political, they leave you feeling that they contain a grain of truth about attitudes if not about facts. One old one, but rather typical, suggested that a Polish Communist leader who died in Moscow had committed suicide. Hence his last words: Don't shoot, comrades.

At the beginning of March, after two months of virtually unrelieved industrial and political unrest, Warsaw Radio itself felt the need of a joke to convey the mood of the moment. 'At a meeting at a factory, a proposal is put forward: From now on we will work only on Tuesdays. Whereupon someone in the hall asks: Do you mean every Tuesday?'

The joke perhaps merits only a wry smile but it is a reminder that the best judgements about Polish affairs tend to be made by Poles themselves. And Solidarity, for all its popularity, was not entirely innocent and undeserving of criticism even in the view of observers who were not for ever looking for 'anti-socialist elements' under the bed. The local radio in Lodz broadcast a very revealing piece by a commentator named Urszula Mikolajczyk, who voiced her gratitude to the strikers of the Baltic Coast.

Thanks to the shipbuilders, all of us, journalists included, can speak the truth. Not the whole truth, perhaps. But our lips are no longer tightly sealed. I am grateful to the people of the coast that I don't have to listen to rapturous speeches about everyday life that have nothing in common with everyday life . . . that I don't have to feel humiliated and helpless when somebody important prattles on and I have to listen to it and reward it with spontaneous applause. I am grateful that I can think out loud, that I am starting to be a subject rather than an object. For that I'm grateful to the people of the coast and respect them . . . Why should I be grateful and respectful to a gentleman colleague of mine who has been sitting in the next room for years, an average colleague who has never done anything special for people? But now this gentleman shouts loudly. He is belligerent. He wants to decide everything . . . He is always right. He wants to be treated like a sacred cow . . . Why should I treat this gentleman with respect and special attention? Because he wears the badge of Solidarity? . . . Let us be sensible. Let us not allow the places vacated by the infallible to be taken over by others who are also infallible. Let us protest against all sacred cows . . . let one sacred thing remain – neither the badge of the Party nor of Solidarity, but man's respect for man, one's good name and dignity.

Places were certainly being vacated. Control commissions of the Communist Party in the provinces were reported to be pressing ahead with the task of getting rid of people who had been more than just fallible. In January in Lublin province alone some 200 cases involving members of the Party apparatus, directors of industrial enterprises and local administrators, had been referred for investigation over charges of abuse of power. Out of all those expelled from the Party in general – nearly 2500 in the second half of 1980 – the largest number were for theft and bribery. Nearly 300 were thrown out, according to official reports, for drunkenness and hooliganism. These charges were not too surprising at a time when the Government was launching an official campaign against alcoholism in a nation said to have 700,000 alcoholics and four million people who simply drank too much. During one broadcast Sunday mass prayers were said 'for the sobriety of the nation'. But the announcement of the campaign brought the expectation of higher prices and drink shops throughout the country were besieged by pre-budget crowds. Those in Warsaw sold more than 100,000 litres every day.

Whatever may have been happening in the great confrontations between Solidarity and the Government, people still had to fend for themselves in the search for food and drink. Sometimes it brought bitter comment. A housewife told Warsaw Radio that she had to do her shopping before going to work, which meant getting up at five.

I'm no longer a mother to my family [she said], I'm simply a provider. Between 1 and 21 January, I succeeded in buying only three packets of butter. I don't even dream about margarine or oil . . . So please don't talk in your programmes about women's social achievements because in our country women have achieved nothing but torment.

The good thing was that people could now say what they

thought with more chance than ever before of being listened to. And more information was coming down from the top. On the sore topic of butter, for example, the Finance Minister, Marian Krzak, revealed on Warsaw Radio that sixty per cent of the country's butter supplies was not only bought in the West but bought with money borrowed from the West. Poland, he said, had been borrowing some 3500 million dollars a year to buy food.

The economic argument against industrial unrest was overwhelming. Not surprisingly the official media – press, radio and television – were anxious to preach the virtues of General Jaruzelski's appeal for ninety days of peace and hard work. They wanted it to work. On 5 March Warsaw Radio was claiming that 'common sense is beginning to prevail', that a 'new climate is emerging in relations between the authorities and the community'. It commented with evident pleasure on the recent surprise visits made by 'the Premier-General' to workers' flats and to shops; these were something unheard of in Poland, 'a symbol of an authority that is strong but at the same time familiar'. The radio even suggested that because of the understanding with which General Jaruzelski's appeal for a moratorium was being received, 'subversive radio stations, like Radio Free Europe and the Polish service of the BBC' were changing their 'propaganda'. After presenting the Polish Communist Party and Government as a 'narrow elite, alienated from society' and the new trade union movement as 'the representative of the national and working class opposition' to it, these radios had decided to 'replace the image of a quarrelling society with that of a disintegrating Party'.

Warsaw Radio proved wrong on all its claims. On the day before that broadcast, the regional leadership of Solidarity in Lodz proclaimed a strike alert throughout the province to support demands for the reinstatement of five of their members who had lost their jobs at an Interior Ministry hospital. A Commission of Appeal had said they should have their jobs back, but they had not been reinstated. Solidarity said that Deputy Premier Rakowski had refused to have talks. Deputy Premier Jagielski had failed to reply to a telexed message. On 11 March, the day after a one-hour warning strike, the men were reinstated. That may seem to have been but a minor disturbance to the general calm, but Jacek

Kalabinski took it seriously on Warsaw Radio and suggested it had been caused by the fact that 'many officials forget that things have changed in this country, that one cannot run things as before'. In a period of calm, he said, they see an opportunity to recover lost ground.

As for General Jaruzelski's unannounced visits, *Zycie Warszawy* published a letter from a reader in the working-class district of Wola pointing out that on the day the Prime Minister went there the shops were offering 'unusually generous quantities' of goods which were normally in short supply. The Roman Catholic daily paper, *Slowo Powszechne*, was reminded of the days when cattle and pigs were shipped to State farms that Edward Gierek was due to visit, and freshly cut carnations were stuck into the ground he was to walk on. General Jaruzelski, the paper was sure, wanted to end such immoral practices but it seemed that not all his staff understood this.

'Revisionist concepts' and 'horizontal structures'

On the final point of the 'disintegrating Party' there were definite signs that Party unity was under severe strain and the cracks were beginning to show. Stefan Olszowski, one of the undoubted strong men of the Politburo, told *Trybuna Ludu* at the end of February that some of the proposals put forward for the Party's new programme would weaken it ideologically. He also claimed that people alien to the Party were trying to tell it what reforms to introduce, 'reaching for the old revisionist concepts and slogans which were suggested to the Party in 1956, 1968 and later'. Olszowski said yes to reforms, but no to 'reformism'.

What Olszowski was saying in the clearest terms yet was that the discussion currently going on inside the Communist Party and outside it had revealed a trend towards turning the Party into something like a social democratic organisation. This was the result, presumably, of all the free debate and discussion sanctioned by the Party leadership in the interests of 'socialist renewal', a new feature of political life generally looked on with favour, as Warsaw Radio reported:

One feature of the preparations for the Ninth PZPR Congress which inspires optimism is the extensive participation of all Poles in the discussion of the programme for overcoming the crisis. In the Party itself there has been a strengthening in recent months of what are known as horizontal links between different organisations. This has been expressed in the creation of platforms for general discussion and the exchange of opinions between members of the Party from various establishments. Discussion clubs and circles are being formed.

Such groups already existed, said the radio, in Szczecin, Warsaw, Cracow, Gdansk, Wrocław, Poznan, Lodz, Torun and Zielona Gora, where a 'discussion forum' was open to people of 'various world views'.

This marked the advent in the Party of the so-called 'horizontal structures'. The term meant simply that, whereas in a strictly orthodox Soviet-type Party policy was formulated after vertical consultation between the leadership at the top of the pyramid and the primary, grass-roots organisations at the bottom, policy discussions were now taking place horizontally between individual basic organisations without reference to the central leadership. Moreover, people outside the Party were also taking part.

It was the flood of proposals coming in from such discussions that had obviously alarmed Mr Olszowski and some of his Politburo colleagues. Olszowski was the man ultimately responsible for the mass media. One wondered whether he completely agreed with Jozef Klasa, his junior, who headed the Central Committee Department for Press, Radio and Television, when he said in a newspaper interview that in his personal view 'the Party press can admit any views provided we also have all the ammunition to argue the Party line'. Doubts were beginning to appear about the ability of the Party to withstand the tide of free debate.

The Party's own history – the skeletons in the cupboard – also added to the difficulties. On 7 March *Trybuna Ludu* suddenly warned that 'some people appear to want to exploit the anniversary of the events of March 1968 to revive old divisions and create new ones'. The anniversary was that of the student demonstrations which turned into riots when the police used violence. More than a thousand students were arrested. Several features of those disturbances were understandably unpleasant memories for the Polish authorities of March 1981. For one thing, the demonstrations had followed the banning of a performance of a classic by the poet Adam Mickiewicz in which uncomplimentary remarks about Russians were loudly applauded. For another, the riots had been used by the so-called Partisan wing of the Communist Party, which had earlier engineered a purge of Jewish Party officials, to seize on the fact that the students involved included the children of leading Communists of Jewish origin. One such student was Adam Michnik, later to become a leader of KOR. The leader of the 'Partisans' in 1968 was now in the Politburo, General Mieczyslaw Moczar.

In the event, two rival rallies were staged in Warsaw to mark the unhappy anniversary. One was organised by the Independent Union of Warsaw University Students, the other by a new organisation of dubious origin calling itself the Grunwald Patriotic Association. Warsaw Radio played both events down, but it did reveal quite a lot by reporting that the Grunwald rally took place outside the Ministry of Public Security and heard speakers recall 'the violation of law and order during the days of the personality cult' – the days, in fact, when Jewish Party officials were in charge of state security.

In subsequent weeks the Party leader, Mr Kania, stated quite clearly that there was no place in Poland for anti-semitism. General Moczar himself dismissed 'tendentious Western commentaries about an allegedly growing anti-Semitic wave' in Poland. 'We shall simply not let it happen.'

But Poland's allies were not against using the anniversary to make their political points. Prague television, for instance, showed considerable sympathy for the Grunwald Association by reporting that speakers at its rally – which was attended by Prague's correspondent – had 'warned the younger generation, above all students, and the working people of a danger which is now emerging'. It also noted with relish that speakers had not only recalled 'the treacherous activity of the Zionists who made a tragic contribution to the abuses of the 1950s', but had also mentioned Adam Michnik 'whose true name is Szechter'.

Moscow Radio had already told listeners in the Arab world that Zionists were directly involved in exacerbating the crisis in Poland. In what is certainly a good example of tailoring one's propaganda to suit the audience, the radio told its 'dear friends' that the Zionists, through such people as Jacek Kuron, Adam Michnik, Mojzesz Finkelsztein and others, had imposed their control on KOR.

'Some elements of destruction'

As March progressed, though, more evidence built up of argument inside the Polish Communist Party. *Trybuna Ludu* conceded that the transformations taking place inside the Party contained 'some elements of destruction', but it was optimistic about the rebirth of the Party which, it said, was starting at the bottom and moving upwards. Society, it said, tended to identify the Party with the top leadership rather than its three million members. It should not be surprising if the Party was identified with 'those who rule us' and with that part of the apparatus of power which was 'blamed for all the sins committed'.

Characteristically the Army paper, *Zolnierz Wolnosci*, was re-emphasising that it was the Party that guaranteed Poland's loyalty to its alliances. It found it difficult to comprehend 'voices heard in some places' revealing a lack of understanding of the 'unity of interests of the Soviet Union and Poland'. Compare that with an article in *Zycie Warszawy* by the leader of the Journalists' Association, Stefan Bratkowski. He claimed that young people in Poland, including those setting the tone in Solidarity, had grown up to see socialism as a screen for rampant bureaucracy, lying propaganda, economic chaos, Byzantine political behaviour and structural ossification. But Bratkowski's most startling remarks concerned the Soviet Union. 'Our attitudes to it oscillate between slogan-laden apology and either covert or overt anti-Sovietism. The range of extremes smacks of political schizophrenia,' he observed. But whether one liked it or not, Poland did lie in the Soviet sphere of security. Poland's alliance with the Soviet Union was not being questioned, but its own sovereign needs did require the preservation of Polish national identity, the right to build socialism in accordance with its traditions and with the support of the entire nation, and also the right to reforms to put the country back on its feet.

'It must be said openly,' Bratkowski added, 'that the political hawks would welcome the prospect of a Soviet intervention in Poland and would have nothing against provoking it, for they know that it would bring them immeasurable political gains.'

It was an astonishing claim to be made in what was, after all, the Government newspaper; but the events of the next few weeks were to provide some support for Bratkowski's view. He – and no doubt others too – were already on the look-out for a 'provocation'. The most likely form such a provocation would take would be an incident involving Solidarity.

Industrially, the situation was relatively calm. Even Moscow Radio reported promising signs of normalisation. But on 13 March *Zycie Warszawy* reported that a strike alert had started five days earlier in Radom, the city that had witnessed perhaps the most severe official crackdown on worker protests against food price rises in 1976. Solidarity was now demanding that the officials deemed responsible for what had gone wrong then should be replaced, and also that two buildings being erected for the Ministry of the Interior should be handed over for public use. General Jaruzelski had received the Solidarity demands just two days after he had had separate meetings with both Lech Walesa and the leader of the old industrial unions, Albin Szyszka, to discuss the restoration of normal working.

On 14 March the First Secretary of the Provincial Party Committee in Radom, Janusz Prokopiak, offered his resignation, and it was announced that General Jaruzelski had accepted the resignation of the Provincial Governor. Two days later Tadeusz Grabski of the Politburo was in Radom attending a session of the Provincial Party Committee. The meeting accepted the resignation of Janusz Prokopiak but went out of its way to stress with Grabski that Prokopiak was not a careerist and that charges that he had misused his position for personal gain had been proved to be unfounded. The same applied to the Provincial Governor and also to Colonel Marian Mozgawa, described now as the 'former' Provincial Police Chief.

Lech Walesa was in Radom that day. After discussions with local Solidarity leaders he told a public meeting that talks with the Government would be held the next day in Warsaw and that the warning strike announced for Wednesday 18 March had been called off. The strike alert itself would be called off once the talks with the Government began.

According to Warsaw Radio, Walesa told the meeting that the Government should be given a chance to govern.

With strikes we shall simply destroy ourselves. We must all stand together at present . . . The economic situation is quite catastrophic. Even bread coupons are being printed. We must hold out mentally and behave in such a way that coming generations will not curse us... Let's learn to sit down with Government representatives at the same table. Let's talk and discuss.

Bydgoszcz incident

Even as Walesa was speaking, a group of a hundred farmers were beginning a sit-in strike in the headquarters of the United Peasant Party in the town of Bydgoszcz. By so doing they set in train a series of events that were to bring Walesa to a very bitter confrontation at the negotiating table and to a crisis which was to threaten Solidarity and the nation and leave the Communist Party in open disarray.

The 'Bydgoszcz incident', as it came to be known, occurred on Thursday 19 March, the day after Warsaw Pact exercises code-named Soyuz-81 began on Polish territory, and the very same day that Stanislaw Kania chose to visit Budapest for a day of talks with his Hungarian counterpart, Janos Kadar. The incident took place on the premises of the Provincial People's Council in Bydgoszcz. The Council met there that morning to consider an agenda covering the nomination of a new Governor as well as the province's social and economic plan. It had been agreed that some Solidarity representative could attend to present their views on the farmers' dispute. Some supporters of Rural Solidarity were taking part in the sit-in nearby. The trouble began when the session was adjourned in the early afternoon to give councillors more time to study economic documents, without the Solidarity representatives getting a hearing. They stayed on in the council hall along with some forty-five councillors who were also surprised by the sudden closure of the session.

They remained in the hall, haggling and arguing, for many hours, until the police were called in. At 8.30 in the evening the Solidarity men were removed from the hall by force and three of them, including the local leader of the union, Jan Rulewski, ended up in hospital. The word was flashed all round the world that they had been beaten up. For the first time since the Polish crisis began, violence had been used and Mr Kania's policy of non-violence had faltered.

Within hours a Government team of experts led by a Deputy Prosecutor General was on the spot investigating what had happened. Lech Walesa arrived on the scene just as quickly and described the affair as an obvious provocation against the Government of General Jaruzelski; he plainly did not mean that Solidarity members had acted provocatively, and his words were therefore specially interesting in view of what Mr Bratkowski had been saying a week earlier. The first tentative report by the Government team of experts was reported by Warsaw Radio on Saturday 21 March. It said that there had been no beating up inside the Provincial Council hall. The uniformed police had been unarmed, without truncheons or helmets, and they had behaved in a firm but not brutal manner. The radio noted that Solidarity's claim was that its three men had been beaten up outside the building, but did not say anything about its other claim that plain-clothes members of the Security Service, the SB, had been involved as well as the uniformed men of the Civic Militia, the MO. A communiqué issued in Bydgoszcz by five members of Solidarity's national leadership – including Lech Walesa and Zbigniew Bujak from Warsaw – said that men of the SB as well as the MO had thrown the Solidarity men out of the building by force into an adjacent closed-off square and there Jan Rulewski, 37, Mariusz Labentowicz, 26, and Michal Bartoszcze, a 68-year-old member of Rural Solidarity, were 'severely beaten'. The Solidarity leaders demanded an objective investigation, a public report and the punishment of those guilty. After originally breaking off all talks with the Government they decided, in response to an appeal from the Prime Minister, to go ahead with immediate talks.

Delegations led by Deputy Premier Rakowski and Lech Walesa did meet on the Sunday but the talks were quickly adjourned. By that time the atmosphere throughout the country had grown tense. There had been brief protest strikes in Bydgoszcz, Torun and Wloclawek, and strike alerts had been declared in many other towns and areas. A statement from the Solidarity organisation in the Lenin Shipyards in Gdansk said that the incident in Bydgoszcz was the work of conservatives in the power apparatus who were opposed to the August agreements. It was therefore an attack both on Solidarity and on the Government led by General Jaruzelski.

That same day a pastoral announcement from Cardinal Wyszynski was read out during the broadcast mass in the church of the Holy Cross in Warsaw:

The State authorities must bear in mind the consequences of every irresponsible step taken by members of the forces of public order. Citizens who are seeking their just social rights . . . must realise that it will take a lot of time, patience and hard work for them to achieve this.

This was all very well but it did not give all that much help to General Jaruzelski as he appointed the Minister of Justice, Jerzy Bafia, to conduct a full-scale enquiry into what could well have been a provocation aimed at discrediting both Solidarity and his own Government's policy of renewal. At the same time, Lech Walesa probably knew quite well that Jan Rulewski, the Bydgoszcz Solidarity leader at the centre of the row, was a radical compared with himself and a bit of a tearaway.

The general atmosphere was not improved by a Politburo statement which took rather a hard line:

There are people in this country who adopt positions of extremism and adventurism and are trying to provoke more and more tension [it said]. Their actions aim at undermining the social order, spreading mistrust in the State authorities and, in particular, in the police and Security Service. The recent events in Bydgoszcz made this even clearer . . . The State authorities cannot and will not tolerate such actions . . . Acting on the orders of the competent authorities, the organs of law and order in Bydgoszcz, according to the information available, acted in accordance with law and order . . . A tendency towards action of a political character has gained the upper hand in the activities of Solidarity . . . The Politburo appeals for a realistic attitude in the present conflict . . . We should resist all possible provocation. The strikes that have been called are clearly political. Party members should not take part in them.

By the time Lech Walesa and Mieczyslaw Rakowski, the Deputy Prime Minister, met again on Wednesday 25 March more strikes were in the offing. The National Consultative Commission of Solidarity, meeting in Bydgoszcz, had decided on a four-hour warning strike throughout the country on the coming Friday, to be followed, if demands were not satisfied, by a general strike the following Tuesday 31 March. The organisation's demands, it is worth noting, were not confined to the Bydgoszcz affair; it wanted legal action against those responsible for acts of violence against Solidarity activists not only in Bydgoszcz but in Warsaw and elsewhere. It also wanted a full guarantee of the security of all its activists and organisations, an end to investigations into people charged with opposition activities in the period from 1976 to 1980, a guarantee that private farmers would be able to form their own trade union, and the repeal of a recent Government decision on strike pay.

Rakowski–Walesa clash
When Deputy Premier Rakowski met the Walesa delegation he described these demands as an ultimatum. He taxed the Solidarity leadership with 'large-scale agitation' against the police and security services, and said that forces inside Solidarity wanted to declare 'a holy war against people's power'. He even suggested that he could detect a desire 'to set General Jaruzelski's Government against the Party to which I belong'. Rakowski also wondered whether Bydgoszcz was the real reason for the present confrontation.

Social peace was disrupted not after the Bydgoszcz incident but much earlier . . . We did not get the ninety days of peace. We got only a few at most. In the few weeks since I took office I have not worked as a Deputy Prime Minister but as a fireman putting out fires . . . The country is flooded with leaflets and broadsheets of an anti-Communist nature. I have seen one leaflet published by Solidarity showing a gallows and an explanation of who is going to hang from it. One factory paper wrote: 'Ninety days of Jaruzelski's Government – ninety gallows for ninety leaders of the PZPR.'
    Perhaps an error of judgment was made [in Bydgoszcz], . . . but that unfortunate incident did not entitle Solidarity to take such colossal action as it has . . . What are you trying to prove? Maybe you want to prove that independent, self-governing trade unions cannot exist in a socialist state because the state collapses as a result. If so, in the name of what, for heaven's sake, do you want to prove that?
    The announced warning strike and the general strike to follow hasten the moment when both East and West, governments and people, will conclude that we are unable to govern ourselves in a wise and sensible manner. Is that the kind of finale we want to the complex and difficult process of renewal? Is that how we are going to bury the hopes of society?

These were good questions from Mr Rakowski, but Lech Walesa had the equally good point to make that the Bydgoszcz incident could not be passed over for the sake of renewal.

On so many occasions in the past – in 1956, 1970 and 1976 – we have had situations like this. In 1980 events would have taken a similar course if we had obeyed you, sir, and your kind of renewal . . . We

140

cannot allow the militia to beat us up . . . Someone in Bydgoszcz has beaten up our members.

The Walesa–Rakowski talks did not resume the next day and did not get under way again until Friday, when the four-hour warning strike took place. In the meantime General Jaruzelski had had a meeting with Cardinal Wyszynski. They agreed that the crisis should be resolved peacefully. It was announced that the Communist Party Central Committee would meet in plenary session on the coming Sunday. The press, radio and television took up the theme that a national disaster was threatening the country and that nothing should be allowed to slow down the process of renewal. In Gdansk a meeting of the local Party executive called for restraint and moderation but took a line that contrasted distinctly with that of the Politburo, if only in emphasis. It had been a great mistake, it said, to replace dialogue with the use of force in Bydgoszcz. There should be a full explanation of what happened and persons responsible should be named.

The delegations of Lech Walesa and Mieczyslaw Rakowski met again on Friday and Saturday 27 and 28 March. Pope John Paul II sent a message to Cardinal Wyszynski saying that voices reaching him from Poland were stressing that working men wanted to work and not to strike. Hoping for a settlement to reinforce calm and the spirit of renewal, the Pope said the Polish people had the inalienable right to solve their problems on their own. Quite possibly he was persuaded to make that remark after hearing that Washington, including President Ronald Reagan, was seriously concerned over the possibility of force being used in Poland and that the Soviet Union 'may intend to undertake repressive action there'. It was part of yet another Western scare, largely sustained by the Americans and quite often contradictory from day to day. In fact, although the possibility of Soviet intervention was there and had been there for several months, it was but one aspect of a situation that was far more complex and interesting.

The Polish authorities were simply not united in their view of the current crisis, let alone the possibility of asking for Soviet help. While *Zolnierz Wolnosci*, the Army newspaper, told readers on Saturday 28 March that Poland was confronted with perhaps its last chance and that 'order and social discipline must prevail', the Government paper, *Zycie*

Warszawy, was claiming that the real task was to thwart extremists on both sides – the 'adventurist and anti-socialist tendencies' inside Solidarity and the 'conservatism and leanings towards confrontation among a few but influential representatives in the Party and power apparatus'.

Further support for the view that the crisis was not entirely the fault of Solidarity came from a meeting of the council of the journalists' union, which claimed, according to Warsaw Radio, that there had been widespread manipulation of information concerning the Bydgoszcz incident, with incontrovertible eyewitness material from local journalists failing to be published. In a letter to all Polish journalists, the Council reminded its members that they did not have to write anything they considered contrary to their professional ethics. Cardinal Wyszynski told journalists at a retreat in the church of St Anne's that they should have the courage to speak the truth. On the same day he had an hour-long meeting with Lech Walesa.

The talks with the Government were not going too badly. Deputy Premier Rakowski even said he saw room for compromise. But they were adjourned again until the Monday, the eve of the planned general strike, so that working groups could examine the first report on the Bydgoszcz incident submitted by the Minister of Justice, Jerzy Bafia. The report was broadcast in full on Polish television on Saturday night. It found that there were no grounds for questioning the legality of calling in the police but it did put on record evidence from a Solidarity eyewitness that Jan Rulewski had been beaten by 'persons in plain clothes'. Regardless of whether this took place inside the building or in the courtyard outside, 'the forces of order . . . had a duty to protect the people removed from the hall'.

Solidarity's immediate response to the report was that, although it needed amplification and correction, it did mark 'undeniable progress'. Mr Rakowski told a television reporter that he had not felt so good for days. But with the talks adjourned until the very eve of the general strike a settlement was being left dangerously late. If that strike were to go ahead, it seemed quite clear that it could mean the end of the policy of talks and renewal espoused by Mr Kania. It could strengthen the hand of 'conservatives' in the leadership who favoured a harder line towards Solidarity and maybe even a request for help to the Soviet Union.

Hardliners denounced

A lot depended on the Plenum of the Party Central Committee which assembled in Warsaw on the morning of Sunday 29 March. The West, it is fair to say, was waiting for word of a crackdown. But the Plenum itself was diverted from that simplistic view by an open letter from a rank-and-file Communist warning the Central Committee that 'hardliners' in the leadership were trying to destroy renewal. The author was Stefan Bratkowski, the journalists' leader, and his letter was published in full by the official news agency PAP.

Let us have no illusions. This is a last-ditch crisis for those who would like to drive our Party from the path of social agreement . . . These are men who do not want agreement even with their own grassroots. They are afraid of them . . . These are the men who want to induce in the Party apparatus a fear of their own Party, pointing to themselves as the only people capable of protecting the apparatus from loss of rank and influence. These are the men who try to set the forces of public order against their own community . . . These are the men who present themselves to our neighbours as the only force capable of guaranteeing the durability of our alliances and the State system.

In reality they constitute no force . . . It is impossible to rule this country in conflict with one's own grassroots – several millions strong – in conflict with several million workers, in conflict with millions of peasants, with the support of no more than part of the apparatus of power . . .

Our hardliners stand for no programme except that of confrontation and disinformation . . . I do not discern even a single proposal which goes beyond the protection of their own positions and the ambition to reach out for still higher ones . . . Today they are trying to involve the whole Party leadership and the Government in a clash with society . . . They are trying to provoke society into behaviour that would justify the use of force . . . I mention no names. But there are, among these men, comrades occupying the highest positions in the Party. They are supported by a group of comrades rallied around the Warsaw Party organisation and also by various people from the apparatus of power. I think their further presence in the Party leadership will result in similar tensions and even worse.

We are all counting on Comrade Kania and on Barcikowski. Nor do we see any alternative to the Government of General Jaruzelski. These men could have won and can still win the acceptance of the majority of the nation for the policy of social agreement . . . It seems to me that we rank-and-file members of the primary Party organisations . . . should say loudly what is our choice.

Bratkowski's letter was a bombshell. It is difficult to judge whether it actually turned the course of events or was only a symptom of what was already afoot. But it is a fact that from then on the whole argument about the crisis was changed and the disarray within the Party came out into the open. At the Central Committee Plenum Kazimierz Barcikowski, who had received what amounted to praise from Bratkowski, delivered the Politburo report and a stinging attack on Solidarity for calling a general strike.

This is no longer a case simply of putting pressure on the authorities, but an open struggle against our Party and State authority and against socialism. It is now a struggle for power . . . Forces have appeared in Solidarity which are pushing the union onto the road of political activity and are engaging Solidarity in a struggle against our Party and our people's State from anti-Communist positions. This results in a threat to the country and to Solidarity itself. We warn the leaders of Solidarity of the consequences of political adventurism.

Barcikowski was tough but he made it clear that the policy of renewal was still on as long as Solidarity eliminated its anti-Communist elements and the Party itself rejected 'extremism both in its conservative and radical manifestations'. Bratkowski's letter, he said, was an example of extremism which introduced deep lines of division inside the Party and its leadership.

Stefan Olszowski, a probable target of the Bratkowski letter, accused the journalists' leader of trying to split the Party and its leadership. He denied any inclination in the leadership to use force but ended his speech by offering his resignation. Two other members of the leadership also offered to resign, Tadeusz Grabski of the Politburo and Roman Ney, a candidate member of the Politburo.

Grabski's speech easily qualified for the description 'hard line'. He accused Bratkowski of 'subversive, anti-Party activity'. He claimed that a counter-revolutionary struggle for power was growing in pace and dismissed the Bydgoszcz incident as merely a pretext, meticulously stage-managed by adventurists. Roman Ney, described in the world's press as a hardliner, did not sound very much like one. He said that criticism of the Party leadership in the debate was quite correct. He offered to resign so that the First Secretary could choose a better team. In the end the resignation offers were rejected and a resolution calling for unity was adopted. It was undoubtedly a disappointment to many who had taken part in the debate. Almost every speech, as reported by the official media, contained some telling point on one side or the other:

Distrust between the rank-and-file and the Party leadership is getting worse and worse.

The Party has lost the trust of the broad masses of the workers.

The responsibility for the events in Bydgoszcz lies with the power apparatus.

It is necessary to give unequivocal approval to the agreements signed in Gdansk, Szczecin, Jastrzebie and elsewhere.

There are too many concessions where determination is needed. Those who cannot cope should resign for the good of the Party.

All extremist forces must be exposed and isolated.

Most of my fellow workers belong to Solidarity but I can see no organised forces hostile to socialism.

The programme based on the agreements of the Coast and Jastrzebie is not feasible. We must sit down and renegotiate.

There are still many in our ranks who give the impression that they have learned nothing of the new and forgotten nothing of the old.

The Politburo cannot decide the future of Party members without their participation. The Central Committee should base its activities on the views and feelings of basic Party organisations.

One repeated demand was that the promised extraordinary Party Congress should not be delayed. The final resolution partially satisfied that by stating that the Congress should take place by 20 July. Equally important was the decision to hold 'a general election campaign in the Party' in preparation for the Congress with the aim of electing Party bodies 'which command respect'. This meant that, although the immediate results of the Plenum were generally disappointing to the rank and file, they would be given the opportunity in the coming weeks to achieve the changes they wanted by what was for them the unprecedented democratic process of the secret ballot.

The plenary session finally rose at dawn on Monday 30 March. It was the day of decision on whether the general strike called by Solidarity for the Tuesday would go ahead. International interest was intense and Moscow had gone so far as to put out a report on Sunday seeming to suggest that counter-revolution was actually breaking out in Poland. TASS reported that roadblocks had closed a motorway in Kielce province and all road signs had been destroyed. It also claimed that anti-socialist forces had seized a television transmitter in Warsaw for a short time. Warsaw Radio simply denied the reports without mentioning their source. One is tempted to wonder whether, with Warsaw Pact exercises continuing in and around Poland, the TASS reports were more than simply mistaken.

The atmosphere for the crucial talks between Solidarity and the Government was probably improved by the speech made to the Central Committee by the Government's chief negotiator, Deputy Premier Rakowski.

Certain comrades tend to look for the source of all mishaps in Solidarity. You can do this if you like, but you must remember that it is an organisation which has millions of working people as members, millions of young workers who are really wonderful people. Solidarity also has Party members within its ranks – several hundred thousand according to some estimates . . . Considerable sections of the Party have formed blocs together with Solidarity organisations. They share opinions on the present situation. They also have common aims.

Agreement averts strike

Warsaw Radio, summing up the atmosphere as the talks began, reported 'tension, expectation and hope'. Hope was rewarded in the evening when the radio announced that the Solidarity delegation had suspended the general strike and that the union's National Consultative Commission would decide the next day whether to call it off completely. The text of the Walesa–Rakowski agreement, quickly broadcast by television, showed that the Government had made some concessions, but not on everything.

On the Bydgoszcz affair the Government agreed that the use of the police had been a hasty action contrary to accepted policy. It regretted that three trade unionists had been beaten up, ordered an investigation into the actions of persons who had failed in their duty, and promised that those held responsible would be taken to court. On the demand for guarantees of security for Solidarity activists, the Government merely promised to speed up the new Trade Union Bill. On the questions of registering Rural Solidarity and granting an amnesty for opposition activity, it was agreed that a special parliamentary commission should examine the issues and report in the near future. It was also agreed that permission should be sought for an arrangement under which workers who went on strike on 27 March should receive the wages normally paid during 'justified absence'.

No doubt there were many members of the Party who thought the settlement gave too much away. But the real quarrel broke out inside Solidarity. When its National Commission met in Gdansk the next day it did call off the general strike, but Jan Rulewski, the Solidarity leader injured in the Bydgoszcz incident, denounced the agreement signed by Walesa as a disgrace. The union accepted the resignation of its spokesman, Karol Modzelewski, but refused to let Andrzej Gwiazda, its Deputy Chairman, do likewise in protest. One secretary of the National Commission, Andrzej Celinski, was said to have been removed from office after a secret ballot.

There was speculation about a split in Solidarity. This was denied by Zbigniew Bujak, the Solidarity leader in Warsaw, and the vote on calling off the strike showed a large majority in favour, with only ten either against or abstaining. But if there was no split there was certainly a realisation that divisions were quite likely to develop.

On the whole, however, Solidarity emerged from the crisis in a better condition than the Communist Party, which had contrived to please nobody. Quite apart from the fact that Moscow reported rather significantly that General Jaruzelski's Government had made 'a number of concessions', the Party was in for an avalanche of criticism from its own grassroots organisations all over the country. This marked a turning point in the course of the Polish crisis. Quite suddenly the spotlight was not on Solidarity but on the Party itself, and it would remain there for months.

9. PARTY IN FERMENT

Even before March had ended, there was news of acute dissatisfaction in Gdansk. The Party organisation in the shipyards disapproved of the Politburo report to the Central Committee meeting and demanded profound changes in the Party leadership. 'Party members feel that there is a group of people within the Politburo whose conservatism and determined opposition to any change is leading to a split in the Party.' Rank-and-file members were said to be facing a dilemma over whether or not to hand in their membership cards. The regional council of the Socialist Union of Students voiced their support for the ideas of Stefan Bratkowski, whatever the Party said about him.

The affair of Bratkowski's letter had been referred by the Central Committee to the Party's Control Commission; but this move, which resulted in a mild rebuke, was immediately criticised, notably by Party members in the editorial offices of Gdansk newspapers, radio and television and by the Party organisation of Wroclaw Radio. The latter specifically condemned attacks on Bratkowski by Stefan Olszowski and Tadeusz Grabski.

The Party leaders took their cue from the rising tide of criticism and attended a series of meetings in primary organisations. Mr Kania himself visited a Warsaw radio factory for what was described in a broadcast as an 'open, polemical and at times very heated discussion'. Mr Olszowski met Party activists in the Warsaw steel works. He said there that Stefan Bratkowski had been wrong to distribute his letter through non-Party channels – though we know it was published by the official Polish news agency. Olszowski also thought that the agreement reached by Deputy Premier Rakowski with Solidarity would probably pave the way for the legalisation of Rural Solidarity. This, he said, would not do the country

148

any good at all. On that very same day Cardinal Wyszynski had a meeting with the young leader of Rural Solidarity, Jan Kulaj, and stated quite plainly that since the authorities had agreed to independent trade unions for workers they should do the same for farmers.

Brezhnev not so sure

In a matter of days Stefan Olszowski was in Prague as Poland's representative at the Czechoslovak Communist Party Congress. There he heard the Soviet leader, Leonid Brezhnev, betray a hint of diminished confidence in the Polish leadership. Instead of saying as usual that he or the Soviet Communist Party were sure or convinced or confident that the Poles would manage, the Soviet President used a curious new formulation: 'Polish Communists . . . will be able, one must suppose, to give the necessary rebuff to the schemes of the enemies of socialism.'

If Mr Brezhnev had to 'suppose' only that the Polish Party would cope, the situation was presumably more uncertain as far as Moscow was concerned. There were without doubt many aspects of the Polish crisis that worried the Soviet leadership. Small but steady progress on the bill to reform censorship regulations was one. The possibility of the registration of Rural Solidarity, which Mr Kania had once so vigorously opposed, was another. But the turmoil inside the Party itself was bound to alarm it even more.

More alarms were in the offing. On 9 April Stanislaw Kania went to Gdansk to attend a Party meeting inside the Lenin Shipyard. The meeting lasted seven hours and the Party leader had a rough time of it. The shipyard's Party Secretary, Jan Labecki, told him that his members had been shocked by the failure of the Central Committee Plenum to take any steps to punish those responsible for the Bydgoszcz 'provocation' or those who had been guilty of manipulating the information put out about it. This, he said, confirmed that renewal was no more than a paper slogan; it would never be carried out. There must, he insisted, be changes at the top. Another speaker told Mr Kania that the Central Committee was unrepresentative. All those provincial Party leaders who had resigned or been forced to do so since August were still in the Central Committee. Whom were they supposed to represent? Certainly not the rank and file who had thrown them out.

Mr Kania appears to have emerged smiling from all this. He promised there would be changes in the leadership when the Central Committee met again. He also gave a pledge that all resistance to renewal would be overcome.

Solidarity Programme

In mid-April Solidarity highlighted the Communist Party's general embarrassment by publishing a long document entitled 'Directions of Union Action in the Country's Present Situation'. It was, in effect, a statement of Solidarity's ideology and a programme of action offered for discussion inside the union. A summary was published by *Trybuna Ludu*, the text by the trade union paper, *Glos Pracy*. The most striking feature of the document was the certainty with which the union, recently described by Mr Rakowski as a mere fledgling, proclaimed the main sources of its inspiration: the nation's best traditions, Christianity's ethical principles, democracy's political mandate and socialist social thought. With equal certainty Solidarity placed the blame for the Polish crisis on the faults of the existing system – the lack of democratic mechanisms, bureaucratic methods of government and the creation of a closed group of 'governors' not subject to the control of the governed. The existing political system, Solidarity said, had not had the strength to reform itself. The way to reform and renewal had been paved by economic crisis, social protest and the establishment of Solidarity. And Solidarity, the document said, was the main guarantee of the renewal process. No other force in Poland was able to replace it in that task.

One can understand Moscow's feelings about that, believing as it did that the Communist Party should play the leading role in the State. But Soviet feelings were due to be further offended in coming days. One development was the virtual legalisation of Rural Solidarity. The Chairman of the special commission of the Sejm in charge of the issue told the leaders of private farmers who were continuing their sit-in in Bydgoszcz that it had been decided to introduce an amendment into the draft law on trade unions making it possible for farmers to set up their own trade union. Mr Olszowski's fears had been proved right. An agreement was signed with the

150

Government on 17 April. Rural Solidarity would be officially registered on 10 May.

Another development was the publication of details of the new draft Party statute. The most striking change, perhaps, was a new section declaring that all elections to all levels of the Party, including leading posts, would be secret and that no member would be able to hold the same post for longer than two terms.

'Anti-Party elements'

The implications of that reform became even more alarming for Poland's allies when considered against the background of an unusual event in the town of Torun on 15 April. Warsaw Radio described it as 'the first pre-Congress, all-Polish forum of Party reconciliation'. It was attended by almost 800 representatives of Party organisations all over the country, who conducted what was described as 'an extensive and critical review of the current situation in the Party and the country'. Speakers were reported to have accused the Central Committee of failing to reflect all the views of Party organisations. The full impact of this occasion is best conveyed by a commentary on Prague television the next day:

Events in Poland confirm that the situation has not become calmer but that new, disconcerting factors have appeared in its development . . . The main onslaught has now been channelled against the leading force in Polish society, the PZPR . . . A curious assembly of right-wing revisionist currents in the PZPR has taken place in Torun. If we take things to their logical conclusion, this is preparing the ground for the formation of an opposition centre within the Party and in the final analysis for the transformation of the PZPR into some kind of social democratic party.

It did not take long before the East German Radio expressed its 'great concern' over developments. It described those who assembled in Torun as 'anti-party elements' and found it significant that the meeting was attended by leaders of Solidarity. As for Solidarity's newly published programme, the radio alleged that the union was laying claim to political leadership of the country. The broadcast also referred to the legalisation of Rural Solidarity as a further field for anti-socialist activities. According to the Polish press, it said, the people behind Rural Solidarity were former landowners and counter-revolutionaries. But it was not so much the Polish press that had said that. Mr Kania had said it, earlier in the year.

In Poland itself, the daily of the United Peasant Party, *Dziennik Ludowy*, hailed the new 'horizontal structures' movement as something seeking 'a universal democratisation of Party life'. It had been accused of factionalism, it said, only by 'some dogmatic Party activists' because it had emerged outside the Party's organisational structure.

Suslov detects revisionism

Moscow was initially reticent about this new development but its interest was left in no doubt when Mikhail Suslov, the Soviet Politburo's leading ideologist and keeper of the Party's conscience, arrived in Warsaw on 23 April accompanied by Konstantin Rusakov, the Soviet Party Secretary in charge of relations with fraternal parties. Their talks with Mr Kania and members of the Politburo were primarily concerned with Party affairs. Mr Suslov, to judge from the communiqué, was given a detailed briefing on how the Polish Party was pursuing the policy it had adopted the previous autumn and how it was preparing for its Ninth Congress. Nothing specific emerged apart from familiar references to fraternal alliance, friendship and cooperation. The talks were said to have been 'cordial and Party-like'.

It was after Mr Suslov had returned home that judgement was passed. While *Trybuna Ludu* in Warsaw was talking about a 'dialogue between friends' making for better understanding, the Soviet news agency TASS in a despatch supposedly coming from Warsaw, was reporting something else:

In a number of places, revisionist elements within the ranks of the PZPR are inspiring a campaign with the aim of discrediting Party officials. They are striving to cause complications between various Party links, between the Central Committee and provincial and primary organisations. Such activity is engaged in, notably, by people who would like to paralyse the Party of the Polish Communists as the leading force in society. It is characteristic that these people include some who were previously expelled from the Party for violating its statutes. The revisionist forces in the Party are putting forward demands for reform of the PZPR, the renunciation of its present organisational structure and the creation, in the guise of so-called horizontal structures, of various forums outside the statutes which would take the place of leading organs of the Party.

It would be difficult to find a better example of a detailed, carefully worded statement of Soviet fears about the consequences of developments in the Polish Communist Party. In Poland, in contrast, the dangers were seen but they seem to have been overshadowed by enthusiasm, even in the highest places, for the intellectual ferment that had replaced the torpor of the past. Professor Adolf Dobieszewski of the Central Committee's Higher School of Social Sciences told the weekly *Kultura* that the Party leadership had received about 700 comprehensive documents containing suggestions for the PZPR programme and statutes.

I regard these documents as something completely new in the history of the Party, as the first such momentous and thorough intellectual movement, which has grown in strength since the end of last year. I regard this grassroots movement in Party organisations as the beginning of a process in which the Party is to free itself from stagnation and a fatalistic outlook on the future . . . The Party's biggest chance is to preserve for ever the atmosphere of intellectual, political and ideological movement. The fact that the resolutions contain proposals which lead to differences of opinion and incorrect suggestions is something I consider normal . . . There can be different attitudes to the horizontal movement, but it is a social fact. It came into being as a reaction to intellectual inadequacy and the lack of political initiative displayed by the vertical structures . . . Sooner or later, the existence of independent structures must lead to a collision. That is why they have to be incorporated into the vertical structures.

Kazimierz Barcikowski, a close ally of Mr Kania in the Politburo, also conceded the intellectual and ideological achievements of the horizontal movement at a meeting in the Karl Marx debating club in Warsaw. But he also warned against the dangers of 'factional activity'. The terminology of all this argument was rather oppressive and maybe also meaningless to the non-Communist ear. But the point at issue, as the bedraggled Polish United Workers' Party approached yet another session of its Central Committee on 29 April, was whether it would be able to control its own members, let alone Solidarity.

Decline in Membership
The state of the Polish Communist Party as it approached the tenth plenary session of its Central Committee in less then eighteen months was difficult to define precisely. Statistics alone revealed that it was in turmoil. According to Mr

Barcikowski, a total of 160,000 members had handed in their Party cards since July 1980. Most of them had been workers. According to official figures, Party membership had declined between October 1980 and March 1981 from 3,158,000 to 2,942,000. The drop was to be explained by dissatisfaction and disenchantment but also by the general purge set in train by Mr Kania in the autumn of 1980. And on that score *Trybuna Ludu* reported that criminal charges of corruption had been levelled against 194 people. They included four former Ministers, eight former Deputy Ministers, six former First Secretaries of Provincial Party Committees, seven former Provincial Governors, and thirty-five people occupying managerial posts in central offices.

These figures summed up, to a certain extent, the record of a Party which still laid claim to be the leading force in Polish society in an unchallenged one-party system. The Communist Party not only claimed a monopoly of power, it knew that it had to claim it, because the Soviet Union and its other socialist camp allies insisted that it should do so and would probably intervene if it did not. This fundamental imperative, the essence of what Polish leaders liked to call the country's 'raison d'état', obliged the Polish Communist Party to stay in power whatever happened. It could not, in theory, be removed and go off into opposition like a Western party to lick its wounds and put itself to rights. It had to stay on and clear up its own mess while still trying to govern, an activity in which it had been signally unsuccessful in the past.

The problems of the Party leader were twofold. Mr Kania had to contend with the danger that Solidarity would turn into a natural opposition party, but now he was also faced with the possibility that the drive for reform inside the Communist Party itself would constitute a de facto opposition while masquerading under the title of Communist. As we have seen, the East Germans had already described the rank-and-file 'horizontal structures' movement as 'anti-Party'. Moscow had denounced 'revisionist' tendencies, which meant, in effect, a leaning towards the ideas of social democracy or another type of party within the Party.

'Protests from the Party masses'
Kania clearly knew the risks of his policy of renewal and greater democracy within the Party. But equally he must have

realised that some of his colleagues in the Politburo were less content than he was to give it a chance. Stefan Olszowski had already issued his own warning about revisionism. Tadeusz Grabski was by now taking a harder line. Andrzej Zabinski, the Party leader in Katowice, rarely had much to say, but his relative silence suggested something less than enthusiasm for the way things were going. Mr Kania never betrayed anything less than the greatest respect for these colleagues, but he was no doubt aware that the opinion in some primary organisations was not so generous. On the very eve of the Central Committee session at the end of April 1981, one of its members made a plea in *Zycie Warszawy* for greater attention to be paid by those at the top to the opinions and feelings of simple, rank-and-file members of the Party. Mrs Jadwiga Nowakowska said this also applied to 'squaring accounts with certain members of the Politburo and Central Committee who do not understand the spirit of renewal and whose conduct continues to excite protests from the Party masses because they are slowing down the process of renewal'.

But once again a plenary session of the Central Committee failed to satisfy fully the demands of the rank and file. The session, which opened on the morning of 29 April and ended in the early hours of the next day, did approve some changes at the top, but they were not very significant. The former Prime Minister, Jozef Pinkowski, left the Politburo at his own request. A candidate member, Emil Wojtaszek, did likewise. A Central Committee Secretary left to become Minister of Agriculture. A member of the Secretariat also resigned. The replacements were meant to be more significant. Two workers joined the Politburo as full members: Gerard Gabrys, a miner, and Zygmunt Wronski from the Ursus plant in Warsaw. A new Secretary, Kazimierz Cypryniak, the Party chief in Szczecin, was appointed. The First Secretary in Opole province, Jozef Masny, joined the Politburo as a candidate member. The changes could hardly be interpreted as a response to the protests from the Party masses.

The grass-roots movement inside the Party was hardly mentioned in Mr Kania's opening Politburo report, not at least as a great problem. He had more practical things to announce: the extraordinary Congress, the first in the Party's history, would be held from 14 to 18 July. He therefore submitted for discussion the Party's 'programme theses on the development of socialist democracy' and a second document on draft changes in the Party's statutes. The latter contained amendments which the Party leader had foreshadowed in the autumn of 1980 – democratic election rules with secret ballots and a stipulation that no member could occupy the same Party post for more than two terms.

As for the election of delegates to the coming Party Congress, a resolution adopted by the Central Committee said that delegates would be chosen by provincial Party organisations, factory and educational establishments and Party conferences in the Polish People's Army. Normally one delegate would be chosen to represent every 1700 members and candidate members. But factory and educational establishments could elect a delegate if they had more than 850 members. As Mr Kania said in his speech, the Party wanted more delegates than usual at the Congress, especially more workers.

Another decision taken by the Central Committee was to set up a special commission, chaired by Tadeusz Grabski, to speed up the work of investigating the responsibility of former leaders for the present crisis. One point in Mr Kania's speech betrayed a certain nervousness. The Party, he said, would never renounce the right to inspire and control the press, radio and television. Certain publications were being accused, not without foundation, of passing from one extreme to the other, from the propaganda of success to the propaganda of doom. A similar point was made by Stefan Olszowski who claimed that 'the social and political consequences of trespassing freedom of speech are multiplying'. Information policy had to be improved, he said, and would be improved.

These remarks from Kania and Olszowski seemed to suggest that the media had been going too far, and no doubt there was hard-line support for that view. But there was no doubt either that many grass-roots Party members believed the media had not gone far enough. As a matter of interest Mr Kania was to be told by a factory Party Secretary that in the past nine months the supply of information had been quite inadequate. 'During this period,' he said, 'a Party member who was not a member of Solidarity and did not listen to foreign radio stations was under-informed.'

As usual when addressing Party meetings, Mieczyslaw Rakowski, the Deputy Prime Minister and Chief Editor of

Polityka, stood out as a politician of practical common sense. He stated quite frankly that, in the opinion of the rank and file, the present Central Committee, elected at the Eighth Congress under Edward Gierek, simply could not lead the country and the Party out of the crisis. However true that may have been, many of the Central Committee speakers had more that was interesting and liberal to say than their leaders. On the sore point of revisionism, for instance, Professor Jerzy Wiatr of Warsaw University reminded the plenum that charges of revisionism had been used in the past as a smoke-screen in order to liquidate political concepts exactly like those being promoted then in Poland. On a more human level, Mrs Zofia Grzyb said that she and her fellow workers wanted nothing to do with renewal if it simply meant 'the renewal of certain comrades who change colour like chameleons to suit the prevailing conditions'.

If we are to believe Warsaw Radio, the Central Committee meeting aroused intense interest in Party organisations throughout the country, with many of them maintaining a night watch to keep abreast of developments. But the general reaction was dissatisfaction. The leadership changes did not 'correspond to the expectation of local Party organisations'. Resolutions telexed to the radio from grass-roots organisations repeated that people who had lost their posts as provincial Party leaders should no longer be allowed to remain members of the Central Committee.

One could understand the thinking behind this. If renewal and the new democratic trend within the Party was to be frustrated by anybody, it was most likely to be halted by diehard elements in the Central Committee who, only a year earlier, had been happily serving the Gierek leadership. Hence the repeated insistence on fixing the date of the Party Congress and getting on with the elections. In the process it was expected that the existing Central Committee would be swept away.

The elections and the Congress represented the greatest hope inside the Party, and outside it as well, of underpinning and consolidating the policy of reform. The elections were already under way and the Congress was less than eighty days away. It was a comparatively short time in which, quite conceivably, someone or something could upset the applecart – though in the prevailing atmosphere of industrial calm it did not seem likely with Solidarity and the Government negotiating in a businesslike fashion on such matters as employment problems and access to the media.

May Day with a difference

The month of May, in fact, represented a high-water mark of sorts, a brief span in which freedom of expression revealed more fully than ever before the state of the national mind. It began auspiciously with celebrations of May Day quite different from those in Moscow, East Berlin or other Soviet bloc capitals. Instead of taking their usual places on a reviewing stand to watch the traditional parade of well-drilled, happy workers – the annual dramatised version of the propaganda of success – Mr Kania, General Jaruzelski and President Jablonski came down to earth and led a procession through the centre of the capital, laying wreaths at the Tomb of the Unknown Soldier and the Monument to the Heroes of Warsaw. Similar celebrations, informal marches in which no one was supposedly under any compulsion to attend, took place all over Poland according to local wishes. *Zycie Warszawy* said it was part of 'the difficult process of restoring dignity to May Day'. There was no open slur on the sort of orchestrated jamboree taking place in 'fraternal' capitals, but Moscow noted that by advising its members not to take part in traditional demonstrations, Solidarity had revealed its 'negative attitude to the international festival of workers'. And in neighbouring Czechoslovakia Prague Radio accused Solidarity of wanting to separate the Polish working class from the international workers' movement in general.

More significant of Poland's mood was the widespread celebration for the first time under Communist rule of a purely national date, the 190th anniversary of the 3 May Constitution of 1791, described proudly by Warsaw Radio as 'the first in the history of our country, and the second in the world after that of the United States, to regulate the organisation of the State authorities as well as the rights and duties of citizens'.

Party, State and Church leaders who gathered in the Wielki Theatre in Warsaw for a gala meeting and concert heard President Jablonski claim that the Poles of 1981, the builders of socialism, were continuing the work begun 190 years before. He spoke of the need to have 'the right attitude

158

to our national past', for that would enable Poles to know themselves better and feel justified pride in the nation's contribution to the treasury of mankind. But Poles did not need any prompting on that score. Already moves were afoot to revise school textbooks following demands made during a strike back in January that children should be able to read 'the whole historical truth'. Some of the most painful moments of modern Polish history involved unpleasant memories of Russian involvement, and 'proletarian internationalism' had required that they be papered over. Resentment on that score and a determination to make sure that the lessons of history should not be forgotten made themselves evident, however diplomatically, during the celebrations of Poland's first democratic constitution.

In a speech in Zielona Gora, broadcast by the local radio, the province's Solidarity leader, Maciej Oltarzewski, made a very pointed comparison:

The 3 May Constitution formed the foundation for the planned renewal of public life in Poland towards the end of the eighteenth century. Unfortunately, this renewal was not to take place, owing to intervention by neighbouring states which saw in this renewal a threat to their own ossified political and state structures. This is why we feel that this day of 3 May is particularly close to our hearts.

In an interview on Warsaw Radio, a historian and writer, Dr Jerzy Lojek, recalled that the Poland of the 3 May Constitution – then between the first and second of its three partitions – suffered under an imposed system of so-called 'foreign guarantee'. This, he said, had been 'a guarantee to those conservative cliques in the republic who wished to maintain the existing social and legal order in Poland and retain their system of privileges untouched'. Dr Lojek noted regretfully that eventually 'there was an intervention; citizens were found who requested this intervention'.

The message, however oblique, seemed obvious: the Poles of the summer of 1981 were fighting an old battle for renewal against the opposition of conservatives at home and of neighbours with ossified political systems who could be requested to intervene.

Sikorski Honoured
There were other signs, too, of a readiness to resurrect the memory of men and women involved in unhappy episodes of

Soviet–Polish history. It was decided to build a monument to the heroes of the Warsaw Uprising of 1944, a touchy subject since it is widely believed that the advancing Soviet Army halted outside Warsaw and waited until the occupying German forces had crushed the rebellion and with it the Poles most likely to challenge Soviet plans to install a Communist government.

Plans were already well advanced for the return to Poland of the remains of General Wladyslaw Sikorski, the non-Communist leader of Poland's wartime government in exile based in London. The idea came originally from ZBOWiD, the Veterans' Association led by General Moczar, and had been quickly supported by the Church, the Government and Solidarity, whose leader, Lech Walesa, said he would willingly go to London to pick up the coffin himself. There was opposition to the idea among the Polish community in Britain on the grounds that the Communist authorities could simply be trying to use the dead hero to bolster their own position. In any event the British Government in July turned down the Polish Government's request for the General's remains, in spite of the fact that a sarcophagus was waiting to receive them next to that of a Polish King in Wawel Cathedral in the ancient city of Cracow. Anyone who was in Poland in May – as I was – would have seen and heard evidence that the desire to recover General Sikorski's remains was not simply a Communist scheme to win favour but another example of the Poland of renewal restoring the clouded image of its own proud history.

On 20 May, the hundredth anniversary of General Sikorski's birth, President Jablonski, General Moczar, Lech Walesa and a Roman Catholic bishop went together to the Tomb of the Unknown Soldier to lay wreaths in his memory, and then left together in the same bus. The radio broadcast hours of material devoted to the man now described as a great soldier, politician and patriot. And yet as a politician and leader of the Polish Government, General Sikorski, shortly before his death in 1943 in a plane crash off Gibraltar, had angered Stalin by demanding an international investigation into the discovery, in the forest of Katyn near Smolensk, of mass graves containing the bodies of some 4000 Polish officers, once held by the Soviet Union. The Russians said the Germans had killed them, the Germans said it was the Russians.

It is interesting to note that the forty-sixth anniversary of the death of Marshal Pilsudski, Poland's leader for a large part of the period between the two world wars, was also commemorated on 12 May, though not on the same scale. But he did feature in a film then showing in Warsaw. Called 'Polonia Restituta', it dealt with the recovery of independence after the Great War and was directed by Bohdan Poreba, the President of the now legally registered Grunwald Patriotic Association, which claimed nearly 100,000 members. The Association took its name from a famous battle in 1410 in which the Poles defeated the German Knights. But for all its harking back to even more distant days of Polish glory, the Grunwald Association remained, in general, highly suspect. More than that, it was openly accused of overt anti-Semitism by the Central Board of the Association of Jews in Poland. More significantly, perhaps, an open letter from a Communist and former inmate of Auschwitz, printed in the Cracow paper *Gazeta Krakowska*, complained that Grunwald members were trying to penetrate Party organisations. The writer claimed that members of the Party leadership belonged to the association and demanded that the Party should break its silence and say publicly what Grunwald was really up to. Nobody seemed willing to answer that question.

In spite of the comparative political and industrial calm and the lack of serious conflict between the authorities and Solidarity, the situation was inherently uncertain. And Solidarity did come in for criticism over its Programme which, as we have seen, described the union as the only guarantee of renewal. But the Polish press, while critical, was rather generous. One article in *Polityka* thought there were signs that Solidarity and the Communist Party could find a common language despite their differences. Daniel Passent, a leading journalist writing in *Zycie Warszawy*, found several faults in the document but concluded that it was a good thing that it existed for it constituted the first alternative manifesto to appear in Poland since July 1944.

Moscow Radio, in contrast, saw the Solidarity document as a sort of rival to the Polish Communist Party Programme, which was just coming out. The Soviet attitude to Polish developments was quietly taking on a different tone: a long article by a recent visitor to Poland in *Literaturnaya Gazeta*, the Soviet Writers' weekly, reported that Communists there were 'fully aware that it is time to go over to the offensive'. Material to back that claim turned up that very week.

Law and order
On Thursday 7 May two young drunks threw stones at a Railway Police post at Otwock, just outside Warsaw. They were arrested but shouted for help, claiming police brutality. A large crowd gathered and tried to set fire to the station. The incident lasted about ten hours and the crowds dispersed only after local Solidarity men intervened to help, advising the Prosecutor to release the two men. The police recorded their gratitude to Solidarity, but even they could not stop another scene of violence the next night when another police station was set on fire by a crowd of youths at one time estimated to number up to a thousand.

In subsequent weeks there were further incidents, some of them spectacularly violent. Two of them involved football hooligans equipped with razors, chains and knives. Others appeared to be plain drunken brawls. The remarkable thing was that they were given so much publicity, with stress laid upon the fact that in several instances the police had been prevented from doing their duty simply because the crowds turned against them in defence of those involved in the violence. Law and order became a big political issue. The Politburo discussed and published figures testifying to an 'alarming' rise in crime. The State Council, after hearing reports from the Prosecutor General and the Minister of Internal Affairs, acknowledged that 'a growth of criminality unheard of hitherto is beginning to threaten the functioning of the State'.

That phrase gave the issue a clear political flavour. Perhaps there was a hint at that, too, in a speech by Stefan Olszowski, who accused KOR, the KPN and 'a certain current in Solidarity' of generating an 'insurgent psychosis'. In another meeting with Party activists in the same week, Olszowski claimed that violations of law and order and the creation of obstacles to the functioning of the police and security services were a very serious matter, placing the country one step short of anarchy. To face this threat, he said, joint police and army patrols were being introduced.

Not everyone, to put it mildly, accepted all the official claims about the reported rise in crime, or indeed the demands

162

for tough action appearing in some press articles. On Warsaw Radio Jacek Kalabinski pointed out that one element that must be remembered was the fact that over the years the police force had earned 'bitterness, dislike and distrust' because some of its members had behaved as if they could do what they liked. 'The community is wise. It remembers every case of brutal beating in dark corners of police stations, every bribe forced out of a driver, every case of police extortion and dealing in vodka'.

It was difficult, too, to find an obvious link between the hooliganism – more easily explained by general dissatisfaction – and the political turmoil attributed to Solidarity. But the East Germans, in broadcasts clearly documenting their growing anxiety, openly accused Solidarity leaders of a 'campaign of incitement against the police', starting with the Bydgoszcz incident in March and culminating in the disturbances at Otwock, one of more than a thousand instances in just a few months in which, according to East German Radio, the Polish police had been attacked. The Solidarity patrols that had assisted the police after the Otwock incident were seen as a demonstration of the union's claim to power.

Allies criticise leadership
But the East German broadcasts were equally significant for their clear demand that the Polish authorities should adopt 'quite different measures, much more decisive than hitherto', to cope with the crisis. One commentary suggested that many people were talking of the possibility of 1,500,000 unemployed because of Solidarity's 'destructive activities'. It noted that the police, 'one of the main targets of Solidarity', were being left 'without the support of the State authorities'. It asserted that people were waiting for a clear word from the Communist Party on how the 'counter-revolutionary forces' could be smashed. The East German Party paper, *Neues Deutschland*, reported that 'some people now in government' in Poland frequently denied that the crisis was becoming increasingly acute.

Reality is often different from the way it is presented by the mass media which are close to the Party and Government . . . There are quite a number of Party Secretaries who firmly defend socialism and people's power at meetings, who protect the police authorities but who, the next day, receive a stab in the back from the mass media.

Life is obviously being determined by Solidarity and the Church rather than by the force qualified to do so, since various factions are operating in the PZPR.

Allied impatience not only with Solidarity but also with the leadership of Mr Kania and his colleagues was obviously growing. So, in spite of the fairly widespread public scepticism over the law and order issue, there was serious concern and some alarm even among the most 'liberal' circles when it was announced that the Independent Union of Students was planning to stage street marches in Warsaw and several other towns on Monday 25 May in support of the demand for the release of 'political prisoners'. To many it seemed a gratuitous and unnecessary demonstration. For one thing, there were only seven people known to be in gaol who could arguably qualify for the title of political prisoner: five members of the Confederation of Independent Poland awaiting trial for anti-state activities, and two brothers, named Kowalczyk, who had served ten years of a twenty-five-year sentence for undeniably blowing up a building in the provincial capital of Opole which had been due to be used for a meeting of the police.

What people feared was a 'provocation'. *Zycie Warszawy* said such a possibility should not be treated lightly, nor its likely repercussions abroad. Stefan Bratkowski issued a warning that any street demonstration, however self-controlled, carried the danger of incalculable consequences, because various groups of people were 'ready for any provocation' to prove that the country was overwhelmed by anarchy.

In spite of appeals, most of the marches went ahead. The students in Warsaw agreed not to march to the Sejm, as originally planned, along a route that would have taken them past Communist Party headquarters. Instead they took a much shorter route from St Anne's Church – where mass was said – to the Tomb of the Unknown Soldier on Victory Square. Student and Solidarity marshals controlled the crowd of several thousand as well as diverting traffic. It all passed off peacefully and impressively. Several Solidarity leaders who had not initially been too happy at the idea marched at the head of the column, as did a priest. What the students achieved was a promise from Parliament that the seven cases raised by them would be examined.

The march was hardly over before even more startling news

emerged. It was announced that two former Ministers had committed suicide. They were Jerzy Olszewski, former Minister of Foreign Trade, and Edward Barszcz, former Minister of Building and Construction Materials, both of whom had served under Gierek and had come in for criticism in the current drive to 'settle accounts'. That, without doubt, was an embarrassment for the Government, but the Government itself caused widespread concern with a surprise statement issued after a meeting attended by provincial governors and city mayors in which it claimed that the dangerous situation created by 'increased crime, disturbances of public order and a slackening of social discipline' was being made worse by numerous politically-subversive acts, including public demonstrations, leaflets and posters hostile to the socialist state and the country's alliances. The statement went on, more ominously:

There have been instances, recently, of an improper attitude to, unjustified accusations against and irresponsible demands – and even individual cases of attacks – on soldiers of the Group of Soviet Armies stationed in Poland. The Council of Ministers states that these are impermissible occurrences. The temporary stationing of Soviet forces in Poland is legally regulated and results from the international obligations of the Polish State which relate to the operation of the defence treaty of the socialist countries. It constitutes one of the conditions enabling the Soviet Union to discharge its rights and responsibility stemming from the Four-Power Agreement on Germany. This is of fundamental importance for stabilising peace and security in Europe and guaranteeing the durability and inviolability of Poland's borders . . . For this reason attempts to spread distrust and to arouse anti-Soviet feelings are in conflict with the spirit and the letter of our allied relationship, and damage first and foremost the interests of Poland.

For some unexplained reason, the official version of the Government statement fairly quickly dropped that reference to 'attacks' on Soviet soldiers and referred instead to mere 'insults'. But the seriousness of the message was unmistakable. If there was one thing the Soviet Union could not be expected to tolerate it was anything that interfered with its ability, under the Warsaw Treaty and other international agreements, to secure its own defence and that of the socialist camp.

As for anti-Soviet or anti-Russian attitudes, one could argue that they were virtually endemic in Poland. But there had been little evidence so far that they had broken to the surface in actual anti-Soviet incidents. One of the effects of the Poles' much-praised 'prudence' was that few such incidents had occurred. But almost immediately after the Government statement, on the night of 25–26 May, a Soviet war memorial in the south-eastern town of Przemysl, close to the Ukrainian border, was daubed with white paint. The act of desecration was immediately condemned by, among others, the local chapter of Solidarity, which called for an investigation. 'Provocation' was again on people's minds.

The Hungarian Communist peper, *Nepszabadsag*, saw the Przemysl incident as the work of 'blackest reaction'. Moscow made no immediate comment, preferring to blame Solidarity for the breakdown in law and order which, it claimed, had led to the students' 'anti-Government' marches. *Rude Pravo* in Prague said the Warsaw march had provided a 'sad if not tragic sight', displaying as much hatred as the recent violence in Otwock. What, it asked, would come next?

10. KANIA SURVIVES MOSCOW LETTER

What did come next was to postpone any consideration of the nagging complaints of Poland's Soviet-bloc allies. It was the death, at 4.40 on the morning of Ascension Day, Thursday 28 May, of Cardinal Stefan Wyszynski, Metropolitan Archbishop of Gniezno and Warsaw, Primate of Poland. He was seventy-nine. Coming so soon after the attempted assassination in Rome of the Polish Pope, the news was undoubtedly a shock. But it was no surprise. The Cardinal had been ill since the middle of March, with what was at first described as a stomach ailment and identified only after his death as cancer. The Cardinal's condition got steadily worse and, when he received the last sacraments on 16 May, it seemed clear that he did not expect to live much longer. According to Warsaw Radio, after receiving the sacrament, 'the Cardinal addressed Roman Catholic church officials who had attended the ceremony, made a public profession of faith and prayed to the Black Madonna of Czestochowa to take special care of the Polish Church'.

Warsaw Radio broke into its programmes to announce the Cardinal's death, but many people guessed what had happened when they heard the bells of St Anne's Church solemnly tolling. As a steady stream of people poured through the gates of the Archbishop's residence in Miodowa Street and filed past the Primate's coffin, some of them in tears, the radio reported that the whole nation was absorbed in grief for a Prince of the Church who was also a great Polish patriot, who believed that supreme wisdom consisted in knowing that it is better to unite than to divide. The leaders of the Communist State – President, Party leader and Prime Minister – described the Cardinal once arrested by their predecessors as a great priest. The nation went into mourning, with flags at half mast, theatres and cinemas closed, and radio and television programmes altered to suit the mood of bereavement. The Primate's body was carried slowly through streets glistening with rain and strewn with flowers to the University Church to lie in state. The procession was headed by children and nuns singing softly and almost silently the prayer 'Sweet Jesus, Our Lord, grant him eternal rest'. The coffin was carried in turns by uniformed firemen and members of Solidarity, whose leaders, in their own tribute, credited the Cardinal with laying the foundations of the present 'moral renewal' and with making the Church the only place where for so long Poles had been able to hear the truth.

On Sunday 31 May the Cardinal was buried in the crypt of St John's Cathedral after an open-air mass in Victory Square, the heart of the capital, witnessed by an estimated 250,000 people, some of whom had taken up positions on window ledges, rooftops and even in trees. It was a colourful national gathering to equal the last occasion that mass was said there under the same huge wooden cross, when Pope John Paul II had returned to his homeland in 1979. But it was also international, with Cardinal Casaroli representing the sick Pope, and many cardinals, archbishops and bishops from all over the world.

Perhaps the most impressive moments came at the very end, after the coffin had been carried down the city's ancient Royal Way, to the tolling of bells and the singing of patriotic hymns, to the Cathedral of St John. There President Jablonski, Foreign Minister Czyrek and Deputy Premiers Ozdowski and Rakowski heard one of the bishops read from the Primate's last will and testament. In it he wrote that he considered it an act of grace that he had been able to bear witness to the truth as a political prisoner and that he sincerely forgave those who had slandered him.

When the coffin had been placed in the crypt, all the official mourners went down to pay their last respects. Some of the cardinals and bishops touched the coffin affectionately with their hands. Others kissed it, as did Lech Walesa before retiring with a sad shake of the head. President Jablonski gave a reverential bow. Bare-headed officers of the Polish People's Army left a huge wreath.

All this was seen at the end of five hours of unbroken television coverage, a remarkable demonstration of national unity and identity. Cardinal Wyszynski had been the Roman

Catholic Primate of Poland since 1948, almost as long as the Communists had been in power. He had been arrested by them in 1953 and kept in confinement in a monastery for three years, dubbed by *Trybuna Ludu* as 'a rowdy pupil of the Vatican'. Now those days were officially described as 'unpropitious times' and the Party paper conceded that 'for Wyszynski, the good of the Church was the same as the good of the nation'. *Kurier Polski*, the Democratic Party paper, almost but not quite suggested that the Primate was the greatest figure of the Communist era.

Gone is the man who exerted on Polish life in the last thirty odd years an influence as great as could be expected from any man in the face of the mighty mechanisms of history. Future generations will surely place him in the pantheon of the greatest national heroes. He served the nation as head of the Church – an institution inseparably linked with the country's life for one thousand years, an institution which has stayed with it through the most tragic and the most glorious turns of its destiny . . . If it were not for all that to which he devoted his long and magnificent life, there would not have been any of our great hopes now.

Those hopes, meanwhile, remained very uncertain, especially if one was listening to the words coming out of Moscow. In a couple of articles in the last few days of May *Trud*, the newspaper of the Soviet trade unions, said that Poland's old trade unions 'did not merit the devastating criticism which was heaped upon them and which paralysed the whole trade union aktiv' in the crisis of August 1980. 'One has to be politically immature', it said, 'not to see that by destroying an ally of the Party, the enemy weakens and drains the lifeblood of the Party itself.'

This was an obvious criticism of the Polish Party leadership, a very belated one, for having allowed August 1980 to turn out as it did. *Trud* followed it up with another article in which its correspondent claimed that 'the majority of Polish Communists' whom he had met kept insisting that the time had come 'to go over to the offensive', and that they had had enough of surrendering one position after another to so-called defenders of the workers who were really 'adventurists who threaten the destiny not only of Poland but of the world'.

Who were these Communists who confided so readily to visiting Soviet correspondents? They did not strike this visiting British correspondent as typical of those then making fiery, idealist speeches, fully reported in the press, at Party meetings throughout the country. The emphasis there was on reform and more of it, plus very bitter denunciation of the Party's errors in the recent past.

A fish always goes rotten from the head [one speaker said]. This is proved by the attitude of many comrades in the leadership who are notorious for their rapacious plundering. Anyone who opposes is dismissed as an idler, or a revisionist, or an anti-Semite or, recently, as an anti-socialist element. But the anti-socialist elements should be looked for in the leadership where some comrades put self-interest before the good of the country.

That, perhaps, represented the opposite extreme. And as for 'anti-socialist elements', lapel badges bearing those supposedly dreadful words had been on sale weeks earlier at a public exhibition of underground literature which took place, unmolested by the police, in the Warsaw Polytechnic. If a serious term of political abuse could be turned into a joke, the age of Communist claptrap, it seemed, could be on the way out.

Katowice Forum
Imagine the surprise, therefore, when *Trybuna Ludu* on Tuesday 26 May published a summary of a number of resolutions adopted by a Party group in the industrial centre of Katowice and couched in terms which seemed to belong to an era long since past. In response to horrified interest the youth paper, *Sztandar Mlodych*, published the texts of the resolutions two days later. Pretty soon protests started to pour in.

It was not surprising. The group, calling itself the Katowice Discussion Forum 'attached to the provincial PZPR committee', accused the Party leadership of 'basic errors, indecision and inconsistency' under the influence of 'right-wing opportunism and bourgeois liberalism'. It protested against the alleged impunity with which 'revisionists and factionalists' were being allowed to split the Party, in which Trotskyite–Zionist views, nationalism, agrarianism, clericalism and anti-Soviet feeling were said to be spreading day by day. The Party leadership, moreover, was accused of remaining impassive in the face of the threat of a revisionist coup d'état inside the Party, of failing to offer resistance to the horizontal structures movement, and of continued passivity and toleration of anti-socialist activities. The Forum even suggested that 'some circles in the supreme organs of power' were interested in encouraging Solidarity to take on the tasks of 'the organs of law and order'. It mentioned points already made by Poland's allies – the incident at Otwock, where Solidarity took on a policing role, and the case of Edward Baluka, the worker who left Poland after the troubles of 1970 but who returned illegally in the spring of 1981, after working for a time for Radio Free Europe, placed himself under the protection of Solidarity, and eventually got his old job back in the Warski shipyard in Szczecin.

The Katowice Forum was particularly critical of the mass media which, it said, should be subordinated to the Marxist–Leninist line. In recent months, it said, the press, radio and television had been dominated by anti-Party centres, and had been used to attack the Party's ideological unity, to place the rank and file in opposition to the Party apparatus, to secure the removal of 'honest Party figures' in the current election campaign, and to facilitate attacks on the internal security apparatus. The Forum demanded that the Party leadership put a stop to all this and take resolute steps against the threat of counter-revolution. It also called for firm measures against all anti-Soviet activities.

On the face of it, this represented the strongest attack on the Party leadership so far. And it looked very much like a hard-line backlash against the policy of renewal espoused by the Party since August 1980. Moreover, the Forum's denunciation of press, radio and television meant that any criticism coming from the mass media could be dismissed as the work of anti-Party revisionists. At last Moscow could, if it wanted, point to a group of Communists ready to back up its claims of general dissatisfaction. For the moment, though, the authors of the Forum documents were virtually anonymous. Indeed, they were denounced immediately by a Party meeting at the giant steelworks at Nowa Huta, outside Cracow, for making 'an anonymous attempt at large-scale subversion' by issuing documents that represented an insult to the Party and a negation of all that was authentic and valuable in the movement for renewal. More than thirty delegates from the Katowice Party organisation told Mr Kania in Warsaw that they did not accept the Forum's declaration which, they said, had been signed behind their backs.

In the midst of what the official Polish news agency described as a 'nationwide Party row', the Forum issued another document, a letter to Mr Albin Siwak, a candidate member of the Central Committee. Siwak had been taken to task by members of Solidarity in an open television debate for some of the things he had said about them during the recent Central Committe Plenum. This was an example, the Forum said, of how the mass media were helping enemies of socialism in their anti-Communist campaign.

Trybuna Ludu published a demand from Cracow that the names of the authors of the Forum's resolutions be made known and that the official Party committee in Katowice should say if it supported them. The Katowice paper, *Trybuna Robotnicza*, obliged the same day by publishing a statement from the Provincial Party Executive – led, of course, by Andrzej Zabinski – saying that it 'does not identify itself totally with the views expressed by members of the Forum'. It described the Forum as a debating club, a term which signified less than approval. *Trybuna Robotnicza* also identified a few of the Forum's leaders, two of them being members of the Silesian Scientific Institute.

It seemed very clear at this moment that the Katowice Forum was unrepresentative of the prevailing mood and aspirations of the Polish Communist Party. That was the unavoidable conclusion reached by anyone reading or hearing the stream of protests coming in from Party organisations all over the country, accusing it of trying to use 'dirty tricks' to split the Party before the coming Congress and, as one resolution put it, of using 'an out-of-date dictionary of epithets and charges such as our press has not tried to use since the beginning of the fifties'.

As for the much maligned press, certain papers gave a display of investigative journalism which made one wonder what would happen in other socialist-camp countries if newspapers were able to function in the same way at times of crisis. *Gazeta Krakowska* in Cracow and *Dziennik Zachodni* in Katowice revealed the names of the Forum's leadership. The Chairman of its 'programme council', the Forum claimed, was Gerard Gabrys, only recently appointed a full member of the Politburo and Secretary of the Central Committee. This undoubtedly was a bit of a shock, so reporters questioned him. All he would say was that he had, indeed, been invited to take up the chairmanship but had not attended any meetings of the Katowice Forum for reasons beyond his control.

But according to the two newspapers, one of which had a reporter at one of its meetings, the Katowice Forum also claimed to have 'made contact' with Stefan Olszowski and Tadeusz Grabski, both of the Politburo, and also with the editorial board of a mysterious new weekly called *Rzeczywistosc* (Reality), which had come out suddenly in May. *Rzeczywistosc*, it must be said, was to be fondly quoted by the Czechoslovak media. It was also closely connected with the equally mysterious Grunwald Patriotic Association, whose secretary had only recently told angry students that Mr Olszowski had said nice things about the Association.

'Sleeping dinosaurs'
Whatever the truth of it all, the plot seemed, very definitely, to be thickening. Mr Olszowski, as a matter of fact, was the first Party leader to say anything in public about the Katowice Forum. He described it as 'dogmatic'. By then, of course, the Forum had been almost totally routed by general opinion inside the Party. The most devastating criticism came from the Polish News Agency, PAP, in one of its special transmissions for seamen – oddly enough one of the most outspoken vehicles of information and comment throughout the period of renewal. The words of commentator Henryk Borucinski are worth quoting at some length because they voiced a general opinion which could not, perhaps, be broadcast so frankly in the mass media.

One could say that the social shock that has racked our country has awakened sleeping, antediluvian dinosaurs. They have made clear their view that our Party should avail itself of the experience of other parties in fighting the threat to the political system. It would seem beyond doubt that at this point they are encouraging the Party authorities to repeat the Czechoslovak experience and ask for assistance.

It cannot be denied that the appearance in Poland of a Party group which glibly speaks in the language of the Stalinist period will encourage some fraternal parties to regard their own rather superficial opinions about events in Poland as true. They may come to believe that the real partners for them in Poland are the members of the Forum.

Borucinski also had something to say specifically about the Soviet Union.

Our Party bears an enormous burden of sins for its attitude to the Soviet Union. Never since the war has it been that of a partner but always that of a vassal. This meant that although the Soviet Union pursued a consistently friendly policy towards us, anti-Soviet sentiments persisted among a large section of society, because a proud, ambitious nation cannot abide manifestations of servility.

The next day, Monday 1 June, the Soviet Union took up the Katowice Forum. TASS and Moscow Radio in its Home Service reported the Forum's stated views in detail and with evident relish and approval. In so doing, the Kremlin signalled its own disapproval of the Polish Party leadership, something underlined by the fact that the Soviet media, in those first reports, did not mention the widespread, almost universal condemnation of the Forum inside Poland itself. Indeed, it contrived to give the false impression that the meeting of the Forum was just one of the many official Party meetings then taking place throughout Poland in the run-up to the Congress. Prague Radio did likewise, though it did in its own way acknowledge the criticism of the Forum. The Forum, it noted, had called for 'all available means' to be used against counter-revolution, but its unambiguous conclusions had been 'answered by a hateful campaign by Polish anti-socialist forces, including Solidarity, who would like to silence every voice that does not agree with their adventurist anti-socialist ideas'.

As it happened, Solidarity had only just issued a statement condemning the Forum's documents as an excuse for Soviet intervention. In Hungary in 1956 and in Czechoslovakia in 1968, it said, the situation was described by the Soviet Union in exactly the same way the Katowice Forum was describing Poland now. This statement received massive publicity in the West. In a sense that was unfortunate, for it tended to reduce the whole issue to the over-simple terms of Solidarity versus Communism; hence it obscured the more important and momentous fact that the Polish Communist Party itself was refusing to be taken in by the antique shibboleths of ideological intimidation dredged up by a small group of unrepresentative Communists who were afraid that the Party could not survive if it gave up the old levers of coercion and control.

It is also worth noting that the first Soviet reports quoted the Katowice Forum as stressing that 'we must use the universal methods of the construction of socialism and not build a Polish socialism', and that more damage had been done to the Polish Party in the months since August 1980 than in the entire ten years preceding it.

Whichever way one looked at it, the Polish leadership was faced with an open quarrel with the Soviet Union. On Tuesday 2 June the Politburo met in Warsaw and stated that, although the documents of the Katowice Forum contained correct statements, their general tenor was harmful to the Party and was not conducive to Party unity. Some of the Forum's generalisations, the Politburo said, were simply false.

In a matter of days it seemed as if the Katowice Forum had been thoroughly defeated. Kazimierz Barcikowski dismissed it as a group of extreme leftists, one of various discussion clubs, including the Grunwald Association which, he said, got things wrong as well as right. Mieczyslaw Moczar, his Politburo colleague, stated his opposition to both the Forum and to Grunwald, which was complaining that very week of a 'gross campaign of slanders and accusations' against it. Gerard Gabrys – the Politburo member reported by Moscow to have presided over the Forum meeting which adopted the disputed documents – announced that he had never attended any meeting or consented to do so and that he agreed totally with the view of the Politburo. Another man to put some distance between himself and the Forum was Jan Konieczny, Chairman of the Miners' Union, originally claimed by the Katowice group as a member of its governing council. On Thursday 4 June the Forum published another statement announcing that it was suspending further meetings until it received an 'unambiguous statement' on its further activities from the Politburo.

Party 'retreating'
But the Forum's 'allies' outside Poland did not give up. Indeed, events inside Poland enabled them to raise the pressure. On 3 June Prague television claimed that the Forum's fears had been justified by an event in Zawiercie, Katowice Province, where it said a Solidarity member, Bohdan Krakowski, had demanded that the town council remove the Red Flag from its building and rename Red Army and Majakowski streets. Moscow Radio said he had threatened violence against Communists. The radio in Prague

alleged that Krakowski had 'said literally that millions of members of the PZPR should be hanged'. Perfect evidence of counter-revolution. Krakowski, when contacted, said he had been misquoted. He denied any threat of violence but insisted that since Zawiercie was in Poland, the Polish flag should be allowed to fly alongside the Red Flag, and that Red Army street should be renamed Paderewski street after the famous Polish pianist and statesman.

But far more substantial problems were also developing. On Thursday 4 June the National Solidarity Commission meeting in Bydgoszcz agreed to back a local call for a two-hour warning strike in a week's time if the Government failed to produce its promised report on its investigations into the beating up of union activists there in March. The Commission reached its decision after a majority vote in the absence of Lech Walesa, who was attending an international trade union conference in Geneva, and in spite of an appeal from the Roman Catholic Church not to strike now. Deputy Prime Minister Rakowski quickly visited Bydgoszcz and arranged for talks in Warsaw on the following Monday. Solidarity agreed that three other northern towns could join in the strike, which would be the first for two months.

Then, on Friday, came news calculated to confirm the worst fears of Poland's allies on the issue of law and order. It was announced that the four members of the Confederation of Independent Poland, the KPN, who were still under arrest, had been released and would be at liberty until their trial on anti-State activities. One other KPN member had been set free earlier without any proper explanation. It had been announced a couple of days earlier, though, that Mr Rakowski had discussed the issue of 'political prisoners' with Bishop Bronislaw Dabrowski, the Secretary of the Polish Episcopate. Moscow Radio was very quick to pick up the news of the release. *Pravda*, the next day, headlined its report 'The Latest Concession'.

Moscow was manifestly unhappy. Faced with the obvious rout of the Katowice Forum, it was forced to report 'a mass campaign' against it. It claimed that this was inspired by 'the right-wing leaders of Solidarity' but had to concede that it had been supported by the leaders of certain Party organisations. Some statements, it said, had described the Forum as 'harmful' – the very word used by the Polish Politburo.

The Kremlin's thoughts on what should be done were made clear when *Pravda* reprinted an article from its Bulgarian counterpart, *Rabotnichesko Delo*, on the progress of 'creeping counter-revolution' in Poland.

The situation calls in the first place for resolute action to strengthen the PZPR and its links with the masses . . . If a Party begins retreating from Marxist-Leninist positions and the laws of class struggle, it inevitably disarms itself ideologically and organisationally, petty beourgeois trends prevail and it loses its leading role . . . The disruptive trends and manifestations of right-wing revisionism and factionalism which have emerged in the Party are particularly dangerous . . . The enemies of socialism do not conceal the hope that the forthcoming Congress of the PZPR will make amendments to the Party rules that will turn it into a reformist party.

It was the state of the Party more than anything else that was worrying Moscow. Reports on the progress of reportback and election meetings in Party organisations throughout Poland suggested the possibility that the existing Central Committee and a fair proportion of the Politburo would be replaced at the coming Congress and maybe even fail to get elected as delegates to the Congress.

On 4 June a Central Committee official reported that the meetings were producing thorough-going changes at all levels, but the higher the body, the bigger the changes. So far, he said, elections in the lowest Party organisations had brought a fifty per cent change as regards first secretaries and forty per cent change in their executives. At municipal level there had been a seventy-five per cent change. At the first three provincial conferences, ninety per cent of those elected were newcomers. Compared with previous campaigns, there was also a change in the social background of those elected. Fewer workers were being elected. Meetings were reported to be stormy, heated, polemical, sharp and almost invariably prolonged, sometimes going on into the night or lasting more than one day. The results locally were striking. In Bydgoszcz province alone 322 out of 393 basic Party organisations got rid of their First Secretaries and replaced eighty-one per cent of the membership of their executives. As for the national picture, President Jablonski seemed to have guessed which way the wind was blowing when he announced that he would not be seeking Party office any more.

The prospect of massive change in the Party through the

medium of secret elections must have been frightening to 'orthodox' Communist observers who were already finding it difficult to digest the astonishing figures just reported by Warsaw Radio. From 1 September to 4 June, it said, people sacked from top posts in the Party and State apparatus included thirteen ministers, forty deputy ministers, eighteen provincial governors, twenty-six deputy provincial governors, twenty-six first secretaries of provincial committees, seventy-two provincial committee secretaries, seven heads of Central Committee departments, and fourteen directors of amalgamations. Eight people had been deprived of their seats in Parliament.

The news that weekend, 6 and 7 June, did not help ease the impression of a deeply divided leadership. In Bydgoszcz the Party report-back and election meeting was told by a delegate from the uniformed police, the MO, that if people wanted to find the sources of the notorious incident of 19 March they should not look at the police but elsewhere.

We wish to serve the Party [he said], but we do not want to serve persons or groups inside the Party or the administration . . . The authors of the declaration of the Katowice Party Forum are taking up the defence of the militia and the security service. We do not need such defenders, people who have on more than one occasion used the police for their own well-known ends.

The political divisions in the top Party leadership were underlined when Tadeusz Fiszbach told a meeting in Gdansk that there was still no real programme for change and there had not been enough change. He dismissed as 'mistaken and vulgar' the theory that reform necessarily breeds anarchy. Every system has its enemies, he said, but it has more of them the more it fails to satisfy the needs of the people. In contrast, Tadeusz Grabski told a meeting in Poznan that the Party's programme was under attack not just from the dogmatic left, which included the Katowice Forum, but also from its right wing, whose views, he said, were of a social democratic or Christian democratic kind.

But the most alarming speech was made at the Bydgoszcz Party meeting by Deputy Premier Rakowski. The man who had so often voiced his hopes in Solidarity now let fly at those elements in it who, he said, were taking a political line. Describing the Bydgoszcz Solidarity leader, Jan Rulewski, as a 'classic demagogue', he accused those like him of seeking a political trial of strength with a view to bringing the Government to its knees.

The existence of Poland as a state is threatened . . . The limit of reasonable compromise has been totally exhausted . . . In the days and weeks ahead, each member of the Party will have to say which side he is on . . . Comrades, we are approaching a very difficult frontier . . . Our allies' patience is running out . . . Anti-Sovietism is manifesting itself not just in tearing down red stars from the graves of Soviet soldiers. It can be seen in many factory news sheets. Many of them have been hissing against the Soviet Union for months . . . I still believe there is a chance to implement the line of accord, but that chance is diminishing.

It was difficult to find an immediate explanation for Mr Rakowski's outburst, which made the situation sound more serious than it seemed. But on Sunday it was announced that the Central Committee would meet again in plenary session on Tuesday. This suggested some urgency since a session of the Sejm had to be postponed. But even the threatened warning strike over Bydgoszcz did not seem to warrant that.

Moscow letter
The real explanation came on Sunday evening when the BBC in Warsaw learned and reported that the Polish Party leadership had received what amounted to a direct warning from the Soviet leaders in Moscow. A letter from the Central Committee of the Soviet Communist Party had been delivered on Friday and quickly distributed in more than three hundred duplicated copies to members of the Polish Central Committee and apparatus. The message, in the simplest terms, said that the Polish Party was losing control and should take stronger action against the threat of counter-revolution. The Polish leaders, the letter said, could count on their Soviet comrades if they needed them.

The existence of the Soviet letter was not confirmed until Mr Kania began addressing the Central Committee on Tuesday, and the text was not published until Warsaw Radio broadcast it on Thursday evening, one day before TASS put it out in Moscow. But it was not intended for the public, it was meant for the Central Committee – the old Committee appointed under Mr Gierek. For some of its members, no doubt, the letter presented an opportunity; for others a threat.

179

Dear comrades, the CPSU Central Committee is writing to you out of deep concern for the future of socialism in Poland and for Poland as a free and independent country . . . We cannot remain unconcerned about the mortal danger which now looms over the Polish people's revolutionary achievements . . . From the first days of the crisis we believed that it was a matter of importance that the Party oppose in a determined manner any attempts by the enemies of socialism to take advantage of the difficulties to further their long-term aims. However, this was not done. Continual concessions to anti-socialist forces and their demands have led to a situation in which the PZPR has been falling back step by step under the pressure of internal counter-revolution, which has been supported by imperialist foreign centres of subversion . . .

The enemies of socialist Poland . . . are waging a struggle for power and are already in the process of achieving it. They have been gaining control of one position after another. Counter-revolution has been using the extremist faction of Solidarity as a strike force. By deceiving them, it has involved workers who have joined a vocational trade union in a criminal plot against the people's power. A wave of anti-Communism and anti-Sovietism is developing. Imperialist forces are making increasingly bold attempts to interfere in Poland's domestic affairs.

The serious danger which looms over socialism in Poland is also a threat to the very existence of an independent Polish state. If the worst came to the worst, if the enemies of socialism were to achieve power and if Poland ceased to enjoy protection from the socialist states, the greedy hands of imperialism would immediately be raised against it. Who then would be able to guarantee the independence, sovereignty and borders of Poland as a state? No one.

At this point the letter recalled that at meetings with Polish delegations in Moscow and Warsaw on 5 December 1980 and 23 April 1981 Soviet leaders had expressed their growing concern, in particular, over 'the fact that the adversary had gained control over the mass information media' and also over 'the need to strengthen the organs of law and order and protect them from the ambitions of counter-revolutionary forces'. On both points the letter was blunt:

Attention was drawn to the fact that the battle had not been won for the Party as long as the press, radio and television worked not for the PZPR but for its enemies . . . To allow attempts to slander and break up the security services, the militia and later also the army almost to succeed practically implies the disarmament of the socialist state and its abandonment to the mercy of its class enemies.

Then came a more specific, personal complaint:

We wish to stress that on all issues that were broached, Stanislaw

Kania and Wojciech Jaruzelski and the other Polish comrades expressed their agreement with our viewpoint. But in fact everything has remained unchanged and no modification has been made to the policy of concessions and compromise. One position after another is being surrendered, without taking into account the documents of the latest plenums which note a counter-revolutionary threat. So far no measures have been taken to counter it and the organisers of the counter-revolution are not directly named.

Recently, the situation within the PZPR itself has become a cause of particular concern. There is not much more than a month left before the Congress. Nevertheless, it is increasingly the forces hostile to socialism that are setting the tone of the election campaign. It is not unusual for individuals chosen at random and openly preaching opportunist viewpoints to enter the leadership of local Party organisations and to be among the delegates to conferences and to the Congress. It is also very disturbing that the delegates to the Congress include only a very small number of Communists from a workers' environment. The preparations for the Congress are being complicated by the so-called 'horizontal structures' movement which is the tool for dismantling the Party being used by opportunists to promote at the Congress the people they need to guide its proceedings in a direction favourable to them. One cannot rule out the possibility that during the Congress itself, an attempt will be made to deal a decisive blow to the Party's Marxist-Leninist forces in order to bring about its elimination.

We consider that there is still a possibility of avoiding the worst and averting a national disaster. Within the PZPR there are many honest and resolute Communists ... It is now a matter of mobilising all of society's healthy forces with a view to countering the class enemy and combating counter-revolution. This demands first and foremost a revolutionary will from the Party, its members and its leadership – yes, its leadership. Time does not wait. The Party can and should find within itself the forces to reverse the course of events and restore them to the right path before the Congress.

The letter ended with a repetition of Mr Brezhnev's promise not to leave a fraternal country in the lurch.

Whichever way one read that letter, it was difficult to avoid the conclusion that Moscow not only wanted tougher measures against the alleged threat of counter-revolution but was also suggesting the reimposition of controls – on the media, for instance – which would help take the stuffing out of reform and at the same time making it perfectly clear that it would not be displeased if there were changes in the Polish leadership.

Intellectual reply
On the morning of Monday 8 June the nation was not sup-

posed to know about this. But a group of more than twenty of the country's leading intellectuals, aware of what was going on, issued a letter of their own. It had been sent to Prime Minister Jaruzelski and to the editor of *Zycie Warszawy*, but when the paper did not publish it it became an open letter. Without referring to the message from Moscow, the intellectuals challenged some of its basic assumptions. Never before, they said, had Poland had such a chance as it had now to devise a programme for national development that would be universally accepted. But they felt obliged to speak now because the opinions being expressed about Poland in the mass media of East and West, but especially in the country's nearest neighbours, could lead to serious consequences. There were no groups of any influence or standing in Poland, they said, which wanted to break the alliance with the Soviet Union. That could only happen if an attempt was made to halt the gradual process of internal reform. But if such an attempt was made, there would be a danger of mass protest and incalculable consequences for Poland, the socialist countries and for Europe. The authors of the letter, who said they believed their views were shared by many Poles, represented a cross-section of the country's intellectual life. Some were Communists, some Roman Catholics, others were MPs or came from the world of arts or academic life. They included the film director Andrzej Wajda, the President of the Academy of Sciences, the journalists' leader, Stefan Bratkowski, and the professor recently appointed by the Prime Minister himself to look at the national economic plan just rejected by the Sejm.

By the next day, when Mr Kania was opening the crucial session of the Central Committee, some of those signatories were among an even larger number who had put their names to yet another open letter. This one came from a group of intellectuals and specialists belonging to a discussion club of long standing known as Experience and Future. The warnings this time were much more startling. The letter stated frankly that, if hardliners were to take over the Party and if the present policy of renewal were to be changed, then the Party would be split. With the moderates losing control, it said, there would be a rapid polarisation of opinion, bringing with it civil disobedience and a wave of strikes. But if force were to be used, internal or external, the results would be worse. Not only would the Communist Party break up, the chance of Poland having any more to do with Communism would be irretrievably lost. Ill feeling towards Russians and Germans would be revived for generations to come and Poland would take on the attitude of an occupied country with underground resistance. Moreover the Soviet Union would become isolated in the international workers' movement and détente would be finally dead.

Mr Kania, one must presume, was well aware of the arguments in these two letters which were, in effect, a vote of support for the policies he and General Jaruzelski were pursuing. He knew the risk of internal reaction if he simply accepted the Soviet criticisms and acted accordingly. He knew too that defiance of the Moscow message could spell disaster, especially with a Central Committee that belonged to the Gierek era rather than his own. In the event, he attempted to tread a delicate middle course that left neither side immediately satisfied.

As for the Soviet letter, Mr Kania said that Poland's friends had every right to react as they had. The Party of Lenin was responsible for the security of the socialist community, and besides there were genuine grounds for alarm over the situation developing in Poland. He mentioned a 'filthy wave of anti-Sovietism and anti-Communism' and the 'barbaric' desecration of Soviet monuments and graves. Poland must give convincing practical proof of its continued commitment to socialism and its alliances. He seemed to admit much else complained of in the Soviet message: that 'honest comrades' were being passed over in the elections, that the grass-roots, 'horizontal structures' movement in the Party had brought out social democratic trends, that Solidarity was turning into an opposition political party, that anarchy threatened to paralyse the organs of state. But his line seemed softer, and perhaps the only point in his speech that seriously disturbed the liberals concerned the media. Negative phenomena had appeared, he said, and there had been a weakening of discipline in editorial teams. 'Personnel decisions' would have to be taken so that the press, radio and television not only reflected opinions but shaped them. This, presumably, meant that some editors would be replaced.

But as regards Poland's general policy, Mr Kania left his audience in no doubt. The present situation, he said, could place a question mark over the line of socialist renewal; but in spite of the difficulties the Politburo believed that there was no sensible alternative to it.

Our Party, the allied parties and the whole front of common sense and political responsibility support this policy. There is room in this front for everyone . . . This policy consolidates the concepts of social justice and restores ethical and moral norms. It creates conditions for shaping humanistic relations between people and respecting the dignity of man, worker and citizen . . . We have acted for the sake of internal calm by using the methods of accord. Today, in the name of defending the socialist homeland . . . we appeal to all patriots to unite their thoughts and efforts in a front of civic responsibility. We are capable of resisting all dangers. We must consolidate the Party and prepare and hold a successful Congress . . . Whoever supports us will pass the test in one of the most dramatic moments of Poland's thousand years of history.

Kania survives challenge

Anyone who saw on television how Mr Kania quickly gathered up his papers and sat down, rather grim-faced, could guess that he was up against it. And first reports of the speeches in the debate confirmed that, with the backing of the Soviet letter, some Central Committee members felt emboldened to attack both the Party's policy and its leadership.

Zygmunt Najdowski, the First Secretary from Torun, said that the plenum should consider revising the formula of solving the crisis by peaceful means and replacing it with that of ending it 'at all costs'. He also suggested changes in the Politburo. Janusz Prokopiak, the man who had lost his job as First Secretary in Radom months earlier and had, incidentally, been defended there by Tadeusz Grabski, also hoped for changes in the Politburo. He suggested that the members of the Central Committee should express their attitude to members of the Politburo in a secret ballot.

Another call for at least a partial change in the Politburo came from the writer, Jerzy Putrament. A member of the Politburo, Andrzej Zabinski from Katowice, spoke of lethargy in the face of an open and tangible threat, of 'our weakness, indecision and constant retreat' in the successive stages of a 'takeover of power'.

Hardliners certainly did not have it all their own way on the first day of the plenum but official reports suggested that they had definitely found a new lease of life. The prospects for Kania were not good. But they improved the next day. The fight back was led by Deputy Premier Rakowski. The man who had scourged the hot-heads of Solidarity only a few days earlier now turned on Comrade Najdowski for making what he understood to be a call for the use of force.

We must not forget that our Party is responsible before history and the nation for the bloodshed in Poznan and on the Baltic Coast. We cannot allow such dramatic events to happen a third time. If that happened the Party would not survive . . . and coming generations would not forgive us.

At one point some members of the Central committee began stamping their feet in protest. Rakowski turned on them.

Comrades, you cannot stamp down reality . . . A lot has been said here about concessions and compromises . . . As soon as a threat passes, the criticisms begin . . . A compromise becomes a concession, then opportunism and defeatism. This has nothing to do with any form of reality. This is an ugly political game . . . I am an ardent supporter of recognising realities . . . A truly great process is taking place today within the Party . . . All this monstrous confusion has produced superb people . . . The Party will not perish, not by any means, if these people direct our Party in the months and years ahead.

Roman Ney, a candidate member of the Politburo, backed Rakowski, saying that a postponement of the Congress would be a tragedy leading to the disintegration of the Party. But his most telling point concerned proposed changes in the leadership. 'If we carried out a change in the Party leadership today, I am convinced this would be regarded by the whole Party and the public as a change forced on us by our allies. Such a change would be regarded as a retreat from socialist renewal. We must not do it.'

A worker from Szczecin voiced his support for Kania's report and suggested that the troubles with Solidarity were exaggerated. After all, he said, the majority of Party members belonged to it. But the genuine loyalist worker's view was presented by Albin Siwak, the construction worker from Warsaw who had been defended earlier by the Katowice Forum. He claimed that Solidarity was 'carrying out elections in our Party how it pleases and wherever it pleases'. More than thirty per cent of the delegates already elected to the Party Congress came from Solidarity, he said, while barely twenty-two per cent were workers. He seemed to imply that Solidarity members could not be classed as workers. Siwak reported fears that after the Congress the Party would never be the same. He warned that if something was not done quickly the Party would not last long, that unless there was a tightening up over law and order, it would soon be impossible to leave one's home at night without fear. He also said the cleansing of the Party was going too far and had an 'element of cannibalism and castration'. This was helping the enemy to break up the Party.

The argument went on on either side, with at least one critical mention of General Jaruzelski's Government and of Stanislaw Kania. But the debate came to a head with the speech by Tadeusz Grabski and what amounted to an open attack on Mr Kania's leadership. Professing full agreement with the Soviet letter, Grabski said the reasons for the continuing crisis should be seen in the leadership itself. For several months, he said, the Politburo had not been a unified body. He had proposed three times that Jozef Klasa be sacked as head of the Central Committee Department for Press, Radio and Television, but nothing had happened. Though a member of the Politburo, he had learned of major decisions – on the Bydgoszcz events and the agreement with the students in Lodz – only from the media. The decision on legalising Rural Solidarity and releasing members of the Confederation of Independent Poland had been taken outside the Politburo. As for the reported condemnation of the Katowice Forum, Grabski claimed that the Politburo had not taken such a stand; it had not been discussed at a Politburo meeting.

In the light of the situation in the Party and the danger threatening our people, I want to answer the question of whether the members of the Politburo are capable of leading the country out of its political crisis. I do not see such a possibility in its present composition under the leadership of Comrade Stanislaw Kania, the First Secretary.

Never before, surely, had the world been allowed to witness a power struggle in a Communist state in such detail and with such immediacy. Even more astonishing was the reaction to Grabski's challenge. Kazimierz Barcikowski sprang to Mr Kania's defence, declaring that his policy was not one of capitulation but the only one possible. He had listened to the debate, Barcikowski said, with sorrow and shame but felt obliged to tender his resignation. As for Mr Grabski, he congratulated him on his lack of awareness. It was odd, he thought, that most of the decisions Grabski complained he knew nothing about actually belonged to the sector for which he was officially responsible.

It was an extraordinary situation requiring extraordinary measures. An intermission was agreed and all eleven members of the Politburo met in special session. Mr Kania then went back to the plenum with a proposal. In line with suggestions made in the debate all members of the Politburo were willing to submit themselves individually to a vote of confidence by secret ballot. If any one of them failed to gain at least fifty per cent of the votes, he would automatically leave the Politburo.

A debate on the proposal followed and according to Warsaw Radio it was a long and lively affair. But there were soon signs that the Kania line was winning. As the evening progressed the radio reported 'views expressing confidence in Stanislaw Kania and Wojciech Jaruzelski' coming from, among others, 'members of the central Party bodies in army uniforms'. Provincial Party leaders asked for a special meeting with Mr Kania. Shortly after midnight the plenum ended. By a majority vote the Central Committee had decided not to go ahead with the vote of confidence. There were to be no changes in the Party leadership. Mr Kania and General Jaruzelski had scored a signal victory by merely surviving.

The only casualty was Jozef Klasa, head of the Central Committee Department for the Press, Radio and Television. He offered his resignation and eventually it was to be accepted. But he departed defiantly. He told the plenum that he had been the victim of 'an unscrupulous campaign' and that he had not been given the necessary assistance and support. A sad exit for a man who had told an interviewer only a few weeks earlier that he had returned to politics after the Gierek era only because Mr Kania had made it clear to him that as long as he was at the head of the Party he would not let anyone shoot at Polish workers.

Mr Kania had survived, but Mr Klasa had become the target of those who disliked and feared the implications of the Party leader's policy.

11. EXTRAORDINARY PARTY CONGRESS

There could be no doubt that Mr Kania and General Jaruzelski had scored a notable victory. Not only had they stayed in power in spite of very pointed criticism of their record by the Soviet Union, they had also managed to win a reaffirmation of the policy of renewal. The Party Congress, which some people had wanted postponed, would also take place as planned. The Soviet letter had made it clear that the Kremlin was afraid that the Congress would change the nature of Poland's Communist Party. There was every reason to suppose that with that letter Moscow had tried to use the Central Committee appointed under Mr Gierek – the one expected to be replaced by the Congress – in a last-chance attempt to secure a change of leadership and policy before it was too late.

One result of Mr Kania's survival as Party leader in the face of Soviet pressure was an increase in support for him throughout the country. Any Pole who stands up to the Russians is bound to be popular anyway. Without saying that in so many words, the Polish radio was quick to report relief and delight at Mr Kania's success. The local radio in Bydgoszcz reported many messages of support for him, including one which said plainly: 'We are grateful to you, Comrade Kania, for not allowing yourself to be ditched.'

Some reactions actually questioned the arguments in the Soviet letter. 'Surely we cannot speak of any counter-revolution in our country,' said one 'man-in-the-street', interviewed by Koszalin Radio up on the Baltic Coast. 'If there are any anti-socialist forces or counter-revolutionaries, please point them out. Who are they?'

In one of his official news agency commentaries for seamen, Henryk Borucinski reported that most Poles could not understand that part of the Soviet letter which spoke of 'the greedy hands of imperialism' being raised against their country.

Can eager hands stretch out to take our independence, when we are surrounded on all sides by friends? Let us not beat about the bush; ever since the famous Brezhnev doctrine on the limited sovereignty of socialist countries and the intervention in Czechoslovakia, we have been living under the psychological pressure that the same will be applied to Poland.

Journalists answer back

Such outspoken comments and questions are worth savouring, for the freedom enjoyed by the mass media for nearly a year was now in danger. Mr Kania's victory had been bought at a price; the evidence of this was in the final resolution of the Eleventh Plenum which declared its agreement with the views of the Soviet Communist Party and promised to use 'all necessary means' to put an end to anti-socialist activities and restore law and order. It could be argued that these were mere words, and Poland's Warsaw Pact allies were to complain bitterly in the coming weeks that such was the case. But there could be no doubt about the resolution's attitude to the mass media.

The Central Committee makes it incumbent on the Politburo and the Secretariat of the Central Committee urgently to take all the necessary political and organisational measures to assess journalistic personnel and to take personnel decisions which will ensure the implementation of the line of the Party and the socialist State by the press, radio and television.

This was one important achievement of the Soviet letter. Another – not immediately obvious but which became clearer as the weeks went by – was that it bestowed respectability on the hard-line views of such groups as the Katowice Forum. The attitudes which had been dismissed as unrepresentative only a week or so before, largely with the help of the media, now had the blessing of a much stronger, bigger brother, who could not so easily be ignored.

Mr Kania, though probably more popular than ever and stronger in that sense, was actually in a difficult position. He now had to cope not only with open Soviet pressure but also with colleagues in the Politburo who, no less than himself, had survived. They included not only Tadeusz Grabski, who had come out openly against him, but Stefan Olszowski, the man ultimately responsible for the media. Olszowski, widely regarded as one of the most talented politicians in the country,

189

was suspected of being more conservative than the Party leader. He had managed not to say anything in public during the critical hours of the Eleventh Plenum. At any rate, it was Olszowski who was soon telling ideological officials and editors of the need to restore Poland's credibility in the eyes of its allies. What that implied was not immediately obvious, and in fact the changes in the Polish press, radio and television took some time to make themselves felt. But it was basically an argument over credibility. The Council of Polish Journalists, led by Stefan Bratkowski, issued a resolution pointing out that the people could hardly trust the authorities if they could not trust the press. Any danger to law and order, it said, came not from the opening up of the press but from its falsification, not from criticism as such but from the suppression of criticism.

Karol Malcuzynski, the man who had spoken out against the propaganda of success, told the Sejm a few days after the Party Plenum that, whilst Polish journalists were neither angels nor sages, 'they do not, citizen deputies, constitute a hotbed of counter-revolution or anti-socialist conspiracies as some would like to present them'. More than that, Mr Malcuzynski said that it was not only the Western press but, regrettably, the press of 'friendly countries' which had been guilty of publishing 'distorted information and commentaries that were either naive or downright false' about the situation in Poland. Such opinions, he said, influenced the assessments and decisions of politicians, and in his view the Soviet letter had in many respects presented a 'one-sided' view of Polish developments. Every word written inside Poland and about it, said Malcuzynski, was worth its weight not so much in gold as in dynamite. 'But does this mean that we are to return to the model of the press of the past decades? Is this press to be accommodating, subservient, well behaved, obedient to all authority – and read by no one, deprived of all prestige within the nation?'

Whatever Mr Kania's intentions towards the media, one change I myself noticed in the first few days after the Party Plenum was that television devoted much greater attention to the person of the First Secretary. He went down to Cracow to attend the Provincial Party Conference and was chosen there, in a secret ballot, as a delegate to the coming Party Congress. This was certainly a tribute to his popularity and a gesture of support for his policies from one of the most 'liberal' Party organisations in the country. Among those chosen as delegates with him were Mieczyslaw Rakowski, Deputy Prime Minister; Jozef Klasa, still described as the Head of the Central Committee's Department for Press, Radio and Television; and Maciej Szumowski, the highly respected Chief Editor of *Gazeta Krakowska*, a paper already accused by hard-line elements of being 'revisionist'. To be elected in such company was, perhaps, a political gesture by Mr Kania himself. But equally striking was the way in which the television cameras seemed to concentrate their spotlight on him. He was shown modestly accepting the applause of enthusiastic comrades and promising that he would remain 'faithful to the end' to the policy of renewal.

Several days later Kania was again in the spotlight when he attended the Party conference of the Pomeranian Military District. The setting was rather different. This time the cameras showed him rising, again modestly, to acknowledge the applause of a forest of uniformed men, clapping rhythmically in a style more reminiscent of the Kremlin Palace of Congresses. One could not be sure, but it did seem possible that, having accepted the Soviet leaders' strictures against the Polish media, Kania had also agreed that television should be used in a very Soviet way to support him and his policies – in the face of patent Soviet disapproval.

The Kania leadership did need support. Life had been difficult enough in the past, but now it was committed to restoring the confidence of its allies and this meant that its margins for error had been narrowed. In a sense it was now permanently on trial. What it had to do, as quickly as possible, was at least to show a readiness to curb the allegedly 'political' activities of Solidarity and at the same time do its best to make sure that the Communist Party did not go completely off the rails. Both tasks were largely beyond the leadership's control. Solidarity had already proved conclusively enough that by its very nature it had a mind of its own. As for the Party, it was now enjoying the unprecedented privilege of free and secret elections in an exercise that could hardly be stopped now.

One remarkable feature of the period between the Eleventh Plenum, which ended on 10 June, and the opening of the Party Congress on 14 July was that for most of it Solidarity did not present any real challenge to the authorities. Indeed, it seemed to go out of its way not to rock the boat. The threatened strike over the Bydgoszcz affair was called off effectively while the plenum was still in session. Lech Walesa, who had gone straight into talks after returning from the trade union conference in Geneva, said that it could not be right to place both the union and the community at risk by going on strike at such a time of national crisis. In subsequent weeks he told a series of meetings throughout the country that it was time Solidarity concentrated on its proper business and resisted any temptation to play at politics. 'There has been too much confrontation,' he said.

Walesa was equally forthright about the rash of incidents in which Soviet war memorials were desecrated over a period of weeks. One such incident happened in Lublin when he was there attending a regional Solidarity conference. But as soon as they heard about it, local Solidarity leaders went to the monument and began cleaning it themselves, before the fire brigade arrived. Walesa denounced the episode as a deliberate provocation designed to give the impression that Solidarity was responsible. He demanded that the authorities should do more to expose the real culprits.

Less obvious to the public, but just as valuable, was a decision by Solidarity not to press its objections on the draft bills on censorship and the trade unions until after the Communist Party Congress. The authorities themselves contrived to avoid one possible occasion of serious trouble. The trial on political charges of four leaders of the Confederation of Independent Poland, which began on 15 June, was adjourned on a defence plea until 2 July.

Kania's electioneering
The effect of all this was that the field was left comparatively open for Kania and his colleagues to concentrate on what was, without doubt, the most immediate and important problem in the run-up to the Ninth Congress – the elections at Party conferences throughout the country. Two sorts of elections were taking place. Party bodies were 'renewing' themselves by electing their officers after hearing reports on the stewardship of their outgoing leaders and executives. The month of June was largely taken up with the big Party conferences in the country's forty-nine provinces. At the same time, though, these conferences were choosing their delegates to the Party

Congress. In all these elections there was more than one candidate and voting was by secret ballot. Given the state of the Party, there was more than a theoretical chance that the elections could sweep away most of the old leadership. The Soviet letter had made Moscow's concern very clear on this point and Kania himself felt obliged to issue an appeal at the end of the Eleventh Plenum. The renewal of the Party at all levels, he said, must be accompanied by an understanding of 'the need to retain continuity' in the leadership of Party bodies. The Party, he insisted, would suffer a great loss if 'experienced activists' were passed over in the formal processes of the elections.

Kania showed particular concern for the election to the Party Congress of representatives of the central leadership – the national Party leadership and apparatus. There should be no artificial barriers created to prevent their nomination, he said, and he would be agitating in their support as much as he could. His motives were probably two-fold. He presumably wanted to make sure that the Party was not deprived entirely of men and women who knew how to run it. He could also have been forced to try to prove to his anxious Soviet allies that a 'recognisable' Party leadership could survive.

On this issue Mr Kania was not to get his way – or not completely. The problem was that some provincial Party organisations were simply unwilling to have candidates foisted upon them from outside, believing that if the new-found democracy was to be genuine all candidates, either for office or for election as delegates to the Congress, should go through the proper procedures starting in their own basic Party organisations. Others were not so obstructive and by 23 June a healthy number of Politburo members and Central Committee Secretaries – eleven in all – had secured their ticket to the Congress. Among them was President Jablonski, who had obviously been persuaded to change his mind about retiring from Party office, but they did not include Tadeusz Grabski, Stefan Olszowski or Andrzej Zabinski, the three men generally considered to favour a harder line. For a little while there was keen interest in the possibility that one or two of these would not be elected to the Congress at all, and this speculation was prolonged by the notable failure of the Polish media to let people know who was standing for election where, or to state quite clearly who had failed. This was, after all, an election campaign, a fact underlined at the end of the month when Mr Kania and General Jaruzelski attended the Katowice Provincial Party Conference and gave their support to their Politburo colleague, Andrzej Zabinski, who was the local First Secretary. Zabinski was re-elected to that post and also chosen as a delegate to the Congress. But even this conference, which Kania thought highly successful, did not go entirely smoothly. The reason was that the Party leader recommended seven people from the Central authorities as candidates for the Party Congress. Why they could not get elected elsewhere was not made clear. At any rate, there was an argument and Kania had to speak twice on the subject before the Conference voted to place them on the candidates' list.

It says a lot for Mr Kania's powers of persuasion that he managed to secure that vote in what was the country's biggest Party organisation and one, moreover, that was trying with great determination to cut itself off from the past. Its two previous Party leaders before Zabinski – Gierek and Grudzien – were now in disgrace.

But things did not go quite so smoothly in Poznan, where Tadeusz Grabski tried to persuade the Provincial Party Conference to accept the candidacy of four more men recommended by the Politburo. They were an interesting group: Stanislaw Zaczkowski, Chief Commandant of the Police; General Edmund Lukasik, Deputy Commander of the Air Force; Leslaw Tokarski, the new Head of the Central Committee's Department for the Press, Radio and Television; and Professor Jerzy Wiatr, of Warsaw University. These were important people, no doubt, but the Poznan Conference refused to consider them, maintaining that only people chosen to attend it had the right to be elected by it either to Party office or to the Congress. Grabski was incensed, a factor which no doubt contributed to the heated quarrel which ensued. After telling the conference that it had violated the decisions of the recent Central Committee meeting on the rules of the election (a matter of profound confusion by now), he telephoned Stanislaw Kania, the man he had tried to oust as Party leader only weeks previously. Kania recommended that the conference think again, but again it refused. Eventually, during a break in proceedings, the chairman of the conference also phoned Kania and received the same message.

After sleeping on it, the conference came back the next day and voted to accept the four men as candidates while re-emphasising that it still retained the right to conduct its own conference as it chose. In the event, only two of the Politburo nominees were actually elected to the Party Congress: the Police Chief and the Deputy Air Force Commander. The new press chief was rejected, although his much maligned predecessor had already been elected.

The whole affair created bad odour. It was not just because of the behaviour of Tadeusz Grabski, though that was striking enough. Quite apart from walking out of the conference in anger at one point, he also made some very harsh remarks about the democratic process being enjoyed by the Party for the first time. He denounced, for example, the 'electoral frenzy' in which he claimed that workers were not doing well enough and worthy activists, as he called them, were being eliminated. In more general terms he claimed that the political situation was getting worse, not better. Statements like that merely underlined the divisions in the top leadership which had been brought to the surface by the Soviet letter. The spectacle of Grabski and Kania actually cooperating to ensure the election of delegates whom local Party bodies did not want to elect suggested to some that, in spite of the new election procedures and the supposed spirit of renewal, the Party was going to insist on 'fixing things' for men of the apparatus to the exclusion of men of the grass roots.

Another conference to receive a telexed list of four Polit-buro nominees to the Congress was the one in Bydgoszcz. It was attended by Deputy Premier Rakowski who said the men, personally recommended by Kania, should be con-sidered in the interests of the Party. The conference agreed but in the end only elected two of them as Congress delegates – a Minister and a Major General. One of those rejected was a Deputy Minister of the Interior, Henryk Pozoga, who was rumoured to be in charge of intelligence.

Allies see no improvement
Probably Kania damaged his reputation among some of his supporters in the so-called 'front of common sense and responsibility' with his efforts to secure the election of some of the more shadowy figures of the apparatus and power structure. And yet for all his efforts he did not manage to

please his Soviet-bloc allies. In fact one of the most remarkable features of June 1981 was the build-up of a steady barrage of criticism and complaint from Poland's allies. For anyone who was in Poland at the time the output of the press, radio and television in the Soviet Union, Czechoslovakia, East Germany and Bulgaria – to name the most outspoken exponents – made interesting reading to put it mildly. The situation they described in increasingly vivid terms seemed rather different from the reality I witnessed in Warsaw. It was comparatively calm. Solidarity was quiet, engaged as it was in elections of its own. There were it must be admitted a few incidents of pure hooligan violence, duly reported on television, and the occasional desecration of a Soviet monument, but there was no feeling at all that counter-revolution was really on the way. At times, indeed, there was an almost idyllic calm in the Polish capital. Such an occasion was the feast of Corpus Christi on 18 June, when families in their Sunday best watched the Blessed Sacrament carried in procession through Krakowskie Przedmiescie, the old street that had seen the processions for Cardinal Wyszynski less than a month earlier, while the rest of the capital, bathed in sunshine, enjoyed that special quiet of a public holiday. The Church, it is worth remembering, was still in mourning for the dead Primate, and almost every night anyone walking through Victory Square would see a small crowd of people gathered round the shape of a cross made of flowers and burning candles laid out on the ground.

One could hardly claim that such scenes represented the total picture but one could adduce plenty of evidence that the Polish people, in spite of their economic privations, were more interested in doing their own thing than in bothering their heads about undermining Communist rule. There were other attractions. For some people the two-week visit of Czeslaw Milosz, the exiled poet and Nobel Prize Winner, had more immediate meaning than the crisis of Poland's Communist leadership.

For other Soviet-bloc regimes, understandably, the crisis was everything. The outcome of the Eleventh Plenum clearly did not please them. They did not say so in so many words. Indeed, Moscow was remarkably quiet in the immediate aftermath. But they all contrived to make it clear that in spite of the plenum the situation was not getting better, but worse.

Again the Czechoslovak media were in the forefront:

The situation in Poland is not being consolidated. On the contrary its danger is intensifying as the consequence of continuing concessions . . . If the situation has not so far come to the worst, it is not, unfortunately, due to the efforts of those with prime responsibility. They are marking time, confining themselves to repeating the right words, quite irrationally closing their eyes to the real state of affairs. (Prague television, 12 June.)

We are disturbed by the fact that the counter-revolutionary danger in fraternal Poland is not being adequately confronted . . . If there is to be a turn for the better, then the words voiced at the Central Committee meeting must be followed by deeds and resolute action against the counter-revolutionary and anti-socialist forces. (*Rude Pravo*, Prague, 13 June.)

Even the Hungarians, remarkable so far for their comparatively moderate and informative style of reporting, felt obliged to comment on the Soviet letter and the desired effects. The Party paper, *Nepszabadsag*, on 14 June:

The particularly difficult situation emphatically demands resolute and united action . . . Regrettably, the attention and energies of Polish Communists have been largely spent on debates about the errors of the former Party leadership . . . The endless discussion is paralysing the struggle against hostile forces . . . To let power slip into the hands of adventurers is not the way to correct errors or renew socialism.

Moscow itself made a very significant contribution to the argument when the Government paper, *Izvestiya*, published a warmly worded profile not of any of Poland's recognised leaders but of a candidate member of the Central Committee and building worker, Albin Siwak, the man once defended by the Katowice Forum. Mr Siwak was, if anything, an old-fashioned zealot, and this was the man *Izvestiya* chose to praise for speaking out against the 'dangerous trends' in Solidarity from its very inception and for not being afraid to speak the truth. According to *Izvestiya* this was now a dangerous thing to do in Poland and Siwak had become the victim of 'a savage campaign of propaganda' by Solidarity members. This meant 'coming face to face with terror as an instrument of political activity'.

Bulgaria also joined in the chorus of disapproval and in some respects excelled its peers in the urgency with which it stated the problem. *Narodna Armiya*, the Defence Ministry paper, gave the impression that the moment of truth had arrived:

We cannot turn a blind eye to a number of outstanding facts which show that the measures undertaken in Poland to stabilise the situation are not effective. The situation is further worsened by the fact that inside the Party itself, groups have appeared who want to review the question of the leading role of the PZPR.

One striking feature of continuing Bulgarian criticism was the impression it gave that the sort of national unity sought by Mr Kania in his plea for a 'front of common sense and responsibility' was just not possible. The writers' paper *Literaturen Front*, for instance, contemptuously attributed the enthusiasm for Solidarity among the Polish intelligentsia to the old 'élite', the old 'aristocracy' of Polish culture which had its roots in a 'reactionary' pre-war past. Another journal, *Pogled*, while insisting that Polish Communists should seize the initiative with 'revolutionary determination', also expressed the rather pious conviction that Poland would not perish because it was in the hands of 'sensible and honest Poles'. 'Real Poles,' it proclaimed, 'can rely on the international assistance of their real friends.'

Even Leonid Zamyatin, the head of the Soviet Communist Party's International Information Department and anything but a simpleton, indulged in this exercise of trying to distinguish, from a Communist Party viewpoint, between good Poles and bad. In a long commentary on Soviet television on 20 June he said: 'There are many honest Communists in the PZPR ready to struggle for a Marxist–Leninist Party . . . But the time is running short.' In the process of commenting on and quoting from letters said to have been received from Poland and the Soviet Union, he put together what amounted to a long indictment.

The picture Mr Zamyatin presented was of a Polish leadership unable to control the situation, for ever retreating in the face of a struggle for power by Solidarity, a supposed trade union association now turning into a political party under the influence of extremists. At first, Zamyatin said, Solidarity had sought to undermine the Communist Party's leading role, but then it had exploited the campaign to correct the errors of former Party leaders by defaming and successfully eliminating 'innocent' middle-rank Party cadres. Meanwhile the Party had preached renewal, a word that was interpreted by everyone in his own way.

Zamyatin virtually dismissed the claim that Solidarity men had been beaten up in Bydgoszcz in March. Their leader, Jan Rulewski, had merely portrayed it that way. 'And incidentally, Rulewski received his wounds several days earlier in a car accident in which he killed a person, and went unpunished. This is how provocateurs behave.' Zamyatin also quoted a letter from a Soviet General claiming that Rulewski had been expelled from a Warsaw military academy in the 1960s for 'activities hostile to people's power'.

According to Zamyatin, Rural Solidarity was a 'kulak party' – a specific term of Soviet abuse, since the kulaks were the Soviet Union's peasant farmers until they were eliminated by Stalin in his campaign for collectivisation. As for the current Communist Party elections, he maintained that Solidarity was trying to 'determine who, in their opinion, should be sent to the Party Congress, and conversely to black-ball those who are unacceptable to Solidarity'. The Soviet spokesman conceded that this seemed 'strange' in what was a 'purely Party affair' but insisted that such were the facts. Why, for instance, had Zygmunt Wronski, a member of the current Politburo, failed to get elected to the Congress? Because he had spoken out openly against Solidarity viola-tions of socialist law at his own plant. That plant, incidentally, was the Ursus Tractor Works in Warsaw, the work-place of Zbigniew Bujak who was re-elected Chairman of Solidarity in the Mazowsze or Warsaw region by a landslide vote at the end of June. Ironically the conference at which Bujak won that vote was held in the very hall where the PZPR had come into being in 1948 through the merger of the Polish Workers' Party and the Polish Socialist Party.

Zamyatin did not conceal the fact that the unwelcome progress of the elections was not the work of Solidarity alone:

Revisionist circles in the Party, together with Solidarity and using those members of the Party – about a million – who have joined Solidarity, want the Congress to be such as to be capable of bringing about the decline of the Marxist-Leninist Party. They are nurturing plans to create some other kind of party, resembling so to speak a workers' party or maybe a social democratic one. Or maybe they can split the Party in two.

This undoubtedly was the nub of the problem for Moscow.

And one had to wonder who exactly were the 'honest Communists' on whom Moscow was depending to defend the Party against revisionists, Solidarity extremists and, of course, the imperialists who were, as always, said to be financing and encouraging anti-socialist counter-revolutionaries. There was the Katowice Forum, which came back to life towards the end of June with a statement that the Soviet letter and the Eleventh Plenum had proved that it had been right. There was also the newly discovered Poznan Party Forum, a similar hard-line group, to which Moscow and Prague Radios gave approving publicity one whole day before Warsaw Radio reported its existence. There were the die-hards of Warsaw who produced the new paper *Rzeczywistosc* (Reality) and claimed on its pages, according to Prague Radio, that 'the right wing, assisted by Solidarity and the Church, is getting ready to assume power and wants to turn the PZPR into a social democratic party of the intelligentsia and the bourgeoisie'. And there was always Albin Siwak. But none of these seemed to have backing strong enough to alter the mood that had taken such a firm hold over the Party in recent months, let alone change the results of democratic elections.

In Warsaw, meanwhile, the magazine *Kultura* had just published the results of a public opinion poll. People were asked which institution inspired the greatest confidence. First came the Roman Catholic Church, then Solidarity, then the Army. Much lower, behind even the police, came the Polish United Workers' Party.

'Labour is not counter-revolutionary'
The mood in the Party largely reflected or was a response to the mood in the nation as a whole. Witness the scenes in Radom on 25 June when the Party, the Roman Catholic Church and Solidarity combined in celebrating the fifth anniversary of the food riots of 1976. Or the impressive demonstration in Poznan on 28 June, when a monument was unveiled on the twenty-fifth anniversary of the workers' march 'for bread and freedom' which ended with the deaths of more than sixty people, including children, after the intervention of Polish troops. *Trybuna Ludu* said that after twenty-five years of silence it must now be stated that what happened in Poznan in 1956 was the first dramatic riot by workers in defence of their dignity. The celebration of the Poznan tragedy became a

celebration also of the new policy that Poles must not fire on Poles. So, whatever *Rzeczywistosc* had to say about the danger from Solidarity and the Church, representatives of both were there on Adam Mickiewicz Square, along with the new, democratically-elected local Party Secretary, to see yet another monument unveiled to the memory of workers killed on the orders of Communist rulers. It was a huge cross with two main stems. On one was the date 1956; on the other all the other dates of mass protest – 1968, 1970, 1976 and 1980.

The Solidarity committee at Poznan Radio and Television wanted the ceremony to be broadcast nationally but, as one of the survivors of the 1956 riots told the radio, Olszowski had categorically banned it. Only an edited version went out on national television but it was impressive nonetheless, mixing shots of the streets crowded for the ceremony in 1981 with still pictures of the same streets filled with demonstrators or occupied by tanks in 1956. What national viewers did not hear was an oddly combative speech at the ceremony by Lech Walesa.

We used to be called troublemakers and vandals and other names that were an affront to our dignity. Today . . . our path lies in solidarity, the solidarity of the world of labour, the solidarity of honest people against those who are dishonest, who try to keep our mouths shut . . . If we do not want to have any more monuments like this, we must not allow ourselves to be divided or to be set against one another, we must not allow any search for anti-socialist or counter-revolutionary forces, which is just another form of troublemaking and hooliganism . . . The world of labour is not counter-revolutionary, it is for honesty and truth . . . Let us remember that victory is already within our grasp, provided we do not allow ourselves to be divided . . . provided that, when the need arises, we march together, remembering the solidarity of labour, the solidarity of honest people against dishonest people and dictators.

This was a rather disjointed outburst by Walesa. At one moment he seemed to be addressing fellow workers in Solidarity, but one could not be sure who exactly was in his mind when he said: 'Could you finally stop insulting us, stop dividing us, because we shall not allow ourselves to be insulted or divided any more.'

Solidarity had come in for some pretty harsh criticism the day before, as it happened, from Stanislaw Kociolek, First Secretary of the Warsaw Provincial Party Committee, at the opening of the Warsaw Party Conference. Kociolek was a controversial figure. He had been in Gdansk during the troubles of December 1970 and had naturally come to be regarded as one of the Party leaders chiefly responsible for the tragic killings there. As a result there had been astonishment when Mr Kania appointed him to the Warsaw post in the autumn of 1980. Now once more he came to his defence. When some delegates at the Warsaw conference objected to the suggestion that Kociolek be re-elected First Secretary, Kania told the conference that a vote for or against Kociolek would be a vote for or against himself. In a speech remarkable for its candour, Kania went through the details of the tragic events in Gdansk and Gdynia in 1970 and stated categorically that Kociolek had not been responsible for ordering the use of force against the strikers. In fact he had stated his view that force should not be used and had been overruled. Subsequently he had been the only member of the Politburo to resign voluntarily, not because of personal guilt but because he felt he bore the burden of 'the moral tragedy of the Party and his own personal tragedy as a Party activist'.

Kociolek was re-elected, but thanks mainly to an extraordinary demonstration of Mr Kania's personal faith in someone he saw as an 'honest Communist'. It was the Party leader's last venture into special election pleading, for the elections, on that last weekend in June, were virtually over. The chief remaining interest, but a diminishing one, was in the fortunes of the two Politburo members generally credited with hard-line attitudes, Stefan Olszowski and Tadeusz Grabski.

Olszowski had chosen to stand for election to the Congress in Warsaw, where he said he was prepared to face his strongest critics. He was duly elected without much trouble after making a speech in which he claimed that the Party's problems dated back to the early days of Communist rule in Poland and the lack of real democracy within it. Shortly before the Warsaw conference Olszowski had revealed that Solidarity leaflets were describing him as a traitor, a 'Targowiczanin', a name taken from Targowica, the place from which Empress Catherine II of Russia was invited to invade Poland in 1792. Curiously enough, a communiqué from the Polish Episcopate read out during the broadcast mass on Sunday 28 June repeated that Poland had the right to shape its own destiny and quoted the words of the late Cardinal Wyszynski who had said months earlier that no one should yield to the temptation of another Targowica. Presumably those who implied that Olszowski was a traitor had their reasons. Yet the evidence of his public pronouncements at that stage suggested, not that he was a likely traitor, but rather a talented politician more aware than most of the need for reform, especially in the economy, and of the dangers inherent in trying to carry it out.

Tadeusz Grabski, on the other hand, had revealed his hand when he tried to oust Kania at the Eleventh Plenum. Since then he had gone on complaining that the situation was getting worse. He had virtually condemned the elections by denouncing 'electoral madness' and he had warned of the danger not just of socialist democracy but of Christian democracy. Grabski, if anyone, was closest to the Soviet-bloc allies and the hard-line groups inside Poland in their assessment of the situation. He too was elected to the Congress, as a 'favourite son' in Konin, where he had been a successful First Secretary some years earlier.

'No Workers' Party without workers'
As the Party elections came to an end there was a hint of anticlimax. Perhaps the coverage provided by the mass media had been imperceptibly tightened up compared with the heyday of reporting that preceded the Soviet letter. At any rate there was far less certainty about what was going on and what the Communist Party Congress would be like. The bare statistics were not enough. Final results showed that a total of 1964 delegates had been elected to the Congress. Of these only 393 were workers, compared with 1202 who were described as white-collar workers. Two full members of the current Politburo, Gerard Gabrys and Zygmunt Wronski, and one candidate member, Jerzy Waszczuk, failed to get elected. Another candidate member, Jozef Masny, had declined to stand.

The failure of Gabrys and Wronski, who had been introduced into the Politburo specifically to increase the number of workers in the leadership, tended to confirm, along with the overall results, the fears only recently expressed by *Trybuna Ludu* about clear evidence of a change in the social character of the Party. Workers, it said, made up a vast proportion of the people leaving the Party. Workers were refusing to stand for

Party office. But 'there is no workers' Party without the workers'.

One other interesting result was the failure of Stefan Bratkowski, the liberal leader of the Journalists' Association, to get elected by the Warsaw Conference to the Party Congress. Coupled with the death of Jerzy Wojcik, Chief Editor of *Zycie Warszawy*, this was an undoubted disappointment to those who believed that outspoken, responsible journalism was one of the strongest and most vital features of renewal. But Bratkowski's defeat was noted by Bratislava Radio across the border in Slovakia as a sign that the 'rightists and revisionists' were now on the defensive in Poland. The final days of the election, it suggested, had shown that the 'healthy forces in the Party' were operating more decisively.

The Katowice Forum was also feeling somewhat happier, and with good reason. A special report issued by the Central Party Control Commission ruled that the Forum's views, while debatable, were dictated by concern for the socialist character of the Party's renewal and a desire to defend it from anti-socialist attacks. The Forum's position, the statement said, lay within the bounds of Party spirit and was not factional. As for the treatment received by the Forum in the mass media, the Control Commission said that it had been 'more often than not one-sided and negative'.

The Forum, meanwhile, was really back in action. In statements publicised at great length by the East Germans and also by the Czechs it expressed gratitude to the Control Commission for having thus stated its 'approval', and also pointed to the Warsaw Conference's rejection of Stefan Bratkowski 'regardless of the forces who supported him' as a good example of how to 'struggle against right-wing opportunism and revisionism'. The members of the Forum – some of whom, by the way, took part in a Polish television documentary about them, part of which was rebroadcast by Prague – insisted at the same time that there had been no adequate change for the better in the performance of the mass media. They called for an immediate check on Party journalists and said it must not be delayed until after the Congress.

Within a week, as it happened, there were changes in some top journalistic jobs. Wladyslaw Loranc, a former editor of the radio in Cracow and more recently an Under-secretary of State at the Ministry of Culture, became Chairman of the State

Committee for Radio and Television. His predecessor was transferred to the Diplomatic Service. *Zycie Warszawy* got a new editor to replace the late Jerzy Wojcik; he was Zdzislaw Morawski, former Foreign Editor of the official news agency, PAP, and correspondent in Rome. The Editor of *Kurier Polski* gave way to his deputy. There was no immediate reason for supposing that these changes actually represented a hardening of line, but they contributed to a growing suspicion that perhaps on the very last leg of the preparations for the Congress the radical voice of renewal was growing more faint.

Mr Gromyko calls
On 2 July came the news that several people had been arrested on suspicion of defiling Soviet monuments and graves. *Kurier Polski* reported that two of them were members of Solidarity, acting under the influence of alcohol. A day later – as foreshadowed in a previous announcement – the Soviet Foreign Minister, Andrei Gromyko, arrived in Warsaw for talks. He left three days later with a communiqué stating that 'certain Western circles' were trying to exploit the situation in Poland in order to 'discredit the socialist system', but that 'Poland was, is and will continue to be a firm link in the socialist community'.

Gromyko was the first Soviet leader to visit Warsaw since the Soviet Central Committee's famous letter of a month earlier. It was a bit difficult, though, to explain why he had to go there. By now one would have thought there was little more that the Soviet Union could do to make its position clearer or its advice more effective. What Mr Gromyko appeared to have done was obtain a repeated recognition from Mr Kania and General Jaruzelski of something they had been repeating for months:

The defence of the gains of socialism in the Polish People's Republic is inseparable from the questions of the independence and sovereignty of the Polish State and the security and inviolability of its borders. These questions not only affect Poland but are vitally important to the entire socialist community.

While Gromyko was still in Warsaw the celebrations planned for the anniversary of General Sikorski's death, 4 July, went ahead but lost a lot of their meaning because Britain had rejected the request for the return of his ashes. At a ceremony in Cracow, where they were to have been buried, a speaker claimed that not for a very long time had one idea so united all Poles as the project for the repatriation of the General's ashes. He hoped they would be returned in 1981. If they had been returned at the time originally requested, the chances are that Poles would have been able to enjoy the tonic of a genuinely patriotic occasion with Western connections to compensate for the prevailing, rather oppressive atmosphere of inter-Communist argument, one dominated by talk of anti-Soviet-ism and apparently unrelieved to any great extent by the announcement of the name of Poland's new Roman Catholic Primate, Archbishop Jozef Glemp.

Rakowski lashes out
The atmosphere, it appears, was rather touchy. On 6 July Mieczyslaw Rakowski addressed a Party meeting in Cracow, the city which had elected him to the Congress along with Mr Kania and the Editor of *Gazeta Krakowska*. He probably knew by now that this paper had been denounced in Bulgaria for defending 'revisionist positions' and fighting 'representatives of the firm and healthy forces'. As a journalist he was also, presumably, well aware of what was being said elsewhere in the Soviet bloc and in Poland. At any rate something goaded him into an outburst of straight talking. He attacked 'extremists in Solidarity' for twisting the arms of anyone who did not agree with them and accused them of being hostile to renewal itself. But then he turned on elements within the Party.

Such enemies of dialogue and compromise can also be found among some members of the Party who are afraid to take an open stand against the policy of renewal and instead have launched a dirty campaign, pursuing it in the same innocuous manner as their kindred spirits on the other side. They are resorting to such well-known arguments as those which place the blame entirely on revisionists, opportunists, anti-Marxists, cosmopolitans, Zionists and such like. These people have their mouths full of socialism but if one reads their documents carefully – the declarations of the Katowice Forum, for example – it emerges that renewal is a disaster, that the working people have achieved nothing through it and that our country is threatened by a revisionist putsch.

Some of the extremists joined forces in setting up the Grunwald organisation. They count the weekly *Rzeczywistosc* among its supporters. In my opinion, what they actually want is power. They have not come up with any proposal or programme, their favourite word being 'No'. The Solidarity extremists say 'everything or nothing'. The Party extremists say 'nothing or everything'.

Mr Rakowski, as we have already seen, was very much in favour of Solidarity in principle. But at that very moment action by Solidarity was about to strengthen the arguments of those fundamentally opposed to it. After a long lapse of industrial calm, it was announced in Gdansk that, after the failure of talks on a long-standing demand for a port workers' charter, Solidarity was calling a one-hour warning strike on 8 July.

On 7 July the Polish Airlines, LOT, announced that services were likely to be disrupted on 9 July because of a four-hour strike to be called that day by LOT's Solidarity organisation in support of the workforce's claim to the right to appoint their own Director General, whom they had selected by competition. On 8 July the strike in all Polish ports went ahead, and at the end of the day the Minister of Maritime Economy announced that the Government had definitely accepted a draft port workers' charter but still had some negotiations to complete.

The next day the LOT strike took place. But the Government, which had let the argument go on for more than a month, now acted promptly, appointing General Jozef Kowalski, until then Commander of the Air Force Higher School in Deblin, to the vacant post. But there was yet another strike on 9 July, when transport workers in Bydgoszcz came out for two hours in support of demands for the dismissal of the local transport chief for alleged abuse of his position. The campaign against him had been led for several months by Jan Rulewski, the local Solidarity leader. The transport chief resigned so as not to cause further disturbances.

However, strikes were not the only point at issue with Solidarity. At the lowest level, Prague Radio had been regaling listeners with ill-concealed suggestions that Solidarity leaders were growing rich on money sent to them from abroad. And Albin Siwak, on a visit to Prague, said on television there that he had been the target of a petrol bomb attack by Solidarity members. *Zolnierz Wolnosci*, the Polish army paper, took up the more pertinent question of a rift in Solidarity itself. The election campaign, it said, had revealed unhealthy rivalry and a recourse to undemocratic methods. Opposition to Lech Walesa was clearly emerging.

A far more serious problem, and an obvious threat of further disputes in the future, was raised by *Trybuna Ludu*. It concerned the draft bill on worker self-management. Solidarity, at a recent meeting with Government representatives, had said that it had not had time to consider the draft properly. But *Trybuna Ludu* maintained that Solidarity had no intention of considering it, and to prove it it quoted from Solidarity documents on the subject. One of them said this: 'Self-government may only be set up on the initiative and with the support of Solidarity . . . Any other initiatives will be in danger of being manipulated by the State authorities against Solidarity.'

Arguments like these promised trouble to come. So did the news that the Government was planning a two-stage increase in prices, including average rises of an astonishing 123 per cent in food prices. The announcement that three of the four leaders of the KPN, the Confederation of Independent Poland, had been rearrested seemed just another indication of a tougher line, part of a readjustment of Polish politics that had been in train since the Soviet letter was received at the beginning of June. The atmosphere had certainly changed in little more than a month. The enthusiasm with which the Party Congress had once been demanded and then looked forward to seemed to have gone. The outline of Mr Kania's 'front of common sense and responsibility' seemed to have become blurred. Some Western commentators suggested that the Extraordinary Ninth Congress of the Polish Communist Party probably would not make such a clean sweep after all.

In the event, the Congress was more surprising than most people ever expected. It was preceded by a final plenary session of the outgoing Central Committee. Among the reports it heard was one from Tadeusz Grabski, as head of the special commission set up to investigate the activities of former leaders. He said that almost 26,000 people had come under investigation and accusations had been upheld against 12,000 of them. The Grabski Commission recommended and the Central Committee agreed that the Central Control Commission should review the question of the continued Party membership of Edward Gierek and five of his former close colleagues. It was also agreed to ask the State Council to deprive Gierek and eleven others of State awards received by them in the 1970s. Other agreed decisions included a strict definition

General Wojciech Jaruzelski, Defence Minister and a member of the ruling Party Politburo, was appointed Prime Minister early in February. He is seen sitting between Marshal Kulikov, the Soviet Commander-in-Chief of the Warsaw Pact forces (left) and General Heinz Hoffman, the East German Defence Minister, during Warsaw Pact exercises in Poland.

Left: Jaruzelski with Mieczyslaw Rakowski, the editor of the weekly Polityka, whom he appointed Demember of the Politburo who was puty Prime Minister with responsibility for negotiating with the trade unions. It was Rakowski who negotiated successfully with Lech Walesa to avert a general strike called by Solidarity in the wake of the 'Bydgoszcz incident' in March, when three union activists, including Jan Rulewski (below left) and Mariusz Labentowicz (below), were beaten up by plain clothes police.

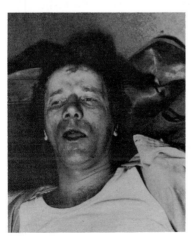

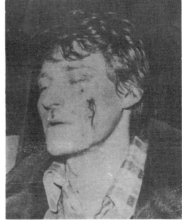

Above left: *Andrzej Gwiazda, for some time Deputy Chairman of Solidarity's National Commission.*
Above: *Jacek Kuron, founder member of the dissident KOR organisation and radical adviser to Solidarity.*
Left: *Zbigniew Bujak, the leader of the Solidarity branch in Warsaw and highest-ranking leader still at large after martial law was declared.*
Bottom: *Walesa with his friend Bogdan Lis, a Communist later to be expelled from the Party.*

Top: *Polish agriculture was dominated by small, privately owned but badly equipped holdings. Following the birth of Solidarity in Gdansk in August 1980, private farmers tried to set up a similar union of their own known as Rural Solidarity.*

Middle: *Students in Warsaw demonstrate for the release of political prisoners, May 1981.*

Bottom: *Archbishop Josef Glemp, Primate of Poland, July 1981.*

Top: *Soviet Foreign Minister Gromyko with Ambassador Aristov in talks with Stanislaw Kania and General Jaruzelski in July shortly before the Polish Party Congress.*
Bottom: *Stanislaw Kania addressing the Ninth Extraordinary Party Congress. From left to right in the same row are General Jaruzelski,* *President Henryk Jablonski and Kazimierz Barcikowski. Just behind Kania's right shoulder are two Soviet guests: Konstantin Rusakov, Secretary of the Soviet Party's Central Committee, and Viktor Grishin, a member of the Politburo who was once in charge of Soviet trade unions.*

Above: *The new Politburo and Secretaries, largely unknown, elected at the Party Congress. The four survivors from the old Politburo are in the front row: Kazimierz Barcikowski (second from left), Stanislaw Kania, Wojciech Jaruzelski, and Stefan Olszowski standing between the first woman member, Zofia Grzyb, and Jozef Czyrek, the Foreign Minister.*
Right: *Stanislaw Kania confers with Albin Siwak, the building worker and critic of Solidarity who was promoted to the Politburo at the Party Congress.*

Right: *August 1980. Hunger marches in Lodz, led by housewives, took food shortage protests on to the streets and culminated (above) in a huge demonstration which blocked one of Warsaw's main road junctions.*

Left: *19 October. General Jaruzelski succeeds Stanislaw Kania as Communist Party leader.*
Middle: *21 October. Police van attacked in Katowice after the authorities stopped the distribution of 'anti-government' and 'anti-Soviet' Solidarity leaflets.*
Below: *General Jaruzelski presides over the Military Council for National Salvation, set up on 13 December when Martial Law was declared.*

Right: Riot police keep back crowds on Mokotowska Street in Warsaw, the home of the local Solidarity headquarters, on the day Martial Law was declared.

Below: The gates of the Lenin Shipyard, Gdansk, 16 December 1981, after troops and police had forced their way in to break up the strike in protest against martial law.

December 1981. Outside the gates of the Lenin Shipyard in Gdansk armoured vehicles stand guard at the foot of the monument built (inset) *and dedicated only a year earlier to those who died in the 1970 food price riots.*

of the rights and duties of Party officials, so as to prevent further 'deformations', and a statement that political responsibility must be borne for political activity and that criminal responsibility must be punished like all common crimes. And just to make sure that former leaders like Gierek did not try to excuse themselves by claiming ignorance, Mieczyslaw Moczar, Chairman of the Supreme Chamber of Control for the past ten years, adduced detailed evidence to the contrary.

Congress debates

This was a fitting overture to the opening of the Congress. The demand that guilty men be brought to account and if necessary face criminal charges had been one of the strongest features of Polish politics since August 1980 but it never represented a true dividing line between liberals and conservatives. Hard-line elements had been just as vehement in their calls for a proper settling of accounts, while warning that the purge should not go too far and touch the innocent. Both Grabski and Moczar had now said that very many activists had in fact been wrongfully accused.

Now the 1962 validly elected delegates who assembled in the monstrously huge Palace of Culture – a gift from the Soviet Union – in the centre of Warsaw had to think more of the future. And the question they had to answer, quite apart from adopting new Party statutes and approving plans to reform the economy, was what sort of leadership the Party was to have. It was not a simple matter. For one thing, most of the delegates were representing the Party for the first time. For another, the choice facing them had been confused and muddied by events, especially the receipt of the Soviet letter. For Poland's anxious allies the choice was plainly between 'healthy' forces defending a Marxist–Leninist line, and 'revisionist, right-wing opportunists' who were allegedly threatening to convert the Party to social democracy.

To the more disinterested spectator the choice seemed to range more widely: from impeccably Communist elements who believed that reform had been too slow, to men of the centre, like Kania perhaps, whose attitudes were shaped by the difficulties and dangers of reform, to more orthodox leaders like Olszowski, and on to hard-line spokesmen like Grabski, and further left to loyalists like Albin Siwak and the Katowice Forum. All of them, however, would say that they stood for the policy of renewal and accord.

The argument for the centre, if we can call it that, was put most energetically not by Mr Kania – who presented the report of the outgoing Central Committee, most of whose members had not been elected to the Congress – but by Mieczyslaw Rakowski, the publicist, editor and now Deputy Prime Minister, who had had more dealings than most with Solidarity. Noting that some people were demanding that the Party 'reverse the course of events' (a reference perhaps to Mr Brezhnev's words in February), Rakowski insisted that the 'policy of understanding' was an 'historical necessity without any reasonable alternative'. The alternative, he suggested,

would be a great conflict, a clash between the authorities and the majority of society, a bloodbath, a national tragedy, after which all our worries would still be there, on a far more threatening scale. The conflict would have ended nothing. It would only have ended us, the Polish nation, the Polish state and us Communists.

According to Rakowski, everyone now said they were in favour of the policy of agreement but not all of them actually supported it in practice. This meant that the authorities had been unable to act decisively. They had been frustrated firstly by conservatives in the Party and its apparatus, by others in the Party using catchwords about democracy to negate its Marxist–Leninist character, by the radicals in Solidarity, and finally by the Central Committee and the Politburo itself which lacked determination. He called for the election of a leadership 'bold in thought and deed', one in which the nation and the allies could believe. 'We have to gather realists favouring a centre policy. Our main enemies are doctrinaire attitudes and ossification.'

No doubt Rakowski had an advantage over his colleagues because of his way with words, but distinctly more radical views were presented, however quietly, by the Party leader from Gdansk, Tadeusz Fiszbach. For too long, he said, the line of accord had represented only an intention, producing no results. It was now becoming an empty slogan, a declaration of intent with nothing to show for it.

In August 1980 I placed my signature on the Gdansk Agreement. Today, after the passage of nearly eleven months, our hopes have not yet been realised . . . The negligible results of our efforts are due

to the Party's shakiness, particularly in its leading links at all levels
. . . We have wasted too much time defending positions we simply
could not defend and did not need to . . . Meanwhile, an historic
union is taking place between democracy in the Party and the
independence of the trade union organisation of the working class.
In the long run none of these important factors can function independently. Without inter-dependence . . . I think the trade unions
must be guaranteed the right to co-participation in taking strategic
decisions . . . Our Congress must map out a political programme for
overcoming the crisis . . . But it will not be possible to regain public
trust by means of a programme, even if it is the best of all possible
programmes. The programme has to be implemented and proved
right.

Fiszbach, as we shall see, had good reason to sound like a
disappointed man as he made that speech on 18 July. But
another speaker on the same day, Albin Siwak, sounded
almost perky as he presented his particular line of argument.
How many workers were attending the Congress, he asked.
In fact there were 438 out of 1962 delegates. 'We are a minority
in the Party,' he said. Having thus established his class position, Siwak proceeded to list the dangers as he saw them:
plans to restore capitalist property; plans to set up large-scale
private farms bringing with them a revival of rural capitalism;
ideas for central planning to be replaced by 'market socialism',
which meant the 'spectre of unemployment'. He spoke rather
disparagingly of the 'so-called alliances of the forces of responsibility and common sense' and warned that it could
turn into 'a common or garden convergence, a Western theory
of bridge-building . . . There is a growing sensation of threat
within the nation. The phantom of civil war, inflation, unemployment and political terrorism is looming. The phantom of
hunger, lack of medicines, fuel and energy is looming.'
     In a jibe at Rakowski, Siwak suggested that some people
were trying not to save the Party but to split it. He also had a
go at others. 'Their mouths are full of renewal and they call
themselves Communists . . . But they have taken good care
of their own interests, in the local election campaign and in
the corridors of the Congress'. He even addressed himself to
Mr Kania: 'I esteem you, Comrade Kania, for solving problems without conflict, without using force. This is a good
trait. But I reprove you, Comrade Stanislaw, for the fact that
there is no law in our country.'
     One would have thought that Albin Siwak's horny-handed

fundamentalism would have had little effect in a country which had witnessed the first successful protest by workers in Eastern Europe and was still trying to cope with the effects of it. Fiszbach's reasoned arguments were surely more to the point. In the event, this view was proved wrong and quite possibly it had something to do with lobbying and manipulation in the corridors. For the key to the Congress lay in its elections. It had to elect a new First Secretary, a new Central Committee and then a new Politburo. This, as much as any Congress resolution, would determine the future.

Election shock
Even before the Congress began there was a move to get Mr Kania re-elected straightaway, before the election of the new Central Committee. His position was not entirely unchallenged and it was made even more uncertain by reports that Congress delegates were being shown a letter said to have been written by Wladyslaw Gomulka, Party leader from 1956 to 1970, alleging that Mr Kania had a part in the decision to use the army against striking workers on the Baltic Coast in December 1970. The Congress rejected the idea of an immediate vote and chose instead to elect the Central Committee first so that it could then choose a First Secretary from out of its number.

The results of the secret vote for the Central Committee, announced on the evening of 17 July, must rank as one of the most astonishing developments in the history of the Soviet bloc. It was an event without precedent. The list of two hundred full members and seventy candidate members read over Warsaw Radio and Television revealed that the Party leadership had been all but swept aside. Out of the existing Politburo only four had been re-elected to the Central Committee – Kania, Barcikowski, Jaruzelski and Olszowski. This meant that most of the men who had led the country for the past eleven months were gone – President Henryk Jablonski, Mieczyslaw Jagielski who signed the Gdansk Agreement, Mieczyslaw Moczar the veteran General who had provided the evidence against former leaders, Tadeusz Grabski who had tried to oust Kania, and Andrzej Zabinski, the conservative leader from Katowice. Also gone were three candidate members of the Politburo, Tadeusz Fiszbach, Roman Ney and Wladyslaw Kruk, along with two Central Committee

Secretaries, Kazimierz Cypryniak and Zdzislaw Kurowski, and a member of the Secretariat, Stanislaw Gabrielski.

Mr Kania had said in his report to the Congress that 'nothing better had been invented than personal elections, carried out in secret', but this was breathtaking. Out of the 142 members of the outgoing Central Committee, only eighteen had secured re-election. They included Mieczyslaw Rakowski and Albin Siwak. They did not include Stanislaw Kociolek, the Warsaw leader, on whom Mr Kania had spent one whole speech only two weeks earlier.

On 18 July the new Central Committee met to elect a First Secretary. At least four candidates were proposed – Kania, Barcikowski, Olszowski and Rakowski. The last two withdrew out of support for Kania. Barcikowski wanted to do the same but was persuaded to run so as to satisfy the rule demanding at least two candidates. Kania was re-elected by 1311 votes to Barcikowski's 568. Interestingly, Albin Siwak's speech about the phantoms stalking the nation was made immediately after Kania's re-election and speech of thanks.

The next day the Central Committee met again to discuss the election of the new Politburo and Secretaries. In a 'lively discussion' in the morning eighteen names were put forward for the Politburo, four as candidate members and seven as Central Committee Secretaries. In the afternoon there was a vote on all these names but a shorter version of the list submitted by Mr Kania won the day.

The Party ended up with a fifteen-strong Politburo boasting its first ever woman member. Apart from Kania, Barcikowski, Jaruzelski and Olszowski, the rest were a mixture of the familiar and the virtually unknown. Tadeusz Czechowicz, First Secretary in Lodz; Zofia Grzyb, a worker from Radom (and incidentally a member of Solidarity); Professor Zbigniew Messner, Rector of the Higher School of Economics in Katowice; Miroslaw Milewski, currently Minister of Internal Affairs; Jozef Czyrek, currently Foreign Minister; Hieronim Kubiak of the Jagiellonian University in Cracow; Jan Labecki, First Secretary in the Lenin Shipyard, Gdansk; Albin Siwak, brigade leader in a Warsaw building combine; Stanislaw Opalko, First Secretary in Tarnow; Jerzy Romanik, coal miner from Siemianowice; and Tadeusz Porebski, Professor and First Secretary in Wroclaw. Two candidate members were elected: Jan Glowczyk, Chief Editor of *Zycie*

Gospodarcze (Economic Life) and Wlodzimierz Mokrzyszczak, First Secretary in Olsztyn. There were seven secretaries:
Barcikowski, Czyrek, Kubiak, Milewski, Olszowski and two
more new men – Zbigniew Michalek, a director of a State
farm, and Marian Wozniak, First Secretary in Siedlce.
    The immediate reaction to these astonishing elections could
only be one of bewilderment. It has been the tradition in
Soviet-bloc countries to keep a steady, virtually unchanging
team at the top, a small group of men remaining in office as
a symbol of continuity and stability whatever the real state
of affairs. Never before had any of these countries introduced
a free, secret vote in Party elections. Now in Poland the
evidence was there for all to see. The distinguished visitors
included Viktor Grishin, the Soviet Politburo member and
Party chief in Moscow, and Antonin Kapek, the Party chief
in Prague, who had seen their Warsaw equivalent fail to get
into the Central Committee. The election to the Politburo of
Albin Siwak must have been welcome to observers in Prague,
Moscow and elsewhere, especially since Mieczyslaw Rakowski
was not elected, but there could be no satisfaction with the
fact that the Party leadership which only a week ago had been
suspected of weakness in the face of revisionism was now
largely an unknown quantity.

Victory for the Centre?
As the Congress came to an end on 20 July after seven days,
Stanislaw Kania told delegates that their work had made it
possible to turn without reservation to the future. In a sense
he was right. Disgraced former leaders had been expelled
from the Party, the old Central Committee was gone, and the
new leadership deserved the chance to forget the past and get
on with the job. But this did not mean that the problems that
had defeated former leaders would be any easier now. Those
problems were still there and some were threatening to come
to a head. Solidarity was planning hunger marches in protest
against plans to double the price of food. The port workers,
still without a satisfactory settlement, were to go on strike on
23 July. The workers at LOT, the Polish Airlines, had also
called a strike for 24 July.
    The danger signals were readily reported by the radios in
Czechoslovakia which still claimed that counter-revolutionary
forces were 'not meeting with the necessary, decisive resis-

tance'. This suggested a strong disposition not to see much chance of improvement under Poland's new leadership. The Hungarians, on the other hand, were more inclined to wait and see. A Budapest television discussion said the new leadership would be judged by its actions. What seemed to have happened, it was said, was that the Congress

in effect reduced the extremes of both right and left. The people elected to leading positions represent the centre of the Party. This would indicate that both the revisionist and dogmatist forces have either been left out or been given a very minor role in these bodies. In spite of this, it appears that there are people in the Central Committee who do not quite agree with one another.

But there was no real reduction, as that programme conceded, in political tension. Kania may have tried to compose a cabinet of the centre, but Albin Siwak hardly qualified for that. And out on the streets Solidarity was getting angry about the prospect of increased food prices. What guarantee was there that Solidarity would be any more amenable to a new leadership, elected largely to satisfy the internal needs of the Party? Exactly one year after the strike wave of 1980 was getting under way, the same economic problems were worse than ever and it looked as though Poland's new leaders, a new team, could be facing them with no certainty of doing any better.

12. THE QUESTION OF POWER

In any history of the Communist regimes of Eastern Europe a special place must surely go to the Ninth Congress of the Polish United Workers' Party. It was an unprecedented attempt by a Communist Party to introduce democracy within its own ranks in the hope of winning public support. True, that attempt had been forced on the Party, ultimately, by its own mismanagement of the economy and the resultant workers' revolt of the summer of 1980. But there was more to it than that. Under the leadership of Stanislaw Kania, and in spite of doubts, suspicions, disapproval and finally warnings on the part of the Warsaw Pact allies, the Polish Communist Party had deliberately chosen reform because it was persuaded that only through reform, only by using all the talents of the nation, could it run the country properly. One other crucial factor in the Party's thinking was the belief that it could not lead the country out of its economic and political crisis without the support of the people, and that, to all intents and purposes, meant the support and cooperation of Solidarity.

The only condition insisted on by the Party was that its leading role, the socialist system and the country's international socialist alliances should not be challenged. This was a big condition, admittedly, but it had been accepted internationally for some thirty-five years and Solidarity had undertaken to observe it.

Poland's allies in the Warsaw Pact were not so sure of this. In fact they were convinced, as far as one could make out, that Solidarity was under the influence of elements dedicated to overthrowing the Communist system. In spite of that the Polish Party managed to press ahead and hold its congress, expelling former leaders considered guilty of causing the crisis, and employing the secret ballot to elect an almost completely new leadership. It was a historic performance and one which might well have given the Party hope, if not confidence, that a turning point had been reached, that now the nation would give it the cooperation it needed to tackle the job of restoring the country's ruined economy. It was not to be. No doubt there were several reasons, but the most obvious was that, for all its splendid democratisation, the Party was fundamentally still the same and the problems it faced were no nearer solution. In fact the situation was worse.

Hunger marches
The Party Congress was hardly over when the Government announced increases in the price of food, arguing that since retail prices were lower than production costs this was the only way of restoring some sense to the situation in the shops. It promised cash or benefits to compensate for an inevitable drop in living standards. As for the increases themselves, butter and bread would be roughly trebled in price, milk would be quadrupled. In addition the meat ration was to be cut by a fifth. Rationing, which started in April, had not worked. Meat production had been falling steadily and the Government no longer had the hard currency to buy extra supplies from the West. The shops, in fact, could not honour the coupons in the family ration book. The Government package was a bitter pill to swallow, coming as it did in the midst of growing shortages of other goods.

Solidarity rejected the price increases and the cut in the meat ration while agreeing to talks. But Solidarity, it seems, had little power to control the angry public reaction. On 24 July hundreds of people – some say more than a thousand – marched in protest through the streets of Kutno, in Wloc-lawek province, to protest against the shortages. Men, women and children, carrying empty pots and pans, marched under banners proclaiming 'We are hungry', 'We want a life worthy of a civilised nation'. In the shipyards in Szczecin workers gathered at a rally organised under a slogan which said, 'Put an end to starving the nation'. A similar protest took place in Torun. Worse was to come, the following week, in Lodz, Poland's second largest city, where butter and flour were the only rationed commodities which could be obtained without difficulty. A local Solidarity representative blamed this on Government 'ineptitude' and claimed that the price stabilisation plan was nothing more than an attempt to solve the crisis by 'the introduction of destitution'.

The atmosphere in Lodz was clearly very tense and the city's anger at not receiving its rations for July was channelled by Solidarity into four days of demonstrations. They included short protest drives through the centre of the city by public transport vehicles covered with 'hunger' posters and a march by women to the Municipal Offices. As it happened, the Sejm, in session in Warsaw, was hearing that very day from a woman deputy from Lodz, Urszula Plazewska.

The picture which best describes Lodz right now is one of endless queues outside shops. In front of meat shops, the waiting time is almost twenty-four hours. We must remember that in this industrial province more than 250,000 women, mothers and wives, work on a three-shift system. After coming off a night shift, they wait in a queue in order to supply their families with life's essentials. Or after spending the night waiting in a queue they turn up for the morning shift. Things cannot go on like this. We have had just about as much as we can stand, physically and mentally.

The mood of angry desperation was conveyed that same day by one of the most distinctively sane commentators on Warsaw Radio, the leader of the capital's journalists' union, Jacek Kalabinski. He told listeners that the Sejm debate, like the conversations in the queues, reflected 'the already universal awareness that everything is falling apart and that the process of disintegration cannot be halted by complaining, shouting or launching slogans about work – that what is really needed is simply action'.

Action of sorts was promised by a meeting of the Government Presidium – chaired by General Jaruzelski and attended, significantly, by the Chief of the General Staff of the Polish Army – which decided to use 'extraordinary means' to fight speculation by reinforcing local authorities with troops. The Military Council of the Defence Ministry met under the Prime Minister's chairmanship to discuss the 'dangerous' situation and the participation of the armed forces in work for the national economy and the fight against speculation and 'other destructive phenomena'.

The Party Politburo approved the Government's plans for 'decisive action', protesting at the same time that 'there is no threat of hunger in Poland'. It claimed that tensions caused

218

by the shortages threatened 'an explosion of conflict on a national scale'; it warned that things would get worse unless there was 'a positive attitude from the trade unions'.

Warsaw blockade

Solidarity did accept an invitation to talks with the Government and the two sides assembled on Monday 3 August. But the talks were completely overshadowed and rendered virtually impossible by a demonstration organised in the capital that morning by the local Solidarity organisation. It was the climax of the protests over food shortages which had been taking place in many towns throughout the country. The demonstration took the form of a procession of public transport vehicles – buses, lorries, cars, taxis and ambulances – which made their way along Warsaw's main shopping street, Marszalkowska, flashing their lights and blowing their horns. The demonstrators intended to turn left down Aleje Jerozolimskie and drive past the Communist Party headquarters before passing on to the building of the Council of Ministers but they were stopped by a line of police blocking the road. The procession ground to a halt at perhaps the biggest roundabout in the city centre, overlooked on one side by the enormous Palace of Culture in which the Party Congress had been held and on another by the tall Forum Hotel, considered ironically to be one of the best places to eat.

And there they stayed for some fifty hours in the most visible and publicised act of confrontation with the authorities since Poland's crisis began. The demonstration ended at midday on Wednesday 5 August after a two-hour strike throughout the city which virtually closed down all but essential services. The procession finally moved off to the cheers of watching thousands with drivers giving the victory sign. At that moment strikes and protest actions were taking place in many other towns.

Looking back, there seems to have been little to shout about. For what the demonstration achieved for sure was not an improvement in the supplies of food but a tougher line against Solidarity. It added extra bite to the anti-Solidarity propaganda of Poland's allies, notably in Czechoslovakia. It strengthened the hand of hard-line elements in the Communist Party, something that was to become clearer from strong statements emanating from the Warsaw Party Committee. But most important of all, it seems to have shocked and disappointed more liberal members of the Party and Government, confronting them with the apparently inescapable fact that, for all their efforts, they were not going to get the cooperation they wanted. The result was a much stronger official line in the media – not, it must be emphasised, a return to the old style of propaganda, but something more like the party political broadcasts of the West. While attacking Solidarity's decisions and 'extremist' elements in its leadership they pleaded the Government case and left the door to continued 'renewal' as wide open as possible. But this important change contributed, in its turn, to a further polarisation of political opinion. Solidarity and the authorities began to move further and further apart.

The media
The media were certainly not niggardly in their reports of chaos in the supply system. Provincial governors were said to be devising their own *ad hoc* schemes to ration the commodities they had. In Krosno, for instance, cigarettes could be bought on ration coupons intended for the purchase of sugar. In Bydgoszcz nappies were rationed to ten for every new-born child. In Koszalin one hapless cashier was reported to have been stripped by a queue of women who suspected her of concealing cigarettes beneath her clothes. At the height of the Warsaw demonstration a series of 'man in the street' interviews broadcast by Warsaw Radio included a damning comment on Communist rule: 'Thirty-six years and still nothing to buy.'

So there was no denying by radio, television or the press that the country was in a mess or that people were unhappy. But the authorities began more and more to use the media to put across statements and 'commentaries' by Government spokesmen. One of the first accused Solidarity of deliberately creating an atmosphere of disquiet, fear and uncertainty; it expressed the fervent hope that 'the majority of citizens' would follow the dictates of common sense and not 'demagogic appeals and slogans'. Obviously the Government felt the need to compete with Solidarity for the nation's support.

In theory, of course, the Government wanted partnership with Solidarity, but even its great advocate, Mieczyslaw Rakowski, the Deputy Prime Minister who had the job of dealing with the trade unions, now admitted to pessimism about the chances of this ever being achieved.

Recrimination

Rakowski's talks on behalf of the Government with a Solidarity team led by Lech Walesa in the first week of August got nowhere; indeed they seem merely to have made the atmosphere more sour. They began in a heated atmosphere, were adjourned for three days, and finally broke up late at night when, according to the official version, Solidarity suddenly refused to sign a joint communiqué drawn up by both sides. The Government accused Solidarity of an 'unprecedented display of arrogance' and of breaking off the talks 'in a manner insulting to the Government'. The Government, the statement said,

well understands the torment of everyday life which is the lot of citizens today . . . but it cannot accept such behaviour by the Solidarity leadership . . . The Government expressed its readiness for compromise many times during the talks. However, there are final limits to concessions and compromises, and these were deliberately crossed by Solidarity with the very clear aim of leading to confrontation . . . The Government cannot be dictated to. The Government of the Republic has sufficient means at its disposal to protect its citizens and is determined to prevent the provocation of anarchy and the continuation of activities threatening the stability of the State.

Solidarity was quick to reply. A statement from its National Consultative Commission, the KKP, denied the charge of arrogance and said that its delegation had rejected not a joint communiqué but an alternative draft. And when it did so, it was Rakowski who broke off the talks. The Solidarity statement was broadcast by Warsaw Television but was followed immediately with yet another Government handout contesting it and accusing Solidarity of lying.

By now, in only the early days of August, the tone had been set for an unremitting argument between the Government and Solidarity which seemed unlikely to end. While repeatedly declaring their readiness to cooperate with the unions on the basis of partnership, the authorities were obviously persuaded that they must no longer pull their punches. And one of the hardest-hitting critics of Solidarity was Mr Rakowski. His opening statement at the ill-fated talks with the union, later broadcast in full by the radio, claimed that new and dangerous elements had been introduced into the political situation. Solidarity had taken protest out on to the streets, thus widening the dangers of conflict, while using children to spread the mendacious slogan that famine was stalking the land. Solidarity had also made a direct attack on the Government. Solidarity, Mr Rakowski said, had a part to play in Poland's life and the Government had no sinister plans against it, but the time had come to define the limits of the union's activities. Was Solidarity going to cooperate in getting the country out of the crisis, he demanded, or was it to go on treating the authorities as the enemy, saying no to whatever they tried to do?

On 7 August a warning strike closed some sixty pits and all but the most essential enterprises in the industrial and coal-mining area of Katowice. The strike, called in protest against shortages, cost the country the loss of more than 200,000 tons of coal, Poland's key export commodity and earner of the hard currency so essential for imports of equipment, spares and food. One can understand what a painful blow this must have been to the Government and also why such publicity was given to reports of violence being used against workers who tried to work and members of management who tried to frustrate the strike. And yet it was difficult to imagine that nearly a million workers could easily be duped into striking. It was Solidarity's claim in general at that time that it was not provoking strikes so much as channelling popular grievances into organised protest; moreover, it had grievances of its own.

'Disinformation'

After campaigning for many months for access to the media, Solidarity now complained that the press, radio and television were giving a decidedly one-sided picture of what was going on in the country. Support for this claim came from a group of the country's leading journalists, five of whom issued a statement accusing the authorities of waging the strongest campaign of 'disinformation' since August 1980. The five signatories, who included Stefan Bratkowski and Jacek Kalabinski, said that the current spate of protests was the 'spontaneous' outcome of bitterness and disappointment over shortages, and also of what they called 'the crisis of hope' affecting all levels of society. At the same time they offered a warning.

> We feel it our duty to draw attention to the fact that the most recent propaganda campaign is helping create the moods of confrontation. Television, radio and some sections of the press are being compelled to act in a way that conflicts with their role as purveyors of social accord. They are dramatising the circumstances of recent events and are stirring up feelings instead of engaging in rational argument. They are condemning a partner who is not allowed to speak for himself . . . A whole series of interventions by the censorship have served to promote a version of events that is out of keeping with the truth . . . What is worse, this campaign is fuelling extremist views in Solidarity and among all people, blocking the way to constructive cooperation.

Significantly, that statement, which was denounced bitterly and at great length by the Government spokesman, was reproduced in *Solidarnosc*, the weekly publication of the independent trade union, but not in the official press. That was just one example of the polarisation against which its signatories had warned and which was to make itself more and more obvious in the coming weeks. The Communist authorities and Solidarity, the supposed partners in renewal, were becoming rivals, a fact emphasised in the second week of August by the simultaneous meetings of the Central Committee of the Communist Party in Warsaw and of the National Consultative Commission of Solidarity in Gdansk.

The Party Plenum ended with a resolution which balanced a pledge of continued dedication to renewal with attacks on 'certain irresponsible advisers and activists in Solidarity' and an appeal to the authorities to act decisively. One of the more striking features of the meeting was the doubt expressed by several speakers about the possibility of being a good Party member as well as a member of Solidarity.

The Solidarity meeting ended on the same day with decisions which prompted the Party paper, *Trybuna Ludu*, to speak of a return to realism. The National Commission appealed for an end to protests over supplies and other isolated industrial action until after the union's Congress. It suggested that workers should go to their jobs on eight work-free Saturdays before the end of the year. It also called for the suspension of a march on behalf of political prisoners which was being planned to converge on Warsaw. This was all very promising from the Government's point of view.

'The system has ceased to function'

But all these appeals were presented in the context of an assessment of the situation which was bound to be interpreted as a challenge to the authorities. At a press conference after their session, later broadcast at length by Warsaw television, the Solidarity leaders made it clear that in their view the present Government, not just their predecessors under Gierek, had failed the nation. Also to blame was the system:

At the root of the crisis lie the system of managing the economy and the method of governing the State. It has been inefficient and wasteful for a long time. At present it has simply ceased to function. It is geared to ruling without democratic freedom.

Solidarity claimed that it would be impossible to overcome the crisis without 'a dramatic reconstruction' of institutions.

For that reason, our union is taking steps to promote self-government reforms. The economic crisis can be overcome most effectively by a combined initiative of the whole community. The instrument of that initiative must be mainly worker self-management, with the right to choose directors . . . The reform should also include local self-government, transforming the People's Councils and the Sejm into genuine representative bodies by way of democratic elections and widening their powers in relation to the State administration.

The full implications of these words do not seem to have sunk in immediately, but looking at them now it is clear that Solidarity was condemning the system of government that had operated in Poland for thirty-six years and calling not just for workers to have the right to manage their enterprises and appoint their directors but also for free elections to representative bodies normally organised by the Communist Party. More than that, the union called for a strike to halt the printing and publication of newspapers on 19 and 20 August.

Solidarity said the strike could be called off if the authorities allowed it to explain its case on radio and television. But the authorities were in no mood for concessions, especially on such a key issue. They argued, on the radio and in the press, that Solidarity had greater access to the mass media than any other trade union in history, pointing out that its weekly, *Solidarnosc*, was printed in 500,000 copies, more even than the long-established *Polityka*, besides which it had some seven other weeklies or bi-weeklies with circulations ranging from 5000 to 100,000. On top of that there were thousands of other publications – local news sheets, factory bulletins and an 'avalanche of leaflets and posters'. The latter were to occasion serious conflict later, but the authorities had already started taking action against them. In Sieradz four unionists had been briefly detained for pasting up in public places what were supposed to be internal bulletins. According to the official media, these were generally anti-socialist and anti-Soviet. Warsaw television told viewers about one such leaflet distributed in Bydgoszcz. Signed, allegedly, by 'the Polish Labour Party' and 'the Polish Democratic Party', it was reported to have said: 'At last the policy of Gwiazda, Bujak, and Rulewski [supposed Solidarity radicals] has won. Talks with the Government must be firm. We can take power into our hands and destroy what exists. We can begin to build a Poland free of the Red plague.' In Katowice the local prosecutor instituted legal proceedings to prevent the publication of caricatures of Soviet leaders in the Solidarity bulletin *Wolny Zwiazkowiec* (Free Trade Unionist) at the local steel plant, which was built, incidentally, with Soviet aid and smelted Soviet ore.

Crimea talks
Such was the atmosphere when the Party Leader, Mr Kania, and the Prime Minister, General Jaruzelski, flew to the Crimea on 14 August to meet President Brezhnev at his holiday retreat. They returned the next day – the first anniversary of Mr Gierek's fateful return – with a Soviet promise to extend the term for the repayment of Poland's debts of some $4200 million until the mid-eighties and provide more raw materials and consumer goods. Such generosity only served to underline the coolness of Mr Brezhnev's comments reported in the joint communiqué. The Soviet Union, he said, wanted Polish Communists to strengthen the PZPR as a Marxist–Leninist Party and consolidate socialism in Poland. External and internal enemies, he is reported to have said, were using anti-Sovietism in the hope of creating an abyss between the Soviet Union and People's Poland.

There was no sign there of any Soviet confidence in either Kania or Jaruzelski, nor could it be expected. They were, after all, the virtual targets of the Soviet letter sent to Warsaw in June, and since then the situation had got worse. Neither was there any recognition in the communiqué of the Polish authorities' attempts to take a tougher line. It was about this time that the Soviet Union announced that Defence Minister Dmitry Ustinov would be in command of major exercises in the Byelorussian and Baltic Military Districts and the Baltic Sea early in September.

Press strike

On 15 August it was announced that Solidarity's printing presses at the Katowice Steel Plant had been closed down by the local Prosecutor. Three days later the two-day press strike began, the 'days without papers' in which printing workers occupied their workplaces throughout the country and, for the first time in Communist Eastern Europe, effectively prevented the publication of national and regional dailies. The strike was not an unqualified success. *Trybuna Ludu* and the Defence Ministry daily, *Zolnierz Wolnosci*, were published, along with some others, on emergency presses, much reduced in size and numbers, but even Budapest Radio reported that most kiosks refused to handle any newspapers.

Radio and television claimed that the strike had failed completely in some areas, and when it was over *Zolnierz Wolnosci* adjudged it a failure overall. But the point was that once again Solidarity had shown its power and proved that the country could hardly be ruled without its cooperation. Although the prospect for such cooperation did not seem good, there were signs that efforts to achieve it would not be easily abandoned. It was largely a matter of trust.

The Polish Bishops had issued a statement insisting that renewal was bound to be difficult but that people would willingly bear sacrifices so long as they could be certain that they would not be wasted. It was a matter of great importance, they said, that the mass media should serve everyone and that all centres of opinion, including the new trade unions and the Church, should have access to radio and television. 'Let none of us clench his fist,' they said. 'Let each of us abandon hatred and a desire for revenge.'

Deputy Premier Rakowski, in an interview with the magazine *Kultura*, repeated that Solidarity could not be excluded from the dialogue on Poland's future. But he justified his tough attitude in the recent abortive talks by saying that he wanted to break their 'resistance and aggressiveness' in order to 'prevent both Solidarity and myself and the whole political system from approaching the point at which the line of agreement would stop functioning'.

The trouble was that no real dialogue was taking place. Indeed, the trade union partner which the Government said it needed so much was being constantly attacked and reviled for what it was doing. In Gdynia, for instance, Solidarity was blocking the export of meat preserves which the Government insisted were necessary if the country was to be able to import greater quantities of food for the Polish people. The printing strike, which actually continued for a long time in Olsztyn, prompted the charge that Solidarity, in spite of all its talk about access to the media, was set on withholding information from the people. In Katowice Solidarity organised a huge rally over the closure of the steel plant's bulletin, *Wolny Zwiazkowiec*, and demanded a vote of no confidence in the works director and his dismissal. It was even suggested that he be carted off in a wheelbarrow, a traditional and humiliating expression of worker disapproval. However farcical that may sound, it was part and parcel of a crucial issue which divided Solidarity and the Government, the right to appoint industrial managers.

In general, papers like *Zolnierz Wolnosci*, which had always taken a hard line, were now convinced that extremists had gained the upper hand in Solidarity and were bent on pushing Poland into 'an abyss of social anarchy and national disaster'. One prize target was Jan Rulewski, the Solidarity leader in Bydgoszcz, described by the paper as 'a morbidly ambitious and mentally disturbed man'. Early in September it was announced that the investigation into the Bydgoszcz incident, in which Rulewski had been beaten up, was being dropped. This prompted an immediate strike alert.

Leadership at the very top of the Communist Party, meanwhile, was not notably firm. Stanislaw Kania, who had been ill for a few days early in August, seemed to be becoming increasingly invisible. When he put in an appearance in Poznan to make a speech, he was asked among other things whether the authorities were not proceeding too cautiously and too gently and again whether they were not behaving too harshly against Solidarity. He did not answer the questions very clearly, but he did point out that it was he who had reported to the Politburo a year ago that new trade unions were necessary. He suggested that nothing could be achieved without Solidarity, but he warned that if street demonstrations went on it would be 'only a question of time before an explosion occurs in Poland'.

Kania was speaking the day after the Solidarity leadership threatened another media strike, this time to last six days and to affect radio and television. The Government condemned the idea, pointing out that Polish radio and television, with their network of transmitters, formed 'part of the general system of allied communications of the countries of the Warsaw Pact'.

'Poverty is knocking at the door'

Whichever way one turned, it seemed, there was argument and conflict as the nation approached the first anniversary of the Gdansk Agreements. The new Primate, Archbishop Glemp, felt the need to call on both sides to cut it out. In a sermon at Jasna Gora in Czestochowa on 26 August – scene of Cardinal Wyszynski's controversial sermon of a year earlier – the Archbishop appealed for a month of peace and said that no side had a monopoly of virtue.

As matters stand here today, there is a division into two social groups, each pleading its innocence while pointing to the mistakes and sins of the other. You only have to switch on the television or the radio to hear how one virtuous and saintly side is condemning the wrongdoing and arrogance of the other. The other side, in turn, deprived of access to the same media, specialises either in caricatures or, not infrequently, abusive words or, prodded by the instinct of self-preservation, resorts to measures described as 'ultimate'. Tensions and emotions are rising while poverty is knocking at the door. Meanwhile, the two contestants tell poverty to wait until one of them wins and can drive it away. Let us look at ourselves truthfully. We shall then see our own sins . . . and this will allow us to see the good done by the other side.

The big fear on the side of the authorities and their Eastern bloc allies was that this was a struggle for power. General Jaruzelski, the Prime Minister, still hoped it was not. He told a passing-out parade of young officers in Koszalin that everyone was looking to the coming Solidarity Congress for the answer to one question: was there going to be constructive cooperation or confrontation? At the same time the General struck a note of firmness. There was no going back on the policy of renewal but, he asked, how long can the line of accord, how long can the patience, moderation and good will of people's power, be put to the test? . . . It is possible to torment the authorities, to incite moods with complaints and endless demands, with printed and spoken words and with posters. But it is impossible to heat flats, build houses or feed people by these means . . . Polish soldiers have the right to say: Enough of this indulgence.

The Solidarity Congress was only five days away when Poland marked the first anniversary of the Gdansk Agreement. The celebrations were modest and rather subdued, in keeping with the state of the nation as it faced higher prices for bread and the prospect of fuel cuts in the coming winter. But in Gdansk the celebrations were not without bitterness. The plan was to hold one ceremony to mark both the Gdansk accord and the forty-second anniversary of the German attack on Poland. It was to take place on the Westerplatte peninsula off which the warship *Schleswig Holstein* had fired the shot signalling the start of the Second World War. Well in advance *Zolnierz Wolnosci* reported with horror that Solidarity were demanding that a memorial cross should be restored to its original place on the peninsula from which it had been removed in 1963 to make way for another monument, a tank used in the liberation of Gdansk by a Polish armoured division formed in the Soviet Union. It was a good story and one which generated a lot of bad feeling, but the paper had to admit eventually that Solidarity had not demanded the tank's removal. When the anniversary ceremony went ahead, in the presence of Lech Walesa, the cross had been restored to its old place, next to the tank. One could not help seeing something very symbolic of the political situation in that incongruous juxtaposition.

The political problems showed no signs of reaching such a compromise. On 1 September, in accordance with an agreement reached with the Government only a few days earlier, four Solidarity leaders, including Lech Walesa, appeared on national television to answer questions from a single interviewer. The effect seems to have been an intensification of the Government's suspicions. Lech Walesa, for instance, while repeating that Solidarity did not want power, also said that 'since the Government has lost public confidence, it has automatically thrust that confidence and the solution of problems onto us'. He said roughly the same in an interview with the

Roman Catholic daily, *Slowo Powszechne*:

Things have now reached a stage at which the authorities are losing the acceptance and support of society. What next? This situation forces us to take upon ourselves responsibility for the fate of the nation. We all have to do that, all social groups, and journalists as well. As Solidarity, we must now think of new, socially effective methods of action.

To judge from those two very similar quotations, Walesa chose his words with care and he must, presumably, have realised that they would encourage the suspicion that Solidarity wanted to push the Government aside, rather as the tank was supposed to be pushed aside on the Westerplatte peninsula. Such suspicions could only have been increased by a remark by one of his colleagues that 'the union must not allow anyone to monopolise access to the mass media'.

Two days later, at the end of another plenary meeting of the Communist Party Central Committee, Mr Kania said this:

The threat of our opponents to paralyse radio and television cannot succeed. Our enemies say that the authorities will definitely not declare a state of emergency in Poland. I want to state with full determination and calm that the authorities will resort to all measures that prove necessary to defend socialism. We do not want this and we are not threatening to use such a weapon. Our declaration of accord amounts to an offer of an alliance with all who are not against socialism.

'A revolution is taking place'

On 4 September the scheduled Soviet manoeuvres, involving 100,000 men, began in the Baltic and Belorussia. In Prague *Rude Pravo* said that 'counter-revolution in Poland is sticking its neck out very far'. On Saturday 5 September Solidarity's first National Congress – or rather the first part of a two-stage affair – began in the Oliwia Hall, a sports stadium in Gdansk. Nearly 900 delegates came from more than forty branches. Archbishop Glemp said mass for them in the Cathedral before they eventually got down to work.

Right from the start there seemed little evidence of the sort of reassurance that General Jaruzelski was looking for. For one thing, Solidarity refused to accredit camera teams from Polish national television after a complex row with the authorities on coverage. The authorities wanted Solidarity to ban all strikes until the congress was finally over, something the union leadership said it did not have the right to do. Solidarity, for its part, wanted its congress to be covered for state television by teams made up exclusively of Solidarity members, which the authorities said no broadcasting organisation would accept. Another point was that no Soviet-bloc trade unions were represented among foreign guests. According to Mr Kania, none had been invited. Solidarity denied this, not very convincingly, by saying that a blanket invitation had been sent to the World Federation of Trade Unions, to which they belonged, and that individual invitations had been sent later – though much too late, as a Hungarian reply was eventually to claim.

The conference began with words from the rostrum which paid no apparent heed to the warning heard in the Sejm back in June – that every word in the Polish crisis was potential dynamite. The report of the union's National Commission, delivered by its secretary, Andrzej Celinski, proclaimed: 'A revolution is taking place in Poland, and its main force is Solidarity . . . Post-August Poland is becoming a different country.' In the minds of many in Eastern Europe that could only be interpreted as counter-revolution. Indeed, the East Germans professed to have found 'proof' that Solidarity was counter-revolutionary in words which they attributed to Lech Walesa in his opening address: 'The fight has only just begun, but we shall win the battle. We will shape Poland the way we want to.'

Polish coverage of the Congress was never so blatantly hostile as that of some Warsaw Pact allies, especially Czechoslovakia. Indeed, there was relief and appreciation of the fact that Solidarity repeated its pledges to remain loyal to the Gdansk Agreement. But even that came under strain when it was reported that Jan Rulewski had initiated a move to delete from the union's statutes the vital clause recognising the leading role of the Communist Party. The move was defeated, but after six days, as it came to the end of the first phase of its National Congress, Solidarity had managed both to dismay and embarrass the Polish authorities and to confirm its allies in their darkest suspicions.

Message to East European workers
Three documents caused all the trouble. One was a brief interim programme statement calling, among other things,

for free elections to the Sejm and the local People's Councils, union supervision of food production and distribution, public control of the mass media, and economic reform; under this last heading it called for authentic workers' self-management and elimination of the Communist Party's right to make appointments. This final point was covered in a separate resolution. It rejected the Government's plans for industrial self-management because they did not give the workers the right to appoint and sack managers. Congress asked the Sejm not to pass the Government bill and instead to organise a national referendum on the subject. If the Sejm refused, Solidarity said it would organise its own referendum and boycott the bill if it was passed.

From the Government's point of view that was all bad enough. But a third document, one it could not have expected, took the challenge beyond the politics of Poland. It was a message to the workers of Eastern Europe:

The delegates assembled in Gdansk at the First Congress of the independent self-governing trade union, Solidarity, send the workers of Albania, Bulgaria, Czechoslovakia, the GDR, Romania, Hungary and all nations of the Soviet Union greetings and expressions of support. As the first independent trade union in post-war history, we are profoundly aware of the fact that we share the same destiny. We assure you that in spite of the lies disseminated in your countries, we are a genuine, ten million-strong representative body of workers, created as a result of workers' strikes. Our goal is struggle to improve the life of all working people. We support those of you who have decided to embark on the difficult path of struggle for a free trade union movement. We believe that it will not be long now before your representatives and ours are able to meet in order to exchange experiences as trade unionists.

The message was at least partly in response to one received, according to a Solidarity news-sheet, from 'The Founding Committee of Soviet Free Trade Unions' declaring that 'Solidarity today is our signpost'. This in itself was interesting enough, since most of the Soviet free trade union campaigners who had come to prominence in the late seventies were by now supposed to be safely disposed of either in prison or psychiatric hospitals or simply silenced by the efficient functionaries of Soviet State security.

The text of the Solidarity message was broadcast in full by Polish radio and television. It was part of the preamble to a calm but white-faced comment by *Trybuna Ludu*. The paper described the document as an 'extraordinary' attempt to interfere in the life of friendly countries, an appeal for changes in the social structures of socialist countries; Solidarity, it said, had expressed a readiness to help in setting up organisations similar to its own in those countries.

A declaration of this type cannot but provoke resolute opposition. It is addressed, moreover, to countries that are our ideological friends . . . countries that guarantee our independent existence, countries that give us aid . . . At the same time, it is known that the activities of Solidarity's leading circles are being observed very critically and with profound distrust in these countries. The appeal may deepen this distrust and thus place certain burdens on Poland's relations with its socialist allies . . . If Solidarity wishes permanently to define its place in socialist Poland, it must also define its place in the socialist world in which Poland lives. The message from Gdansk . . . places Solidarity not in this socialist world but against it. It thus does harm to Solidarity itself and, what is worse, to Poland.

The Polish Foreign Ministry followed that up with a statement accusing 'the inspirers' of the Solidarity message of violating the principles of Poland's foreign policy and her *raison d'état*. 'Does Solidarity wish to emphasise in this way that it belongs to a different world?' It was a good question, for Poland itself once used to belong to a very different political world before it became a member of the Soviet bloc. And what had Lech Walesa said in his speech winding up the first stage of the Solidarity congress? 'We have a great chance to make Poland the sort of country that our fathers failed to bring about.'

Moscow was in no doubt about the answer to the question posed by the Polish Foreign Ministry. In a vitriolic and comprehensive indictment of what it disparagingly called 'the Gdansk assemblage' the Soviet news agency, TASS, claimed that Solidarity's 'villainous appeal' had been inspired by 'a whole conglomeration of counter-revolutionaries of various types, including agents of imperialist secret services, all who hate socialism and people's power in Poland'. Their ultimate aim, said TASS, was 'the restoration of the bourgeois order in Poland'. The Gdansk congress, it claimed, had been turned into 'an anti-socialist and anti-Soviet orgy'. The Solidarity leaders had issued an appeal for 'struggle against the socialist system' not just in Poland but throughout Eastern Europe. 'Just like their Western masters, they imagine that it is possible to impede the progress of socialism in the countries which are allied with the Polish People's Republic.'

The old speculation, much relished in the West, about the spread of the 'Polish disease' had suddenly been strengthened out of the mouth of Solidarity itself. Czechoslovakia talked of 'the export of counter-revolution'. In Warsaw the Soviet Ambassador, Mr Aristov, called on Stanislaw Kania.

Taking stock

This was a good moment to look back. One year had passed since Communist Eastern Europe's first free trade union had come into existence, a year in which many preconceptions and predictions had proved to be wide of the mark. Originally, for instance, there were serious doubts about the possibility of a free trade union with the right to strike ever being allowed in a Communist state supposedly modelled on the Soviet Union. If the Soviet authorities imprisoned and harassed anyone who tried to form a free trade union and if they managed through tight control of the media to pretend that strikes were unnecessary and therefore did not happen, surely the Polish authorities could do the same. They did not do the same, because they chose deliberately to do otherwise. Under the influence and later the leadership of Stanislaw Kania, the Polish Communist Party chose to allow the strikes to be reported by Polish and foreign journalists, something the Soviet Union would never permit. It also decided to avoid bloodshed by opting for negotiation rather than using the police and the army for confrontation. It was influenced, no doubt, by the memory of Poznan in 1956 and Gdansk and Gdynia in 1970, and also by the disastrous economic situation, which could not be put right without the cooperation of the country's work force. Nonetheless the Communist Party's decision was historic. And the evidence of much that was said in the early months of Solidarity's existence suggests that the Communist leaders, while determined to maintain their leading role, were also enthusiastic and hopeful about the new union's ability to revive the country's fortunes.

Mr Kania and his colleagues undoubtedly took a risk when they launched their policy of renewal and the line of accord. They did so against the wishes of their Soviet-bloc allies. What they set out to achieve, if one wishes to be cynical, was the survival of Communist rule in spite of its abject failure hitherto. To be more generous, they seemed to want to create a state in which the Communist Party remained supreme but where prosperity was based on the use of all the talents of the nation whether Communist or non-Communist. To pursue that policy, the Kania leadership had to face distrust on all sides – in the Party, in Solidarity and among its allies in Eastern Europe. But it pressed on with a purge of the Party, with an Extraordinary Party Congress based on democratic elections, with bills to codify the rights of free trade unions, relax the censorship and introduce self-management in industry. All, apparently, to no avail. One year after the great experiment began, the Communist leadership found itself still under fire from a disappointed Party, opposed on vital points of practical economic policy by Solidarity, and under greater pressure than ever from its comrades in Moscow.

From the very start the possibility of a Soviet intervention had been a constant feature of all assessments of the Polish crisis. The example of what had happened in Czechoslovakia in 1968 had been regularly raised, more often than not by the Czechoslovak media, as a warning to the Poles. But no intervention had taken place. The great military super-power, which at that moment had 100,000 men engaged in exercises round Poland's northern coast and eastern frontiers, had been helping to keep the Polish economy going by postponing the repayment of loans totalling several thousand million dollars and, unlike the other Comecon allies, by supplying Poland with extra goods while receiving only a fraction of the commodities, notably coal, which Poland was supposed to supply to the Soviet Union. According to Mr Kania, the Soviet leaders had also agreed in August to supply small quantities of grain, despite their own poor harvest, and 2000 million cigarettes.

The economic aid was certainly not entirely disinterested. The Kremlin could not entertain the prospect of a member of the socialist commonwealth simply collapsing in ruin. At the same time the Soviet leadership could hardly be expected to sit back and watch Poland descend into political chaos. The fact remained, though, that it had not intervened. One can speculate fairly convincingly about the reasons why. Intervention was perhaps too costly economically for a country already finding it difficult to feed its own people while waging a war in Afghanistan. Maybe it was also considered too damaging, politically and diplomatically, to be worth the risk. The Kremlin may well have agreed with the warning, issued by Polish intellectuals in June, that the use of force would turn Poland into a resentful, occupied nation with its people taking to underground resistance. Communism in Poland would be permanently discredited, while on the international plane détente would be pronounced clinically dead and the Soviet Union would become isolated in the international workers' movement.

The arguments were certainly persuasive but they left quite a number of Western observers unconvinced. If the worst came to the worst, they said, the Soviet Union would go in, even though it might be the last thing it wanted to do.

At the end of the first stage of Solidarity's Congress in the early days of September 1981 one would have thought that the Polish authorities and the Soviet Union had been pushed as far as they could be. Solidarity had not only challenged the Government's plan to rescue the economy, but was also apparently setting itself up as the only organisation with enough public support to carry the nation through the crisis. At the same time it had called for free elections to Parliament and local councils and for public control of the media; it had also offered its support to aspiring free trade unionists in the Soviet Union and other East European countries.

If all that seemed unnecessarily provocative, it must also be said that Solidarity did enjoy the continued support of the great majority of the population and could not compromise itself by not responding to popular dissatisfaction over increasing food shortages. Moreover, the stronger line against Solidarity in the official media, introduced very gradually but ultimately as a result of the Soviet letter received in June, was bound to provoke a stronger line in reply. The result, as Stefan Bratkowski and other leading journalists had warned, was that Solidarity and the authorities had moved farther apart. This, in itself, was very definitely in the interests of the Soviet Union. The men in the Kremlin had made it perfectly clear that, while they disliked and feared Solidarity, they were also very dissatisfied with the leadership of Stanislaw Kania and General Jaruzelski. If the two sides could come to blows and so prove that the renewal they espoused could not work, then the Soviet Union might simply have to sit back and wait for the Poles to do their work for them. No one could say whether such calculations formed part of the Soviet strategy, but it seemed perfectly clear that Solidarity's latest pronouncements, particularly its message to the workers of Eastern Europe, had weakened Mr Kania's position in relation to the Soviet Union.

Soviet workers answer back

A whole week passed before the Polish authorities revealed what the Soviet Ambassador, Mr Aristov, had had to say to Mr Kania. In the meantime Moscow's propaganda machine moved into top gear and organised the sort of campaign traditionally reserved for moments of crisis, with mass meetings of protesting workers at factories around the country. Such meetings, last brought into play at the time of the campaign against the American neutron bomb at the end of the seventies, are supposedly spontaneous expressions of popular 'anger and indignation'. In reality they are the product of careful organisation and orchestration. This is not to say that there was no genuine anger at all at the meetings at the Likhachev Motor Car Works in Moscow, the Kirov factory in Leningrad, at Uralmash in Sverdlovsk, the iron and steel plant in Magnitogorsk, or the several other plants that were moved to protest against Solidarity's message to Eastern Europe. There is never much love lost between Russians and Poles, but these rallies had little to do with such atavistic attitudes. They were highly organised affairs which merely used the mouths of Soviet citizens to give voice to official anger about their fellow workers in Poland.

The language of condemnation grew more vivid and ferocious as the protests multiplied. In a letter to Polish workers, the metal workers of Magnitogorsk said:

Under whatever mask counter-revolution in Poland hides itself, however it disguises itself from the friends of the Polish people, its brutish, bared fangs cannot be hidden by any means. The so-called congress of the trade union association Solidarity . . . revealed itself as an open struggle against the PZPR and the Polish Government . . . The end has come for all patience and tolerance towards the actions of Poland's enemies. The Polish working class . . . must seize all provocateurs and accomplices of imperialism . . . The time has come to tear the masks off these 'friends' of the people and give them their just deserts.

The Soviet reaction was perhaps predictable, as was the fact that its example in organising workers' protests was followed by Czechoslovakia and Bulgaria. But the serious offence caused by Solidarity's message to Eastern Europe can be measured by the fact that the Hungarians, whose coverage of events in Poland had always been notably more objective, also reported rallies at which both workers and intellectuals condemned what were described as 'the destructive ambitions of the extremist elements in Solidarity'. Even the Yugoslavs rejected the message as 'interference'.

'Insane provocation'

In Poland itself the argument against Solidarity built up further with the announcement from the Anti-Crisis Operational Team, set up by the Government in August, that unless there was a marked increase in coal output in the remaining months of the year a considerable number of industrial plants would have to be closed down, there would be severe reductions in the generation of electricity and even a danger of 'total economic collapse'. All this was attributed to the introduction of the five-day working week in the coal mines. Solidarity was also in trouble over its publications. The Prosecutor General's office announced that the authorities in Ustrzyki Dolne, in the south, had impounded an illegal, anti-Soviet publication distributed by Solidarity and allegedly containing material on 'The Fourth Partition of Poland', the Soviet invasion of Eastern Poland on 17 September 1939 in the wake of the German attack from the west. The confiscated material had not been handed back in spite of a warning strike. In Wroclaw a delegate to the Solidarity Congress had been arrested and then released on bail on connection with the illegal sale in a news kiosk of the union's 'Lower Silesian Bulletin' which was said to contain an appeal to Soviet troops stationed in Poland not to obey orders. In Warsaw the censors placed a ban on one of the pages of *Solidarnosc* because it contained material connected with the Congress Message to the Working People of Eastern Europe.

Such was the climate in which the Party Politburo met and issued a statement claiming that the first part of the Solidarity Congress had destroyed the hopes of many people.

The Congress raised to the level of an official programme adventurist tendencies and phenomena that appeared to be only extremist undercurrents. The agreements concluded in Gdansk, Szczecin and Jastrzebie were unilaterally violated. They were replaced by a programme of political opposition which strikes at the vital interests of the Polish nation and State. This means a course aimed at confrontation threatening bloodshed . . . The so-called Message to the Working People of Eastern Europe was an insane provocation against Poland's allies . . . Solidarity's negation of all the efforts of the state authorities . . . threatens a further inevitable decline in the Polish economy. At the Solidarity Congress victory went to the line of building an opposition political organisation which openly sets itself the goal of taking over power and changing the social and political system in Poland.

Solidarity's reaction to that, through its spokesman Janusz Onyszkiewicz, was to accuse the Politburo of a 'lack of realism'. That, at least, is what Warsaw Radio quoted him as saying.

Moscow protests

But the Party leaders were aware, when they made their statement, of what the Soviet Ambassador had told Mr Kania the week before. Details of this, published two days later, revealed the coldest and sternest warning yet to pass between Moscow and Warsaw. It was not a fraternal letter from one Party to another, but was more like a diplomatic protest, delivered as it was by the Ambassador. Its main complaint was over the growth of anti-Sovietism in Poland which, it said, had reached dangerous proportions. The charge was that a coordinated and unbridled campaign against the Soviet Union was being waged 'openly, extensively and with impunity', so that it penetrated various spheres of life including education and culture. The history of Soviet–Polish relations was being distorted in publications, in the cinema, in theatres and on public platforms in speeches by members of KOR, the Confederation of Independent Poland and Solidarity. Solidarity's message to Eastern Europe was described as 'an outrageous provocation'. But that seemed just part of the catalogue of anti-Soviet acts which included the desecration of Soviet graves and threats against Soviet troops stationed in Poland. The message from Moscow alleged that anti-Socialist forces were stirring up an atmosphere of extreme nationalism with a distinct anti-Soviet flavour. Then came the point of the message.

Why have the official Polish authorities not taken any effective steps so far to put an end to the hostile campaign against the USSR? We do not know of any case of the instigators of anti-Soviet provocations meeting with a sharp reaction from the authorities and being punished . . . They are being given easy access to state-owned premises to hold their meetings, the mass media are being made available to them . . .

We have repeatedly drawn the attention of the leadership of the PZPR and the Government of the Polish People's Republic to the rising tide of anti-Sovietism in Poland. We spoke about it during the meeting in Moscow in March, and in Warsaw in April. We wrote with complete openness about it in the CPSU Central Committee letter of 5 June. We also talked about it during the meeting in the Crimea in August this year . . . The Soviet people . . . have every moral right to demand that an end be put to anti-Soviet impudence in Poland . . . Further tolerance of any kind of manifestations of anti-Sovietism will inflict immense harm on Polish-Soviet relations and will be in direct contradiction of Poland's obligations as an ally . . . We expect the Polish Party and Government leadership to take immediate, resolute and radical steps to stop the malicious anti-Soviet propaganda and actions which are hostile to the Soviet Union.

At roughly the same time, Warsaw Radio broadcast a grim statement from the Polish Government. It maintained that the resolutions adopted by the first round of the Solidarity Congress amounted to 'a *de facto* rejection of the offer of constructive cooperation' and confirmed the 'anti-socialist course of the extremist forces in Solidarity'. The Government still spoke of a struggle to preserve the policy of renewal, but delivered what seemed to be a blanket condemnation of Solidarity. 'Today the intention of the Solidarity leadership gradually to take over power is obvious. This is no longer a supposition. This is not a hidden intention but an action that became overt by virtue of the Gdansk deliberations.' The Government said that, if the need arose, it would not hesitate to take 'all means that accord with the state prerogatives'. It had considered concrete measures 'which may turn out to be essential to defend socialism and the basic interests of the Polish State and nation'.

One could be forgiven at that moment for concluding that it was all over. Yet in the midst of the massive onslaught on Solidarity there were still voices suggesting that all was not lost. Deputy Premier Rakowski, in a speech at Nowa Huta near Cracow, said he would like to believe that there was still the possibility of stepping back from confrontation. Janusz Zablocki, a Roman Catholic member of parliament, told Warsaw television that everything should be done to save the policy of accord. It would be wrong, he advised, to draw premature and over-generalised conclusions from the first round of the Solidarity Congress. A full assessment could be made only after it was all over. In the meantime, one must not lose faith in the discretion of Solidarity activists.

Far more astonishing was a statement to the youth paper, *Sztandar Mlodych*, by Walerian Solinski, who was elected to the Communist Party's Central Committee in July. He said that the Party would do well to think about relinquishing power for some time and going into opposition – a suggestion condemned in Prague as 'outright betrayal'.

Solinski's words were not reported by Polish radio or television. Nor was an appeal for compromise by Stefan Bratkowski, the journalists' leader, who warned that the people reaching for the levers of power, coercion and violence would be condemned for centuries if they had their way. The official media, and especially television so far as I can tell, were more concerned with reporting a wave of approval for the line taken by the Party leadership in its most recent statement. The views of Solidarity hardly got a look in though the Polish News Agency, PAP, did attempt some kind of balance. However, a Yugoslav correspondent reported that, for all the reports of support for the Party line, initial reactions among Party members indicated that they were not disposed to break off all contacts with Solidarity. This was an important point and a crucial one, for a total break, though satisfying the hard-line elements and pleasing Poland's allies, could hardly help solve the country's economic problems. Solidarity was too big to be ignored.

13. APPEALS AND WARNINGS

In the week that preceded the resumption of the Solidarity Congress in Gdansk there were faint signs of a more conciliatory approach. But it struggled to survive amidst increasing calls for a harder line. From East Germany came the view that the Polish authorities were still not being tough enough. When, asked *Neues Deutschland*, would they realise that 'you cannot discuss things with the enemy but have to fight him with all means available'? The paper added for good measure that Solidarity had para-military gangs all over the country harassing those who were willing to work. The East German radio described such alleged groups as storm troopers, modelled on the SA, the Nazi brown shirts. In subsequent weeks there were to be more allegations of Nazi leanings – especially against Zbigniew Bujak and Jan Rulewski, the Solidarity leaders in Warsaw and Bydgoszcz.

In Warsaw itself, however, the hard line emerged clearly in a statement from a so-called Marxist–Leninist seminar at the local Party headquarters. The line of agreement, it said, had turned into one of agreement with counter-revolution. It demanded a purge of Party ranks. This was the old line of the Katowice and other forums, now changing their names to Marxist–Leninist Seminars. There was a distinct contrast between that and a television speech by Stefan Olszowski, the supposed hard-liner of pre-Congress days. He warned against Solidarity extremism and also, more startlingly, against the possibility that the Soviet Union might be tempted to reconsider all its extra economic aid. But Olszowski also appealed for national agreement, for the participation of all patriotic forces in the National Unity Front. This should be a meeting place, he said, for everyone, members of the Communist Party, the United Peasant and Democratic parties, all trade unions including Solidarity, representatives of the

Roman Catholic Church, and so on. 'All patriotic forces should unite for the salvation of the homeland.'

The possibility of such a last-minute appeal succeeding in spite of everything seemed to be strengthened by the news that the presidium of the National Commission of Solidarity, quite independently, had come up with a new formula on the disputed issue of the appointment and sacking of factory directors under the plans for industrial self-management. Directors, it said, should be appointed and dismissed either by the workers' council or by the founding body, meaning the State, and each side should have the right to challenge the decision of the other. This formula was roughly the same as the latest proposal from the Government.

Then came yet another surprising development. An appeal from Poland's leading intellectuals for an immediate resumption of negotiations for the sake of the nation was published in full in the press and given wide coverage on the radio. Its authors – men like Karol Malcuzynski, Stefan Bratkowski and Andrzej Wajda – had been taken to task and severely criticised in the army paper *Zolnierz Wolnosci* only a week earlier for a similar appeal they had issued at the time of the Soviet letter in June. But now, for some reason, their words, in an appeal to the nation and a message to the Foreign Ministry, were listened to. They condemned 'anti-Soviet excesses' and stated clearly that Poland's place was in the socialist camp. But they insisted that the line of agreement was the only way. Poland was more important than the ambitions of individual men. Solidarity was capable of magnanimity in the face of 'the campaign of insinuations'. The Government was capable of putting the supreme interests of the nation above those Solidarity activities which caused alarm. 'The great chance of Polish socialism, the great chance of national rebirth . . . is still before us,' the appeal said.

This was, as General Jaruzelski told the Sejm, 'a really decisive moment'. The first round of the Solidarity Congress had created a new political crisis but he left the door open for negotiation.

The Party, the people's power, do not intend to leave the road of socialist renewal. There can be no return to the evil pre-August days. Their costs are too great for our generation to forget them. Nor will there be a rehabilitation of those guilty of the distortions of that time . . . While we remain ready to defend the socialist state, we are waiting for an answer, for the standpoint of the Solidarity leadership, for a change in that line which reached its culmination in the first round of the Congress . . . Everyone who is not against socialism can create with us new forms of constructive cooperation . . . One cannot accuse the Party or Government of a lack of moderation . . . But how long can one operate in such conditions?

'A worse Totalitarianism'

A proper Solidarity response to General Jaruzelski's appeal, which was backed up by a resolution of the Sejm, would have been more possible, perhaps, had the union been a more homogeneous organisation. But, as Mr Kania had frequently said, it was not homogeneous at all. So the second part of the congress got under way without apparently paying any attention to what the Government or intellectuals had said in their appeals. The union was distracted, for one thing, by the recent arrest of the Solidarity leader in a coal mine near Katowice; his offence had been to allow his members to cart the rival leader of the industrial mineworkers' union off in a wheelbarrow for allegedly talking to television behind Solidarity's back. The result was another strike, which some thought might be used as an excuse to ban the congress.

But even when the Congress went ahead, it plunged almost immediately into a bitter wrangle over the recent decision of the National Commission's presidium to reach a compromise with the Government on the sore topic of the appointment of industrial managers. It was revealed that only four out of the presidium's eleven members had been present to take that decision, one of them being Lech Walesa, and that the vote had been three for and one against. Jan Rulewski had been against and was still against, demanding a motion to reject the decision which was described by another radical, Andrzej Gwiazda, as 'an unpardonable political error' which violated the previous resolution calling for a national referendum.

Very clearly this was a fundamental challenge to the leadership and line of Lech Walesa. Many speakers were reported to have attacked 'autocratic views' on the part of some members of the leadership. The offending decision was condemned as 'undemocratic'. But Walesa fought back and in the process became the man in whom Government's best hopes for moderation lay. PAP quoted Walesa as saying that the union must define its position now. 'Some people are trying to break down the Sejm, break down the Government and take their place and be more totalitarian than them. That would produce a worse totalitarianism than we have today. I will not take that bait'.

After three days of the congress PAP, in an anonymous commentary which was obviously authoritative, reported regretfully that the Prime Minister's appeal had been 'ignored as if it did not exist'. The Government had also compromised on self-management, it said, but this and all other compromises had been attacked.

Can any authority in the world treat seriously appeals for cooperation from a congress that breathes hatred? Can a State which wanted to be a partner of Solidarity cherish such illusions after a congress which, in every word, declares war on the government of its country and the political and legal principles which it solemnly swore, before the court, to respect?

The Government was either tempted to accept the hard-line view advocated by its allies and their supporters in Poland or perhaps just wanted to give the impression that it was. At any rate *Zycie Warszawy*, which had retained a more hopeful line in the midst of the thickening gloom, maintained still that of the two sections in Solidarity – the radical and the centre – the moderate centre under Lech Walesa would definitely win. This depended on the union's elections.

The Congress had first to choose a new Chairman, a post for which Walesa had three challengers. One was Andrzej Gwiazda, one of the organisers of the Gdansk strikes, who had tried to resign in March when he disagreed with the decision to call off the threatened national strike. He was a prime target for criticism by Moscow. So too was the second challenger, Jan Rulewski, the maverick leader of the Bydgoszcz chapter of Solidarity, one of the men who was beaten up there in March and now described by Moscow as 'fascist'. The third was Marian Jurczyk, the Solidarity leader in Szczecin, where he signed the August agreement with the Government ahead of that in Gdansk. All four had to appear before the Congress, as before a selection board, and give a brief statement of aims and policy before answering questions. This episode provided a striking contrast between Walesa and Rulewski. While Walesa, according to Poznan Radio, urged the union to seek 'simple, workers' paths' and not to underestimate the Government, Rulewski launched into delicate international affairs.

He claimed that the union was too preoccupied with an imaginary threat of Soviet intervention and suggested that the Final Act of the Helsinki Conference of 1975 should be included in the union's statute. He pointed out that this provided for the voluntary nature of affiliation to political systems or military blocs. He was hinting, it seems, at the possibility of Poland leaving the Warsaw Pact.

When it came to the vote, Walesa was re-elected Chairman of the National Consultative Commission of Solidarity. He received 55 per cent of the vote compared with 24 per cent for Jurczyk, 8.84 per cent for Gwiazda and 6.21 per cent for Rulewski.

This must have been a relief for the Government, but a lot depended on who would be elected to serve under Walesa in the National Commission and the Presidium of the Commission. A lot, too, depended on the programme to be adopted by the Congress. But the Government made matters a little more difficult by suddenly announcing a rise in the price of cigarettes, by some 80–90 per cent on popular brands. The Solidarity Congress exploded in anger. Walesa sent a letter of protest to General Jaruzelski who immediately despatched his Minister of Finance along with the Chairman of the Prices Commission to Gdansk to face the Congress and charges that the union had not been properly consulted. Once again Solidarity made it clear that no such decision could be taken without prior consultation and approval. The union demanded that prices not only on tobacco but on fish should be frozen until agreement could be reached, otherwise there could be unrest. The authorities said this was impossible.

The row over cigarettes overshadowed the voting to fill the places on the National Commission. Sixty-nine people had to be elected to join Solidarity's regional leaders, more than thirty of them, to make up what was vaguely the equivalent of the Communist Party's Central Committee. It took six ballots to settle it, with several leading nominees failing to get elected and Bogdan Lis, the Communist from Gdansk, only just scraping in. Walesa's challengers for the Chairmanship were elected to the National Commission but they were not included in a nineteen-man Presidium headed by Walesa and consisting of six regional leaders and eleven elected members. Significantly, Walesa said that these new men were not discredited in the eyes of the authorities. The Presidium, it seems, was more moderate than its National Commission.

'Restructuring the State'
The Government may well have considered the election results a mixed blessing. But its final judgment depended on the union's programme, adopted on the twelfth and final day of the congress. It consisted basically of eight chapters defining the union's role and its aims, and inevitably there was much to disturb the Government. For instance, Chapter Two, as reported by PAP, said that in the face of national tragedy Solidarity could no longer restrict itself to waiting for the authorities to meet their obligations.

We are the only guarantor for society and that is why the union considers it to be its basic duty to take all short-term and long-term steps to save Poland from ruin, poverty, despondency and self-destruction. There is no other way to attain this goal except by restructuring the State and the economy on the basis of democracy and all-round social initiative.

The programme claimed that Solidarity did not want to violate international agreements, but it also said that it could not support the Government's plan to overcome the crisis and stabilise the economy because it was not good enough and did not have the support of the public. It demanded the abolition of centralised management of the economy and the separation of the economic administration from the political authorities. The union also called for a social council for the economy empowered to pass judgement on the Government's policy. It said that democracy should be based on the principles of philosophical, social, cultural and political pluralism. State legislation should guarantee basic civil liberties. The media should serve society and be under its control. As for economic reform in general, Solidarity said it should ensure that workers managed factories. It should also reconcile market laws with socialised planning. The programme ended by admitting that the union did not have a monopoly of truth and declaring its readiness to hold honest and loyal talks with the authorities.

Moscow, for the record, condemned Solidarity's programme as 'a counter-revolutionary document in which Solidarity places itself above the Party, the Government and the Sejm'. Moscow Radio told Polish listeners that the pluralism mentioned in the document was just another word for capitalism.

National coalition

The authorities in Warsaw were not so prompt with their reactions, possibly because it was too important a matter to be treated hastily or lightly. Besides, Lech Walesa had said that Solidarity had already accepted an invitation to preliminary talks. *Zycie Warszawy*, in a comment of its own, said that it seemed as though common sense was still prevailing. At the same time *Trybuna Ludu* published a strange article canvassing the idea of a sort of national coalition. It said an idea was taking shape of an agreement embodying the prospect of

a coalition government providing a platform for all who are not opposed to socialism and who, although not themselves ideological supporters of socialism, do uphold the Polish *raison d'état* and espouse the idea of social justice and public ownership of the basic means of production. The creation of such a front is dictated by the national instinct of self-preservation.

The next day, 10 October, the Government Presidium met. While commenting that the Solidarity Congress had made the situation 'even more disquieting', it went on to propose as a matter of urgency the formation of a joint commission, composed of representatives of the Government and also of the trade unions, to discuss and agree on market supplies, rationing and prices. On the face of it, this looked like a response to Solidarity's call for a 'social council for the economy' and also to its demands for consultation on price changes.

The proposal produced no immediate reply. Indeed, there was a distinct but pregnant pause in which one noticed that unrest was building up throughout the country. Strikes had been called by Solidarity in Piotrkow Trybunalski over food shortages. Another non-Solidarity union leader had been carted off in another wheelbarrow in Krosno for altering a Solidarity poster. Teachers were threatening strikes over their draft charter. Solidarity members began a sit-in at a plant in Suwalki, again over food shortages.

While all this was going on, *Pravda* in Moscow was composing a considered article to appear on 13 October under the name of Aleksey Petrov. It was one of those published in full by TASS on the eve of actual publication, so it was important. What it said, in brief, was that Solidarity was making 'a grab for power', that its aim was 'the destruction of the entire socialist system in Poland'. Solidarity was 'a stepping stone to the seizure of state power'. The Polish counter-revolution, the paper said for the first time, was also 'supported by reactionary Catholic clerics'. The ultimate aim of the imperialists was 'to shatter the socialist community starting with Poland'. Once again *Pravda* repeated that this was not just a domestic Polish affair. Poland's workers and leaders should give counter-revolution 'an effective rebuff'.

The required rebuff seemed a long way off. The Government met and expressed the view that the Solidarity Congress had had a negative effect. But it repeated that it was still ready for talks and that its offer of a joint commission was still open. *Trybuna Ludu* carried another article on the need for a broader Front of National Unity, for a 'democracy of understanding between Communists and Catholics'.

Government offer rejected

The Solidarity National Commission, meeting in Gdansk, said nothing about this or the Government's offer. It called instead for an end to local protest actions and strikes which had spread to at least seven more towns and were to go on spreading.

The Government's offer of a joint commission had been telexed over the signature of Mr Rakowski to all union head-quarters on 12 October. The next day it received a non-committal reply from Solidarity's negotiating Chairman, Grzegorz Palka, suggesting talks on 15 October. By the time that date arrived, however, the Government was under pressure not just from Moscow and the spreading wave of strikes but from hard-line opinion in the Party. At a meeting of the Warsaw Party committee, the central Party leadership was openly criticised for incompetence and accused of being isolated from the masses. The line of accord was fine, speakers said, but the Party had gone too far by 'going along with everyone, even with those who spit on us'. It was at this moment that Lech Walesa chose to go ahead with a visit to Paris.

On 15 October the Government announced that its proposal to set up a joint commission had been accepted by the Industrial Unions, the Confederation of Autonomous Unions, the Solidarity Union of Private Craftsmen, Rural Solidarity, the Polish Teachers Union and the Public Utilities Union, but it had been rejected by Solidarity itself. According to the

Government spokesman, Solidarity did not want to sit round a table with other unions. The Government was astonished and shocked. It could not understand why Solidarity should be reluctant to help tackle the food shortages and the problems of the coming winter. Nonetheless it went ahead with separate talks with a Solidarity team led by Grzegorz Palka, who outlined the union's own plans for a social council on the economy.

Details of the plan emerged as the Central Committee of the Communist Party, meeting in plenary session, was debating a report from Mr Kania. What Solidarity wanted, according to Warsaw television, was a council completely independent of the Government so as to ensure credibility. Mr Palka was reported as saying that to support the Government's activities would be to betray the interests of the nation. The council should be set up by trade unions independent of the Government, it should be able to help shape economic policy and reform, it should have powers to check on Government activities, and also have the right to veto erroneous decisions by the Government.

This, it seemed, was the last straw. Not surprisingly the Government angrily rejected the plan as an undemocratic attempt to install a 'totalitarian dictatorship of the Solidarity union'. No opposition party in any country behaved like this, it said. The union which had denied any aspiration to become an opposition party was now displaying 'a desire to exercise arbitrary dictatorship'. The Government spokesman concluded that the Solidarity document 'fully and clearly confirms the accusations that the union's leadership is after all striving to seize power'.

Kania resigns
Two days later, at the end of the Central Committee meeting, Stanislaw Kania offered his resignation as First Secretary. It was accepted by 104 votes to 79 in a secret ballot. General Jaruzelski was appointed to replace him with an overwhelming 180 out of 184 votes cast.

It all happened rather quietly and, as General Jaruzelski was to say, in a civilised atmosphere. That atmosphere, in fact, was of Kania's own making for it was under his brief leadership, little more than a year, that the system of the secret ballot was introduced. But Kania stood for far more than that. He had virtually launched the policy of renewal, he had led the way to the acceptance of free trade unions and the right to strike, he had reformed and purged the Party, stood up to the pressure from Moscow, and survived. Now he had finally gone at a moment when the most noticeable feature of political life was not so much the pressure from Moscow or the criticism of hard-line elements in the Party, which was strong enough and increasing, but Solidarity's inability to make any concession to the Government in the way of cooperation for the national good. That at least is how the authorities saw it and one could understand why they did. Kania resigned, it seems, because his leadership was considered too cautious and ineffectual. Perhaps he was also tired and disappointed. Perhaps the man who once said that Poles would not shoot at Poles while he was in power preferred to go before that danger came any closer.

The signs were certainly not good. Half the country's provinces were said to be affected by strikes and the Solidarity leadership seemed incapable of stopping them. Politically the climate was getting much colder and Kania was not the only casualty. Bogdan Lis, the Communist in the Solidarity leadership, the sort of person who once embodied the possibilities of renewal, had been expelled from the Party. So too had Stefan Bratkowski, the journalists' leader, the man who had so often spoken out bravely and sensibly for honest reform. And the editor of the youth daily, *Sztandar Mlodych*, had been sacked for publishing an interview with Jacek Kuron, one of the leaders of the dissident organisation, KOR, which was now dissolved. At the Central Committee session the recent highly publicised appeal by thirty-five intellectuals, including Bratkowski, was denounced by one speaker, Marian Orzechowski, as 'ideologically vicious'. Another, Albin Siwak, asked when there would be changes in such papers as *Gazeta Krakowska*, one of the great papers of the high days of renewal.

The big question was whether General Jaruzelski, who said he would continue the Kania line, would be able to stem the tide. The Central Committee resolution, adopted unanimously, suggested that it would be difficult. Accusing Solidarity of unilaterally violating its agreements, it called on the Polish Government to resort to constitutional powers if necessary and to renegotiate the agreements concluded with the unions. It also suggested that the Sejm should be asked temporarily to suspend the right to strike. Jaruzelski himself told the committee: 'We have never sought confrontation, indeed we have always avoided it. We are not seeking it today. One thing, however, is certain – that the possibilities for retreat are already exhausted.'

Strangely enough the Government and Solidarity had agreed, while the Central Committee was in session, on freezing prices until they could agree on price changes and a system of compensation. But there was little else to be cheerful about. Solidarity rejected the Party charge that it had broken its agreements, but at the same time it was unable to stop the wave of strikes, mainly over food supplies, that was sweeping the country. Then there were incidents which made matters worse. In Katowice on 20 October crowds stoned the police after three men had been detained for selling 'provocative posters' and 'anti-Soviet' publications from a Solidarity van. In Wroclaw the next day there was more trouble when police broke up a crowd listening to 'communiqués of an anti-state content' allegedly being broadcast from a loudspeaker van belonging to Solidarity.

On the very same day the Czechoslovak News Agency, CTK, quoted Stefan Olszowski as telling Soviet-bloc journalists that unless Solidarity responded to the demands of the Central Committee and dissociated itself from 'rightist' forces, then the union would have to cease to exist. One could, perhaps, treat this as an example of partial reporting, but there was no denial in Warsaw of its accuracy. One could also treat it as a huge bluff. How, one might have asked, could such a powerful and popular organisation as Solidarity, with its membership of just under ten million, be made to cease to exist? That may have seemed to be an impossible venture, but the Central Committee of the Communist Party had already spoken of using 'all constitutional means' and suggested that the Sejm should think of suspending the right to strike.

Whichever way one looked at it, General Jaruzelski's Government seemed determined to do something to ease the effects of the economic crisis with Solidarity's help or without it. It was announced that he was setting up 'local operational groups' with plenipotentiary powers to go to work in the country's basic centres of administration, more than 2000 parishes and towns. The groups would be led by professional soldiers and would include, but not consist exclusively of, privates and NCOs, whose national service had just been extended by two months. Extraordinary situations, the announcement said, required extraordinary measures.

Not surprisingly in such a fraught situation, first reports of this created an impression among many in the West that troops were being sent in to quell the increasing local disturbances, that this was the beginning of a 'crack-down'. However, a careful reading of the original announcement and of subsequent reports, including a television broadcast by Lieutenant General Tadeusz Hupalowski, the Minister of Administration and one of a small number of army officers brought into the Government, suggested that the new groups would be small, numbering as few as three or four members, and that their main task was to help local administrations overcome mounting problems of supplies on the threshold of what promised to be a severe winter. They would, if necessary, assist in matters of law and order, but they were primarily 'trouble shooters', designed to help rather than coerce.

National strike
General Jaruzelski's move came a few days after a decision by the National Commission of Solidarity to call a national one-hour warning strike on 28 October. The strike followed a heated debate. It was intended as a protest against general Government mismanagement and its refusal to consider Solidarity proposals on solving the problems of the economy. It was also a protest against what the union described as a campaign of defamation against it and against 'arrests and repressions' of its activists. Solidarity certainly had plenty to worry about on that score. An increasing number of union members were now facing charges, generally over the public distribution of bulletins and leaflets deemed to be anti-socialist or anti-Soviet. The violent incidents in Katowice and Wroclaw were simply more dramatic manifestations of a determined Government campaign undertaken most probably in response to increased pressure from the Soviet Union. And Solidarity fears of strong-arm tactics against the union were strengthened on 27 October, when persons unknown threw canisters containing a noxious gas into a crowd attending a Solidarity rally in Sosnowiec near Katowice. The immediate result was another local strike.

The national warning strike went ahead as planned. Many

millions of workers – in the first such exercise since the crisis of March – responded to the call of the Solidarity leadership. But many at the same time ignored the leadership's call for an end to local, regional strikes undertaken without the approval of the men in Gdansk. The wave of wild-cat strikes continued.

The national strike was a success in terms of support, though General Jaruzelski claimed that this was far from total. But it had also dealt considerable damage to the ailing economy. Lech Walesa, for one, was very conscious of that. But his public expression of concern was double-edged. 'This is the last time we go on strike like this,' he said. 'We must change our methods to ones which do not result in production losses – such as, for instance, an active strike.' An active strike was one in which workers would seize control of their factories or enterprises but keep production going. To the authorities this was little consolation for, as *Trybuna Ludu* pointed out, the ultimate result of such sit-in strikes, if they became general, would be a takeover of power in the national economy.

In a week in which the Sejm was expected to be asked to consider banning strikes, pronouncements by Solidarity activists did little to encourage the Government to feel that there was much chance of conciliation. Walesa himself caused considerable consternation by telling workers in Zyrardow, where a strike had been in progress for weeks: 'Today we are approaching the finale of the decisive showdown. Either we really win and have the Poland we want or we shall be defeated.' Marian Jurczyk, the Solidarity leader from Szczecin and the man who came closest to Walesa in the voting for the union Chairmanship, caused anger and an official investigation with a speech in Trzebiatow on the day of the national strike which he was later to claim had been quoted out of context. But parts of what was claimed to be a recording of the speech were broadcast by Warsaw Radio and listeners heard what seemed to be Jurczyk's voice describing the Sejm, the Government and the Central Committee of the Communist Party as 'traitors to Polish society' and 'Moscow's representatives'.

Both statements were striking. Walesa gave the distinct impression, whether intentional or not, that what was happening was a struggle that would end with one side winning and the other losing. Jurczyk, the man who signed the Szczecin agreement of August 1980, showed himself totally distrustful of the authorities, although he conceded that they included just 'a few honest and wise men among them'. The big question, though, was whether continued Solidarity militancy would benefit either the union or those few honest and wise men who had undoubtedly helped the union grow into a powerful, ten million-strong organisation with its own premises and printing facilities and so on in little more than one year. Was it not possible that continued strikes and continued opposition to Government plans would strengthen the hand of those who had no liking for Solidarity at all while weakening the position of General Jaruzelski and others who still wanted to prove out of sheer necessity that a Communist government could work with a free trade union?

A great deal was at stake. There was much to lose and much to be saved from a year of change and reform which few had ever imagined possible, and many more had thought would never last. A great deal had also survived in spite of a palpable tightening up of controls by the Communist authorities. The press, radio and television had again become more obviously the instrument of Government and Party policy and propaganda, but they still found room to report what in a normal Soviet-bloc state would be unpalatable facts. Stefan Bratkowski, the journalists' outspoken leader, had been expelled from the Party, but protests against this unpopular move were reported by the official media from his own Party organisation, from Gdansk and Cracow. He was even allowed to go with a journalists' delegation to Moscow. In any real crack-down that, surely, would never have been allowed. Much still remained of the renewed Poland that the Party, Solidarity and the overwhelming majority of Polish society had espoused.

The next big question was how it could be preserved. One of the astonishing features of the last few weeks of October 1981 was the way in which, in spite of all the confrontation and defiance on both sides, the idea of some sort of coalition persisted and received publicity. One Roman Catholic version of the idea, as reported by *Slowo Powszechne*, came from Ryszard Reiff, leader of the PAX association. Rather daringly, he suggested that the present power system, based on the Army, the Communist Party, the Sejm and the other – normally impotent – parties of the National Unity Front could no longer solve Poland's problems. What was needed, he said, was a grand coalition, a broadening of the social base of power to take in Solidarity and the Roman Catholic Church. That, he added, would involve an abdication of a monopoly of power. That was too much, presumably, for the Communist authorities.

But when General Jaruzelski addressed the Sejm in the final days of October, besides calling for legislation granting extraordinary powers if necessary, he also proposed the formation of a Council of National Accord to examine and agree on the programme of a new National Unity Front, in which patriots from all sectors of life, from the parties, the trade unions and social, academic and artistic organisations could take part. 'We can save our country,' he said, 'and lead it out of the crisis by joint action.' General Jaruzelski said he expected the support of the Church.

The offer applied equally to Solidarity. As Jaruzelski was speaking, the Presidium of the union's National Commission was meeting in Gdansk for what seems to have been a heart-searching session. Its outcome was a statement which admitted that the protest actions then taking place throughout the country in an 'elemental and unorganised' manner were threatening the union with 'disintegration and loss of public support'. The National Commission's appeals were not meeting with understanding and 'the name of Solidarity is beginning to become an empty term'.

The Presidium which, as we have said, was considered to be more moderate than its National Commission, appealed for an immediate end to strikes. 'Nobody can take from us the right to strike, and we shall never allow it. But it is we who must programme the use of this weapon, and we must do this in a considered, planned way.' This appeal did not go unnoticed in the Sejm, which did not move to ban strikes but demanded instead that they should stop immediately. At the same time, at the suggestion of Deputy Karol Malcuzynski, the Sejm noted 'with approval' the latest appeal from the Solidarity Presidium. If there was no response, the Sejm said, it would proceed to consider granting the Government whatever legal powers the situation might require.

The session of the Sejm, a body which had most definitely been revived in the process of renewal, gave Solidarity a breathing space in which to think hard on the future. General Jaruzelski, for his part, gave a token of his intentions over the idea of national coalition by bringing three non-Communists into the Government, among them the leader of the Democratic Party, Edward Kowalczyk, as Deputy Prime Minister. The pressure was on Solidarity to make some sort of gesture to General Jaruzelski and the stakes could prove to be very high. But when the union's National Commission of more than a hundred members met some days later, the arguments and divisions inside the leadership were bitter and fundamental. Lech Walesa, in particular, came under fire. One of his deputies, Miroslaw Krupinski, argued that the union could not allow a conflict to occur without first exhausting the possibilities of reaching agreement with the authorities. Andrzej Gwiazda warned that if the union were to refuse to do anything about the grievances of its members, the union itself would be carted away in a wheelbarrow. Walesa replied that local strikes themselves could destroy Solidarity.

The National Commission eventually ended its discussions by passing several resolutions, including one on negotiations with the Government. It contained a warning that if agreed topics were not jointly solved after three months, the Commission would call for action which might include a general strike. No doubt it was a serious warning but the term of three months, in itself, gave grounds for some hope of industrial peace in the near future.

But the National Commission was still rather aggrieved. Before it had concluded its business its Chairman, Lech Walesa, informed its members that he was leaving for Warsaw to meet General Jaruzelski and Archbishop Glemp. His announcement caused a tremendous row. Walesa was accused of being autocratic, of conducting secret talks above the heads of the Commission. Walesa gave as good as he got, apparently, accusing some members of trying to set up an opposition political party. Having said that, he left.

On the evening of 4 November 1981, for the first time, the leaders of Poland's three main forces, General Jaruzelski, Communist Party leader, Prime Minister and Defence Minister, Archbishop Jozef Glemp, the Roman Catholic Primate of Poland, and Lech Walesa, Chairman of Solidarity, the Soviet bloc's first legally recognised free trade union, met in Warsaw for talks lasting more than two hours. They discussed, to quote Warsaw television, 'the possibilities of setting up a front of national accord which would be a platform for dialogue and consultation between political and social forces, based on the precepts of the Constitution of the Polish People's Republic'. The meeting was said to be useful and a prelude to further discussions.

It seemed an event of great moment, holding out the possibility of conciliation but at the same time the germs of damaging dissension inside the ranks of Solidarity. In the course of more than a year Poland had frequently stepped back from the brink of disaster. This, it appeared, could prove to be yet another example of that dogged sense of survival in what was once rightly described as a 'crisis of hope'. Crisis persisted, but hope survived.

But on a practical level, three Party appointments at the end of October must not go unnoticed. Two new Central Committee Secretaries were named: Marian Orzechowski, a Wroclaw university professor, and Wlodzimierz Mokrzy-szczak, already a candidate member of the Politburo. The third appointment – to candidate membership of the Politburo – was that of General Florian Siwicki, Chief of the General Staff.

14. DESCENT TO MARTIAL LAW

The day after his historic meeting in Warsaw with the Prime Minister, General Jaruzelski, and the leader of Solidarity, Lech Walesa, Archbishop Jozef Glemp was in Rome, addressing Polish priests in the church of St Stanislaw. The situation at home was extraordinarily complex, he said, but one got the impression that there was a great opportunity to fulfil one of the predictions of a former Polish Primate, Cardinal Hlond, that Poland would be the first country capable of combining elements of revolution and stability, the past with the future and technology with the spirit. 'It may seem that this amounts to an effort to join fire with water,' the Archbishop said. 'And yet all it amounts to is a harmony between the spirit and the flesh.'

The attempt to create a Front of National Accord was, indeed, going to be difficult, but there is no denying that the Polish media gave it all the publicity they could. Warsaw Radio spoke of the need for 'a Polish historical compromise'. *Kurier Polski*, the Democratic Party paper, insisted that the country's problems could be overcome only through 'the authentic cooperation of the whole of society'. The Government Presidium described the meeting between Premier, Primate and Solidarity leader as momentous. The weekly *Polityka* said the move to set up the Front was 'the last attempt' to reverse the course of events. *Trybuna Ludu* claimed that Poland's Communist leaders had shown their good will; now it was for Solidarity to make the next move. A Solidarity statement, signed by Lech Walesa, said that the union's National Commission would be ready for concessions and compromises that could be justified by the supreme good of the community.

On the face of it, prospects may have looked good. And optimism may well have been encouraged by the spectacle of the Communist State publicly celebrating for the first time the anniversary of 11 November, the day in 1918 when Poland regained her independence after one hundred and thirty years of partition by Prussia, Russia and Austria. The main ceremonies were in Warsaw, where President Jablonski laid a wreath at the tomb of the unknown warrior, but there were celebrations in many towns throughout the country. Mass was said in Wawel Cathedral in Cracow and flowers were laid at the tomb of Jozef Pilsudski, the leader who once fought against the Russians but was now described by *Zycie Warszawy* as 'the embodiment of the struggle for independence'.

But even this occasion prompted unfavourable comment. According to the East German news agency, Solidarity and the Confederation of Independent Poland (KPN), used the anniversary to organise 'a counter-revolutionary mob' in a demonstration in Warsaw during which Seweryn Jaworski, one of the local union leaders, was said to have called for 'true independence'. The agency noted the 'glorification' of Marshal Pilsudski and said that he had been largely responsible for the attack on Soviet Russia in 1920.

As for the proposed Front of National Accord, Moscow had by now barely mentioned it. Other allies, though, were more outspoken. The Bulgarian radio warned that some forces wanted to exploit the idea for anti-national and counter-revolutionary aims. Prague Radio reported that the project had given rise to unjustified optimism. *Rude Pravo* suggested that agreement was an illusion. All optimistic talk of a basis for national understanding, it said, was built on sand.

As far as one could see, such allied criticism had little obvious effect on events in Poland. Warsaw went on talking about the Front in spite of the sniping off-stage, just as the Government went on negotiating for re-entry into the International Monetary Fund while *Rude Pravo* in Prague denounced the Fund as a 'bastion of capitalism' and 'one of the most important instruments of neo-colonialism'.

But one of the weaknesses of the initiative to set up a Front of National Accord was its loose definition, and different ideas on what it actually stood for now began to emerge. The Party Politburo, meeting on 10 November 1981, decided that the notion should be the subject of further consultations among all Party organisations and all other organisations concerned. The next day, in a speech in Legnica, Stefan

Olszowski, one of the Politburo's leading members, declared openly that the idea of the Front was based essentially on Poland's existing political system and had 'nothing in common with the concept of a coalition government launched by Solidarity extremists'. The Party, he said, would not allow that.

Deputy Premier Mieczyslaw Rakowski, in an interview with *Zycie Warszawy*, rejected what he called the Party–Church–Solidarity formula as an over-simplification which would debar other organisations from Government. At the same time he revealed some of the argument inside and outside the Communist Party. He denied that the initiative to create a Front was a tactical move to make it easier for the Party to survive. As for the Party's authority in a Front, that, said Rakowski, would depend not on the Constitution which endorsed its leading role, nor on strong words and appeals, but on the force of its arguments. Some elements in the Party were clearly unhappy and maybe diffident about this, to judge by Rakowski's words: 'In my own ranks, I hear voices alleging that the line of agreement is a sell-out of socialism. But what alternative has there been? What is proposed in its place? Perhaps only the use of force.'

Once again, as on so many occasions throughout the Polish crisis, Rakowski had stated the issue clearly for both sides as one of choice. A week later Kazimierz Barcikowski, who defined the Front of National Accord as 'a political platform for consultation', said that the nation faced the alternatives of conciliation or confrontation. He also claimed that Solidarity was now shaping towards a joint search for solutions.

Tragedy in instalments

It was true that Lech Walesa, on the first anniversary of Solidarity's registration as a union, had sent a letter to all its members in which he spoke of new prospects for national agreement. 'I beg you,' he said, 'to maintain dignity and prudence.' But the signs were that Solidarity was as divided as the Party and also incapable of imposing prudence on its local bodies. It was difficult enough to assess the union's views and activities on the basis of Poland's official media, which were ultimately controlled by Mr Olszowski. But throughout this period when all the talk was of the Front of National Accord, the picture that emerged was one of widespread strikes. At one point Walesa himself was reported as saying that there were sixty-five major and minor conflicts, as he called them, still unresolved. The situation was bewildering and confusing, worse possibly than at any time since August 1980. And the strikes were not simply industrial. One of the most important started at the Higher Engineering School in Radom over the new education bill and spread to universities and colleges throughout the country. As early as 12 November Warsaw television was drawing sad conclusions.

Only a few days ago the attainment of internal calm seemed at last to be a real possibility. But even these hopes are beginning to peter out. There is hardly a Pole who understands what is really going on. No foreigner can understand any more why it is that a nation of thirty-six million people in the centre of Europe which has so many enlightened and intelligent citizens who have had so many bitter experiences in history is tightening the noose around its own neck. Poland is full of strikes again. When some come to an end, another flares up. Some are so absurd that foreigners with a liking for Poland are ashamed to write about them so as not to confirm the view current abroad that Poles are mad . . . These are no longer disputes between the Government and Solidarity. This is a national tragedy taking place in instalments, a conflict between the need to save the nation and the State and a plethora of irresponsibility . . . There have been various predictions about Poland, but no one forecast that Poles would want to dig their own graves.

Meanwhile the Solidarity leadership, in the shape of the Presidium of its National Commission, had offered talks with the Government. It proposed discussions on several topics including its ideas on a so-called 'social council for the national economy', economic reform, price reform, industrial self-management, elections to the People's Councils and union access to the mass media. These were not subjects on which any agreement could be expected to be readily available. Talks did begin on 17 November and Government and Solidarity delegates met several times before the end of the month. But by that time, before any sign of substantial achievement, events far removed from the negotiating table – events, it must be noted, reported by the media from the official point of view – had begun to take on the appearance of a steady deterioration very like the instalments in a national tragedy of which the television had spoken so eloquently.

One of the first signs of this was the news that Solidarity had started a propaganda campaign to back its demands for access to the media by sticking up posters and handing out leaflets on the streets of most Polish cities. According to Warsaw television, the Party and Government were being accused of 'Goebbels-type propaganda'. All this was presented as something very disappointing and most inappropriate for a union which was, at that very moment, starting talks with the Government on access to the media. But to add to the confusion Warsaw Radio reported that in some towns the contents of the Solidarity posters had been agreed with the Censorship Office.

A far more damaging report came from the radio on 20 November. Quite simply it stated that the Solidarity organisation in the Ponar factory in Zywiec had sent a letter to the works management demanding that the Communist Party should vacate its premises in the factory, that it should be banned from carrying out activities on factory premises during working hours and not be consulted over any factory decisions.

In a country where the Party was still supposed to play the leading role this report, if true, marked without doubt another escalation of the Solidarity challenge. But it was somewhat obscured, in terms of Western reporting, by an appeal for food aid addressed by Lech Walesa to workers and trade unions in Western Europe. The Solidarity leader warned that a drastic shortage of food could trigger dangerous social tensions and a spontaneous outburst of popular discontent. The Polish News Agency, in a commentary on the appeal, speculated that the West might well be wondering why Poles could not feed themselves instead of wasting time on strikes.

It was at this time that the authorities announced that the small military operational groups which had been working in the villages with some success would shortly be withdrawn and that larger groups would soon be appointed to operate in the cities. *Zycie Warszawy* commented that the Army had proved itself 'a political force which enjoys public backing'. It was reassuring for the public, the paper said, 'to realise that there is somebody who can be relied upon'.

Police and Party

A stiffening of official attitudes became apparent on 22 November, when it was announced that police had raided the Warsaw flat of Jacek Kuron, one of the founders of the dissident organisation KOR, and prevented the holding of 'an illegal gathering'. According to Warsaw Radio, the aim of the gathering was to set up a political organisation which went under the name of 'Clubs of the Self-Governing Republic – Freedom, Justice, Independence'. The organisation's founding declaration, confiscated during the raid, was said to be 'a platform of a political grouping hostile to the State'. Moreover, Solidarity representatives were said to be at the gathering.

It is worth noting here that KOR's leaders had publicly dissolved their organisation at the recent Solidarity Congress, on the grounds that its aspirations were adequately represented by the union itself. But soon after that the radios in Prague and Budapest reported that a new organisation had been set up called the Club in the Service of Independence. Now the authorities were claiming that the organisation under a slightly enlarged title amounted to a new anti-Communist political party. Brushing aside Solidarity denials, they claimed that union activists, whether they liked it or not, had been 'drawn into a political game'. Quite apart from the political implications of this development, it was significant, surely, that the police, who had largely ignored the activities of the technically illegal KOR for so many months, should now be acting so decisively.

In Radom, meanwhile, the Ministry of Internal Affairs and the General Prosecutor's Office simply placed a ban on a planned national convention, organised by the local Solidarity chapter, in support of political prisoners. The convention was declared illegal. This was another example of firm and decisive police action of the sort that had become rare since August 1980. Perhaps such moves had been avoided in the recent past for fear of offending Solidarity. Now there seemed to be no such hesitation.

On 24 November a statement from the Secretariat of the Communist Party's Central Committee hit out at Solidarity:

Certain links of Solidarity have recently stepped up their campaign against committees and members of the Polish United Workers' Party. Implementing the political concepts of illegal, anti-socialist organisations, they have been voicing, among other things, slogans about forcing the Party out of factories. This has been followed by cases of members of the Party being persecuted in certain factories and of various forms of psychological pressure being applied, particularly against factory committees . . . This is dangerous political adventurism which is not only directed against the Party. It also strikes at the vital interests of the working class and the idea of the nascent Front of National Accord . . .

Let no one count on separating the Party from the workers. The leading role of the Party constitutes the principle of the political system formulated in the Constitution of the Polish People's Republic. Whoever strikes at or attempts to restrict the application of this principle strikes at the legal order of the State . . . The Secretariat of the Central Committee condemns the witch-hunt against Party members, the attempts to force the Party committees out of factories . . . Our Party will resist these hostile acts with all its strength.

One wondered how widespread was the alleged move against the Party in the factories; we had been told only about Zywiec. At the same time one noted that only 'certain links of Solidarity' were accused. A week earlier *Trybuna Ludu* had suggested that the fight for national agreement would, in effect, be 'a fight for Solidarity, a fight to draw this most powerful social force in Poland towards a front of cooperation'. Now, after the Secretariat's statement and the raid on Kuron's flat, the Party paper revealed an interesting attitude to Solidarity. It claimed that the document found in Kuron's flat accused the union of being ineffectual 'in the struggle to form another Polish republic' and condemned 'the realistically minded Solidarity leaders for their awareness of the vital interests of the State and nation'. This attack, according to *Trybuna Ludu*, was 'clearly directed against those persons in the Solidarity leadership and also against representatives of the Catholic hierarchy who are in favour of a national accord'.

Eleventh hour
There was nothing unusual in the claim that the influence of Jacek Kuron was bad for Solidarity and the Communist State. But *Trybuna Ludu* did seem to be suggesting more frankly than ever before that the Party had less fears of the Catholic-inspired wing of the union. Stefan Olszowski, in a subsequent interview with the paper, backed this up when he said that the people involved in the 'Clubs of the Self-Governing Republic' were 'opposed to less radical concepts such as, for instance, the socio-Christian ones and to the possible chance of Solidarity cooperation with the State'. In the same interview, Olszowski sounded another warning:

265

Only political reactionaries and counter-revolutionaries can launch a provocation leading to bloodshed. If we are to be realistic, we must consider such a development.

Such was the mood when the Central Committee of the Polish Communist Party began a two-day plenary session in Warsaw on 27 November. The session began with two main reports, one by Marian Wozniak on behalf of the Politburo and the second by Wlodzimierz Mokrzyszczak for the Central Committee Secretariat. It was the latter which caught the eye.

Mokrzyszczak said the Party was concentrating on four basic tasks – consolidating the Party itself, developing its ideological and propaganda activity, resisting 'the anarchisation of life' and fighting the crisis in the economy. Almost in passing he mentioned that the activity of many divisions of the Voluntary Civil Militia Reserve (ORMO) had been revived. Repeating the Secretariat's line on Solidarity's alleged attempts to oust the Party from factories, Mokrzyszczak conceded that the Party was weak, with some organisations showing ideological and political instability. He called for opposition to 'right-wing opportunist revisionist views' and also to 'sectarian–conservative attitudes' inside the Party. As for Solidarity, Mokrzyszczak recalled that the Sejm had issued an appeal for social peace in October and repeated it some weeks later. 'Now it is the eleventh hour, a time to make a categorical choice. Does the Solidarity leadership intend to answer this appeal positively? Not just the Party but the entire nation is waiting for this answer.'

It was difficult to assess the overall mood of the session on the basis of Warsaw television and radio reports alone. There were certainly disagreements but these were not exactly highlighted. One speaker, for instance, said that there would be no economic reform without the support of the work forces. But more than one speaker called for the restriction or suspension of strikes by law. And one of them, Julian Kraus from a car factory in Bielsko-Biala, said a remarkable thing. His members were confident, he said, that the Party would manage. 'But this can be done only in one way – if we find the man who will tidy things up in public. This is because people today refuse to follow any organisation; they will only follow a man, a person who sets this country to rights. This is the only chance of salvation. This is the only chance for us to remain a Party.'

266

If that does not convey a sense of deepening crisis, consider the words of Deputy Premier Zbigniew Madej, the Chairman of the Planning Commission. According to him some people had suggested it was pointless to draw up a plan for 1982 because 'one does not know what might happen in a couple of weeks' time'. Later he said:

If the economy is anarchised to such an extent that we have to resort to confrontation based on force, then we will have to resort to this. But no one will resort to it of his own free will, because a war economy is also a decaying economy as many of us know from our own experience. A war economy might be a necessity, a periodic necessity, but when all is said and done one must try to make sure that the economy flourishes.

The session's final resolution, while declaring the Party's will to build a Front of National Accord and also to continue the process of socialist renewal, put it on record that the continuing unrest was 'a direct threat to the existence of the nation and to the external security of the State'. The resolution recognised the need to equip the Government with 'full powers' and asked Party members of the Sejm to seek a bill on 'emergency measures in the interests of protecting citizens and the state'. The closing speech was by General Jaruzelski.

Let no one try to use manipulation or pressure or threats or force to remove the Party. The Party cannot be removed by force. There may be force to meet force . . . There are only two ways for Poland and for Poles. One leads straight to doom through further strikes, tension, chaos, anarchy and lawlessness . . . That road ends in confrontation. The second road will lead gradually to overcoming the crisis . . . This is the way of national accord . . . The present situation cannot be tolerated any longer. The process of disintegration must be stopped. Otherwise it would inevitably lead to confrontation, to a type of state of emergency.

These were, without doubt, the most newsworthy of General Jaruzelski's phrases. But he too said he thought 'realistic' elements in Solidarity were under attack from the forces opposed to the idea of national accord just as much as the Party was.

The question of Solidarity's final attitude was influenced, though, by another quite separate incident.

Fire Brigade College raid
On 25 November cadets at the Fire Brigade College in

Warsaw began a sit-in strike. They were demanding that the college be removed from the jurisdiction of the Ministry of Internal Affairs and were said to be supported by the Warsaw region Solidarity organisation. On 30 November the Government declared the college closed. The college was surrounded by police and on the morning of 2 December, after the failure of mediation efforts by the President of the Academy of Sciences, the authorities acted. Special groups of riot police forced their way into the building through its main gate while others descended from a helicopter to secure the roof and upper floors. Within two hours the building was cleared. The cadets were allowed to go home but eleven 'outsiders' were briefly arrested for being on the premises illegally. One of them was Seweryn Jaworski of Warsaw Solidarity. It was alleged that during the strike Mr Jaworski had actually placed the Deputy Commandant of the college under arrest.

From that moment events began to move more swiftly. According to Warsaw Radio Lech Walesa appealed on the evening after the raid for 'reason and discipline'. But according to *Zycie Warszawy* the local Solidarity chapter in Warsaw had declared a strike alert on the grounds that the attack on the college was further proof of 'an increasing tendency on the part of the authorities to resolve social conflicts by force'. In a speech to Party workers in the Ursus tractor plant in Warsaw, Stefan Olszowski claimed that the Fire Brigade College had been used 'as a testing ground of what could be done against the forces of law and order'. He also spoke of 'brutal' attacks on the Party and mentioned another factory, the Fadroma plant in Wroclaw where, he said, there had been an attempt to oust the Party Committee. Olszowski also alleged that Zbigniew Bujak, the Warsaw Solidarity leader – and incidentally an electrician at Ursus – had once said that the first Solidarity broadcast transmitted by a Polish radio station would mean that the regime had fallen apart. 'Such a broadcast will not be made,' Olszowski said, 'and the regime will not fall apart.' Olszowski was asked about the possibility of 'a state of war', the Polish phrase for martial law. That, he said, would be the last resort. *Zolnierz Wolnosci*, the Army paper, said that 'extraordinary measures must be taken to stop the process of degeneration'.

There was a very strong impression that someone was spoiling for a fight. And the atmosphere was not helped by a report in *Zycie Warszawy* that on the day before the raid on the college the founding declaration of the so-called 'Clubs of the Self-Governing Republic – Freedom, Justice, Independence' had been presented at a press conference on the premises of the Warsaw region Solidarity organisation. This, the paper said, was 'an immeasurably alarming fact'. *Zycie Warszawy* was also alarmed by reports of a declaration by the Solidarity commission in the Adolf Warski shipyard in Szczecin. This said, according to the paper, that if the Government refused to allow free elections Solidarity would organise its own – to the Sejm and the People's Councils – after which 'the existing authorities will lose all attributes of legality'. This sort of thing, the paper maintained, only served to strengthen the hand of extremist conservative forces.

Radom meeting

But worse was to come. On 3 December the Presidium of the National Commission of Solidarity held a meeting in Radom with the chairmen of the union's regional boards. The meeting produced a hard-hitting statement from the Presidium which, according to radio and television, made the following points:

The authorities had exploited the idea of national accord in order to mislead the people. By increasing anti-union repressions, by threatening the adoption of emergency powers which would limit civil liberties, and by planning provisional arrangements for the management of enterprises without any consultation, they had effectively ruled out all possibility of national accord. Should extraordinary measures be introduced, the union would reply with a 24-hour national strike and in the event of repression it would consider a general strike.

Solidarity, the meeting insisted, could not be an ornament behind the façade of the authorities. The minimum conditions for national accord were an end to anti-union repression, a trade union bill acceptable to Solidarity, the introduction of genuine economic reform, democratic elections to the People's Councils, the creation of a Social Council for the National Economy, and access to the media for that Council, for Solidarity, for the Church and for other 'centres of opinion'.

The official response was one of horror and anger. Warsaw television said straightaway: 'This statement would seem to deprive us of any illusions whatsoever.' Later it commented that it was difficult now to believe in any assurances given by certain leaders of Solidarity. 'The statement confirms unambiguously that the idea of accord and agreement in the interests of the nation as a whole is alien to the union's governing body.'

On the same day as the Radom pronouncement, 3 December, General Jaruzelski was visiting miners near Katowice on the feast of St Barbara, their patron saint. He was still talking of national accord. 'Never before has so much depended on the capacity for national accord. May history not record that this opportunity went unfulfilled. There is no shortage of such occasions in Polish history and we have always paid an enormous price for them.' An announcement that night said that the Prime Minister had instructed ministers and lower officials that attempts to prevent the Communist Party from working in the factories were illegal and punishable by law.

On 4 December Solidarity postponed until further notice any talks with the Government. Stefan Olszowski, certainly one of the most publicised of Communist leaders at that crucial moment, told the Warsaw Party organisation that the Radom statement from Solidarity represented 'an open drive to take power'. On Saturday 5 December the Party Politburo met but no details of its discussions were revealed. Lech Walesa had a meeting with Archbishop Glemp. And Stanislaw Kania was reported to have addressed a meeting in Cracow on extricating the country from the crisis through national accord, 'thereby uniting the Party with the nation'.

The storm broke out again the next day. The Warsaw Solidarity organisation announced that 17 December would be a day of rallies on the streets in protest against the use of force. At the same time Warsaw Radio broadcast what it said were recordings made at the recent Solidarity meeting in Radom. For the record, the quality of the recordings was too poor for the BBC's monitors to put anything down with any certainty. But the official Polish News Agency and the papers were not slow to record what they said they had heard from the mouths of several Solidarity leaders:

Lech Walesa: Confrontation is inevitable and it will take place. I wanted to reach it in a natural way when virtually all social groups would be with us, but I miscalculated . . . It turns out that we shall not follow that road any more. So we are picking a road for a lightning-speed manoeuvre . . . We are aware that we are dismantling the system.

Jacek Kuron: The ground must be well prepared to overpower the authorities.

Grzegorz Palka: The Party can delay confrontation because it has power. Solidarity lacks such power. Therefore, we must set up a so-called workers' militia, groups of people armed with helmets and batons.

Zbigniew Bujak: The first action of the workers' militia will be aimed at liberating the radio and television headquarters. The Social Council for the National Economy must be established immediately. It will be something like a provisional government. The Government must at last be overthrown, laid bare and stripped of all credibility.

Jan Rulewski: An attack must be launched on the provincial authorities to discredit them completely before the elections.

At this point one feels bound to say that for many weeks now, if not for much longer, it had been virtually impossible to feel sure that the Solidarity view had been presented quite as dispassionately or honestly by the official media as it might have been. That perhaps is an understatement. Certainly the Polish Bishops, in a statement issued before the end of November 1981, felt the need to stress that one of the conditions for creating national agreement was true information. 'The mass media – radio, television and the press – cannot use half-truths or ignore some problems, for this leads to falseness and awakens anger. In such a difficult period all sides must observe responsibility for the word.' My impression was that the media treatment of Solidarity became sharper as the union failed to make a united and wholehearted commitment to General Jaruzelski's project of a Front of National Accord and proved incapable of controlling its striking members.

Whatever the ultimate explanations of what went wrong, the authorities' reaction to the reported statements from Radom were predictable. A Government statement accused the supreme authorities of Solidarity of breaking the agreements of Gdansk, Szczecin and Jastrzebie, of violating solemn pledges and assuming the role of a political opposition engaged in a struggle for power. After a long period of appeals and persuasion, the Government would have to equip itself with 'the indispensable means of action'. *Zolnierz Wolnosci* concluded that the Solidarity masks had finally been removed, revealing that all the fine slogans had been fraudulent and that the point all along had been to take over power. *Trybuna Ludu* maintained that Lech Walesa, who had never before rejected national accord, had now become evasive, probably under pressure from the Solidarity 'hawks'. *Zycie Warszawy*, the paper that had won much popularity in the heyday of renewal, expressed 'concern, protest and grief' and hoped that the hard resolutions of Radom would not be accepted by Solidarity's National Commission when it met in Gdansk in a few days' time.

In the meantime, Solidarity's national spokesman, Marek Brunne, published a reply to the Government denying that the union's Presidium had rejected national accord. The official media found his arguments unconvincing. Lech Walesa, who had another meeting with Archbishop Glemp, was denounced by *Zolnierz Wolnosci* as 'a great liar'. The Archbishop was reported to have written a letter to General Jaruzelski, Walesa and the Sejm. No details were revealed but the Czechoslovak News Agency accused him of 'rude interference and shameless threats' and of 'going willingly to the aid of Solidarity'.

Gdansk
The National Commission of Solidarity began its crucial two-day session on Friday 11 December in the Lenin Shipyard in Gdansk. The point at issue was whether the Commission, as the union's policy-making body, would endorse the attitudes reported to have been adopted at the meeting of the Presidium and regional chairmen in Radom eight days earlier. At an opening press conference Lech Walesa insisted that reports of the meeting put out by the official media had been misleading. They had distorted the meaning of individual statements and picked out only fragments of a ten-hour debate. He and other Presidium members denied that Solidarity was trying to remove the Communist Party from the factories. Walesa said:

I want to state with full emphasis that we are for agreement, we shall continue our programme for renewal, we do not want confrontation. In union language, the term confrontation means only a strike . . . National accord is indispensable, provided it is honest. Taught by experience we trust nobody any more. We want to have the right to exercise control over all vital matters of society and we shall fight for this.

All of that was reported by Warsaw Radio and the Polish News Agency and it is on them that we have to rely for details of what took place at the National Commission session. Given the circumstances of intense crisis and animosity, their fragmentary reports did not give an entirely convincing impression of a gathering set on counter-revolution. On the contrary the impression was, as usual, of an uncoordinated and disorganised debate which threw up a variety of proposals. Several speakers called for a national truce as long as attacks on Solidarity ceased. One speaker repeated that the triad of Solidarity, Church and State should play the main role in national agreement. Only three speakers – Jacek Kuron, Karol Modzelewski and Bronislaw Geremek – were reported to have urged the adoption of the Radom programme. But individual contributions contained phrases to alarm the Government. Jan Rulewski spoke of a provisional government of experts until free elections. Grzegorz Palka advocated a referendum and a vote of no confidence in the Government. Zbigniew Bujak, advising caution, favoured a political struggle as opposed to one on an open front. Seweryn Jaworski – the man reported to have said at Radom that he would knock Walesa's head off if he retreated any more – suggested the formation of a workers' guard. Walesa himself said that the union was not retreating, but admitted that the Radom meeting had changed his outlook.

The meeting, according to Warsaw Radio, seemed likely to go on into the night. But long before that the Polish News Agency was reporting that 'the Solidarity leadership is clearly leaning towards the adoption of political actions bearing all the signs of a direct struggle for power'.

Last warning
The Government in Warsaw had also issued an important statement:

The Executive of the Warsaw Region Solidarity organisation is organising a rally in the centre of the capital on 17 December. Similar preparations are in progress in some other regions . . . Poland is experiencing a serious economic crisis magnified by winter difficulties; strikes are continuing throughout the country and disturbances abound . . . In such a situation bringing masses of people out on to the streets is tantamount to putting a match to a powder keg . . . The demonstrations are being arranged under slogans hostile to people's power and to socialism which has for thirty-six years

273

been the system for regulating the life of the Polish people and will remain so . . . Appealing for the abandonment of street demonstrations which may lead to unexpected and incalculable consequences, it is necessary to warn, with full decisiveness, that the entire responsibility for the outcome will rest with their organisers. All acts against people's power will be counteracted by the organs of public order.

Late that Saturday night, 12 December, international news agencies reported from Warsaw that in spite of the Government appeal the Solidarity meeting in Gdansk had decided by a majority vote to declare 17 December a day of national protest. Warsaw Radio said nothing about this or any of the developments which swiftly followed. Solidarity representatives in Warsaw told Western journalists that their communications had been cut off. Soon it was discovered that all public telephone and telex links between Poland and the outside world had also been cut. Private telex lines operated by Western news agencies told us that the Solidarity headquarters in the capital had been surrounded by riot police carrying shields. Both ends of Mokotowska street, where the building stood, had been cordoned off. Police began carrying away sacks of documents. One wondered what might be happening in Gdansk where the entire Solidarity leadership were gathered in one place.

I myself went up to the BBC Monitoring Service at Caversham. At 0500 GMT I heard General Jaruzelski announce in a broadcast to the nation that Poland had been placed under martial law.

15. STATE OF WAR

'It is six o'clock. This is Polish radio, Warsaw calling. Today is Sunday 13 December 1981. A special day in the history of our State and in the life of the nation has begun. In a moment, Army General Wojciech Jaruzelski will make a speech at the microphones of Polish radio.'

Those were the words, followed by the national anthem, that ushered in a new and more frightening stage in the Polish crisis.

Citizens of the Polish People's Republic, I turn to you today as a soldier and as Head of the Polish Government [General Jaruzelski began]. Our country finds itself on the brink of an abyss. The achievements of many generations, the house erected from Polish ashes, are being destroyed. The structures of the State are ceasing to function. New blows are being struck every day at the dying economy . . . Chaos and demoralisation have assumed disaster proportions. The nation has come to the end of its psychological endurance. Many people are beginning to despair. Now it is not days but hours that separate us from national catastrophe . . .

The initiative of the great national accord won the support of millions of Poles. It created a chance to deepen the system of democracy and broaden the range of reforms. These hopes have now been dashed. The Solidarity leadership was absent from the common table. The words uttered in Radom, the session in Gdansk, have fully revealed the true intentions of its leading circles . . . How long can a hand stretched out towards accord meet with a closed fist? I am saying this with a heavy heart, with immense bitterness. Things could have been different in our country; they should have been different. Further continuation of the current situation would inevitably have led to catastrophe, to complete chaos, to poverty and famine . . . In this situation failure to act would be a crime against the nation . . . An early date has been set for mass political demonstrations in the centre of Warsaw in connection with the anniversary of the December events. We must not, we cannot allow these demonstrations to become a spark from which the whole country could flare up. The nation's instinct for self-preservation must be heard;

the adventurists must have their hands tied before they push the homeland into the abyss of fratricide.

General Jaruzelski, one of the most respected advocates of 'socialist renewal', then announced what had been done. Martial law had been imposed from midnight and a Military Council of National Salvation had been formed. This was not a military coup or an attempt to establish a military dictatorship. The Military Council would be dissolved, he said, once it had achieved its aims of restoring the rule of law, order and discipline and creating guarantees for the normal working of the State administration. There would be no weakness or vacillation, the General warned. A group of people believed to represent a threat to the State – 'extremist Solidarity activists and activists of illegal anti-State organisations' – had been interned. Also interned were several dozen people held personally responsible for the crisis of the seventies and for abusing their positions for personal gain. They included the former Party leader, Edward Gierek.

The General promised a drive against crime and speculation and said that anyone guilty of failure in leading posts would be dismissed at the suggestion of plenipotentiary military commissars who had been appointed to supervise the State administration from ministries down to parishes. Martial law, he went on, was only a temporary measure. 'Our soldiers have clean hands . . . They have no goal other than the good of the nation . . . The Army will not act outside the normal mechanisms of socialist democracy.'

As for the Communist Party, General Jaruzelski said it must rely on 'people who are honest, modest and courageous, people who will deserve the name of fighters for social justice'. On this above all would the Party's authority depend. At the same time, the Prime Minister hoped that 'the healthy trend in Solidarity' would reject the 'prophets of confrontation and counter-revolution'. Professing support for national accord, respect for a 'multiplicity of world views' and recognition for 'the Church's patriotic attitude', he said there would be no return to the erroneous methods of government practised before August 1980 and promised that reforms would be continued. 'History would not forgive this generation were this chance to be wasted.'

For anyone who had not already assumed the worst, General Jaruzelski's 23-minute speech, though undoubtedly a shock, still contained a few grains of hope. He still spoke of reform, national accord and socialist renewal. He had not dismissed Solidarity out of hand. His words on the Party indicated a candid recognition of its failings and the need for it to find good men before it could earn a good reputation. As he closed his speech with words from the national anthem – 'Poland has not perished so long as we are alive' – it was just possible to hope that the General was thinking of the nation and not just of Communist supremacy. On second thoughts, though, it could be assumed that for him the two concepts of nation and Party were ultimately the same. And how, one asked, could renewal survive when one of its essential ingredients – the rejection of the use of force – had been cast aside. How could the nation contemplate accord when leaders of its most representative trade union had been interned, detained without trial?

Doubts and fears multiplied as the day wore on and the radio began to pour out an avalanche of regulations, restrictions, prohibitions and orders. From the Military Council of National Salvation, soon to be identified as twenty-one senior army officers including its chairman, General Jaruzelski, came the news that all trade unions were being suspended temporarily. The head of State broadcasting announced that all regional stations were being switched off. There would be just one 24-hour radio programme, and one television programme, both run from Warsaw by a specially selected team of employees. Other employees were being given a special holiday.

Radio and television were on the list of industries said to have been militarised or placed on a military footing. These included the railways, motor transport, the ports, telephone and telegraph services, all refineries, eventually also the mines, and even factories producing military uniforms. Anyone employed in these industries was to consider himself on national service subject to military discipline. Anyone failing to report for duty or refusing to carry out instructions was liable to a military court sentence ranging from two years imprisonment to death. Anyone between the ages of sixteen and sixty could be 'called up' by local authorities at any time to perform 'emergency work' or be instructed to make his property or equipment available for defence purposes.

Pretty soon it became evident that Poland was in an iron grip, deprived of communications externally and internally. Frontiers were closed and permission was needed to go near them. Even sailing off the Baltic Coast was forbidden. All flights were cancelled until further notice. Private telephone and telex facilities were closed down or subject to censorship in emergencies. Mail was also censored and parcels would not be accepted unless they contained only food or medicines and were presented unwrapped for inspection and then wrapped in the presence of an official. Prior permission was required to move from one town to another and one had to report within twelve hours of arrival. Travel anyway was made more unlikely by a ban on the sale of petrol to private motorists. And everyone over the age of thirteen moving about town in the ordinary way was required to carry an identity document. All gatherings apart from religious services were banned. There were to be no public entertainments, sporting events or public rallies. The use of printing presses was also banned and the only publications allowed to appear were the Party paper, *Trybuna Ludu*, the Army paper, *Zolnierz Wolnosci*, and a few papers in the provinces. All firearms and radio transmitters had to be surrendered. People were forbidden to carry 'weapons of cold steel' or air guns, gas guns or other objects that could be deemed to be offensive. The authorities also took powers to prohibit photography, filming and television recording. Curfew was imposed from ten o'clock at night to six o'clock in the morning.

All this, as the martial law decree signed by President Jablonski admitted, represented a suspension of basic civil rights. Anyone over seventeen could now be interned 'for the duration' if he or she was deemed to present a threat to the state. Trade unions and the right to strike were suspended and punishments were listed for anyone carrying on with trade union work: up to five years for organising a strike, up to ten years for sabotaging industrial equipment. A sentence of up to eight years awaited anyone disseminating information thought likely to weaken the country's defences. For spreading information which could cause anxiety or lead to riots the sentence could be five years.

Reporting events in Poland was clearly going to be difficult and maybe dangerous. But on the first day of martial law there was a press conference for foreign journalists given by

Jerzy Urban, the Government spokesman, and for the military by Captain Wieslaw Gornicki, one of General Jaruzelski's advisers. Gornicki reiterated that the Military Council, which had not replaced the constitutional authorities, had been formed because recent Solidarity meetings in Radom and Gdansk and the plan to stage demonstrations on 17 December – the anniversary of the bloody food riots in Gdansk in 1970 – indicated an attempt to seize power. Mr Urban could not say how many people had been interned but he made the point that they were not imprisoned and that no penal proceedings were being undertaken against them. Lech Walesa, Mr Urban said, had not been interned. He was in Warsaw, being treated 'with all the respect due to the Chairman of Solidarity'. Meanwhile the Politburo and Secretariat of the Communist Party's Central Committee were functioning normally. The line of accord, he added for good measure, had not died. Mr Urban's statements were to be seriously doubted in the weeks to come.

One of the first casualties of martial law was suffered by the Roman Catholic Church. Because of the tightening up on radio programmes, Sunday Mass was not broadcast – as it had been ever since September 1980 – from the Church of the Holy Cross in Warsaw. But as the people of Poland entered their first night of curfew, they were able to hear on the one surviving radio channel a recording of a sermon delivered that evening by Archbishop Jozef Glemp, Primate of Poland, in the Jesuit Church in the capital's old town. It was a remarkable thing that the authorities chose to broadcast the sermon, a sign of just how much they needed the Church's help. It appealed for non-violence, although it offered no hint of approval for the imposition of martial law.

The Archbishop, without doubt, was in a difficult situation as he tried to answer the question of what people should do following the imposition of martial law, which he said had astounded him and which he saw as 'something dangerous'. God's answer was in the Sermon on the Mount. For many people, he knew, it meant a retreat from achievements, an admission of defeat. But martial law was a fact. Opposition could bring bloodshed. 'We can be indignant, shout about the injustice, protest against the violation of civil and human rights. However this may not yield results.' Some, he said, might accept that the authorities had chosen the lesser of two evils. Many others would not and would oppose 'the existing evil'. He went on:

The Church wants to put itself in the place of every man and understand him. That is why it received with pain the severance of the dialogue . . . the switch to the path of force. This cannot happen without the infringement of basic civil rights. It carries with it, in many instances, the trampling of human dignity, the arrests of innocent people, contempt for men of culture and science, anxiety in many families. Representatives of the Church will continually demand, as far as they are allowed, the release of citizens detained without justification . . . There also remains the most important matter, that of saving life and preventing bloodshed. The Church will be unyielding when it comes to defending human life. It does not matter if someone accuses the Church of cowardice . . . The Church wants to defend each human life and therefore, in this state of martial law, it will call for peace, for an end to violence, for the prevention of fratricidal struggle.

There is nothing of greater value than human life. That is why I myself will call for reason even if that means that I become the target of insults. I shall plead, if I have to, even on my knees: Do not start fighting, Pole against Pole. Brother workers, do not give your lives away.

Whatever the Archbishop said, it seemed clear that there would be resistance to the military authorities from Solidarity and its members. The union, which had been hailed as Poland's great hope by Party and non-Party people alike, had suffered considerably in just one day. Apart from losing leaders through internment, it had had all its splendid premises with their printing facilities seized and the decree on martial law, by speaking of the need for every employee to work six days a week, seemed to have undone the union's achievement of the five-day week. But it was always understood that Solidarity had contingency plans ready for just such an eventuality as martial law. These included the occupation of factories and sit-in strikes.

Reports of resistance

The problem was: how could foreign correspondents in Warsaw adequately report such developments deprived as they were of telephones and telexes, many of their contacts and of any prospect of refilling their petrol tanks to get around in their cars? During the first Monday of martial law, Western news agencies that had managed to keep their lines open reported strikes at at least four plants in Warsaw – the steelworks, the Ursus tractor plant, the Swierczewski precision tools factory and the big car factory. In the evening the last lines went down when the Reuter news agency ceased to file.

What this meant, in effect, was that all information from or about Poland was from now on at least partially discredited. Henceforth correspondents were supposed to base their reports on official information and present them for censorship before they could be sent. If they managed to get anything out that was uncensored there was still bound to be some element of doubt simply because they were confined to Warsaw, they could see little apart from that for themselves. Moreover, whatever sources they might find for reports on what was happening elsewhere could not automatically be accepted as above suspicion.

As a result the Western news media did the best they could by resorting to sources which in normal circumstances they might have paid little attention to – travellers from Poland, Solidarity representatives abroad, even a British ham radio operator who had talked to a fellow enthusiast believed to be in Poland operating what was by now illegal equipment but reporting on developments which no one could vouch for.

Whatever the truth or otherwise of much of the news from such sources, Warsaw Radio and the television themselves revealed that resistance was widespread. Clearly they did not mean to do so. Their style from the start was that of good news programmes: as might be expected from media engaged in propaganda during a state of war, they always reported the better side of things. Thus on the first working day of martial law – when Solidarity was expected to attempt a general strike – radio and television consistently claimed that 'calm prevailed in the greater part of the country's centres'. But they admitted something when they reported that 'most' Poles had turned up for work. When they had to concede trouble they tended to play it down as an exception to the general rule. In this way, it took them twenty-four hours to say that on that Monday 'professional agitators' in several plants throughout the country, including a few in Warsaw and also in Plock, had made normal work 'more difficult' by calling for opposition to martial law. In the early days the media always reported strikes or attempted strikes when they were over. Thus a sit-in at the Katowice steel works had been 'frustrated by the forces of law and order'. Equally revealing though not as specific were reports that in Rzeszow 'almost all work forces' turned up for work, or that Lublin was 'almost normal'. In Poznan, the Cegielski works – where the 'bread and freedom' riots started in 1956 – was reported in one bulletin to be working normally, but another admitted that there had been some breaks in production requiring a visit by the local Party Secretary. In the first three working days of martial law, reports like these and others on the arrests of people accused of organising strikes made it clear that there had been trouble in some twenty cities and towns, sometimes involving more than one factory. The places in question were Warsaw, Lodz, Katowice, Gdansk, Szczecin, Poznan, Lublin, Cracow, Wroclaw, Plock, Piotrkow Trybunalski, Rzeszow, Nowy Sacz, Gorzow Wielkopolski, Lubin, Jaworzno, Gorlice, Bedzin, Bialogard and Rybnik.

It was at this time that the authorities announced that four provincial governors had been replaced by officers for incompetence and that several industrial managers had been sacked for failing to perform their tasks under martial law. One could see these changes as the fulfilment of General Jaruzelski's pledge to get rid of those guilty of incompetence or corruption. But there was a suspicion that the men were removed because of opposition to martial law. And it was admitted officially that one of them, the manager of a hosiery factory in Lodz, was dismissed after starting 'strike agitation'.

One of the first indications of resistance came from across the border in neighbouring Slovakia, where Bratislava Radio reported on Monday morning that troops had prevented strikes in about a dozen factories. It also said that Miroslaw Krupinski, one of Lech Walesa's two deputies, had called for a general strike. Warsaw Radio confirmed the next day that Krupinski, with three other Solidarity leaders, had taken refuge in the Gdansk shipyard and issued leaflets which had reached students in Warsaw calling for the strike.

That report suggested that the police swoop on Solidarity leaders assembled in Gdansk on the night of Saturday to Sunday could not have been all that comprehensive. And this impression was confirmed by the news that Andrzej Slowik and Jerzy Kropiwnicki, who had been speaking at the Solidarity meeting in Gdansk, had been arrested in Lodz, where they headed the union's organisation, on Sunday for addressing a large crowd and calling for a strike. How could they have got to Lodz from Gdansk if the authorities' internment net had been drawn so tight?

Further doubts about the Military Council's grip on Solidarity arose when the radio published what it called the 'first list' of union members and dissidents interned. Fifty-seven people were named, among them several top leaders of Solidarity – Andrzej Gwiazda, Jan Rulewski, Seweryn Jaworski and Marian Jurczyk. But the list was almost equally divided between Solidarity men and members of KOR, such as Jacek Kuron and Adam Michnik. This was admittedly only a first list but many names one would have expected were conspicuously absent. Lech Walesa, now reported by the Polish Ambassador in Sweden to be under house arrest, was not listed, as was to be expected. But neither was Zbigniew Bujak, the union's charismatic leader in Warsaw, nor the leader from Wroclaw, Wladyslaw Frasyniuk. Both proved to be still at large.

Bloodshed

By the middle of the week, the authorities were proving less than bland. The Military Council of National Salvation broadcast an appeal against the rally planned by Solidarity for Thursday 17 December.

We have, in these early days, avoided incidents which could have driven Poland to tragedy. We must realise that groups of provocateurs who seek shelter in colleges or factories have not discontinued activities that present a danger to the entire community and every family . . . The Warsaw rally can only be a provocation. All of us, especially women and mothers first and foremost, must protect children and young people from getting involved in the consequences of the provocation planned by the extremists. Let us not expose our dear ones to danger.

The broadcast confessed to being 'not without unease' and revealed that on Tuesday the forces of order, as it called them, had had to enter several enterprises where there had been attempts to organise strikes.

One could understand the unease. On 16 December 1980, as *Trybuna Ludu* recalled, the nation had erected a monument in Gdansk to those who had died back in 1970. 'Never again,' it said, 'should it be necessary to erect that sort of monument in Poland.'

On Thursday evening came the news that the worst had happened. Warsaw Radio announced that seven miners had been killed at the Wujek colliery, near Katowice in Silesia, on Wednesday. It happened, it said, when police attempting to break up a strike had been attacked allegedly with stones, crowbars and pickaxes and, as it put it, 'recourse was had to arms'. Forty-one uniformed policemen and thirty-nine civilians were injured. On the same day, the radio reported, 160 policemen and 164 civilians had been injured in street disturbances in Gdansk. It was a tragic irony that the very thing that Polish leaders had said should never happen again had happened again on the eve of one of the most painful anniversaries in the country's Communist history. The media placed the blame firmly and squarely on the 'provocateurs' who had 'stirred up the miners'. Warsaw Radio confessed: 'The authorities will not retreat since there is nowhere to retreat to.'

The news from Gdansk followed diplomatic reports that the army and police had broken down the gates of the Lenin Shipyard at dawn on Wednesday 16 December and broken up the sit-in strike there along with the skeleton leadership of Solidarity under Miroslaw Krupinski. Confirmation of the action if not of the detail came two days later in the local newspaper, *Glos Wybrzeza*, as quoted by Warsaw Radio. According to this version, the strikers were removed without incident and several hundred people who did not belong in the shipyard were detained, among them a citizen of a Western country. That same morning, the paper reported, many people tried to gather near the Monument to the Fallen Ship-builders outside the shipyard in response to leaflets calling for a rally. The army and police blocked access to the area but by noon the crowds had grown. They refused to disperse so tear gas and water cannon were used to break them up.

There was more rioting in Gdansk the next day. It started in the morning and lasted for several hours. This time twenty-seven people were injured, but the paper emphasised that there were no deaths. The incident, the paper went on, showed a terrifying lack of imagination and a complete decline in the instinct for self-preservation. At one point a van was over-turned and set alight. Later there was another attempt to set a car on fire. Two officers were said to have leapt out with their clothes ablaze. They were saved, the paper said, only by the water cannon. In mid-afternoon the situation became very dangerous. In the central streets of the city youths were said to be hurling abuse and stones while people erected barricades. Water cannon and tear gas were again used and the 'rowdies' as they were described were said to have dispersed as dusk fell at about six o'clock.

Gdansk was not the only scene of serious demonstrations on 17 December. Water cannon and tear gas were used also in Warsaw and Cracow. And it was now clear that the 'forces of law and order' had had to intervene not only in Gdansk and at Wujek but also in the steel works in Warsaw, Katowice and Cracow and the shipyards in Szczecin. There had also been trouble with crowds in Lublin.

As Poland approached the end of its first week of martial law, the military-controlled media, in their continued reports of general calm, revealed that there had been strikes or attempted protests in a growing number of places, among them Bydgoszcz, Tarnow, Jelenia Gora (where nine factories were suddenly reported to have ended strikes), Walbrzych and Bialystok.

In spite of their efforts to present a picture of a country returning to a normal, well-disciplined, hard-working life, the official media had in fact provided a picture of protest and resistance in virtually every corner of the country. Radio and television broadcast throughout the first week a series of statements by Solidarity members or officials voicing approval for martial law or condemning so-called extremist elements in the union. One of the first was by Zdzislaw Rozwalak, Chairman of Solidarity in the Wielkopolska region. Another was said to come from the Solidarity leader in Leszno, a man already reported to have been interned. But some of these public recantations conveyed more than simply a change of heart. Stanislaw Zawada, Solidarity leader in Huta Lenina, the steelworks near Cracow, described the tension as the security forces prepared to break up the sit-in strike on the night of Tuesday–Wednesday.

Just imagine it. One o'clock at night. Fifty or sixty motor vehicles parked near the fence. Sirens wailing – an agreed signal to indicate that the forces of order have entered the combine. Telephones cut off. Groups of people in the production shops, confused, frightened because rumours were flying about. We knew anything could happen in this sort of situation. At the same time, we knew that two kilometres away in the town, our wives, our mothers, our children could hear these sirens, could see the lights. This was a terrible experience. I do believe – although I witnessed the incursion of the security forces, into the small rolling mill to be precise, where 1500 people were gathered, praying, singing, seeking a sign of hope – that at this particular mill nobody was beaten up. It was just a question of this group of people being rounded up by ZOMO [motorised units of the civil militia], but ZOMO units equipped with shields, batons, helmets and visors. Just imagine the feelings of the people waiting there knowing that practically anything might happen. I really believe that no matter how this all turns out, this image will stay in people's memories for ever.

As Poland began its second week under martial law the resistance was far from over. Although it was announced that strike leaders from Gdansk and Szczecin and elsewhere – including Miroslaw Krupinski – were under arrest and being charged, the resumption of work at the shipyards of Gdansk, Gdynia and Sopot was put off till the first Monday after Christmas. Although curfew was reduced by two hours on 19 December, it was maintained in its original length in Szczecin, Elblag, Lublin, Katowice and Wroclaw and actually extended in Gdansk province by two hours.

The Baltic Coast, it seemed, was the area giving most concern to the authorities. But suddenly all attention switched to the Katowice area. On Sunday 20 December, the Soviet News Agency, TASS, and later the East German News Agency, ADN, reported that Solidarity 'counter-revolutionaries' had blown up one of the exits at the Ziemowit colliery at Tychy near Katowice and were threatening to blow up the other exit with explosives already planted. As a result some 1300 miners were trapped underground.

The next day Warsaw Radio confirmed that nearly 1200 miners were still underground at the Ziemowit pit – at one time there had been more than 2000 – and more than 1700 underground at the Piast mine nearby. The radio said nothing about the explosives but alleged that strike organisers were intimidating fellow miners, refusing to admit doctors, experts or priests.

While Warsaw was admitting that, the East Germans and Czechoslovaks were reporting more trouble at the Katowice steel works. Quoting Polish reports, they said that counter-revolutionaries had barricaded themselves in and were threatening to blow up the furnaces by means of oxygen and acetylene. The next day Warsaw reported that the strike at the steelworks was continuing. It was supposed to have ended a week earlier.

286

These were the last major instances of industrial protest admitted by the authorites. On 23 December, Warsaw Radio announced finally that police and soldiers had restored order in the steelworks. Some 2000 employees, said to have been kept in the foundry for many days by Solidarity 'terrorists', had gone home. No one had been hurt. Most of the organisers of the strike had been arrested. A search was continuing for the rest of them.

But the authorities were facing quite a different dilemma at the Ziemowit and Piast mines. It seemed logistically impossible for them to force the men out and they were no doubt wary of occasioning any further bloodshed to add to the Wujek tragedy in an industry so vital to the economy. They adopted the tactics of persuasion. The strikers who were allegedly being terrorised by Solidarity extremists, abused and even stripped naked and doused with icy water if they wanted to give up, were subjected to very telling psychological pressure from the authorities on the surface. Food parcels from wives and mothers were sent down to the men below. Relatives were encouraged to talk to their men by telephone. The strikers were given assurances that no one who had been forced to strike would be punished. This obvious attempt to divide the strikers was backed up by thoughts of Christmas. One letter sent down said: 'Don't stay below any longer. The country is calm. Everybody is working. End the strikes. Christmas is drawing near. Your families are waiting for you.' Late on Christmas Eve, the radio reported that all the miners had left the Ziemowit pit. Experts had found ten and a half tons of explosives inside it.

The strike at the Piast mine ended only on 28 December when the strike committee was said to have disbanded itself and the last 900 men came up to the surface. First reports said all of them had been sent home after medical checks. The next day, though, the radio reported that four of them had ended up in hospital and that the twelve most active organisers of the strike had been arrested. By now we had been told that four men had been detained for organising the Ziemowit sit-in and that seven were under arrest as ringleaders of the Katowice steelworks strike.

As they approached the new year, the military authorities had cause to feel some satisfaction. Indeed, they claimed that their first objective had been achieved after two and a half weeks. Tuesday 29 December, they said, had been the first day without any strikes or protests. Most of the shipyards around Gdansk had resumed work on the Monday but the Lenin Shipyard and the Adolf Warski Shipyard in Szczecin where the agreements of August 1980 had been signed would not be opening again until after the new year.

'State of shock'
That, to all intents and purposes, marked the end of the story in terms of dramatic action. Quite naturally the official version of events had, from the start, been in conflict with the reports published by the Western news media. Both versions were in doubt. But even if the official Polish sources were considered the worst possible, the fact remained that they had provided a picture of widespread resistance. If we remember how at one time the official media were saying that all was well in this or that area, only to admit later that things were bad – the sit-ins at the Ziemowit and Piast collieries, for instance, started in the first few days of martial law – then we can legitimately speculate that the resistance may have been greater than the authorities were obliged to admit. Even what they did admit by the end of the year was bad enough. Eight dead – one of them in the Gdansk riots as it was eventually announced – and some 5000 interned, plus a steadily growing number of people arrested on charges of organising strikes and industrial sabotage, these were statistics that only months earlier would have seemed unthinkable.

One remembered the warning issued by a large group of intellectuals back in June within days of the receipt of the letter from the Soviet Communist Party Central Committee. They said then that if the policy of renewal were to be changed by a hard-line takeover the Polish Party would be split. They also said that if force were to be used, internal or external force, then the Party would break up and the chances of Poland having anything more to do with Communism would be lost for ever. Poland, they said, would become in effect an occupied country with underground resistance. It is a significant fact, perhaps, that out of the sixty-nine intellectuals who met General Jaruzelski two days before Christmas only a few names were recognisable as those of the signatories of the intellectual statements of the summer and autumn.

As for the predictions of underground resistance, Warsaw

Radio and the official press had themselves revealed the possibility of it by reporting attacks on soldiers and police, the existence of 'hide-outs' for so-called Solidarity extremists and the discovery of arms caches in a variety of places, including the shipyards in Szczecin. Towards the end of 1981, however, the word from Solidarity leaders still at large seemed definitely to be on the side of passive rather than violent resistance. And Warsaw Radio gave a strong hint of that before Christmas when it reported the conclusions of a gathering of industrial directors. 'The atmosphere among factory workers is not good everywhere. It is characterised by suspicion and taking one's time. People who were previously full of talk now work in silence. One can observe a state of shock after what happened in Silesia.'

The conclusion of the directors was that success in the future depended among other things on an improvement in supplies and the consistent introduction of economic reform. General Jaruzelski, as he said he would, did try to press ahead with economic reform. It was a makeshift affair because it had not been completely agreed with Solidarity. But the official view was that when independent trade unions started functioning again, divested of their extremist, political elements, all the rough edges could be smoothed out. If this seemed a forlorn hope, the economic problems themselves were daunting. The General knew, and statistics were soon to reveal, that in 1981 Poland's national income had dropped by nearly fifteen per cent, with exports down by fourteen per cent and imports by seven per cent. Industry had produced less than in 1980.

But the military regime, which had a distinctly puritanical air to it, seemed determined not to flinch from subjecting industry and the nation to the shock of what it saw as a necessary cold shower. Industry was told that from 1 January 1982 it would have to pay far more for basic raw materials and fuels. The prices would be roughly those obtaining on the international trade market. Regulations were introduced making it necessary to pay for certain consumer goods, such as washing machines, for three years before actually obtaining them. It was announced that meat and butter rations would be cut in January for everyone except manual workers. Great publicity was given to the regime's drive against economic speculation and crime. At the end of 1981, the Government passed a decree on the universal obligation to work. It applied to men between eighteen and forty-five and seems to have been directed in particular against those 'whose sources of livelihood cannot be documented'.

General Jaruzelski's strong work ethic was also expressed in the dismissal in the first three weeks of martial law of some ninety senior administrators. In keeping with the General's promise to 'cleanse Polish life of evil irrespective of its source', it was announced that the Military Council would ask the Sejm to set up a Tribunal of State to examine the cases of people considered responsible for leading the country into crisis in the seventies. This was yet another move designed to show that the military Government meant what it said about there being no return to the corrupt practices of the Gierek regime.

All this left one with the impression that General Jaruzelski did indeed want the Army – the soldiers with clean hands – to step in and sort out a chaotic situation with military efficiency and discipline, dismissing the incompetent, scourging the corrupt and neutralising the 'political adventurists'. But he took a great risk in imposing martial law, for he could not be sure how it would ever end.

That, we had been told, could only happen when order was restored and the administration was functioning normally. But that was more easily said than done. For the country to function normally the workers had to work; to win their cooperation it seemed obvious that some accommodation would have to be reached with Solidarity, an organisation claiming some ten million members who, with their families, represented the greater part of the Polish population. General Jaruzelski's aim was to separate Solidarity from its extremists and then let it carry on a simple trade union function. To persuade the population that this could happen, a small number of Solidarity men appeared before the microphones of radio and television to recant and voice support for what the Military Council was doing. Their statements may well have been honest and sincere, although one man was to claim later that his recantation had been extracted under duress, but the authorities needed more of them if the great conversion of Solidarity was to take place. And there could be no hope of that unless and until Lech Walesa, the hero of the Lenin Shipyard, decided to back the General and say so in public. And even if that happened there would be other Solidarity leaders who would not agree. As the year ended, Lech Walesa was still in the Government's hands, in Warsaw, enjoying the comforts of radio and television according to an official spokesman, but refusing still to say anything in support of the military authorities. It seemed unlikely that he could ever change his mind after the deaths of the miners in Silesia.

The killings at the Wujek colliery no doubt weighed heavily on General Jaruzelski's mind. Other Communist leaders before him had presided over Polish governments that had killed fellow Poles – in Poznan and on the Baltic Coast – but none had survived. He spoke about it in a broadcast to the nation on Christmas Eve.

I state with all resolution that the reports alleging tens or even hundreds of fatalities, thousands of people arrested and being held in freezing conditions, beaten up and tortured, are lies. The truth about Poland cannot be concealed in Poland. Sooner or later it will be known to the whole world . . . We did not want as much as a single drop of blood to be shed . . . Unfortunately we were not successful. We all grieve over the events at the Wujek mine. It is also my own personal tragedy.

General Jaruzelski told his listeners that night: 'I cannot wish you a merry and prosperous Christmas. This year's holiday is a modest one, but a safe one.'

Beyond martial law
Christmas brought some concessions. Mass was broadcast at midnight and the following morning, and with it came further evidence of the Church's opposition to martial law. In the first week after its imposition there were unconfirmed reports of dissatisfaction with the Church's attitude. But the Polish bishops had rapidly issued a statement which spoke of a nation 'terrorised by military force' and 'deeply wounded by the drastic curtailment of civil rights'. The nation, the bishops said, 'cannot give up the democratic renewal. It must seek the release of those interned and the restoration of the trade unions, in particular Solidarity.' Vatican Radio, which broadcast the statement, explained that it had received it from the French News Agency because its own channels were cut off. Archbishop Glemp raised some eyebrows in the Western news media when he issued a statement admitting that 'we are helpless in the face of suffering and evil'. First reports placed

the emphasis on the helplessness rather than his plain identification of evil. On Christmas night, in a message read out at Mass, the Primate offered the consolations of religion to families who, he said, had been 'harmed, disappointed, imprisoned, and slandered without reason'. Look at the manger, he said, and the Child Jesus facing the uncertainty of tomorrow. All He had was his mother, St Joseph and 'the solidarity of the shepherds and the wandering intellectuals, the wise men. This was not much, considering the absolutism of Herod. But it was enough.'

One cannot say for sure, but perhaps the Archbishop meant this to be understood as a parable. At any rate, as subsequent statements were to make clear, the Church wanted martial law to end as soon as possible and Solidarity to be given back its rights. Indeed the Archbishop's message hoped that martial law would end at Christmas. A later statement by Pope John Paul referring to the extension of martial law suggested that maybe the two Vatican envoys who had visited Warsaw just before Christmas had returned home with some expectations on that score.

But one of the biggest obstacles to the repeal of martial law concerned a body that we have hardly mentioned since the Military Council took over – the Polish Communist Party. Technically, the Party was still supposed to be exercising its constitutional role as the leading force in society. In fact, it was not. The Army was running the country, something not supposed to happen in a Communist country. The excuse for that was the alleged need to save the nation, but that amounted, in effect, to the need to save the Communist Party and Poland's place in the so-called socialist camp, the Soviet sphere of influence. Until the Communist Party was strong enough to rule without the help of tanks and troops, there seemed to be little chance of martial law ending.

Several factors seemed to make that an unlikely possibility. One was the probable attitude of the people, as forecast by the intellectuals back in June: could a Party that had so signally failed and at the cost of so many lives over a period of nearly forty years have any hope of winning public confidence after being propped up yet again by military force? For General Jaruzelski to replace the Army with the men of the Security Service, strengthened and more active as a result of the martial law exercise, would not surely be the best way of securing his declared aim of continued 'renewal'.

The big question, of course, was what the General meant by renewal and whether the Party, with a breathing space to regroup and reorganise itself, would eventually emerge still in favour of the sort of renewal we all imagined we knew, or in a distinctly tougher frame of mind. Towards the end of the year *Pravda* in Moscow reported problems inside the Polish Communist Party itself. Not all its members or organisations, it said, had withstood the test of acute political struggle. Now the Party had to strengthen its militant ranks.

Such expressions of concern will probably be interpreted differently by different people, but to this writer, at least, they did not suggest the sort of certainty or confidence one might have expected from the Kremlin if it had indeed imposed martial law on the Poles. And if there has been little mention of Moscow in this book since the beginning of November 1981 it is because it was Warsaw that was making all the running and Moscow was following. But *Pravda* was right to report trouble inside the Polish Party.

Practically nothing was said about the Party in the early days of martial law. Then it came back, very gradually, into the news. 'Experienced activists' were said to be getting together at grass-roots level. The Party was reported to be freeing itself of 'alien, vacillating and ideologically uncertain people'. Albin Siwak, the worker fundamentalist member of the Politburo, said in an interview with Prague Radio that there was still 'a sharp polarisation of attitudes within the Party'. If it was to regain confidence, he said, the Party had to 'rid itself of all who do not belong there'.

All this, coupled with reports that rank-and-file Communists were volunteering to join public order patrols, suggested a return to something like a 'class war' mentality and possibly a hard-line purge. The word purge was being used quite freely by the end of the year but there was no clear indication of a controlled purge directed from the centre. Some expulsions from the Party reported, for instance, from Koszalin concerned men who belonged to the Gierek era and had already lost their jobs.

Kazimierz Barcikowski, a centrist member of the Politburo, did not say anything in public until the last day of the year, but in an interview with *Trybuna Ludu* he made it fairly clear that any purge should be of the sort of people who were being purged under his old ally Stanislaw Kania – 'opportunists, careerists and immoral people'. Also very active still and working closely with General Jaruzelski was Mieczyslaw Rakowski, the journalist turned Deputy Prime Minister, whose broadcasts since August 1980 had played a considerable role in the process of liberalisation.

The complexities of the Polish political crisis sometimes made nonsense of facile divisions into hard-liners and liberals or moderates and radicals. The imposition of martial law no doubt necessitated some adjustment by anyone blessed with such titles, but in the absence of any clear indication of the way the Party was going it seemed fairly safe, at the end of the year, to speculate that the future could depend very much on what happened to some of the Party leaders dealt with in this book. These would include Tadeusz Fiszbach, the sanely liberal leader in Gdansk, Mieczyslaw Rakowski, Kazimierz Barcikowski in the centre, Stefan Olszowski who was flexibly further to the left, then Albin Siwak, the voice of the worker as opposed to the intellectual, and maybe also Marian Orzechowski, the professor who became a Party Secretary in October after urging the Central Committee to discard the power of argument in favour of the argument of power.

At the same time, it was worth remembering that many Party members were also members of Solidarity – as many as one million according to one Soviet estimate. And when Jerzy Urbanski, the Chairman of the Polish Party's Control Commission, was asked what would happen to members who joined in strikes in protest against martial law, he replied simply: 'They will cease to be members of the Party.' The possibility that many resigned from the Party as a result of martial law could not be discounted. The evidence of this book suggests that Party members wanted renewal as much as members of Solidarity. For many of them martial law was no doubt just as much a shock.

For anyone like that the prospects for 1982 were probably as bleak as for Solidarity men in internment or ordinary people filled with uncertainty and doubt. Official talk of the Party going back to the 'historic, patriotic traditions of the Polish Workers' Party' – which meant the 1940s – and of a 'reborn' Party guaranteeing that this crisis will be the last, may not have persuaded many people. Any hope seemed to depend on too many improbable contingencies – on Solidarity agreeing to the unthinkable, on the Party feeling strong enough to restore the 'line of dialogue', on the Soviet Union supporting further hazardous attempts at reform.

What could be said, though, was that no solution had yet been found to the fundamental problems that made up the Polish challenge. Elements now apparently defeated might still be needed. Who, for instance, had ever believed that free trade unions would have been allowed in the first place? And who could forget some of the brave and honest things said in Poland over the previous eighteen months, many of them said by Communists?

Appendix A

Text of the Gdansk Agreement

Text of protocol agreement between the Government commission and the Inter-Factory Strike Committee concluded on 31 August 1980 at the Gdansk Shipyard

Having examined the twenty-one demands submitted by the striking work forces, the Government commission and the Inter-Factory Strike Committee adopted the following decisions:

With regard to point one which says: Accept free trade unions independent from the Party and employers as provided for by ILO Convention 87, which was ratified by the Polish People's Republic and which concerns trade union freedom, it was agreed:

1. The performance of trade unions in the Polish People's Republic does nót fulfil the hopes and expectations of employees. It is considered expedient to establish new self-governing trade unions that would genuinely represent the working class. No one will have his right to remain in the present trade unions questioned and it is possible that the two trade union movements will establish co-operation in the future.

2. In view of the establishment of new, independent and self-governing trade unions, the Inter-Factory Strike Committee declares that they will observe the principles laid down in the Constitution of the Polish People's Republic. The new trade unions will defend the social and material interests of employees and do not intend to play the role of a political party. They approve of the principle that the means of production are social property – a principle that is the foundation of the socialist system in Poland. Recognising that the PZPR plays the leading role in the State and without undermining the actual system of international alliances, they seek to ensure for the working people suitable means of control, of expressing their opinions and of defending their interests.

The Government commission declares that the Government will guarantee and ensure full respect for the independence and self-government of the new trade unions both as regards their organisational structure and their performance at all levels of activity. The

296

Government will ensure for the new trade unions every opportunity to fulfil their basic functions in defending the interests of employees and implementing their material, social and cultural needs. At the same time, the Government guarantees that the new trade unions will not be subjected to any discrimination.

3. The establishment and activity of the independent, self-governing trade unions are consistent with ILO Convention 87 which concerns trade union freedoms and the defence of trade union rights, and ILO Convention 96 which concerns the right of association and the right to collective negotiations. Both Conventions have been ratified in Poland. The diversity of trade union and employees' representation will entail suitable legislative amendments; in connection with this the Government pledges itself to making legislative proposals, particularly concerning the law on trade unions, the law on workers' self-government and the labour code.

4. The established strike committees can, if they wish, transform themselves into bodies for the representation of factory employees such as workers' committees, employees' committees, workers' councils or the founding committees of the new self-governing trade unions. As the founding committee of those trade unions, the Inter-Factory Strike Committee is free to choose the form of a single union or association within the coastal region. The founding committees will function until new authorities are elected in accordance with the statutes. The Government pledges itself to create the conditions for the registration of the new trade unions outside the register of the Central Trade Union Council.

5. The new trade unions should enjoy genuine opportunities to evaluate publicly new decisions which affect the working people's working conditions: the principles for dividing the national income into consumption and accumulation; the distribution of the social consumption fund for various purposes – health, education, culture; the basic principles of remuneration and the lines of wage policy – particularly the principle of an automatic adjustment of wages under conditions of inflation; long-term economic plans, investment policy and changes in prices. The Government pledges itself to ensure conditions for the exercise of these functions.

6. The Inter-Factory Committee is establishing a centre for social and labour studies, whose task will be to analyse objectively the employees' situation, the working people's living conditions and the ways of representing employees' interests. The centre will also prepare specialist opinions on the wage and price indices and will propose forms of compensation; it will also publish the results of its research. The new trade unions will also have their own publications.

7. The Government will ensure that the provisions of Article one Paragraph one of the 1949 Trade Union Act, which stipulates that

workers and employees are guaranteed the right to voluntary association in trade unions, are observed in Poland. The new trade unions will not join the association represented by the Central Trade Union Council. It is agreed that the new law will preserve this principle. At the same time, representatives of the Inter-Factory Strike Committee or of the committees that will found the self-governing trade unions and representatives of other workers' bodies will be ensured participation in formulating this law.

With regard to point two, which says: Guarantee the right to strike and guarantee security for strikers and for persons helping them, it was decided: The right to strike will be guaranteed in the trade union law which is now in the course of preparation. The law should define the conditions under which a strike is proclaimed and organised, the methods of settling disputed issues and responsibility for violating the law. Articles 52, 64 and 65 of the Labour Code cannot be applied with regard to the participants in a strike. Also, the Government guarantees strikers and persons helping them personal security and the maintenance of their present working conditions until the law is passed.

With regard to point three, which says: Observe freedom of speech and the printed word, that is, not to repress independent publications and to make the mass media available to representatives of all religions, it was decided:

1. Within three months the Government will introduce in the Sejm a draft law on control of the press, publications and entertainment which will be based on the following principles. Censorship should protect the interests of the State. This means the protection of State and economic secrets, the extent of which will be more closely defined by legal enactments, and the protection of the State's security matters and important international interests. This also means protecting religious beliefs and, at the same time, the convictions of non-believers and preventing the dissemination of morally harmful material. This draft law would also deal with the right to appeal to the Supreme Administrative Court against the decisions of the organs responsible for control of the press, publications and entertainment. This law will be put into force by amending the Administrative Procedure Code.

2. Denominational groups will be given access to the mass media for religious purposes through agreement between State bodies and the interested religious associations on substantive and organisational problems. The Government will ensure that the radio will transmit a Sunday mass under a detailed accord with the Episcopate.

3. Radio, television, the press and publications should be used to express a plurality of ideas, views and opinions. This use should be subject to social control.

4. Like citizens and their organisations, the press should have access to public documents, especially administrative documents, socio-economic plans and so on, issued by the Government and its administrative bodies. The exceptions to the principles of the openness of the Administration's activities will be defined in the law as stipulated in point one.

With regard to point four, which says: (i) Restore the former rights of people dismissed from their jobs for the strikes in 1970 and 1976 and of students banned from higher schools for their convictions; (ii) Free all political prisoners (including Edmund Zadrozynski, Jan Kozlowski and Marek Kozlowski); and (iii) End the persecution of people for their convictions; it was decided:

(a) To examine immediately the propriety of the job dismissals after the strikes in 1970 and 1976. In all cases, if irregularities are ascertained, immediately to restore the people concerned to their jobs, provided they want to return, and to take into account the qualifications they have acquired in the meantime. A corresponding procedure will be used in the case of the students banned from higher schools.

(b) To refer the cases of the persons mentioned above to the Minister of Justice who will examine them and will within two weeks institute the necessary proceedings: in the cases in which the listed persons have been deprived of freedom, their punishment will be interrupted until proceedings have been completed;

(c) To examine whether their detention is justified and to release those mentioned in the supplement;

(d) To observe fully the individual's freedom to express his convictions in public and professional life.

With regard to point five, which states: Publish in the mass media information about the establishment of the Inter-Factory Strike Committee and publish its demands, it was decided:

This demand will be fulfilled by publishing this protocol in the national mass media.

With regard to point six, which says: Take genuine action to extricate the country from its state of crisis through (i) fully informing the public about the socio-economic situation, and (ii) enabling all social communities and sections to participate in the discussion about the reform programme, it was decided:

We deem it necessary greatly to accelerate the work on economic reform. The authorities will outline and publish the basic tenets of this reform within the next few months. It is necessary to ensure that public discussion of this reform is extensive. In particular, the trade unions should participate in formulating the laws on socialist economic organisations and on workers' self-government. The economic reform should be based on radically increased self-dependence of enterprises and on genuine participation in management by the workers' self-government groups. The necessary enactments should guarantee the fulfilment by the trade unions of the functions defined in point one of this agreement.

Only a nation that is aware of its problems and that has a sound perception of reality can sponsor and implement a programme for streamlining the economy. The Government will radically expand the range of socio-economic information available to the nation, the trade unions and economic and social organisations.

In addition, the Inter-Factory Committee demands that: lasting prospects be created for developing peasant family farms, which are the foundation of Polish agriculture; all sectors be ensured equal access to all means of production, including land; and conditions be created for the rebirth of rural self-government groups.

With regard to point seven, which says: Pay wages from Central Trade Union Council funds for the duration of the strike and for annual leave to all those who are striking, it was decided:

Employees in the striking work forces will receive for the period of the strike an advance payment of 40 per cent of their normal remuneration and, after they have resumed work, they will receive the outstanding balance of their remuneration, calculated as for a period of annual leave based on an eight-hour day. The Inter-Factory Strike Committee appeals to the work forces associated within it that – after the strike has ended and in co-operation with the managements of factories, work enterprises and other institutions – they should take action to increase productivity, economise on materials and energy and enhance conscientiousness in every job.

With regard to point eight, which says: Increase the basic wages of each employee by 2000 zloty a month in compensation for the present price rises, it was decided:

Gradual increases will be effected in the wages of all groups of employees, above all in the lowest wage groups. It was agreed in principle that wages will be increased in individual factories and in groups of branches. These increases are being implemented and will be implemented in keeping with the specific characteristics of trade, professions and branches, the aim being to raise all salaries by a single increment or to increase other elements of remuneration or of the wage group. As for office workers in enterprises, their remuneration will be raised by a single increment in their personal wages. Pay rises now under discussion will be completed by the end of September this year in accordance with branch accords.

Having analysed all branches, the Government, in co-operation with the trade unions, will by 31 October this year present a programme for increasing, as of 1 January 1981, the wages of the lowest paid, giving special consideration to families with many children.

With regard to point nine, which says: Guarantee an automatic

300

increase in wages parallel to increases in prices and deterioration in the value of money, it was decided: Increases in the prices of staple goods must be checked by increasing control over the socialised and private sectors, in particular by stopping so-called creeping price rises. In keeping with the Government's decision, research will be conducted into the development of living costs. This research will also be conducted by the trade unions and scientific institutes. By the end of 1980 the Government will work out the principles of compensation for increases in the cost of living. These principles will be subjected to a public discussion and, when agreed upon, will be implemented. They should take into account the issue of the social minimum [minimum subsistence level].

With regard to point ten, which says: Ensure adequate supplies of food for the domestic market and only export surpluses; and to point eleven, which states: Abolish commercial prices and sales for hard currencies under the scheme of so-called internal export; and to point thirteen, which states: Introduce the rationing of all meat – food coupons – (until the market situation is mastered), it was decided:

Meat supplies to the public will be improved by 31 December this year by various measures, including: increased profitability of farm production, restricting meat exports to the necessary minimum, and additional meat imports. Within the same period a programme will be presented for improving meat supplies to the public and for eventual meat rationing through coupons.

It was agreed that the Pewex shops [selling for hard currencies] will not sell those staple consumer goods produced in Poland that are in short supply. The nation will be informed by the end of the year about the decisions and measures concerning supplies to the market. The Inter-Factory Strike Committee has asked for the ending of commercial shops and for the streamlining and standardisation of meat prices at an average level.

With regard to point twelve which says: Introduce the principle by which leading and managing cadres are selected by virtue of their qualifications not their Party affiliations, and abolish the privileges of the citizens' militia, the security service and the Party apparatus by equalising family allowances, ending special sales and so on, it was decided: The demand is accepted that leading and managing cadres should be consistently selected according to qualification and ability, both among members of the Party and non-Party people. The programme for equalising family allowances for all trade groups will be presented by the Government by 31 December 1980. The Government commission states that, as in other work establishments and offices, there are only staff restaurants and canteens.

With regard to point fourteen which says: Lower the retirement age of women to fifty and of men to fifty-five, or thirty years worked in the Polish People's Republic by women and thirty-five years by men regardless of their ages, it was decided: The Government commission regards this demand as impossible to fulfil now in view of the country's present economic and demographic situation. The issue can be discussed in the future. The Inter-Factory Strike Committee has asked that this issue be examined by 31 December 1980, and that consideration should be given to allowing employees doing strenuous jobs to retire five years earlier, after thirty years for women and thirty-five for men, and in the case of particularly strenuous jobs [to advance retirement] by at least fifteen years. This should take place only at the request of the employee.

With regard to point fifteen which says: Equalise the pensions and annuities of the so-called old scheme so that they are equivalent to the pensions and annuities of the present scheme, the Government commission declares that the lowest pensions and annuities will be increased annually, consistent with the country's economic potential, and will take into account increases in the lowest wages. The Government will present an implementation programme by 31 December 1980. The Government will propose that the lowest pensions and annuities be raised to the level of the so-called social minimum determined by research carried out by the appropriate institutes, presented to the public and controlled by the trade unions. The Inter-Factory Strike Committee stresses the extreme urgency of this issue and maintains its demand that the pensions and annuities of the old and new schemes should be at the same level and that increases in the costs of living should be taken into account.

With regard to point sixteen which says: Improve the working conditions of the health services so as to ensure complete medical care for working people, it was decided: It is considered necessary to increase immediately the investment capacities of the health services, to improve the supply of medicines through additional imports of raw materials; to increase the wages of all health service workers (to change the wage structure for nurses) and to draw up urgently Government and departmental programmes for improving the state of the nation's health. Other measures in this field are listed in the supplement to point sixteen:

1. To implement the Charter of Health Service Employees' Rights.
2. To ensure suitable quantities of cotton protective clothing for sale.
3. To pay from the material costs fund an amount equal to the cost of work clothing.
4. To secure such a wage fund as to make it possible to award the necessary extra payments to all people who distinguish themselves in their work – to award them in keeping with theoretically valid considerations.

5. To set increasing additional payments for completion of twenty-five and thirty years work.

6. To set additional payment for work under conditions that are a strain or harmful to health, and to introduce additional payment for shift work for non-medical employees.

7. To re-introduce additional payment for working with patients with infectious ailments and for handling infectious biological materials, and to raise the wages for overnight nursing.

8. To recognise spinal ailments as an occupational disease of dental surgeons.

9. To ensure supplies of good quality fuels for hospitals and creches.

10. To equalise service benefits for nurses without full secondary education with benefits for nurses with diplomas.

11. To introduce a seven-hour working day for all specialist employees.

12. To introduce free Saturdays without the need to work them off later.

13. To pay double rates for Sunday and holiday work.

14. To provide free medicines for Health Service employees.

15. To make possible a partial repayment of housing loans from social funds.

16. To increase the size of apartments for Health Service workers.

17. To enable single nurses to obtain apartments.

18. To convert the bonus fund into a thirteen-month wage.

19. To grant six weeks leave to Health Service workers after twenty years of service, and to make it possible for them to obtain paid annual leave to improve their health, as is the case for teachers.

20. To ensure paid leave of four weeks for those studying for a doctor's degree and of two weeks for those specialising.

21. To ensure the right to a day off after a spell of duty as a physician.

22. A five-hour working day for employees in creches and kindergartens, and free food.

23. Cars for employees of the basic health services and kilometre allowances or lump payments for official trips.

24. Nurses with higher education should be treated and paid as are other personnel with higher education.

25. To set up specialised repair teams in the factory trade union organisation (ZOZ) in order to protect Health Service installations against further depreciation.

26. To raise the standard allowance for medicine for hospital patients, from 1138 zloty to 2700 zloty, since this is what treatment actually costs; to raise the food allowance.

27. To issue food coupons for the bedridden.

28. To double available medical transportation because this is a pressing need.

29. To ensure the cleanliness of air, soil and water, especially of the

coastal waters.

30. Parallel with the completion of new housing settlements, to complete facilities such as out-patient clinics, chemists and creches.

With regard to point seventeen which says: Ensure the necessary vacancies in creches and kindergartens for working women's children, it was decided: The Government commission fully agrees with the importance of this demand. The provincial authorities will present the necessary programme by 30 November 1980.

With regard to point eighteen which says: Grant maternity leave for three years in order to raise a baby, it was decided: By 31 December 1980 an analysis will be made – in cooperation with the trade unions – of the national economy's potential and the length of maternity leave and the amount of monthly payment will be determined for women (now unpaid) to take care of their babies. The Inter-Factory Strike Committee demands that such an analysis should consider a payment equivalent to the full wages in the first year after the baby is born and that 50 per cent of these wages be paid in the second year, but that these should amount to not less than 2000 zloty a month. This demand should be met gradually, beginning with the first six months of 1981.

With regard to point nineteen which says: Cut the period of waiting for apartments, it was decided: By 31 December 1980 the provincial authorities will present a programme for improving the housing situation in order to cut the waiting time for apartments. This programme will be extensively discussed by the people of the province who will consult with the appropriate organizations: the Association of Polish Town Planners – TUP; the Association of the Architects of the Polish Republic – SARP; the chief technical organisation – NOT; etc. The programme should also consider the present utilisation of the existing plants manufacturing housing components and the further development of the construction trades' production base. The same measures will be taken nationwide.

With regard to point twenty which says: Increase daily travelling allowances from 40 zloty to 100 zloty and increase the family separation allowance, it was decided: As of 1 January 1981 travel allowances and the separation allowance will be increased. Proposals regarding these will be presented by the Government by 31 October 1980.

With regard to point twenty-one which says: Make all Saturdays work-free, and compensate employees working round the clock or on a four-shift pattern with increased annual leave or by other paid days off, it was decided: We will work out and present by 31 December 1980 principles and methods of implementing the programme for paid work-free Saturdays as well as other methods of regulating a shorter working period. This programme will provide for a larger number of paid work-free Saturdays by as early as 1981. Other measures in this regard are contained in the supplement listing the demands of the Inter-Factory Strike Committee.

Having made the aforementioned decisions, the following agreement was reached: The Government pledges itself: to ensure personal security and honour the present working conditions of the participants in the present strike and of the persons helping them; to examine at ministerial level the specific problems of the branches as submitted by the workforces of all the striking factories that are associated with the Inter-Factory Strike Committee; to publicise immediately the full text of the protocol of this agreement in the national mass media – the press, radio and television.

The Inter-Factory Strike Committee pledges itself to end the strike at 1700 hours on 31 August 1980.

[Signed] The Presidium of the Inter-Factory Strike Committee: Chairman Lech Walesa; Vice Chairman Andrzej Koloziej, Vice Chairman Bogdan Lis; members: Lech Badkowski, Wojciech Gruszewski, Andrzej Gwiazda, Stefan Izbedski, Jerzy Kwiecik, Zdzislaw Kovylinski, Henryka Kizywonos, Stefan Lewandowski, Alina Pienkowska, Jozef Przybylski, Jerzy Sikorski, Lech Lobieszek, Tadeusz Stanny, Anna Walentynowicz, and Florian Wisniewski.

The Government commission: Chairman Mieczyslaw Jagielski, Vice Chairman of the Council of Ministers of the Polish People's Republic; members: Zbigniew Zielinski, member of the PZPR Central Committee Secretariat; Tadeusz Fiszbach, Chairman of the Provincial People's Council in Gdansk; Jerzy Kolodziejski, Provincial Governor of Gdansk.

Supplement to point twenty-one:

1. To change the decree issued by the Council of Ministers on the methods of calculating payments for annual leave and sickness benefits for workers working the four-shift system; the present method is to use an average of thirty days (whereas the workers work twenty-two days). This method of calculation reduces the average working day when workers are on short sick leaves and lowers the equivalent for the annual leave.

2. We demand that a single legal enactment – by the Council of Ministers – should streamline the method by which payments are calculated in individual cases for a given period of absence from work. The vagueness of the present regulations is used against the employees.

3. Workers working the four-shift work system should be compensated by an additional leave allowance for their work on Saturdays. The fact that these workers are given more days off than others on different work systems does not mean that they can enjoy real days off. Their present days off are just an opportunity to take a rest after very strenuous work. The arguments submitted by the

administration, maintaining that real days off should be granted only after the amount of hours worked under the two work systems is the same, are not correct.

4. We want all Saturdays work-free every month as is the case in other socialist countries.

5. We want Article 147 of the Labour Code to be abolished. This Article allows for extending the average work norm by nine hours a week when additional days off are due. We also want Article 148 to be abolished; our work norms are among the longest in Europe.

6. To increase the importance of the contracted decisions concerning payments by making changes in the Labour Code, namely: that not only a change in a worker's own wage group or in other elements of his remuneration, but also changes in the methods of payments (from daily wage to piece work) must be notified by the employer. It is also necessary to introduce the principle that all jobs done by a worker on a piece work basis should be paid for in accordance with his actual wage group. At the same time, it is necessary to sort out the issue of employing young workers in keeping with their qualifications so the aforementioned decision does not become an obstacle to professional advancement.

7. To introduce in the shift system an increase of 50 per cent in the allowance for night work in the day system and to increase by 30 per cent the actual earnings under the piece work system. We also want an allowance for work during the afternoon shift (as is the case in the chemical industry). We want the Government to examine these demands by 30 November 1980.

Appendix B
Martial Law

Broadcast by General Wojciech Jaruzelski, 13 December 1981
Citizens of the Polish People's Republic! I turn to you today as a soldier and as Head of the Polish Government. I turn to you on matters of supreme importance. Our country has found itself on the brink of an abyss. The achievements of many generations, the house erected from Polish ashes, are being destroyed. The structures of the State are ceasing to function. New blows are being struck every day at the dying economy. Living conditions are placing an increasingly harsh burden on people. Lines of painful division are running through every work enterprise and many Polish homes.

The atmosphere of endless conflict, misunderstanding and hatred is sowing psychological devastation and harming the traditions of tolerance. Strikes, strike alerts, protest actions have become the norm. Even school-children are dragged in. Yesterday evening many public buildings were occupied. Exhortations to a physical settling of accounts with the 'Reds', with people who hold different views, are being made. Acts of terrorism, threats and moral mob trials and also of direct coercion abound. A wide-ranging wave of impudent crimes, assaults and break-ins is sweeping over the country. The fortunes, amounting to millions, of underground economic sharks are growing.

Chaos and demoralisation have assumed disaster proportions. The nation has come to the end of its psychological endurance. Many people are beginning to despair. Now it is not days but hours that separate us from national catastrophe.

Honesty compels one to ask: Did things have to come to this? On assuming the office of Chairman of the Council of Ministers, I believed that we could raise ourselves up. We have accordingly done everything to stop the spiral of the crisis. History will assess our activities. There were slips; we are drawing conclusions from them. Above all, however, the past months were a busy time for the Government, a time of wrestling with enormous difficulties.

Unfortunately, however, the national economy has been turned into a platform for political struggle. Deliberate torpedoeing of Government activities has meant that the results are not commensurate with the effort put in, with our strivings. It cannot be said we lack good will, moderation and patience. Sometimes, perhaps, we even showed too much of these. One cannot fail to notice the respect displayed by the Government for social agreements.

We went even further. The initiative of the great national accord won the support of millions of Poles. It created a chance to deepen the system of democracy and broaden the range of reforms. These hopes have now been dashed. The Solidarity leadership was absent from the common table. The words uttered in Radom, the session in Gdansk, have fully revealed the true intentions of its leading circles. These intentions are confirmed on a mass scale by everyday practice, by the growing aggressiveness of extremists, by an open striving for complete partition of the socialist Polish statehood.

How long can one wait for a sobering up? How long can a hand stretched out towards accord meet with a closed fist? I am saying this with a heavy heart, with immense bitterness. Things could have been different in our country; they should be different. Further continuation of the current situation would inevitably have led to catastrophe, to complete chaos, to poverty and famine. A severe winter could have multiplied our losses and engulfed numerous victims – especially among the weakest, whom we most want to protect.

In this situation failure to act would be a crime against the nation. It is necessary to say 'enough', to prevent, to block the path to confrontation which the Solidarity leaders have openly announced. We must announce it this very day, when an early date has been set for mass political demonstrations, to include the centre of Warsaw, which have been called in connection with the anniversary of the December events. That tragedy must not recur. We cannot, must not, allow the announced demonstrations to become a spark from which the whole country may flare up. The nation's instinct for self-preservation must be heard; the adventurists must have their hands tied before they push the homeland into the abyss of fratricide.

Citizens! Great is the burden of responsibility which falls on me at this dramatic moment in Polish history. It is my duty to assume this responsibility. Poland's future is at stake; the future which my generation fought for on all fronts of the war, and for which it gave the best years of its life.

I announce that a Military Council for National Salvation was formed today. The Council of State, in accordance with the provisions of the Constitution, introduced martial law throughout the country at midnight today. I want everyone to understand the motives and the aim behind our action. We are not striving for a military coup, for a military dictatorship. The nation has sufficient strength, sufficient wisdom in itself to develop an efficient democratic system of socialist rule. In such a system, the armed forces will be able to remain where they belong – in the barracks. No Polish problem can in the long run be solved through force. The Military Council for National Salvation is not replacing the constitutional organs of power. Its sole task is to protect the legal order in the State, to create executive guarantees which will make it possible to restore order and discipline. This is the last possible way to start extricating the country from the crisis, to save the country from disintegration.

The Committee for National Defence has appointed plenipotentiary military commissars at all levels of the State administration and in some economic units. The plenipotentiary commissars have been granted the right to supervise the activity of the State administration, from ministries down to parishes. The proclamation of the Military Council for National Salvation and the decrees published today define in detail the norms of public order for the duration of martial law. The Military Council will be dissolved when the rule of law reigns supreme in the country again, when conditions appear for the normal functioning of the civil administration and the representative bodies. With the stabilisation of the internal situation, restrictions of freedoms in public life will be eased or lifted.

Let no one, however, count on weakness or vacillation. In the name of the national interest, a group of people presenting a threat to the safety of the State have been interned. This group contains extremist Solidarity activists and activists of illegal anti-State organisations. On the instructions of the Military Council, several dozen people who are personally responsible for bringing about the profound crisis of the State in the 'seventies and for abusing their posts for personal gain have also been interned. These people include, among others, Edward Gierek, Piotr Jaroszewicz, Zdzislaw Grudzien, Jerzy Lukaszewicz, Jan Szydlak, Tadeusz Wrzassczyk and others. A full list will be published. We shall consistently purge Polish life of evil, irrespective of its source.

The Military Council will ensure conditions for a ruthless stepping up of the struggle against crime. The activists of criminal gangs will be summarily dealt with by the courts. Persons who engage in large-scale speculation, benefiting from illegal profits and violating the norms of social coexistence, will be pursued and brought to book with all severity. Fortunes amassed illegally will be confiscated. Persons occupying leading posts who are guilty of negligence, waste and pursuing their own narrow interests, abuse of power and callousness towards the public will, at the suggestion of the plenipotentiary military commissars, be relieved of their posts after disciplinary procedures have been followed.

We must restore respect for human work, ensure respect for law and order. We must guarantee the personal safety of everyone who wants to live and work in peace. The provisions of the special decree provide for forgiveness and leniency for certain crimes and offences against the interests of the State committed prior to 13 December this year. We are not looking for revenge. Those people who, without ill intention, allowed themselves to be carried away by emotion and yielded to false incitement can avail themselves of this opportunity.

Citizens! The Polish soldier has faithfully served and serves the homeland. He has always been in the forefront, always there when society needed him. Today too he will discharge his duty with honour. Our soldiers have clean hands. Private interests are alien to them, hard service is not. They have no goal other than the good of the nation. Our resorting to the help of the Army can be and is only a temporary measure, an extraordinary one. The Army will not act outside the normal mechanisms of socialist democracy. Democracy, however, can be practised and developed only in a strong State ruled by law. Anarchy is a negation, an enemy of democracy.

We are but a drop in the stream of Polish history. It is composed not only of proud pages, it also contains dark pages, the liberum veto, the pursuit of private interests, quarrels. As a result we had decline, fall and disaster. This vicious circle must at some stage be broken. We cannot afford to let history repeat itself. We want a great Poland: great by its achievements, its culture, its forms of social life, its position in Europe. Socialism – accepted by society and constantly enriched by practical experience – is the only path. This is the Poland that we will build, this is the Poland we will defend.

Party people have a special role to play in this cause. Despite the mistakes that have been made, despite bitter reverses, the Party, as far as the process of historical change is concerned, continues to be an active and creative force. In efficiently discharging its leading role, in cooperating fruitfully with allied forces, it must rely on people who are honest, modest and courageous, on people who in any milieu will deserve the name of fighters for social justice, for the good of the country. It is this above all that will decide the Party's authority in society, this is its prospect.

We shall cleanse the ever living sources of our idea from deformations and distortions; we shall protect the universal values of socialism, enriching them all the time with national elements and traditions. On this path, socialist ideals will become closer to the majority of the nation, to working people who are not Party members, to the younger generation and also to the healthy trend in Solidarity – especially the working-class trend which, with its own forces and in its own interests, will reject the prophets of confrontation and counter-revolution.

This is how we view the idea of national accord. We support it.

310

We respect multiplicity of world-views. We recognise the Church's patriotic attitude. There is a higher goal which unites all thinking and responsible Poles: love for the homeland, the need to strengthen our independence which we fought for and gained with such difficulties, respect for our own State. This is the strongest basis for genuine accord.

Citizens! Just as there is no turning back from socialism, so there is no going back to the erroneous methods and practices prior to August 1980. Steps taken today serve to safeguard the fundamental premises of the socialist renewal. All important reforms will be continued in conditions of order, businesslike discussion and discipline. This also applies to economic reform.

I do not wish to make promises. We are facing a difficult period. In order that tomorrow may be better, we must recognise the hard realities of today, we must understand the need to make sacrifices. I would like to attain one thing: calm. This is the fundamental condition from which a better future should begin. We are a sovereign country. From this crisis we must, therefore, emerge on our own. It is with our own hands that we must remove the threat. If this chance were to be wasted, history would not forgive the present generation.

We must put an end to the further degradation of our State's international position. A country of 36 million inhabitants, situated in the heart of Europe, cannot remain indefinitely in the humiliating role of petitioner. We cannot fail to notice that today derisory opinions about our Republic, supposedly ruled by anarchy, are springing to life again. Everything possible must be done to ensure that such opinions are thrown into the rubbish heap of history.

At this difficult moment I address myself to our socialist allies and friends. We greatly value their trust and constant aid. The Polish–Soviet alliance is, and will remain, the cornerstone of the Polish raison d'état, the guarantee of the inviolability of our frontiers. Poland is, and will remain, a lasting link in the Warsaw Pact, an unfailing member of the socialist community of nations.

I address myself also to our partners in other countries with which we wish to develop good, friendly relations. I address myself to the whole of world public opinion: we appeal for understanding of the extraordinary conditions which have arisen in Poland, of the extraordinary measures which have turned out to be essential. Our measures do not threaten anyone. They have but one goal: to remove the internal threats, thereby preventing the threat to peace and international co-operation. We intend to observe the treaties and agreements to which we are a party. We wish the word 'Poland' always to give rise to respect and sympathy in the world.

Poles! Brothers and sisters! I appeal to you as a soldier who remembers well the horrors of the war. Let not another single drop of Polish blood be spilled in this tormented country which has already experienced so many reverses and sufferings. Let us jointly put paid to the spectre of civil war. Let us not erect barricades where bridges are needed.

I appeal to you, Polish workers! For the sake of the homeland, abandon your inalienable right to strike for as long as may prove necessary to overcome the gravest difficulties. We must do all we can so that the fruits of your hard work are not wasted.

I appeal to you, brother peasants! Do not allow your fellow countrymen to go hungry. Show concern for the Polish land, so that it may feed us all.

I appeal to you, citizens of older generations! Rescue from oblivion the truth about the war years, about the difficult time of reconstruction. Hand it down to your sons and grandsons. Hand down to them your ardent patriotism, your readiness to make sacrifices for the good of your native country.

I appeal to you, Polish mothers, wives and sisters! Spare no effort to see that no more tears are shed in Polish families.

I appeal to young Poles! Show civic maturity, deep reflection on your own future, the future of the homeland.

I appeal to you, teachers, creators of science and culture, engineers, doctors, publicists! Let reason take the upper hand over inflamed emotions at this dangerous point in our history. Let the intellectual function of patriotism win over illusory myths.

I appeal to you, my comrades-in-arms, soldiers of the Polish Army on active service and in reserve! Be faithful to the oath you made to the homeland for better or for worse. It is on your attitude today that the fate of the country depends. ,

I appeal to you, functionaries of the civil Militia and Security Service! Protect the State against the enemy, protect working people against lawlessness and violence.

I appeal to all citizens! An hour of hard trial has come. We must prove equal to this trial. We must prove we are worthy of Poland. Fellow countrymen! For the entire Polish nation and all the world to hear, I wish to repeat these immortal words [first words of national anthem]: Poland has not perished so long as we are alive!

Proclamation by Military Council for National Salvation, 13 December 1981

Men and women of Poland! Citizens of the Polish People's Republic! The Military Council for National Salvation is appealing to you.

Our homeland is threatened by deadly danger. The anti-State, subversive action of forces hostile to socialism has pushed the community to the brink of civil war. Anarchy, arbitrariness and chaos are ruining the economy, rendering the country powerless and endangering the sovereignty and organic existence of the nation.

The already overt preparations for a reactionary coup, the threat of terror, may lead to bloodshed. The efforts of the Sejm of the Polish People's Republic, the Government and the organs of State administration have proved ineffective. Appeals for patriotic prudence and all well-intentioned acts are disregarded. The aggressive actions of the anti-socialist forces, often inspired and supported materially from abroad, strike at the constitutional principles of the political order, and are torpedoeing the national accord. These forces, in the name of the NSZZ Solidarity, are deliberately boycotting initiatives which could help to lead Poland out of the crisis.

It is time to abandon the road to disaster, to avert national ruin. The time has come to take firm measures which are of the utmost necessity. As of now, the carrying out and respecting of the decisions of the legal authorities and State organs must be ensured. Discipline, harmony and order must prevail.

Moved by the supreme national interest and the seriousness of the historical moment, the Council of State, on the authority of Article 33 of the Second Paragraph of the Constitution of the Polish People's Republic, introduced on 13 December 1981, has declared martial law throughout the entire country.

The restrictions which martial law entails are essential for a transitional period. Everyone who wants to prevent the disintegration of the State and enable the reform of the means of exercising authority and of the economic system to continue, everyone who desires socialist renewal, will understand this.

Fellow countrymen! On the night of 12/13 December this year, a Military Council for National Salvation was formed. Army General Wojciech Jaruzelski has assumed the chairmanship of it. Having behind it the armed forces of the Polish People's Republic and counting on the confidence and support of all patriotic and progressive social forces, the Military Council for National Salvation is resolved to ensure the internal calm and safety of the country. The Council is a temporary body which will operate until the situation is normalised. It is composed of higher-ranking officers of the Polish Army. It does not violate the existing areas of jurisdiction and does not replace any segment of the people's authority.

The Council's task will be to foil a coup d'état, to stabilise the situation, to ensure and carry out within the framework of the law the efficient functioning of the administrative and economic units.

The Council declares the maintenance of our political and defence alliances, and the fulfilment of international agreements and obligations which have been concluded and accepted by the Government of the Polish People's Republic.

The Council supports the creation of conditions for the development of socialist democracy. It will assist in making economic reform

313

a reality according to the main assumptions which have been adopted so far.

The Council, bearing in mind the rights and interests of the working people, will combat with all severity and through the appropriate bodies speculation, wastefulness and profiteering by individuals at the expense of the community. It will combat misdemeanours, the breaching of public peace and order and the deliberate shirking of work.

Citizens, the Military Council for National Salvation is acting through departmental, provincial, municipal and parish plenipotentiary commissars of the National Defence Committee, appointed on the basis of Paragraph 15 of the law of 21 November 1967 on the general duty of defending the Polish People's Republic.

The Military Council for National Salvation calls on all representative bodies of the State administration to understand that the extraordinary situation renders their normal functioning impossible. The Council will do its utmost to ensure that the conditions for them to resume normal work are created as soon as possible.

It calls on legal, political and social organisations for serious work to help stabilise life in Poland. It is the duty of the leadership of these organisations to ensure that their cells and members carry out their duty in accordance with their statutes and official work schedules. It calls on the bodies of the State administration to implement promptly and consistently tasks and undertakings resulting from the introduction of the state of martial law. At the same time, the Council warns those guilty of failing to perform their duties of the possible consequences, and reminds them of the principle of individual responsibility.

At present the most important issue for all of us is to ensure the population is supplied with basic foodstuffs, medicaments and other medical supplies, and to alleviate the results of wintry conditions.

The state of martial law involves the need to suspend the activity of trade unions. The Council expresses its conviction that they will soon be able to resume their statutory activity in the interests of the working people.

Fellow countrymen! The Military Council for National Salvation wishes and intends to remove the threat of the State collapsing and losing its sovereignty, to speed up the emergence from the crisis, to ease difficulties which weigh on all citizens. What Poland needs above all is strenuous, fruitful work, a grand, universal civic deed. Calm is essential. This is not a time for quarrels and disputes.

Society and the State can no longer tolerate the work of subversives, instigators and adventurers. They must be isolated till sense returns. The people responsible for leading the country into the state in which it found itself in August 1980 and for embezzling social resources must be punished. Until such time as the appropri-

314

ate organs have carried out this action they should not be at liberty. In this crucial situation various other punishable deeds committed but not yet brought to court can and should be unconditionally forgiven and forgotten, on the strength of the Abolition Decree passed by the State Council.

Persons guilty of action against the interests of the socialist State and the working people will from now on be punished with all severity, using all means and powers arising from the martial law.

An historic moment has arrived for the Polish people and the last chance for them to put their house in order through their own forces. This chance must not be wasted.

The Military Council for National Salvation.

Announcement by the Head of the Radio and TV Committee, 13 December 1981

In connection with the exacerbation of the political situation caused by the forces hostile to the socialist state, aimed at taking over the Radio and TV, conditions have arisen which make it impossible to carry out normal work and which endanger the safety of the employees of the Polish Radio and TV. In order to ensure the correct and essential functioning of the Radio and TV, on the basis of paragraph one of resolution number 185/81 of the Council of Ministers of 28 August 1981, I order the following:

(1) Production and broadcast of one, central, 24-hours radio programme and one central TV programme.

(2) Cessation of other radio programmes and the Second TV Programme.

(3) Switching off of the regional broadcasting stations and regional TV centres and limiting the activity of the TV centre and the Central Radio Station in Warsaw to the minimum which is essential in the current situation.

(4) The undertaking of programme, technical and organisational work by an assigned team of employees of the Committee. The persons assigned to this work will report to their agreed places immediately.

(5) Other employees are given special leave until further notice.

(6) The order is valid as from the date of signing.

Appendix C

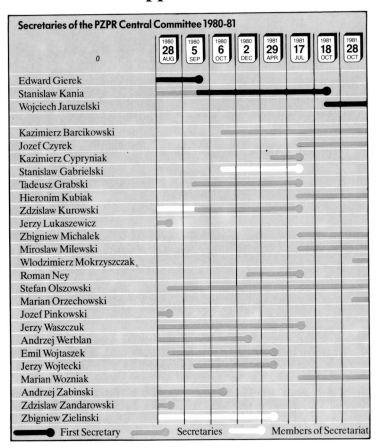

Secretaries of the PZPR Central Committee 1980-81	1980 28 AUG	1980 5 SEP	1980 6 OCT	1980 2 DEC	1981 29 APR	1981 17 JUL	1981 18 OCT	1981 28 OCT
Edward Gierek								
Stanislaw Kania								
Wojciech Jaruzelski								
Kazimierz Barcikowski								
Jozef Czyrek								
Kazimierz Cypryniak								
Stanislaw Gabrielski								
Tadeusz Grabski								
Hieronim Kubiak								
Zdzislaw Kurowski								
Jerzy Lukaszewicz								
Zbigniew Michalek								
Miroslaw Milewski								
Wlodzimierz Mokrzyszczak								
Roman Ney								
Stefan Olszowski								
Marian Orzechowski								
Jozef Pinkowski								
Jerzy Waszczuk								
Andrzej Werblan								
Emil Wojtaszek								
Jerzy Wojtecki								
Marian Wozniak								
Andrzej Zabinski								
Zdzislaw Zandarowski								
Zbigniew Zielinski								

First Secretary   Secretaries   Members of Secretariat

Turnover in Party leadership

Poland's ruling Politburo, normally consisting of fewer than twenty full and candidate members, used up forty-four people between February 1980 and October 1981. Twenty-seven lost their places – among them two Party leaders, Edward Gierek and Stanislaw Kania. By the end of 1981 only two remained of those elected at the Party Congress in February 1980 – General Wojciech Jaruzelski and Kazimierz Barcikowski. Along with Stefan Olszowski, sacked in February 1980 but reinstated the following August, they are the only survivors from the Politburo of the seventies.

Politburo of the Polish United Workers' Party 1980-81

	1980 15 FEB	1980 24 AUG	1980 6 SEP	1980 6 OCT	1980 2 DEC	1981 30 APR	1981 19 JUL	1981 18 OCT	1981 28 OCT
Edward Babiuch									
Kazimierz Barcikowski									
Tadeusz Czechowicz									
Jozef Czyrek									
Tadeusz Fiszbach									
Gerard Gabrys									
Edward Gierek									
Jan Glowczyk									
Tadeusz Grabski									
Zdzislaw Grudzien									
Zofia Grzyb									
Henryk Jablonski									
Mieczyslaw Jagielski									
Gen. Wojciech Jaruzelski									
Stanislaw Kania									
Alojzy Karkoszka									
Wladyslaw Kruczek									
Wladyslaw Kruk									
Stanislaw Kowalczyk									
Hieronim Kubiak									
Jan Labecki									
Jerzy Lukaszewicz									
Jozef Masny									
Zbigniew Messner									
Miroslaw Milewski									
Mieczyslaw Moczar									
Wlodzimierz Mokrzyszczak									
Roman Ney									
Stefan Olszowski									
Stanislaw Opalko									
Jozef Pinkowski									
Tadeusz Porebski									
Tadeusz Pyka									
Jerzy Romanik									
Albin Siwak									
Gen. Florian Siwicki									
Jan Szydlak									
Jerzy Waszczuk									
Andrzej Werblan									
Emil Wojtaszek									
Tadeusz Wrzaszczyk									
Zygmunt Wronski									
Andrzej Zabinski									
Zdzislaw Zandarowski									

Full members   Candidate members

Index

Italic figures refer to illustrations

138; denies split in Solidarity 147; elected chairman of Warsaw Solidarity region 199; attacked by East German radio 242; contradicted by Olszowski 268; speaks at Solidarity meeting in Radom 271; favours political struggle 273; escapes internment 283; *10*

Bulgaria 97

bus drivers 9

butter supplies 130–1

Bydgoszcz 43, 137–40, 176–8, 207

'Bydgoszcz incident' 137, 140–2, 144–7, 163, 227; *9*

Carrington, Lord 76

Carter, President 96

Casaroli, Cardinal 168

Catholic and Social Circle (Znak) 70

Catholicism 80–1; *see also* Roman Catholic Church

Ceausescu, Nicolae 70

Celinski, Andrzej 147, 231

censorship 16, 32, 35–6, 79, 116–17, 298

Central Committee of Polish Communist Party 19–20, 27, 30, 56, 143–4, 212–13; *see also* Communist Party, Polish

Central Statistical Bureau 33

Central Trade Union Council (CRZZ) 20–1, 47

Chelm 5, 7

child benefits 16

Church–State Commission 44

cigarettes, prices 246

'Clubs of the Self-Governing Republic' 264–5, 269

coal production 46, 222, 238

'commercial' shops 2

Communist Party, Polish: organisation and authority xii; fear of independent unions 24–6, 55; mistakes admitted 25; Kania admits need for changes 40–2; purged by Kania 42–4; attitude of Solidarity towards 72, 82–3; provincial purges 130; internal

divisions 135; extraordinary (Ninth) Congress 145, 155, 188, 191–4, 208–17; decline in membership 153–4; Eleventh Plenum 189–91, 196; role under martial law 292–3

Communist Party, Soviet 126, 179, 180

Confederation of Independent Poland (KPN) 66–7, 176, 260

corruption 43, 58, 154

cost of living 5, 11, 16, 301

Council of National Accord 256

crime 162, 165

curfew 279, 286

Cypryniak, Kazimierz 155, 213

Czechoslovakia: Soviet intervention in 1968 30, 34, 64, 76, 90, 127, 235; radio condemns Walesa 70, 118; radio condemns Solidarity 88, 158; condemns Poland 90, 98, 101, 197

Czechowicz, Tadeusz 213

Czestochowa 12, 24

Czubinski, Lucjan 84

Czyrek, Jozef 97, 168, 213; *13*

Dabrowski, Bishop Bronislaw 102, 121, 176

Dabrowski, Jacek 54

Daily Telegraph 63

Daily World 31

Democratic Party xii, 17, 95

'Directions of Union Action in the Country's Present Situation' 150

Dobieszewski, Adolf 153

dustmen 9

Dziennik Baltycki 54

Dziennik Zachodni 172

East German Radio 120, 151

East Germany 63–4, 91, 242

Elblag 19

elections 177–8, 191–6, 199, 202–3, 212–14

Experience and Future club 182

Falin, Valentin 99

family allowances 4, 34, 301

Finkelsztein, Mojzesz 134

Fire Brigade College 267–8